Bringing Englis

Studies in Curriculum History Series

General Editor: **Professor Ivor Goodson**, Faculty of Education,
University of Western Ontario, London,
Canada N6G 1G7

The series aims to fill a gap in the literature of education and schooling; we do not have any comprehensive studies of the history of curriculum. The books will aim to respond to the growing wave of interest in curriculum history on both sides of the Atlantic.

Studies in Curriculum History Series: 14

Bringing English to Order: The History and Politics of a School Subject

Edited by
Ivor Goodson and
Peter Medway

The Falmer Press
(A Member of the Taylor & Francis Group)
London · New York · Philadelphia

UK   The Falmer Press, Falmer House, Barcombe, Lewes,
        East Sussex, BN8 5DL
USA   The Falmer Press, Taylor & Francis Inc., 1900 Frost Road,
        Suite 101, Bristol, PA 19007

First published 1990

British Library Cataloguing in Publication Data

Bringing English to order: the history and politics of
  a school subject. – (Studies in curriculum history)
  1. Schools. Curriculum subjects. English language.
  Teaching. Sociopolitical aspects
  I. Goodson, Ivor   II. Medway, Peter   III. Series
  420'.7'1

  ISBN 1-85000-474-9
  ISBN 1-85000-475-7 (pbk.)

**Library of Congress Cataloguing-in-Publication Data
available on request.**

Typeset in 10$\frac{1}{2}$/12 Bembo by
Mathematical Composition Setters Ltd, Salisbury.

Printed in Great Britain by Taylor & Francis (Printers)
Ltd, Basingstoke.

Contents

To Jeremy Hein, English teacher
The Jack Kerovac of Kingston-upon-Thames

Bringing English to Order: Introduction

Ivor Goodson and Peter Medway

In constructing a history and politics of schooling the case of English is especially significant and revealing. English is a subject alongside others such as history, physics, art and mathematics, but it is also in unique ways more than a subject. This is apparent in the distinctive relationship which English bears to the rest of the curriculum and to schooling in general. Whereas other subjects import into school the knowledge and procedures of disciplines whose centre of practice lies outside, English, as part of its responsibility, teaches the literacy on which the practice of other subjects is based. Moreover, by taking as its matter and assiduously cultivating those processes of reading and writing through which education itself is conducted, English confirms their legitimacy. For reading and writing, rather than the more 'natural' means of learning such as oral discussion and practical engagement, are the established modality of schooling. Thus, if English teachers decide, as from time to time they do, to reorder the priorities of their subject and accord legitimacy to new forms of writing or to the spoken vernacular or non-standard dialect, more is involved than the in-house arrangements of a specialist subject community. Attempts to control and define the subject move beyond the subject community because changing English[1] is changing schooling.

And not only schooling: at stake is the order of things more generally. Changing English (or stopping it changing) has consistently, and across many countries, been a matter with which the state has concerned itself. From the studies in this volume we can learn a great deal about how curriculum is made, maintained and transformed, and specifically about the extent to which others besides the professionals are involved.[2] Debate within the English community has typically proceeded on the assumptions that, first, English curriculum is made by English teachers acting on their best judgments about what and how children need to learn; and, second, what matters is its content and pedagogy, what is taught and learnt and by what methods. Debate beyond the English community has, in continuity

with these assumptions, presumed a disinterested and dispassionate definition of intellectually and pedagogically worthwhile content. These
assumptions are challenged in the papers that follow. Those who have
made English what it is have not only, perhaps not even primarily, been
English teachers but have included agencies with purposes quite other than
those of the teachers. What has been most significant about particular
curricula has often been who they have been taught to (and not been taught
to) in what contexts, by whom, with what powers and purposes, and to the
exclusion of what and whom.

Versions of English,[3] the papers make clear, have *always* been something more than alternative approaches to competence and knowledge in
English language and literature. English has been the means through which
powerful groups, especially governments, have sought to achieve ends
which were ideological and political and not neutrally 'educational'. Where
other groups with other agendas — including, sometimes, English teachers
with their own values and priorities — have resisted, English has been a
battleground. And this, indeed, is what English *has* been continuously since
mass schooling began. Thus, to examine the texts and tasks of English is
only the beginning of understanding the subject. The belief informing
these papers is that English can only be seen for what it is if its 'context' is
also clearly seen. What it in different ways substantiates is the embedded-
ness of English curricular practice within wider social and political projects.

The reason for the state's interest in English has partly been functional:
the demand of both administration and the economy require a literate
population. But English is important for more than the personal competence required in modern societies. In the nineteenth and early twentieth
centuries, as we learn from the papers by Morgan and by Ball, Gardner and
Kenny, part of its purpose was the formation of national and imperial
identity. Bob Morgan sees the 'Englishness' celebrated by English in the
colonies not as a stable national identity, solidly there to be drawn upon,
but as a shifting set of relations with subordinate groups. English teaching
in schools has served first to secure the dominance of the English language
against the other mother-tongues of children in Canadian, Australian,
American, South African and British schools (part of the motivation behind
Benjamin Franklin's English School in mid-eighteenth century Philadelphia was, according to Burns, the wish to secure the dominance of the
English-speaking community against the influx of foreigners); and then to
suppress variant forms of English in the interests of establishing the
'standard' form of one class as the national language. As a foreign language
in the curriculum of other countries, English may likewise serve as a means
of asserting and instilling national identity. Gundem relates how the
significance of English in Norwegian education has been not simply that it
has provided access to trade, but also that it is *not German*. The choice of
foreign language for school study expresses a choice of national identity.

One of the most striking findings of Morgan's paper is the way in which the creation of personal and of national identities is seen as one and the same process. Identities are based on perceptions of what is 'I' and 'not I', 'us' and 'not us'. The authorization of forms of English (typically the 'standard' dialect) and types of text (typically 'literature') is always by implication the de-authorization of other forms and texts. As Bob Morgan puts it, constructing what counts as English is at the same time constructing 'otherness'.

The state, then, has concerned itself with producing not only national identities but also subjectivities. English is relevant to this process because forming and controlling young people's language is forming and controlling identities; the meanings embodied in language 'shape our perceptions and our experience of the world' (Donald, quoted by Green, p. 140). English has therefore been relevant to the desire of states to determine how people perceive themselves, what they desire and fear, how they comport themselves within the structure of roles in the society, who they regard as 'us' and who as 'them' and how they regard the state itself. English, in other words, has more than other subjects in state schools been a medium of popular surveillance and socialization. Hunter argues, in a paper referred to by Ball, Kenny and Gardiner, that practices which English teachers regard as distinctively their own, such as the provision of 'a unique vehicle for personal expression and individual growth' within 'a special relation to the English teacher whose supervision is not coercive but is, apparently, "drawn from the pupil" himself', was actually 'a late mutation in an apparatus of moral training' developed without any literary concerns in the first half of the nineteenth century.[4] It is this practice of scrutinized self-expression which makes English 'a field of infinite and intimate self-correction' (King, quoted by Green, p. 151). (To state this is not to make any assumptions about the effectiveness of those processes, a point we will return to at the end of this introduction.)

English has not always been seen by governments as a convenient instrument of control. Within largely anglophone societies English had at first to be urged on governments by rising class interests concerned to challenge the upper class curriculum of Greek and Latin. Burns relates how Franklin attempted to increase middle class power through the empowering which an English curriculum would bring, and how the realization of this purpose in the United States had to await the arrival of the powerful nineteenth-century middle class of 'professional, experts and administrators'. In contemporary South Africa, according to Hilary Janks, the demand of Black communities for English teaching has been an oppositional claim. English is thus quite clearly a two-edged sword: a means of control over, but also of resistance by populations. This is yet another reason why, where English teaching exists, it tends to be more tightly superintended than other subjects. That English is a world language makes it yet more powerful or dangerous, depending on your point of view. Victorian imperialists saw the worldwide dissemination of English as a means of securing hegemony, but, in the event, the *lingua franca* of English turns out to be under no one's control. Thus, for black South Africans, English is a medium of contact with potential allies in the rest of Africa and beyond.

Where the maintenance of English teaching in schools is established state policy, it is undeniable that English teachers have a degree of autonomy and discretion in the way they go about their work. But what and how they teach may be, in Bill Green's words in this volume, 'with' or 'against the grain' of the structuring within which their room for manoeuvre is located, or, more often, in complex and contradictory ways both with and against that 'grain'. This structuring — 'structuration' is Giddens's useful concept, referred to by Green — derives in important measure not from explicit government policy but from the *social* ascription of degrees of legitimacy to elements of curriculum. The significance of a practice (such as group discussion, or poetry writing) is a matter not only of its intrinsic character and pedagogical effectiveness but also of whether it 'counts'; whether for instance, it is endorsed or disregarded by certification procedures, teacher education programmes, resourcing and timetabling and so on. The structuring of legitimacy is the work largely of *external* 'constituencies' (Meyer)[5] or 'publics' (Wright Mills).[6] The discourse about school curriculum is heavily determined by these constituencies and publics, which include, but are broader than, the specific interest groups — parents, employers, trade unions and universities, and so on — in terms of which schools' external relations are normally conceived. They include, for instance, scholars, politicians, administrators and others.

> These interested publics which pay for and support education hand over its work to the professionals in only a limited and unexpected sense. For a while it may appear that the professionals have power to determine what is taught (at school, district or national level, depending on the country in question) their scope is limited by the fact that only the forms and activities which have significance for external publics can, in the long run, survive.[7]

So pervasive and even constitutive in educational practice are these powerful discourses which originate outside the schools, that it is almost a misapprehension to speak of 'external' and 'internal' factors. The external *is* internal, appearing in the consciousnesses of the teachers themselves and influencing their aims, criteria and practices, though in tension, to a greater or lesser degree, with other discourses and other values, some of which may be special to the English professionals.

A number of practices in the teaching of English are identified in these papers as enabling formative power to be exercised in the interests of the state or powerful groups over individuals exposed to schooling. These are the imposition of 'standard English', the teaching of grammar, the selection and handling of literary texts, and the eliciting and guided reconstruction of students' written, spoken and enacted expressions of their experience. Pervasively, there is the very designation of 'English' as matter for a subject, with all the panoply that implies of syllabuses, textbooks, examinations, specialist teacher training and so on. The general point is well put by Morgan that 'The pedagogic space within which students read and write is always within the agendas of a whole culture, particularly as these are defined by the state'.

The ways in which larger discourses in the society bear on English down to the detail of its content is illustrated by the case of grammar. On the face of it, the desirability of the teaching of grammar is a technical matter, to be decided in the light of considerations about how children best acquire proficiency and command of the conventions. The argument, however, has never been merely technical. The teaching of grammar has consistently been a plank of social and political programmes of a particular colour, and its aims have gone far beyond the promotion of grammatical knowledge or even of linguistic competence in the population. In Deborah Cameron's words, grammar 'is only secondarily about language at all'.

> Historically and synchronically, 'authority' is the significance grammar has usually had whenever the subject has erupted into public consciousness.... Grammar is meant not as a tool of reflection on one's language but as a means to restore order in place of chaos.
>   And it is not always *linguistic* chaos which is most relevant. Extraordinary as it may seem, grammar has become a symbol for order and discipline in all spheres of life; it stands for all the traditional rules of conduct which are perceived as being in decline.

Cameron quotes from an article by John Rae, then Headmaster of a prestigious English public (i.e. private) school:

> There is a further claim that can be made for the restoration of the teaching of correct English. Attention to the rules of grammar and care in the choice of words encourages punctiliousness in other matters. That is not just an intellectual conceit. The overthrow of grammar coincided with the acceptance of the equivalent of creative writing in social behaviour. As nice points of grammar were mockingly dismissed as pedantic and irrelevant, so was punctiliousness in such matters as honesty, responsibility, property, gratitude, apology and so on.[8]

Having been eclipsed for a generation, the teaching of grammar is now returning. This is a case in which history genuinely throws light on current states of affairs. The meaning of this return to nineteenth-century practices is discussed in these papers in relation to earlier debates in Ontario (Morgan) and the United Kingdom (Ball, Kenny and Gardner). It is happening in Australia and the USA too. Most recently, in England and

Wales, since the papers were written, we have had a series of official reports culminating in the draft orders which specify the content of English in the National Curriculum. In prescribing the learning of grammatical terms by five to seven year olds the government has gone beyond the recommendations of the three (government-appointed) bodies which have given advice, the Kingman Committe,[9] the National Curriculum English Working Group[10] and the National Curriculum Council.[11]

Changes in education occur at different levels. At the school level, English, we have argued, is realized both pervasively as 'modality' across schooling and locally and specifically within the boundaries of a subject. There may also be changes of focus and intent at the level of systems of state schooling. The Kingman Committee, in the manner of its constitution, as much as in the nature of its findings,[12] has shown how thoroughly the contest over versions of English is interlinked and implicated with the more general contest (partially played out at the level of governance) over the versions and structuration of schooling. Sometimes, changes at the two levels work in broadly similar directions, as in the moment at the end of the 1960s in England when common schooling was pursued within the newly reorganized comprehensive schools and when English as a subject took common everyday experience as its material and students' everyday language as its vehicle of expression. For a time, aspects of the restructuration of schooling and the redefinition of the subject seemed to work in symbiotic process. (Gundem's paper shows such a process at work within another culture — Norway — with a more protracted commitment to democratic schooling.)

In about the mid-1970s in England and Wales (a salient moment was the Prime Minister's Ruskin College speech of 1976) the tide of change at system level turned, with a move to restructure schooling for more utilitarian purposes. English did not spontaneously change itself in sympathy: for a time, versions of English more in harmony with the earlier democratic moment persisted and were unchecked, relations between the levels being characterized by a loosely-coupled apparent autonomy. Now, however, we are witnessing a move towards a tighter coupling and an imposition of government wishes down to the detail of classroom transactions. This tighter coupling, however, is not simply a matter of bringing English into line with the demands of the economy as rationally conceived. Certainly, the justifications are expressed in the neutral language of 'the needs of society' and 'closer attention to the needs of industry', yet the relevance of the changes to these needs is by no means always obvious. Indeed, the British government's education policy differs in significant ways from the recommendations of leading industrial and business bodies. It is not simply that the learning of grammar has dubious relevance to the language *competence* which industry requires; requirements for the study of English literary classics and the learning by heart of poetry appear to reflect a different order of purposes. More lies behind current attacks on approaches deriving from the sixties and early seventies, when concerns with social justice and common schooling were running strongly, than worries about their economic dysfunctionality. As we noted earlier, commentators have drawn the connection between the reinstatement of grammar and the reinstatement of discipline, 'punctiliousness in other matters'. As the leader of the National Association for the Teaching of English has said

> The teaching of grammar seems to be associated in the prime minister's mind with picking up litter. [13]

The new curricular prescriptions are consistent with a broader cultural reversal — a concern not with enabling more pupils to gain access to higher levels of education and work but with early division and exclusion. The underlying intention appears to be about re-establishing hierarchy and social discipline and restoring the older social configurations which had been partially disrupted. Effects of the emphasis on grammar, on Standard English and on the English 'national heritage' will clearly be to increase once again the relative disadvantage and sense of exclusion of pupils from working class and ethnic minority backgrounds, and it is hard not to conclude that this may be part of the intention.

A perhaps disproportionate emphasis has been given in these papers to those aspects of English which derive from the need of government and powerful groups to exercise surveillance and form identities in ways which suit their purposes. At the present stage in the development of our awareness of the ways in which English has been and is being made, the first necessity has been to challenge the prevalent view that changes in English teaching have resulted largely from changes in ideas about the nature of language and learning and about developmental psychology. 'Bringing English to order' has been a necessary emphasis. But it is important also not, in Green's words, to 'fall victim to the rigid and doctrinaire logic of the reproduction thesis'.

One of the moments when the directions of the profession and those of the external constituencies appeared less out of phase than they later became was the 1960s. This was a time when, in Britain certainly, teachers' priorities and purposes appeared to have a greater than normal influence over the English curriculum, resulting in the emergence of the version of English teaching which has come to be known by the label 'personal growth'. Three of the papers discuss the significance of this phenomenon. In the paper by Ball, Kenny and Gardner it appears as the 'progressive' version of the 'English as Language' approach which emerged as an alternative to Leavisism, 'focusing upon personal aspects of experience, stressing the relevance and validity of each child's culture, language and self-expression'. The careers of both 'progressive' and 'radical' versions are traced into the 1970s when their concerns, at least in the cities, became respectively multiculturalism and the roots of inequality, and when they came under violent attack from the Right. Medway identifies the traditions within English which gave rise to 'growth' and the transformations they underwent in doing so, and speculates on the meaning of the striking, though hitherto largely unremarked, congruence between tendencies in English and tendencies in the culture more widely. While aspects of English practice were in clear accord with the official policy of comprehensivization or the institution of common schooling, others were decidedly associated with quite other 'authority poles'. Values of spontaneity and self-expression celebrated in English in the sixties were not essentially oppositional and may represent a capitalist economy shifting gear from a production to a consumption basis, but nevertheless were not at all those of the groups exercising formal power over the schools.

Green finds in 'personal growth', despite its limitations, a potentially liberating belief in *agency*. Whereas English has normally been a 'dividing practice', producing social differentiations harmful to subordinate groups, 'growth' represents a partial refusal of such divisions. For refusal, too, is a possibility, though one, quite clearly, which is more or less sustainable at different historical conjunctures. In Green's view the construction of curriculum is essentially contestable, so that it is not futile for teachers to seek to move towards a 'critical pedagogy'. Against structuration there is the agency of teachers and students who are not simply acted upon. Change can begin in classrooms, and there is 'no use in sitting back and waiting for the Millennium, or even a change in government'. By no means all changes in the structuration of schooling represent an intensification of oppressive control; some can liberate new potentialities and make possible new subjectivities.

What has not been explored in this volume is the degree to which the use of English teaching to form identities along preferred lines has in fact been effective. To what extent is Foucault's government by individualization' achieved, through individual students coming, in Morgan's words, 'to unconsciously adopt the institutionalised norms embedded in the habitual daily performances of "English"'? In a brief aside Morgan comments that 'the ideology sold' was not necessarily 'the ideology bought by the pupils', and argues for the need for research into pupils' experience of English teaching; in one suggestive sentence he outlines a possible agenda. A study of the role of the agency of the taught in determining the nature of the *enacted* English curriculum is perhaps the next major task for studies in the history and politics of English teaching.

Bob Morgan speaks of a disabling 'historical blindness to the social and institutional conditions which gave rise to English studies'. We hope that this collection will help teachers and others concerned with English teaching to gain the awareness they need to understand what is happening to English and to find ways of keeping alive the valuable alternative discourses which many of them have developed.

Notes

1. The title of a collection of essays: M. Meek and J. Miller (ed.) *Changing English: Essays for Harold Rosen*, London, Heinemann, 1984.
2. The series 'Studies in Curriculum History' has sought to address these issues in an historical manner. The concern is to understand the social construction of curriculum. See I. F. Goodson, *The Making of Curriculum*, Lewes, Falmer Press, 1988.
3. Also the title of a study of English teaching in England: Douglas and Dorothy Barnes with Stephen Clarke, *Versions of English*, London, Heinemann, 1984.
4. I. Hunter, 'Culture, education, and English: Building "the principal scene of the real life of children"', *Economy and Society*, 1987, vol. 16, no. 4, pp. 568–88. Quotations from pp. 574 and 576.
5. J. W. Meyer [ref]. The concept of constituencies has been further developed by W. A. Reid, 'Curriculum topics as institutional categories: implications for theory and research in the history and sociology of school subjects', in I. F. Goodson and S. J. Ball, *Defining the Curriculum: History and Ethnography*, Lewes, Falmer Press, 1984.
6. C. Wright Mills [ref].
7. Reid, *op. cit.*, p. 68.
8. From a talk by Deborah Cameron, a version of which is to appear in J. Bourne and D. Cameron, *Grammar, Nation and Citizenship: Kingman in Linguistic and Historical Perspective*, Occasional Paper No. 1, Department of English and Media Studies, University of London Institute of Education, 1989. Quotation from J. Rae, 'The decline and fall of English grammar', London, *Observer*, 7 February 1982.
9. Department of Education and Science, *Report of the Committee of Inquiry into the Teaching of English Language* [the Kingman Report], HMSO, March 1988.
10. *English for ages 5 to 11: Proposals of the Secretary of State for Education and Science and the Secretary of State for Wales*, Department of Education and Science, November 1988.
11. *National Curriculum Council Consultation Report: English 5–11*, York, National Curriculum Council, 1989.
12. H. Rosen, 'Struck by a particular gap', in M. Jones and A. West, *Learning Me Your Language*, London, Mary Glasgow, 1988, pp. 1–15.
13. *The Observer*, April 2, 1989.

Chapter 1

Into the Sixties: English and English Society at a Time of Change

Peter Medway
University of Leeds

The Point of Studying English in England and Wales

In any study of a general phenomenon, there is a particular interest in the deviant case. In the history of school subjects and of the processes by which they emerged, were sustained, flourished or failed to flourish, adapted or failed to adapt, the case of English in England and Wales provides such a special instance. The first way in which English is special is that certain characteristics generally attributable to academic subjects are notably lacking. The most obvious example is that English does not essentially comprise a body of facts and concepts to be communicated; those specifiable items which *are* taught — spellings, for instance, or grammatical structures — do not constitute the substance of what English is seen by its practitioners as being about. Much of what English 'teaches', moreover, is not new to the learners, nor is it exclusively obtainable from the lessons, since English is in a sense what all native speakers are doing all the time already. Indeed, not only is English being continuously learnt outside school; it is also learnt *in* school in other lessons wherever reading and writing are practised. In these ways English seems not quite a subject in the usual sense.

A second area of interest is the unusually ambivalent *status* of English. The department is often the largest in the school and is seen as being at the core of the curriculum; it is regarded as indispensable for all students in compulsory schooling; it has tended to have the largest number of students preparing for the prestigious GCE O and A level examinations at ages 16 and 18, leads directly into a university subject, and is relatively well off for above-scale salary points and financial resources. English is one of the subjects from which teachers commonly rise to be headteachers. Yet there are a number of signs that English is not classed as a subject of first rank. One is that in post-compulsory schooling and higher education English

1

tends to be avoided by boys — predominantly female subjects generally ranking lower in the hierarchy. Another is that it is regularly staffed partly by non-specialists drafted in to use up periods left over from their specialist timetables.[1] The main reason why this policy has appeared feasible to administrators, and a factor which doubtless lowers the standing of the subject in the eyes of other teachers, is that English is seen as having no formidable body of technical knowledge which would disqualify lay persons from attempting it. This impression is strengthened by the lack of obvious connection between university English studies and the school subject, except in its specialist literature strand with older students. Most of the teachers give little sign that they locate the source of their professional identity, values and criteria in the advanced academic discipline.

The territory of English seems in general ill-defined and weakly defended: it may or may not include drama and the library, and, particularly in recent years, elements which might seem its rightful preserve have appeared elsewhere on the timetable and under other management: discussion of social and ethical issues (e.g. the Humanities Curriculum Project), 'communications' courses, reading programmes and study skills are examples. Also, the fact that English is taught to everyone, while clearly making it important educationally, may tend to lower its status against subjects taught only to selected groups of older students. Finally, we may note that unlike two other major subjects of the core curriculum, mathematics and science, English has received no large injections of development money from government and industry.

Yet another notable feature is the pretensions of the subject: English teachers have not uncommonly claimed that English is more than a subject and has far-reaching importance for students' lives and the health of society: 'English is hard to plan because we are teaching a way of life; we are teaching children to enjoy life to the full.'[2]

A final reason for treating English as a highly significant case within the school curriculum is that, at least in certain of its contemporary forms, it is manifestly strange. It certainly *appears* strange to people outside the subject subculture, who find it puzzling that English lessons are not about English but about old people, getting into trouble, gender or space adventures. Equally strange, in the context of a generally acknowledged remit to develop language abilities, and especially writing ability, is the preoccupation of English with a particular selected subset of the forms of writing, mainly ones, moreover, such as stories, which have no likely utility in the future existences of most of the students and are not widely regarded as deserving privileged attention. This is one aspect of the pervasive *literariness* of the subject.[3]

It is hard to believe, in short, that if a subject were being freshly invented to meet the commonest identified language needs of the school population it would look anything like English. The factors which have gone into producing such a specific and unexpected cultural form are clearly worth investigating. How is it that, in relation to the demands and expectations placed upon it, and upon school subjects in general, this subject could have ended up so eccentric?

The Need for a Study of a Recent Period

It is clear from studies[4] of the construction of English as a subject in schools and universities that several of the features I have noted are traceable to its nineteenth- and early twentieth-century origins. (And behind this specific history lie two others which profoundly affected English: those of the teaching of rhetoric from antiquity to the nineteenth century, and the 'construction' of literature as a cultural category.[5]) But not all the explanations of the nature of present-day English lie way back. The aspect of strangeness, for instance, which the subject presents to those who are not inside the subculture, is a recent phenomenon. Before the 1960s English was more intelligible to the lay public, and some of the puzzling elements which now form part of normal practice were sixties innovations.

My purpose in this paper will in fact be to examine a recent period, one in which there was a particularly interesting interaction between the traditions which historians have traced to the early days and new impinging circumstances, resulting in changes of which some have proved lasting. This is the period from the late 1950s to the late 1960s. The clear consensus of the historical accounts is that there was considerable continuity from the time when the subject was decisively established in schools, around the end of the first world war, to the 1960s, but that significant changes then occurred. Through this analysis I hope to account for aspects of English as practised today, to throw light both on what is distinctive about English in relation to other school subjects, and, more generally, to provide a case study of how curriculum is made in England and Wales.

One problem with the histories covering the entire timespan or extended periods of the subject's existence is that the basis on which sources were selected has often appeared unsystematic. Understandably, none draws on all available sources, but one is never confident that sources not considered were excluded by any clear rationale. In the present study I adopted a contrasting methodology, which was to concentrate, where there was differentiation in the sources, on the younger secondary years and to confine myself, even within my short ten-year spread, to restricted time stretches — two separate years, in fact, 1958 and 1968; and for these to attempt to examine all published sources. Evidence from this limited slice could obviously be partial or atypical, but if this is taken with the existing broader histories and with a less systematic reading of other texts from the general period — some of which I refer to — the exercise is, I think, illuminating.

The choice of years was inevitably somewhat arbitrary. My earlier year needed to fall within the long post-war period during which change in the education system and the curriculum was relatively slow and inconspicuous.[6] 1958 was chosen simply because it was a round twenty-five years before an ethnographic survey I had conducted.[7] The second point selected was ten years later, when accelerated change, much of it promoted by public policy, was well under way. The year happens also to be symbolic of those notable developments within western societies sometimes referred to as the Counterculture; the question of the effects on curriculum of changes in the wider culture is one which this paper will consider.

My procedure, then, was to seek to examine all the books and articles which were published in Britain about the teaching of English as a first language in the years 1958 and 1968, with the exception of material which clearly related specifically to age groups other than 11-13. Little direct evidence is available of what English consisted of in practice in the diversity of settings in which it took place: gaining reliable knowledge of that would require a major research study employing such methods as the collection of school syllabuses, stock lists and surviving pupil work, interviews with former teachers and pupils and a study of textbook sales. From the published sources to which I have been restricted may be inferred (a) what was taken to be normal practice, and (b) what bids for changes were being made. Two functions of 'method texts' — that is, books or articles for English teachers about English teaching — may be distinguished: 'technical' texts support the implementation of aspects of English which fall within normal practice, while 'proselytizing' texts present advocacy for, or aim to facilitate, changes in practice. (Advocacy may also be necessary to confirm the convictions of a group of teachers who have made changes which are not yet securely established as 'normalcy'.) Accounts written for teachers by academics of relevant theory, from disciplines such as psychology or the study of language development, may often be taken as advocacy also, the particular selection of theory implying suggestions for changes in practice.[8]

English in 1958

The Scene as a Whole

The main sources for 1958 consist of one periodical (*The Use of English*), two 'method' books[9] and numerous textbooks. What the documents reveal is consistent with the existence, established by previous subject histories, of two traditions originating from the separate secondary and elementary school sectors, and manifested now in somewhat different versions of English for the selective grammar and non-selective secondary modern schools. (There were only forty-six comprehensive schools in January, 1958. Three-quarters of all pupils attended secondary modern schools.[10])

It is characteristic of orthodoxies that, unless they come under serious attack, they do not need to be justified with rationales. Within the prevailing grammar school and secondary modern 'normalcies' writers did not debate the aims of the subject. English was simply the sum of its well established parts: literature, composition, instruction and exercises in written language, and (less universally) speech training. There were, however, clear differences in the *implicit* aims of English in the two types of institution. Some secondary modern prescriptions unambiguously emphasized preparation for subordinate roles in life: the skills and values taught were to be such as would produce a useful, responsible and inoffensive citizen with a respect, based on slight acquaintance, for literary culture. In these schools the content of the English lesson might be determined by reference less to a conception of the subject than to the school's socializing function.[11]

Besides the prevailing grammar school and secondary modern school normalcies, which were largely implicit in practice and not systematically explicated, two other coherent positions can be discerned. Adherents of the view of English associated with F.R. Leavis at Cambridge and the literary critical journal *Scrutiny* saw themselves as representing a distinct embattled position.[12] In fact this 'Cambridge' position comprised a group of teachers large enough to sustain (since 1939) a quarterly journal, *The Use of English*,[13] which, while constantly affirming the need for struggle against the prevailing (mainly grammar school) orthodoxy, afforded ample indications of the gains that had been secured by 1958. The Cambridge position was well on its way to becoming an alternative normalcy. The core of English, in this view, was the reading of literature as an active, creative and essentially moral pursuit through which the degeneracy of contemporary mass society might be combated.[14]

The other coherent view of English was that advocated by Percival Gurrey, formerly of the University of London Institute of Education, in his book, *Teaching the Mother Tongue in Secondary Schools*.[15] For Gurrey the unifying centre of English is not literature but language as a human function, integral to development in general and intellectual development in particular. Gurrey does not explicitly criticize the Cambridge position, but it is a measure of the distance between them that nothing in his account of what an English teacher needs to know and do indicates a need for a literary training. Gurrey has an explicit and sophisticated view of the role of language in cognition. He states unambiguously that language organizes experience so as to make it accessible to mental operation, and draws the implication that this is a need which English must address. There is nothing in the literature to indicate how far Gurrey's views were shared by teachers in schools.

Of the textbooks of the period, some covered a single aspect of the curriculum and some were general course books. The latter were organized in two different ways, either in sections each of which covered the range of curricular strands in a given period of time (usually a week), or in sections based on instructional topics. In some books a linking narrative, about a boy and girl or a family, runs through the chapters and provides material for exercises — a characteristic today associated with foreign language courses for the lower secondary years and prompting the comment that the pedagogies of English and modern languages were once more similar. Visually, the overall impression is of drab covers, cheap paper, cramped print and bad artwork: the few illustrations, when they are not simply matchstick figures, are crudely drawn, with people in strangely distorted postures.[16] Cover designs are likely to show emblems of reading and writing — a pattern of marching inkwells, for example.[17]

In this account, as in that of 1968, there will be space to deal in detail with only two aspects of the English curriculum, literature and writing, omitting language instruction, drama and spoken English.[18] The point must briefly be made, however, that in 1958 grammar and instruction and exercises in the conventions of written English were *major* components of most of the curricula of which the documents provide evidence.

Literature in 1958

Nowhere in the sources is it explicitly questioned that all students need to study literature. In practice, however, the importance ascribed to literature varied considerably. We have no accounts of the 'normal' place of literature in either the secondary modern or the grammar school. Certain secondary modern textbooks purporting to provide complete courses omit literature altogether, though teachers may have supplemented them with readers and anthologies. Gurrey's views may well be representative of a tradition of grammar school thinking about literature: while by no means seeing English as centrally about literature, and while wanting reading to range well beyond the usual literary texts, his answer to the question posed by one of his chapter headings, 'Is literature so important?' is an unequivocal yes. Gurrey values literature in the first place because it gives knowledge of human nature and of the ways of the world: 'we perceive and understand the ideals that move people to fine action, and the evil intentions and thoughts of the ill-disposed.'[19] This is a traditional, classics-derived justification; the concern is a moral one in the sense that literature teaches us lessons. Literature also fulfils what Gurrey sees as a basic human need for a life of the imagination: his most heartfelt plea is about the deprivation suffered by ordinary people denied access to the visions and sustaining myths it offers:

> And those who live a life full of learning, salty-humoured dis-
> course and fine aesthetic experience may not believe how starved
> the imagination of children, and of many older people too, can be,

and how blindly these may crave for something beyond their immediate material existence, and for something worthy to strive for that is better than the everyday routine of their lives in town, village or country.[20]

The strength of this position is that it does not make literature a matter of the cultivation of 'taste' for an elite. Its weakness, as the quotation strikingly displays, is that it drains people's everyday lives of significance and value; aspiration and vision depend on access to 'something beyond'.

Gurrey's final point is that literature contributes to the cultivation of intelligence: poetry has 'the power of nourishing and quickening a perceptive mind'; 'the reader ... becomes accustomed to precision and vitality in this thinking'; it is in reading 'biography, history, exploration and travel, and especially literature that the mind can be kept supple, free from rule-of-thumb thinking, alive to unusual possibilities and well out of the rut of preconceived ideas'.[21] It is in this high valuation of intellectual qualities, rational thinking and a lively mind, as opposed to moral and affective responses, that Gurrey's stance is most clearly at odds with the Cambridge position. Gurrey's view of the place of literature, and especially perhaps his stress on intelligence and rationality, is essentially that which seems to have sustained the endeavours of many grammar school teachers of English since before the Newbolt Report of 1921.

Teachers of the Cambridge persuasion were in no doubt that literature was of paramount importance amongst the elements of the English curriculum. For them, too, the activity was moral, but in a different sense from Gurrey's: not for the 'lessons' it taught but because reading an authentic text was itself a formative act of moral engagement. A second contrast was that the pursuit of literature, certainly in the view of F.R. Leavis and of some writers in *The Use of English*, was an explicitly elite activity in that only the finest minds were capable of full appreciation of the best literature[22] — which was not to say, for teachers such as David Holbrook, that ordinary people could not benefit from it.

The Cambridge view of literature was evidently gathering strength, but several writers make us aware of the persistence of the traditional literature canon. M. Spencer complains that in students' teaching practice preparation (presumably for secondary modern schools), the poems '"Meg Merrilies", "Sea Fever" and "The Pied Piper" reappear until one is heartily sick of them'.[23] Spencer blames the students' weak reading background and suggests that the third training year shortly to be added be used to remedy this: modern texts such as *Lord of the Flies* might be read. (It is interesting to see how this book, later to be adopted on a large proportion of O level and CSE courses, made its tentative entry onto the educational scene.[24]) Britton's *Oxford Book of Verse for Juniors* is praised for not being just 'a milder "Oxford Book of English Verse"' and for excluding 'the pixie-and-toadstool nonsense'.[25] The tone of the older, pre-I.A. Richards approach to literature is illustrated by K.P. Thompson's account of teaching Byron's 'The destruction of Sennacherib': 'How graphic is the picture of the noble animal with its distended nostrils and how apt the comparison of the foam at its mouth to the cold spray of the surf ...'[26] In the grammar school textbooks the corpus is modified *Golden Treasury*, the anthology which was still, according to a contemporary survey,[27] the most used in secondary modern schools.[28]

In prose literature, Gurrey's prescriptions for eclectic reading not confined to fiction were being met in the grammar school course books, mainly through extracts from nineteenth-century sources. The survey referred to above reported also on the full length prose texts in use in the secondary modern school. Notable for their absence are not only the classics but contemporary children's literature and, with one exception,[29] contemporary fiction.

Indeed, of the thirteen most used texts only six are fiction and fully five are books of real life travel and adventure (two of them about Everest).[30] Cheshire County Council, advising secondary modern teachers against the classics, which 'often fail to appeal', recommend biographies of famous and worthy figures as 'of more interest to many' and indicate that 'the Cheshire Agreed Syllabus of Religious Instruction has valuable suggestions to offer on this matter'[31] — clear evidence of the subordination of English to the requirements of socialization into a set of mainstream values.

Writing in 1958

Viewed in the light of developments since 1958, practice in the teaching of writing appears bound by restrictive convention. The normalcy implied by the textbooks (both secondary modern and grammar school) is that writing occurs in the context of a programme of instruction, with assignments often constructed to provide practice in systematically introduced skills.[32] In class, it appears that compositions were generally assigned in two ways. One was for the teacher to provide detailed guidance in the form either of step-by-step instructions or of an outline.[33] An alternative to the textbook outline for the prepared composition was evidently oral preparation in class — what Rosen calls the 'class prepared composition': 'a run up in class discussion and the pupil left at the take-off board'.[34]

The other method, according to Rosen, is 'the bolt from the blue', the 'one-off' composition, normally outside the context of the instructional programme, specified by no more than a title or phrase. As an alternative to both methods Rosen argues for a two or three sentence elaboration of what is required.[35] (This later became the standard form for composition rubrics in CSE examinations, while GCE O level English Language tended to retain the short title form.[36])

One notable 'new method' in writing instruction is the subject of considerable advocacy and attention. 'Free writing' had been developed in the late 1940s by Dora Pym of Bristol University, initially as an assessment technique for the Wiltshire eleven plus examination and then, through a curriculum development project involving teachers from all types of schools, as a regular classroom technique for use with secondary as well as primary school pupils.[37] The 'freeness' (from imposed form and content) of 'free writing' was only one of its defining features; the other was its origination by 'the use of a starting point (usually an object of sense perception)'.[38] The practice was thought by now to be widespread amongst *Use of English* readers.[39] It is significant that adherents of the Cambridge position found 'free writing' acceptable: reasons for this will emerge below.

Rosen offers an informal classification of the composition subjects available in the standard repertoire. First there are 'what are called the time-honoured subjects ... picnics, bicycle punctures, pets, character sketches, hobbies and whimsies'. Then there are the (from the students' point of view) 'this-is-just-up-my-street' assignments: 'Alone in the house at night', sports topics, 'An exciting chase'. There are also school topics, such as 'Speech Day'; and finally there are the large issues for the argumentative essay: 'What about the problems created by TV, admass, subtopia, the colour bar, competitive international sport? What about Culture, Economics, Society, Life, Time and the Cosmos?'.[40] In fact I found few examples of the last category in the textbooks for the younger secondary pupil, and no bicycle punctures. Other bicycle topics, however, and all the rest of the list were there in abundance, as were school and sports topics and conventional 'exciting' stories.

The 'World' of 1958 English

The terms of the discourse which constitutes the repertoire of extracts for reading and topics for writing centre around an opposition between on the one hand everyday normality, and on the other perturbations within it, realities outside it, and alternative realities. The reading extracts in the textbooks are drawn almost entirely from the latter area: I found no representations of everyday life as it would be lived by the students themselves or their families. The topics covered were: the exotic historical; feats of daring and adventure; children in out-of-the-ordinary settings (living in a barn, on a boat, on an island); moral tales; sporting prowess; set-piece descriptions (old building, fire); travel, topography, exploration; amusing social incidents, comic low life; detective/mystery fiction; ethical philosophizing (the 'game of life'); social-political philosophizing (democracy); true spectacles, disasters (Titanic); patriotic history; marvel of technology (submarine cables); and worthy institutions (post office, lifeboats).

The historical figures about whom reading is provided constitute an official pantheon of non-contentious, non-political figures who may stand as examples of heroism and Christian service. Cheshire County Council, for instance, suggest 'biography and autobiography dealing with real figures such as Florence Nightingale, Grenfell of Labrador, Barnardo, Booth, Wilberforce, Shaftesbury, Livingstone, Schweitzer'.[41] This is what a curriculum looks like which is based on the view, articulated by Gurrey, of literature as nourishment in the desert of ordinary existence. Everyday life is implicitly represented as banal and uninteresting except when the unusual happens (a fire, being chased by a bull, finding a hare); significance and interest are to be found only in exotic settings (geographical or historical), physical prowess and great deeds.

Topics from the world of everyday first-hand experience do appear in the writing assignments, but in a way that confirms the message about its banality: I was struck by the number of items apparently selected because they were in no way interesting or out of the ordinary; their significance was precisely their lack of significance; they were emblematic of routine, unruffled normality. These assignments were usually descriptions: 'either a postage stamp or a pencil', the town or village you live in,[42] a postman,[43] a summer's morning.[44] Within a familiar world, events and situations were otherwise deemed worth describing either because of their *publicly ascribed*, conventional significance (the winning goal[45]), or as disruptions to normality. These might be trivial, calling for writing with a light touch (the dog who stole the sausages at the Scout Camp[46]); or more serious (house on fire, burglar observed by neighbour and caught by police[47]). The effect of acknowledging these occasional incursions of disorder, far from making normal reality appear precarious, was to confirm that they were containable within the order of normality and did not constitute a threat to it.

It was a world in which the postman and milkman on their rounds threaded reality together every morning, children went to school, scored winning goals and played with train sets, yachts and cricket bats and mischievous animals got into trouble, while policemen and firemen at home and lifeboatmen and lighthouse keepers at sea, following the examples of Albert Schweitzer and Grace Darling, made things safe for us where the wilder forces beyond our world threatened to encroach. There were, in contrast, zones of excitement and high endeavour, but they were hopelessly remote, in the Napoleonic wars, the Gilbert and Ellice Islands and storybook worlds of jungles and caves. Little hint of the real world was admitted — the conflicts and tensions of Korea, Malaya, Cyprus, Mau Mau, Hungary, South Africa and Ban the Bomb, or even of the everyday world most students lived in. It was a world without cities ('Loamshire' is the typical address of one of Burton's model letters), and there are constant references to bulls, hens, swans, ponds and rivers. The ethic is vaguely Christian: life is generally good and we should be thankful for its pleasantness and take a lighthearted attitude to its small crises. English, moreover, identifies itself totally with the school, celebrating and amplifying its culture and values: prizes, exam-passing and school sports success are common topics in the textbooks, while Towers's 'Form Newspapers' and Gurrey's 'Reports' on school activities[48] contribute directly to the expressive order of the institution. The composition topic 'A popular head of school receiving a prize' is not unusual, and a sentence offered for working on is, 'The present prefects of our school are all very popular, and well known for their success either in work or play'.[49]

Some Minority Tendencies

Against this general picture of a rigidly conventional curriculum there are a few deviant phenomena to be noted. One of these is a textbook by J.H. Walsh, *Graded Exercises in English*, the assignments in which display two unusual features: firstly, children's real concerns appear to be taken seriously ('Write about an occasion in your life when you were really concerned for your own or for someone else's safety'), and, secondly, the everyday is not assumed to be banal and uninteresting — or significant only for its non-significance; publicly unimportant events may nevertheless be special in an individual's view of his or her own life. The invitations to write about family photographs, a time when all the rest of the family were ill, the interesting visitor and the climb to a 'high top' are unusual in the textbooks of 1958.

Although a matter of emphasis rather than a fully realized alternative, underlying Walsh's assignments was a view of experience which was essentially different from the prevalent one in seeing elements of everyday life as worth recording not simply for practice in recording ('describe a fountain pen') but because the texture of experience was interesting in itself. There was a respect, of a kind we associate with D.H. Lawrence, for the detail of ordinary life. Despite the elitism of the Cambridge position (Walsh was deputy editor of the Leavisite *Use of English*) the rejection of conventional criteria of significance and the substitution of authentic response had democratic implications.

We see these implications being borne home also on Frances Stevens and David Holbrook. Stevens expressed a haughty worry that the problem of the uprooted 'Scholarship Boy', incapable of acquiring a true sense of literature, would be multiplied as pupils 'without first-rate intellectual equipment' were forced through A level and training college, to pass on 'their muddle and insincerity' to the next generation. Clearly, the appreciation of fine literature could not be the basis of education for the majority. But Hoggart's (1957) *The Uses of Literacy* had convinced her that something needed to be done about that education, and she identified a possible principle in another value which she found implicit in the Cambridge view, namely honesty and straightforwardness about one's own experience. The solution was thus that 'children must be encouraged from the very first to speak and write frankly out of their own experience...'.[50] We can already see the transmutation which the Cambridge style of literary education will undergo in order that its essential values may be enacted in the comprehensive schools: for the subtle intelligence and fine discrimination cultivated in the elite would be substituted a plain and decent honesty about real experience.

David Holbrook,[51] criticizing the archnesses and posturings of some amateur plays he had to read, implied as his positive alternative model not great literature but the qualities for which Stevens was reaching: '... *common life and common decency are everywhere absent.* The joys and difficulties you and I encounter everyday are absent. The kind of people, good and bad, you and I would meet if we went out into the street for ten minutes are absent, too.'[52]

Two quite different considerations led Rosen to the same conviction that children's experience and honest accounts should be treated with a new respect. The first was practical: topics to do with home produced good writing where the standard topics failed: 'Keep sending them home — to mum, to dad, to the family; at meals, quarrelling, having a laugh, getting up, going out, buying something.' The second derived from a view of language and experience as organically connected. As a member of the London Association for the Teaching of English Rosen undoubtedly knew Gurrey's ideas: 'Because they know and feel about these things they have the language to write about them. The springs of language are being tapped...'[53]

Related to this new attention to experience we note in the advocacy of the period a move away from general subjects towards a concentration on the particular. The generalizing essay is rejected[54] while descriptive assignments of a new particularity are proposed: 'Let's describe when we turn on a cold tap full and strong into an empty tin bowl.'[55] A strong Leavisite undercurrent contributed to the sweeping away of generality. L.C. Knights articulated it in his critique of contemporary culture: '... what is in question is the substitution of a surface awareness for awareness of depth, the substitution of general notions for a living response to the individual and unique, the obscuring of a whole dimension of consciousness'.[56]

Theory in English Method Discourse

English method was relatively 'untheorized'. *Use of English* writers refer almost exclusively to the discipline of English studies, the exceptions being allusions to cultural studies (Hoggart) and American academic and popular sociology: Whyte's (1957) *Organization Man* and Packard's (1957) *Hidden Persuaders*.[57] Psychology, in the form of psychoanalysis — never of cognitive or developmental psychology or the psychology of language — is sometimes in the background, but without specific references.

The lack of any generally available theory about English teaching leads Frank Whitehead to comment, in a review of Gurrey's book, that 'To write at length about the teaching of English is a difficult task. After all, so much depends on the human imponderables — the here and now of this particular class in this particular classroom.'[58] It is precisely because, exceptionally, Gurrey has a more developed theory that he is able 'to write at length about English'. This theory clearly derives from sources beyond those he names (mainly classical philosophers and 'thinkers') and particularly from more recent work in cognitive and developmental psychology. What Gurrey brings to English teaching as a result of his reading is, to put it at its simplest, the notion of language. Through this concept English teaching is able to be related to those universal processes whereby, as revealed by psychology, individual cognitive potential is constructed and, as revealed by anthropology, culture is maintained. Uniquely amongst those writing in 1958, Gurrey understands that what we experience is in part an effect of our language. 'It is by using language to express his experience, even when the language used is imperfect and incomplete, that the child is able to form concepts related to his experience, and so to perceive it and to understand it...'[59] We note the very significant acknowledgment that the functional importance of language is not necessarily related to its status as 'good' or 'bad' English, well-formed or ill-formed.

While Gurrey's perspective addressed people's common emotional and personal needs and their intellectual potentialities, Cambridge saw language as primarily the carrier for values and ways of feeling, and, moreover, failed to find relevance in those insights from other disciplines which were revealing the place of language in the production of all human individuals and, historically, of the human species.

English in 1968

No major formative book on English teaching was published in 1968, but one book on language had important implications for English: Denis Lawton's *Social Class, Language and Education*. There were now two journals exclusively devoted to the teaching of English: to *The Use of English* had been added *English in Education*, the journal of the National Association for the Teaching of English which had been founded in 1963.

Although there is plenty of evidence of the persistence of the traditions, the overwhelming impression is of change. Cambridge values still pervade *The Use of English* but its formerly characteristic note of high moral seriousness is rarely struck and, when it is, has overtones of religious mystery ('deep and hidden energies', 'strange ... powers', 'the mystery of "being"'[60]), suggesting that as the main tradition has become more tolerant, an extreme and strident form has developed to preserve the movement's original purity.[61]

The definition of English is no longer taken for granted but has become a preoccupying topic. It had been the main issue at the Anglo-American Dartmouth Seminar of 1966.[62] The writers who offer analyses of what currently counts as English share a sense that things have changed and are in some agreement that a 'new English orthodoxy'[63] has emerged. Its main characteristic is that it is literature-based, either in the sense that much of the work is centred around the reading of literary texts or in that what is read and written is almost exclusively 'imaginative' texts,[64] or both.[65] There is a greater emphasis on active language production: 'Writing (particularly imaginative writing), talking, interviews, improvised drama have all become increasingly important.'[66]

The 'new orthodoxy' is not monolithic but exists in a number of varieties which, despite differences of emphasis, are informed by essentially similar principles. Peter Doughty, working on the Nuffield Programme in Linguistics and English Teaching,[67] who offers the most clear-sighted critique, identifies within the current consensus three different emphases: moral formation, the cultivation of imagination and ordering of experience, and social competence.[68] Moral formation was not in fact proposed in the 1968 literature, but the development of imagination, the ordering of personal experience and social competence are all advocated. The fostering of imagination is the theme of Marie Peel's *Seeing to the Heart* (1967) (though the most influential book taking this position had been Creber's (1965) *Sense and Sensitivity*).[69]

The major advocates of English as the ordering of experience are John Dixon and James Britton with his colleagues in the University of London Institute of Education and LATE. John Dixon's 'growth model', from his (1967) *Growth through English*, is recognized as having growing influence.[70] This view held that English was about the ordering, through language, of significant personal experience in the interests of the development of the student as a person. While literature was by no means neglected, the emphasis was undoubtedly shifted onto the spoken and written language generated by the student. For James Britton, 'The experiences that are structured in English lessons are those in which individuals differ ... By saying "unique and personal" we put a stress, clearly, upon relations of feeling.'[71] Both Britton and Dixon stood for the ordering of experience as the function of English, as they affirmed in their joint Schools Council paper: '... the English lesson is becoming a time in which order may be brought to some of these bewildering elements (of the adolescent situation), and the individual encouraged to make sense of his personal world'.[72]

Doughty objects that this approach involves a 'limited interpretation of "pupils' needs"' as 'what is necessary for the personal development of the pupils "as people"', rather than as 'what is publicly expected of those who have passed through the educational system'. He sees the currently approved English programme as one which 'makes excellent sense ... (for) a closely integrated and non-industrial society of three or four million people'.[73]

Nobody refers to Gurrey, but we might take the textbook series *Structural English* by Robert Druce and Margaret Tucker as in some respects a contemporary, 'new orthodoxy' enactment of the position he repre-sents.[74] Like the texts which arise from a Cambridge perspective,[75] *Structural English* includes a varied sample from the historical range of English literature, but it intermingles these with non-literary texts without in any way privileging the former. The intention is less to introduce English literature than to develop awareness of (a) aspects of human existence and (b) a wide range of language uses. As in Gurrey's work, *intellectual capabilities* — 'the techniques of successful thinking', speculation and a 'lively mind' — are accorded importance.[76]

Doughty's third variant, 'social competence', exemplified by Flower's (1966) *Language and Education*[77] (primarily for colleges of further edu-cation), covers both competence in social communications and understand-ing the social world. It is notable how readily writers take the latter as an evidently acceptable purpose for English, on its own or alongside personal development: to have claimed ten years earlier that this was what English was centrally for, before even language skills, would have seemed bizarre. So far has English come from having even to *say* that it is about English or language, that Butts and Watkins, describing their fifth year theme on 'violence', express their aims entirely in terms of students' understandings of that topic.[78] Doughty finds it necessary to present a forceful argument why 'the English teacher must concern himself with the development of a pupil's total linguistic resource, his power to talk, listen, read and write'.[79]

Some writers feel that it is in classroom organization and teaching and learning styles that English has most strikingly changed. There is evidence of a great deal of experiment with workshop methods, group work, diversification of tasks and pupil choice.[80] Marland finds that '... the main organizing principle is a natural flow, with periods and homework devoted to a run of work that is linked closely together, often by theme'.[81] Excitement is expressed about what pupils are capable of doing on their own.[82]

While some of the textbooks could have been published ten years earlier, from others one gains an impression of eager innovation. The books are more expensively produced and more like 'trade' books, photographs are plentiful, and drawings are self-consciously arty.[83] Although the unreconstructed secondary modern pupil of 1958 and earlier lives on as a textbook stereotype, with his or her (mainly his) restricted experience, unexciting destination and need for the firm instructional hand with touches of avuncular humour, in a number of texts the student is accorded a new status. The imperative mode of address has been softened into suggestion or invitation ('Perhaps you could...') and a fiction is maintained that the students are free consumers who have come to the book and to the work by choice, in a search for interesting things to do.

Doughty characterizes the new orthodoxy in terms of a dependence on spontaneously arising interests and activities: 'The notion of "creative" writing — writing for oneself, or writing out of one's immediate experience, is a major instance of this, as is the strong emphasis now placed upon the value of class room work in drama that is unscripted or improvised ...' There is a reluctance to impose tasks, and an absence of planning, principle or analysis in the organization of teaching:[84] he quotes Summerfield on the 'ad hoc excitements' of English.[85] It has to be said that this picture is not supported by any of the published accounts from that year[86] or by the three books he cites as recent key texts which suggest student choice within a thoroughly planned and resourced framework. Doughty's impressions probably come, however, from direct knowledge of teachers' work and must, I think, be taken seriously.

According to Marland, '... the major preoccupation is with content ...';[87] courses and anthologies address themselves explicitly to this need. Since nobody had raised this as a problem ten years earlier, the question has to be asked why the material which had evidently then sufficed to occupy students for four and sometimes five years was no longer deemed adequate. I suggest three answers: that a reduction in the time devoted to language exercises and instruction left a large space to be filled;[88] that to the requirement that the content provide opportunity for practice has been added the new criterion that it stimulate interest and motivate a committed engagement; and that teachers' cultural preferences have changed. The last point is speculative, based on the conspicuous changes which had occurred in the mainstream culture in which many English teachers would have participated: in literary — especially paperback — publishing, in the content of arts and documentary television and film and the 'quality' Sunday papers, and in the interests and preferences of student culture.[89]

One effect was that the bland tranquillity of the fifties textbook was replaced by a preparedness — indeed, eagerness — to dwell on disturbing aspects of life, especially violence.[90] The main impulse was certainly to engage the interests of the students, but it may be that a new generation of teachers felt unwilling to associate themselves with the message that the world ran on basically well-ordered lines, and preferred to acknowledge that conflict and disorder were endemic.

While themes such as war were important, the main source of content was now, according to Doughty,[91] students' own experience, while the Schools Council wanted not only an English course but a whole curriculum for the young school leaver which 'starts from *individual learning* based on *experiences* related to *needs and interests*'.[92] In their suggestion that the work should move beyond experience into 'the objective world' and 'wider human issues'[93] they were, ironically, criticizing as inadequate a 'normalcy' that had barely been achieved: that English was 'personal' was certainly not the general view in the late fifties.

Literature in 1968

While there is evidence of the continuing strength of the grammar school normalcy,[94] the dominant impression is of an eager search for and receptiveness towards new material. Overriding concern with students' interests leads, according to Butts and Watkins, to a prevailing note of 'social eagerness' and to the widespread 'exclusion of some kinds of imaginative literature (e.g. poetry and especially literature produced before 1900)'.[95] Undoubtedly the most adventurous new collection is the three-volume *Voices* by Geoffrey Summerfield. This drew on previously untapped sources: small magazines, casual and ephemeral verse, folk verse, poetry in translation, and the lesser works of well-known poets. Accompanying the poems were photographs and drawings of a quality unprecedented in school publications.

Writing in 1968

Like the subject as a whole, writing is never for the mere attainment of competence, the aims being variously stated as 'imagination',[96] organizing experience,[97] social understanding,[98] expressing feelings, and therapy.[99] Noting, for instance, that grammar school students do not express feelings in their writing, Garnett straightforwardly assumes that this is because they are unable to, not that they choose not to.[100] She ascribes this failure to the over-intellectual diet they have received.

The term 'free writing' is heard no more: its contemporary equivalent, 'creative writing', has not only taken its place but has expanded to comprise, it sometimes appears, simply 'the writing done in English'. The procedure is well summarized as 'a stimulus set up, discussed and used as a starting point for writing, supported or followed by evocative passages of prose or poems'.[101] Critics of the practice characterize the 'stimulus' aspect as the display of arbitrarily chosen attention-catching phenomena — Summerfield's 'ad hoc excitements'. The stock examples are 'bubble-blowing' and 'the well known ritual burning of a piece of paper'.[102] Activities prescribed in Shaw's textbook read like a caricature of the impracticality and desperation which marked some of the bids for student involvement in course books of the period: 'If you can, go out in the playing field and do some serious running, competing against one another. Wear your ordinary shoes, which should give you something of the feeling of what it is like to race in wellingtons ... Then make notes of how you felt ...'[103]

Amongst the many criticisms[104] those of Doughty are particularly important: whereas the advocates of what Britton and his London Writing Research colleagues were by now calling 'expressive' writing appeared to see it as spontaneous and convention-free, the direct expression of thoughts and feelings, Doughty was aware of the part which models played in all writing and was almost right in characterizing 'the only kind of written work acceptable to many teachers at present' as 'one variety of the language of literature, that is, intensely autobiographic, densely metaphoric, syntactically highly informal, and devoted to the accurate reporting of personal response to experience'.[105] ('Densely metaphoric' is questionable.) That this was indeed a literary language, and not simply the 'natural' language of unplanned expression, was an insight which failed to be widely registered. The corollary of this bias was, in Doughty's view, the neglect of non-literary uses of language and particularly of 'the varieties of English appropriate for analytical processes, and for rational discourse ...'[106] — a neglect of which Gurrey would certainly have disapproved.

We learn something of pupils' preferences. The new popularity of poetry writing[107] is a cause of concern to one HMI: while he cannot complain that '... there has been a remarkable increase in the writing of poetry by children, so much so that many now take it for granted...' he is suspicious of adolescents' motives: 'Their poems are poems of rebellion, protest, disenchantment. Sex, death, modern materialism, disappointment in relationships — anything which seems to sour them, or to spoil their conceptions of perfection.'[108] What Clark is contemplating, with such evident distaste, is the face of the Counterculture. Clark's is an interesting observation. A possible chain of causation suggests itself: teachers feel a need to provide opportunities for their students (especially their difficult adolescent students) to engage in activities which are congenial to them as well as capable of educational justification; the activities which are congenial are those which permit the expression of subcultural themes and values; thus English, through the exigencies of the teachers' classroom situation, comes to admit and, in effect, legitimate the articulation of ideas which are antithetical to the established ideology of schools — in the process gaining a staffroom reputation for subversiveness.

The trend, noted in 1958, towards the representation of particulars and away from abstractions and generalizations is strongly confirmed. The observation (or imagining) of the physical appearances of individual objects and scenes is accorded importance in many textbook writing assignments and, implicitly, in photographs which draw attention to the unique texture and configuration of a particular tree trunk entwined with creepers,[109] a dandelion seed head,[110] or an owl's eye.[111] The celebration is of 'things being various'[112] and Chanan detects a cult, satirizing it as a belief that only the most concrete and minute specification can catch the reality, even names being suspect as veiling the vision. He cites a passage from a Wesker play as exemplifying this spirit:

ADA: ...Tell me what you see.

DANNY: Hedges!

ADA: No, no, Daniel, That's a name, that's not what you see.

DANNY: I see thin pieces of wood. Going all over the place. With bumps on them, and thin slips of green like paper, and some funny soft stuff on them.

ADA: Now you can use names.[113]

This shift in the level of abstraction affects even the treatment of social issues. Whereas in 1958 the model essay on a large social theme would be written in the judicious generalizing style of a newspaper leader, in 1968 the material used in preparation would be 'experiential' (filmed or photographed representations of concrete experiences) and the students' 'exploration' of the theme would typically remain at the same level, e.g. through fiction and poetry writing and dramatic improvization. If the general 'truths' arrived at in the 1958 essay might often have been vacuous, in 1968 there appears to have been little interest in extracting any formulated transferable understandings — only a vague 'awareness'.[114] It is as if general knowledge itself has come to be mistrusted.

One other tendency incipient in 1958 (notably in Walsh's textbook) has become normalcy. Subjectivity — what it feels like to be the unique experiencing subject — is now a central writing topic. The tone is no longer unusual which we find in assignments such as, 'Try and remember a time when you felt sad, really sad, when you could easily have burst into tears — perhaps you did burst into tears...'.[115]

Features of the 'English Method' Discourse

In the years immediately preceding 1968 the number of books being published about English had notably increased,[116] and the 'method' literature showed a wider range than in 1958 of references to work outside English studies. Other disciplines explicitly drawn on were psychology, sociology, sociolinguistics and linguistics. Specific psychologies were systematically brought to bear on the teaching of English. Lawton provides the first extended account of the relevance for education of recent psychological research, especially that of the Russians Luria and Vygotsky, which supported Gurrey's view that through the symbolizing process language made possible cognitive operations on representations of the world.

The considerable appeal of the work of Basil Bernstein clearly lay in his explanation why working class children did less well at school (or, more cynically, in the confirmation he seemed to offer to those already inclined to subscribe to the traditional view of the inadequate working-class home) and in the agenda it implied for English teachers: get working-class children habituated to elaborated code. Lawton's own research provided grounds for believing this to be a practicable proposition.[117]

Linguistics was also by 1968 beginning to affect the teaching of English in schools. Like the disciplines mentioned above, it did this by placing in a new light the job which English teachers seemed called upon to do. By offering a model of the range of human language functions and presenting literary, scientific, conversational and all other uses of language as aspects of the same human phenomenon, linguistics suggested both that competence in the whole range was the goal which needed to be aimed at and that language itself in its variety was a fit object of study. (M.A.K. Halliday, director of the Programme in Linguistics and English Teaching, was emphatic that this did not imply the teaching of linguistics in schools.) Linguistics made it more possible to see English teachers' near exclusive concentration on literary language as unreasonable, and to maintain the belief that no variety of English was inherently superior to any other. Of immediate practical importance was the assertion that 'correctness' was a matter of no more than arbitrary social convention.[118]

'Feeling' has become a key term in the discourse. Britton and Newsome, in an article setting out the rhetorical model developed by the Writing Research team at the London Institute of Education, offer what is essentially a development of Gurrey's line of thinking.[119] The psychologists Luria and Vygotsky supported Gurrey's view of language as ordering experience in the most general sense and, specifically, in providing the organism with a means of self-regulation. They did not, however, explicitly point towards the ordering of experience in Britton's special sense — that is, representing and 'coming to terms with' particular, deeply affecting remembered experiences. Britton selectively emphasized the capacity of language to organize feeling and contribute to the individualization of each child's identity and personality: it was this function which for him defined English as a subject. To underpin this specialized function of English Britton had to supplement these Soviet theories with those of psychologists engaged in personal therapy, such as George Kelly, D.W. Winnicott and Carl Rogers.

That Britton and his London Institute colleagues were fully aware of the cognitive implications of the newly won understandings of language, and understood that the symbol system of language enabled not only feelings and affectively loaded experience but experience in the broader sense of knowledge of reality to be represented and thus mentally manipulated, is shown by their language across the curriculum policies.[120] It was only in English that learning through active language use was to be concentrated within the realm of the 'personal' and the affective.

It was, however, from a quite different quarter than cognitive psychology that the value-commitments originated which sustained feeling in this privileged position. For Bantock, the writer to give the most explicit expression to this ideology, the main source is D.H. Lawrence (a subsidiary one is Nietzsche). Expressivity — the capacity spontaneously, directly and without intellectual or conventional filtering to express feeling — is associated with unconsciousness or a quiescence of the conscious rational mind, and is seen as a desirable and fulfilling mode of existence for those for whom the life of the intellect is not a possibility. For the working class, therefore, hope of happiness, coinciding with the best prospects for a stable social order, lies in 'building up a genuine folk culture of the future', fostered by a separate education based on feeling. [121] It is easy to see how, in a cultural context pervaded by such ideas, the implications which the new theory held for the use of language for a *general* extension of cognitive power, knowledge and rational understanding, might well fail to be grasped. [122]

Interpreting the Changes: The Significance of the Growth Model

In the remainder of the essay I propose an interpretation of the changes which took place in English between 1958 and 1968. Referring to the version of English which was regarded in 1968 as a new orthodoxy and has since come to be known as the 'growth' model, I offer a critique of earlier accounts and then attempt to explain the emergence and success of the new model in terms of changes first in the institutional environment and then in the surrounding culture.

Of the writers who have given the main accounts of the history of the teaching of English, [123] Hodgson, Hamley and Ball have claimed to identify distinct traditions, models or 'paradigms'. Both Hodgson and Ball see English as marked since the beginning of the century by a basic opposition, one term of which, though present as a minority consciousness since 1900, has only recently achieved real institutional power. Ball identifies the conflicting paradigms as 'language' and 'literature', the recent manifestation of the former being the 'English as language' position, [124] associated with Britton and the London Institute and deriving from the 'grammarian' tradition but now emphasizing the use rather than the study of the mother tongue; while 'literature' has taken the form of the Cambridge position. Hodgson sees on the one side a conservative 'transmission' or initiation model, informing the teaching of both language ('Explicit Language Skills') and literature ('Cultural Heritage'), with Cambridge as a 'compromising' version within Cultural Heritage, and on the other a radical 'Growth rationale'. If these binary representations are appropriate at all, Hodgson's is the more plausible. Amongst other advantages it attributes some effectiveness to the progressive tradition (he calls it 'Personal expression'), which Ball loses track of after Marjorie Hourd's *The Education of the Poetic Spirit* (1949).

Hamley,[125] like Hodgson, sees the 'skills' and 'cultural heritage' models as the unargued normalcy until the late 1940s and also distinguishes a progressive and a Cambridge line of development. Unlike Hodgson, however, he rightly sees Cambridge as antagonistic to the traditional curriculum, and not as a new variant of 'Cultural heritage', and he then rightly characterizes 'growth' as a fusion of Cambridge with his 'Romantic-progressive' tendency. This is an important insight, and one which the other writers, and not only Ball and Hodgson, miss. Hamley explains that although progressivism and Cambridge have separate nineteenth century progenitors in Froebel and Matthew Arnold, further back their origins are intertwined in early Romanticism. It is thus not surprising to find the two streams merging again in the 1950s and 1960s[126] in the 'literature-based progressives', who represent one form of the 'growth position'.[127]

Hamley is surely right to see Cambridge and progressivism as having much in common. Clearly Romantic values which stand behind both the literature-centred and the growth approaches to English are those of the authority of individual response and the priority of an intelligence of feelings over one of rational thought. We first see their fusion in Ford's (1960) *Young Writers, Young Readers* in which, as Hamley points out,[128] progressive ideas are taken into account so as to admit as educationally valid literature other than great works, and specifically children's fiction, which rapidly became accepted as the principal genre up to the examination years. Pradl provides an interesting demonstration of one way in which progressive and Cambridge lines of thought came together: David Holbrook, a major representative of the Cambridge position, took from the psychologist D.W. Winnicott the notion that moral development in the older child comes about through the exercise of creativity 'when the child's inner world is permitted to interact "with the storehouse of man's cultural achievement"'.[129] English could thus value *both* the child's creativity *and* the cultural heritage of literature.

That the connections between 'growth' and the Cambridge spirit were close is indicated also by other evidence not noted by Hamley. Firstly, as we noted earlier, the model of English associated with Britton and Dixon was literary in orientation. Secondly, it was a central tenet alike of the Cambridge view of literature and of Britton's philosophy that feeling and thought were not inherently distinct functions, that affective response was as much a source of 'knowledge' as was intellectual cognition[130] and that the feeling responses could be refined and sharpened through expression in language. Both James Britton and David Holbrook were powerfully influenced by the object-relations psychology of D.W. Winnicott and others.[131] Thirdly, a point of fact is that Leavis himself approved of the Institute of Education English department[132] and advised Downing

College students who were planning to teach to go on there. Squire and Applebee observe that

> Somewhat joshingly (but not pejoratively), Cambridge graduates talk of having been 'deliteratized' at such institutes (postgraduate institutions of education). One of the most influential alliances affecting the teaching of English in Britain was that formed between the Cambridge graduates of F.R. Leavis and the one-year graduate program in English education directed by James N. Britton at the University of London ... [133]

Finally, the survey report from which that quotation is taken provides convincing evidence that an emphasis on active language *production*, justified as contributing to pupils' overall personal development, provided an acceptable basis for many whose socialization had been through the Cambridge version of English. A team of American observers visited forty-two English departments which in the view of a group of British 'experts' showed the best current practice. This practice, as the observers described it, was unmistakably that of the new 'growth' orthodoxy: while literature had a large place, [134] creative writing had a larger one; the guiding values were to do with the importance of response and spontaneity: 'The teaching of English in British schools is the teaching of creative response. Involvement in the creative act seems to be the primary goal... Feeling and doing, not knowing, are the critical concerns.' [135] 'Intellect is out; feeling is in'; 'Every class ... was a kind of happening ...' are other comments. [136] About the teachers who administered this 'growth' regime the authors offer the highly significant fact that '... a majority of the chairmen (heads of department) and many teachers in the schools selected for visitation took their university work at Cambridge. A typical pattern was a B.A. at Cambridge followed by a year's work at the University of London Institute of Education.' [137] In other words, 'growth' was what 'Cambridge' — or a significant branch of it — had now become.

It has been important to insist on the point that 'growth' was less remote from the Cambridge school than has often been suggested. Nevertheless, it is correct to see the work of Britton and Dixon as basically the expression of a different tradition, that of which Gurrey was an earlier representative, [138] with his understanding of the importance of language as the function on which largely depends our cognitive grasp of the world. A firm believer in the role of literature, Gurrey had stood also for rationality and clear thinking, a value which was perhaps the most highly prized of all in some grammar school varieties of English, [139] and the importance of which the historians do not seem to have realized. It was out of this tradition that the socially critical English of *Reflections*, by Dixon and his Walworth colleagues, and of Fred Flower's *Language in Education* derived; and it is evident in other writers associated with the London Institute, such as Nancy Martin and Druce and Tucker, in the respect their work expresses for rational thought, knowledge and the ability to generalize, and in their rejection of the current overemphasis on feeling.

The practice of Dixon, and also of Rosen as represented in his 1958 article, was informed at the same time by an elementary school tradition[140] which acknowledged the pupils' real location in their world, did not require them to pretend to genteel sensibility and placed them in the role of responsible observers and commentators. The informing aim, as in Gurrey's English, was a broad range of written and spoken language competence (not excluding an initiation into literature), while the method was the promotion of active, motivated and enjoyable uses of language, together with a certain amount of study of grammar in the context of use. This is certainly not Ball's 'grammarian' or Hodgson's 'basic skills' paradigm; but it is not exactly the 'progressive' tradition either, if by that we mean the one to which such figures as Lamborn, Hourd and Langdon were central, with their emphasis on spontaneity, free expression and the child as seer. It is not in fact identified as a 'model' at all by those writers given to such an approach; it is Shayer who first gives it due recognition. Yet it is important for contributing to the English of the 1960s both an emphasis on the range of language uses and a down-to-earth, humorous and democratic tone that was quite different from the harrowing intensity by which Cambridge work was sometimes marked. It underlay that cheerful, *angst*-free writing about home and neighbourhood of which Rosen gives us a taste in the late 1950s and which continued to be a distinctive feature of the Walworth and similar lower school English courses. This celebration of the general texture of ordinary working-class lives — the street markets, totters, bagwashes, stray cats, hiding places and nagging neighbours — had behind it a socialist optimism.

The insight informing this tradition — intuitive in most teachers, but becoming explicit with Gurrey — that language was a means of organizing experience and that in its use for that purpose lay the best means of extending pupils' competence — received valuable corroboration from the already mentioned studies of Vygotsky (1962) and Luria (1961), and also of Bruner (1964) and Chomsky (1957, 1959).[141] The theoretical basis was thus to hand for an English centred on the immediately intelligible purpose of general language competence, to be achieved, as in early childhood, through the student's pursuit of cognitive mastery and understanding.

Such a theory was indeed adumbrated, though perhaps never fully articulated. It provided the basis for the 'language across the curriculum' movement, with its paired objectives of language extension through motivated learning and more effective learning through motivated language use. It was only, however, in an interestingly modified form that the theory was taken up for English itself. By a selective reinterpretation of the key insight, typically expressed in the formula that language organized experience, experience was taken to mean not the sum total of what is in fact experienced but experience as inner events occasioned by interactions with the environment. What essentially *needed* to be organized, according to the most influential accounts, was the feelings. This sidetracking of 'language and experience' thinking away from the possibilities it offered of a broad rationale for English and into a preoccupation with feelings and a narrowly constructed notion of 'personal experience' seems in part an effect of the complex fusion of the tradition just described with the Lawrentian-Leavisian inheritance. Other factors will be mentioned below.

The version of English which now became dominant had great strengths. The purpose of full personal development (regardless of students' assigned destinations) lent a new dignity and seriousness to English teachers' work with the full range of abilities. An approach based on personal experience and social issues did indeed motivate many pupils, with the result that impressive new achievements in writing and drama were recorded.[142] Ordinary lives of ordinary children were dignified as worthy matter for the English lesson. English became more enjoyable and less redolent of a stuffy official culture. Of all the school subjects except perhaps art, English was most in tune with the styles and preoccupations of youth culture.

As against these gains, the adoption of the personal growth concept also entailed losses and the closing off of possibilities. The emphasis on feelings and on the prime value of the individual's authentic response could sometimes override the rationality and respect for general ideas which the London Institute took from the grammar school tradition, and led to the continuation in English teaching of the anti–intellectualism implicit in late Leavisite readings of Lawrence — what Mulhern has called the 'irrationalist kernel of Leavisian "analysis and judgement"':[143] 'Everywhere, from every source I encountered, there came a genuine anti-intellectual cry for a negation of the cognitive dimensions of learning', said a member of the US delegation.[144]

The Environment of English

Traditions of pedagogical thought and practice do not transform them-selves, or fuse with each other, simply on their own. Why changes in English took the form they did, and why they came then rather than earlier or later is the matter we must now address. I consider two sets of factors: changes in the institutional environment of education, and cultural changes in society.[145]

Foremost amongst the institutional changes was comprehensivization. Some of the effects on English were immediate and obvious. The writing of syllabuses, for new departments which often comprised a mixture of staff from secondary modern and grammar school backgrounds, meant that 'The comprehensive situation ... required us to go back to first principles, to a rethinking of our whole attitude towards the teaching of English'.[146]

Teachers of the Cambridge persuasion, who had hitherto worked almost exclusively in the grammar schools with 25 per cent of students selected on academic ability, felt they had to come up with a radical modification to their programme, not least because of their perception that 'The low verbal ability, and the cultural poverty of many pupils in a system of compulsory universal education has made it hard to find accepted works of prose literature which can in fact be read with understanding and enjoyment in the classroom.'[147] For graduates from Cambridge and similarly oriented university English departments there must have been a problem in constructing the job as a pursuit worthy of such a high-calibre training. The perceived low ability of many of the pupils appeared to rule out a definition in the grammar school tradition of the fostering of rationality. Yet the pastoral social-moral ethic of the secondary modern would not do either, since it was associated with low-status institutions and manifestly did not call for the qualities which English graduates distinctively possessed. The solution lay in the Cambridge notion of *sensibility* — that capacity for responding, feeling and living which all humanity was felt to possess in common.[148] The cultivation of sensibility, albeit through writing and 'children's literature' rather than through great works, was an enterprise which was (a) deeply worthwhile, since on it the cultural health of the nation was felt to depend, and (b) commensurate with the capabilities of graduate English specialists since that criticism of life and literature which constituted their training involved the utmost rigour and discipline.

In placing feelings rather than intellect at the centre of their subject English teachers at the same time provided themselves with a democratic ideology which consorted well with the official aims of the comprehensive schools. Those emotional resources which in the secondary modern schools had been developed as a compensatory alternative[149] were elevated to become the most important element in all children. Squire and Applebee confirm that in the schools they visited democratic sentiment was indeed a powerful ingredient in the teachers' motivation: 'They [British teachers of English] were all working to make their society a more democratic one, and they were all convinced that English was an important basis for the changes to be made.'[150] A corollary of a defining purpose centred on feeling would be a necessity to resist any tendency to make the subject more 'intellectual', since that would imply that to be landed, as the teachers in question now were, with pupils who were generally regarded as lacking intellectual ability, would be a diminution of one's professional scope — a consideration which might partly account for the sustained rejection we have noted of anything smacking of generalizing or abstracting.

The problems facing English, however, lay not only at the level of teachers' professional identities and their personal survival in classrooms which presented unaccustomed challenges. The place of the subject as a whole, at least as a well-resourced section of the curriculum, regarded as essential for all pupils and taught by a large department, was placed in question. If a curriculum suitable for the full range of children had not been found to take the place of the grammar school literature course, embody its values and command the allegiance of the literature teachers, English might have survived only in a much weakened form as two separate elements: a minority literature option reserved, like physics, for the ablest, and a literacy programme, principally for the younger and less able children, deriving its content, method and status from the elementary school tradition. It may be that the survival of English as a well-endowed core subject with generous capitation, a large share of the school's salary points, access to sixth form work and good prospects of promotion to headships, depended on the invention of a new version of the subject as a single unified and distinct enterprise which was readily justifiable as a central component in the education of the entire population.

As we have seen, the only adequate potential theory of English capable of being developed at the time pointed in the direction of intelligence and cognitive power developed through a wide range of language competencies, for reason, analysis, reflection, argument, inquiry and the regulation of practical activity as well as for personal expression and literary discourse: that is, a reformulation of one strand of the traditional grammar school programme. We have suggested one reason why such a rationale was never seriously considered. Even, however, had objections not been felt towards the promotion of thinking and knowing rather than feeling, a further difficulty remained, namely that such a programme would best be realized *across* the curriculum, without any particular need for English, since other subjects provided ample contexts for communication and learning in which language might be developed.

Perhaps what 'growth' had decisively to offer, then, was a specialist and *different* role for English, one which, with its distinct content of 'a personal experience' hardly touched on in the rest of the curriculum, and its methods and models drawn in part from the prestigious and mystique-laden sphere of literature, was able to ensure that English stood no risk of being 'integrated out' through diffusion across the curriculum. The strategy was quite different from that which has been well documented for other subjects, the pursuit of academicization. Nothing could be more remote from such an intention than to define one's content as the rest of the pastry after the other subject shapes have been cut out.[151] Rather, non-specialism itself became a sort of specialism, one for the handling of which a literary background and trained sensibility were prerequisites.

At the start of this chapter I itemized some features which I took to be distinctive of English in England and Wales today. We are now in a position provisionally to enumerate which of them were acquired between about the last quarter of the 1950s and the last quarter of the 1960s.

The 'non-specialist' appearance of English is nothing new. It was always the complaint of English teachers that specialist qualifications were not judged necessary for teaching the subject. The turn, however, which the subject took in the 1960s, in making a specialism out of non-specialism, while securing the *place* of English in the comprehensive school, did little to improve its status as a 'discipline'. Although the leading advocates insisted that dealing with personal experience and encouraging unconstrained communication was a highly skilled business requiring a specialist training (with literary criticism and the study of language development alternatively claimed as the best preparation), this was not obvious to those outside the subculture. Features which accrued to English in the period we have considered in fact made it appear both less specialist and less intelligible. In 1958 it was evidently a rare teacher who did not provide a great deal of direct instruction, particularly in the area of grammar and language usage. By 1968 English teachers did not obviously *teach* anything. By this date also the language, spoken and written, which was the valued output of the English lesson was no longer so recognizably special. Literary models certainly informed writing practice, but at the same time the emphasis on authenticity meant that continuity with students' own vernaculars was sought: students were not, or at least were much less obviously, taught a refined linguistic 'best behaviour' only obtainable from school and from 'cultured' milieux. Lastly, the matter which formed the content of the English lesson was already in the students' possession: no longer was it a central purpose of English to *introduce* students through literature to inspiring and ennobling human achievements beyond the realm of the everyday.

There is one further respect in which the nature of present-day English was decisively settled in the sixties. English in the 1950s promoted a range of written language which was certainly not wide but which included argument and analysis. While the forms these took might be regarded as essentially literary, it is clear that over the ensuing years English became 'literary' in a narrower sense in focusing almost exclusively on the language of fiction, poetry and personal expression.

There were, then, numerous reasons to do with the changing institutional context which might account for developments in the subject between 1958 and 1968. At the same time, however, it strikes one forcibly today that the period of rapid educational change was also one of conspicuous cultural change and that, moreover, there are striking congruences between the shifts in English teaching and cultural developments in the wider society. The issue seems important yet none of the histories have addressed it. In breaking new ground, the discussion which follows will necessarily be exploratory and speculative.

It is the phenomenon commonly known as the 'Counterculture'[152] which most immediately presents apparent parallels to what was happening in English. The Counterculture, all writers are agreed,[153] though anticipated by the Beats and by a popular interest in existentialism, was a movement which peaked in the mid- to late sixties and involved mainly middle-class youth. Zicklin calls it a 'full scale revolt against the values and institutions of the society', by American youth 'experiencing a collective role moratorium, testing and experimenting with much of their lives, from the way they dressed to what they believed to be the ultimate truths of existence'.[154] There is agreement too about the central themes of the Counterculture, prominent among which is (in Zicklin's terms) 'the Expressive Mode, about spontaneity and 'opening up': ("...we will know and love our own nature, far beyond words or political thoughts, know what we are a part of, just a part; we will be together with each other..."'[155]); while for Gussner the key imperative of 'the new individualism' is: 'Learn to feel the fantasy ego, the animal aspect of the psyche, develop directness of feeling and sensory awareness, be open to whimsy, creativity, humour and dreams.'[156] Bernice Martin finds that:

> The romantic counterculture of the 1960s attacked (the) classic elements of form and found reason compromised by its bourgeois and instrumental connotations. In assaulting the restraining frame they thus freed egoistic individualism to pursue anarchic subjectivity and let loose romantic idealism to assert the superiority of collective being over disciplined ratiocination. Knowledge transmuted from the objective to the subjective mode.[157]

Bernice Martin suggests a direct influence from the Counterculture on education. Of the features which we earlier noted as characteristic of the emerging English of the 1960s those which strikingly recall Countercultural phenomena are: the anti-rational emphasis on feeling; the stressing of the cultivation of individual unique identity rather than socialization into approved values; the concern with the expression of suppressed or unarticulated needs; the dissolving of categories and lowering of boundaries; and the valuing of choice and spontaneity over discipline and the mastery of conventional forms. Educational trends which Martin notes as signs of Countercultural influence are a general mistrust of categories and boundaries, an emphasis on student self-determination and 'learning through exploration, feeling, self-discovery', and a de-emphasis of rituals of collective identity, such as uniform and speech days, and of 'Hierarchy, authority, and honourable, achieved leadership roles'.[158]

'Collective being' or communal solidarity, the last point in the passage quoted from Martin above, is central to her account of the Counterculture: she identifies in it the essential structural complement to the urge to 'antinomian subjectivity'. But it is here that the analogy with English breaks down, since while the 'growth' model exhibited plentiful manifestations of the expressive mode it showed no tendency to promote a merging of individuals into a collectivity. Martin indeed has to acknowledge the almost total absence from schooling of the aspiration towards collective totality. In addition, her account of the mechanisms by which

Peter Medway

Countercultural influences might have been transmitted to teachers in schools is unconvincing.

The evidence which Martin cites in fact points rather to the conclusion that education was experiencing a strong pull towards expressivity in any case, and that the Counterculture was not itself an important cause of change. As she says, 'the axial principles of the Expressive Revolution had already put down deep roots' in teaching.[159] Teachers, she argues, were already predisposed towards expressivity because status in education attaches to the expressive activity of pursuing knowledge and experience for their own sakes and not for use, while little self-regard is to be derived from those instrumental functions which are mainly what is expected of them by the outside world and, indeed, by the students.[160]

Of greater interest, therefore, are accounts of underlying tendencies in the society, some of which are adduced as explanations of the Counterculture and which may in a parallel manner have affected education. As Bernice Martin puts it, 'The argument is that the counterculture was a particularly colourful symptom, herald and agent of structural changes which were occurring in the fabric of advanced industrial societies. The sixties' aspiration to let the jinn out of the bottle was itself the product of social change.'[161]

The first theory we will note is that the Counterculture was essentially a response born out of frustration with the constrictions and tensions induced by industrial societies. In an industrial economy 'feelings, intuition and fantasy are subordinated to capacities of the rational mind to measure, analyze, compare and calculate ...' leading to a demand for the right to give full rein to the emotions.[162] Young people acted in rejection of 'older virtues of thrift, hard work, competition to accumulate surplus, and the drive for career success ...' and in affirmation of those parts of themselves which had previously not been validated.[163] Gussner notes that this 'technocracy theory' which 'charges that technique and production ... subjugate the human spirit and life itself to bureaucratic organization', is 'a virulent strain breeding new variations almost monthly'.[164]

For other writers, however, such as R.H. Turner, summarizing and quoting Shils, '... mass society opened up opportunities for an augmented range of gratifications. As existence became less precarious, people could afford to act on their impulses. More of society's resources could be applied to creating avenues for the gratification of impulse:

The individual organism has become a seeker after experience, a repository of experience, an imaginative elaborator of experience. To a greater extent than in the past, the experience of the ordinary person, at least in youth, is admitted to consciousness and comes to form part of the core of the individual's outlook. There has come about a greater openness to experience, an efflorescence and intensification of sensibility ... In a crude, often grotesque way, the mass society has seen the growth, over wide areas of society, of an appreciation of the value of the experience of personal relationships, of the intrinsic value of a personal attachment ...[165]

In parallel vein Berger *et al.* note that 'the individual's subjective reality ... becomes increasingly differentiated, complex — and "interesting" to himself'.[166] But it is not simply that goods have become abundant so that people are released from 'the immediate disciplines of survival'.[167] Changes in the basic nature of the economy have had direct implications for the biographies and identities of individuals. The long-term trend has been 'away from production orientation and toward consumption orientation'. Instead of disciplined work habits, 'the cultivation of personal tastes, expressive style, and distinctive psychological "needs" was at a premium...'.[168] Economic change thus leads to changes in the personality structures which are socially valued. In Rose's terms, the population's characteristics as a market become more important than its characteristics as a labour force: '... modern economic performance depends ultimately on avid consumption'.[169] Accordingly, not thrift but indebtedness, not deferred gratification but immediate satisfaction are the values now urged on the population.

Berger and his associates argue that these changes in the economic structure affect the construction of identity in even more profound ways: 'Identity ceases to be an objectively and subjectively given fact (assigned by work and community), and instead becomes the goal of an often devious and difficult quest.'[170] This 'identity work'[171] takes place in 'the interstitial areas left vacant, as it were, by the institutions',[172] and especially the family, one of the few settings in which, according to Martin, 'it is unequivocally legitimate to be an integrated person with full affective and expressive rights'.[173] The sphere of operation of the 'true self' is thus confined to the margins of the society's central activity.

Turner's preoccupation is with changes in the way we determine which of 'the various feelings and actions that emanate from my person' I recognize as 'my real self'. The essence of these changes — over 'recent decades' — is 'a shift in the locus of self' away from those 'feelings and actions with an institutional focus' — that is, those which manifest public societal values, such as achievement, altruism, self-discipline or loyalty — and toward 'ones they identify as strictly impulse'.[174]

Changes in the economic structure have borne with particular force on the young. Bauman points out that in advanced industrial societies '... the period during which young people [remain unproductive] is becoming longer and longer', but that the dominant 'cultural precepts' continue to stress the existence of absolute moral standards and the duties and values appropriate to productive roles, leading to 'inner cultural discord', stress and mental crisis.[175] Gussner's theory to account for 'the generation gap' centres on the notion of 'de-authorization' — the 'withdrawal of legitimation from pursuits, ideals, institutions, and cultural absolutes'.[176] Traditionally, the overwhelming influences on a young (American) person were those of the three 'norm-projecting centres' of the society — 'his home', 'his institutional experience' and 'his peer group',[177] of which the third, although always to some degree in conflict with the other two, was heavily outweighed. In the 1950s and 1960s, however, a fourth 'authority pole' emerged, that of the media, which 'began to adopt values opposed to mainstream America'.[178] This new influence aligned itself with the peer group, with the result that 'About 1969, poles 3 and 4 achieved a parity of influence with the traditional ones. There was a balance of power; fully half the young people were for peace and love.'[179] The effect was that the young person, instead of being straightforwardly socialized, was now forced to make an existential choice of values. 'The pluralization of authority poles relativizes the power of all of them, and much of it then drains to the individual... *The new individual is bound only by the sense that he ought to be true to his inner state of being as it is in the present moment.*'[180]

It is beyond the scope of this paper and my own competence to attempt to trace the channels through which influence flowed between the wider society and the subculture of English teaching. While the influence of the Counterculture may not have been decisive, it was nevertheless presumably felt: young teachers would have imported it, if only as 'latent culture',[181] and expressive tendencies in education could only have been reinforced by analogous manifestations in the Counterculture itself and in other professions such as social work and psychiatry.

The existence of wider cultural influence, which is all that I hope to suggest here, may be somewhat melodramatically illustrated if we attempt, if only as a heuristic device, to characterize the changes in English teaching between 1958 and 1968 in the terms employed by the sociologists of culture. Viewed from this perspective, English has jettisoned its function of inculcating the values and norms of Gussner's 'authority poles 1 and 2', those of the traditional family and of school, church and the official public sphere. The dominant 'criterion of significance' in English teaching has ceased to be that of public and conventional significance and has become that of personal significance. English no longer, as in 1958, helps the student to identify his or her 'real self' in conformity to institutional values. It does not prepare children for approved roles, whether of subordination or leadership, or for work in an industrial society: English students enjoy a 'role moratorium' while they investigate existential possibilities of living. An explicit claim of English is to help students with a central predicament of modern youth, that of making their own order and learning to cope with the 'inner cultural discord' induced by a pluralist society. 'De-authorization' has, moreover, extended beyond moral authority to linguistic authority: it is for students to choose the language appropriate to their purposes.

Instead of transmitting a legitimated and authorized set of values

English now helps students with the 'identity work' inescapably demanded of members of a plural society, and required by a consumption-based economy. What is to be recognized as the 'real self' is decisively the private self. In the literature studied the 'axis of individualization'[182] swings away from notable public heroes towards the private individual, often the child. English is directed towards an exploration of the inner self — 'we will know and love our own nature' — and one's experience in the private sphere; 'the experience of the ordinary person, at least in youth, is admitted to consciousness'. Experience becomes 'a positive, sought-after value'. Through literature, talking and writing, children come to 'an appreciation of the value of the experience of personal relationships'. Self-actualization is aimed at through 'opening up' and the expression of feelings; the spontaneity of first responses is valued; rational analysis is subordinated to 'feelings, intuition and fantasy', to 'directness of feeling and sensory awareness' — while new anthologies like *Voices* celebrate 'whimsy, creativity, humour and dreams'. Previously neglected aspects of the personality are validated. As in the family, so in the English lesson the student may be 'an integrated person with full affective and expressive rights'. In some versions there is, rather than an explicit preference for feeling over thought, a denial of that dichotomy: the ideal of the integrated person is captured in the notion of 'sensibility' — there was 'an efflorescence and intensification of sensibility'.

Finally, not only does English not align itself with establishment values; it displays a tendency to anti-authoritarianism. Attention is paid to oppressed groups and to their expressions of protest, and older students are allowed or encouraged to express nonconformist or rebellious sentiments, sometimes in their own voices, sometimes in those of groups with whom they are encouraged to identify.

We can cautiously conclude that explanations for change in English which rest exclusively on changes in the material and institutional conditions of teaching are not enough. Influences from the wider economy and culture, though diffuse and hard to track through specific channels, appear at certain times also to be of critical importance.

Notes

Abbreviations used:
EE English in Education
LATE London Association for the Teaching of English
NATE National Association for the Teaching of English
UE The Use of English

1 DEPARTMENT OF EDUCATION AND SCIENCE (1975) *A Language for Life* (The Bullock Report), London, HMSO, pp. 8 and 414.

2   TAYLOR, P.H. (1970) *How Teachers Plan Their Courses*, Slough, NFER, p. 13, summarizing views expressed to him by a group of English teachers. Ten Brinke finds such claims to be typical of mother tongue teaching not only in Britain but in the USA, Netherlands and West Germany: 'It seems to deal with almost everything that is valuable in life, leaving only small fragments for the other subjects to take care of. In its extended form MMT [mother tongue teaching] is a kind of all-comprising subject — a subject with, in a manner of speaking, a supernatural status. It is almost a pity to think that any attempt would ever be made to shed this half-divine position ...' TEN BRINKE, S. (1976) *The Complete Mother-tongue Curriculum*, Groningen, Netherlands, Wolters-Woordhoff-Longman, p. 243.

3   MEDWAY, P. (1986a) 'What gets written about', in WILKINSON, A. (Ed.) (1986) *The Writing of Writing*, Milton Keynes, Open University Press, pp. 22–39.

4   Historical accounts are: ALLEN, D. (1980) *English Since 1965: How Much Growth?* London, Heinemann; BALL, S. (1982) 'Competition and conflict in the teaching of English: a socio-historical analysis', *Journal of Curriculum Studies*, Vol. 14, No. 1, pp. 1–28; BALL, S. (1983) 'A subject of privilege: English and the school curriculum 1906–35', in HAMMERSLEY, M. and HARGREAVES, A. (Eds) (1983) *Curriculum Practice: Some Sociological Case Studies*, Lewes, Falmer Press, pp. 61–88; BALL, S. (1985) 'English for the English since 1906', in GOODSON, I. (Ed.) (1985) *Social Histories of the Secondary Curriculum: Subjects for Study*, Lewes, Falmer Press, pp. 53–88; GRACE, G. (1978) *Teachers, Ideology and Control: A Study in Urban Education*, London, Routledge and Kegan Paul; HAMLEY, D.C. (1979) 'Changing principles and recommended practice in the teaching of fiction in elementary and secondary modern schools from 1902 to the present day: with special reference to the age group 11–13', unpublished Ph.D thesis, University of Leicester; HODGSON, J.D. (1975) 'Changes in English teaching: institutionalisation, transmission and ideology', unpublished Ph.D. thesis, University of London; MATHIESON, M. (1975) *The Preachers of Culture: A Study of English and Its Teachers*, London, Allen and Unwin; MULLINS, W.R. (1968) 'A study of significant changes in the theory of the teaching of English to older pupils in elementary and secondary modern schools, 1860–1966', unpublished M.Ed. thesis, University of Leicester; SHAYER, D. (1972) *The Teaching of English in Schools 1900–1970*, London, Routledge and Kegan Paul; and WRIGHT, E. (1986) 'English teaching: classics in the vernacular', in PRICE, M., *The Development of the Secondary Curriculum*, London, Croom Helm, pp. 49–76. HANSEN, I.V. (1960) 'The teaching of English: an examination of its growth in the grammar school curriculum and its present practice, and an assessment of its success in giving a command of the mother-tongue', unpublished M.A. (Ed.) thesis, University of Southampton, includes an interesting historical section, of use in relation to the early history of the subject, which draws on histories of individual schools. Other writers who deal with English as a university subject are BOARD OF EDUCATION (1921) *The Teaching of English in England* (The Newbolt Report), London, HMSO, pp. 242ff; POTTER, S. (1937) *The Muse in Chains*, London, Cape; PALMER, D.J. (1965) *The Rise of English Studies: An Account Of The Study Of English Language And Literature From Its Origins To The Making Of The Oxford English School*, London, OUP for the University of Hull; MULHERN, F. (1979) *The Moment of 'Scrutiny'*, London, NLB; DOYLE, B. (1982) 'The hidden history of English studies', in WIDDOWSON, P. (Ed.) (1982) *Re-reading English*, London, Methuen, pp. 17–31; EAGLETON, T.

(1983) *Literary Theory: An Introduction*, Oxford, Blackwell; and BALDICK, C. (1983) *The Social Mission of English Criticism, 1848–1932*, Oxford, Clarendon Press.

5 On the latter see WILLIAMS, R. (1977) *Marxism and Literature*, Oxford, OUP; DAVIES, T. (1978) 'Education, ideology and literature', *Red Letters*, No. 7, pp. 4–15, and Eagleton (1983) *op. cit.*

6 'As recently as 1960 English as a school subject was in a state of suspended animation which had hardly changed over forty years': ALLEN, G. (1973) 'English past, present and future', in BAGNALL, N. (Ed.) (1973) *New Movements in the Study and Teaching of English*, London, Temple Smith, p. 30.

7 Reported in MEDWAY, P. (1986b) 'What counts as English: selections from language and reality in a school subject at the twelve year old level', unpublished Ph.D thesis, University of Leeds.

8 It is not always obvious from the text alone into which category a textbook falls, since the teaching material tends to be provided without comment. Indications may, however, be sought in accompanying teachers' manuals, in advertisements and in contemporary reviews. The interpretation of textbooks is generally problematic. Clearly, a textbook is not necessarily evidence of practice — it may not have been bought by schools in significant numbers. Sales figures, however, are not easily obtained. Some indication may be gained from the number of impressions and editions a book went through, but one still does not know what proportion of sales (it was often considerable) was to overseas markets (GARNETT, E. (1968a) 'Your fifty favourite books', *UE* Vol, 19, No. 3, pp. 119–206).

9 GURREY, P. (1958) *Teaching the Mother Tongue in Secondary Schools*, London, Longmans, Green; REEVES, J. (1958) *Teaching Poetry: Poetry In Class: Five to Sixteen*, London, Heinemann.

10 NATIONAL UNION OF TEACHERS (1958) *Inside the Comprehensive School: A Symposium Contributed By Heads Of Comprehensive Schools In England And Wales*, London, Schoolmaster Publishing Company, Appendix A; DENT, H.C. (1958) *Secondary Modern Schools: an interim report*, London, Routledge and Kegan Paul, p. 20.

11 That subjects may simply subserve this function is evidently the view taken by the committee (including sixteen head teachers) set up to advise Cheshire Councily Council on the curriculum of the secondary modern school. Their report is organized not by subjects but by the functions of the school: under each of these the contributions of the various subjects are specified, so that prescriptions for English are found in the chapters on 'Spiritual and Moral Development', 'Emotional Development', 'Mental Development' (relegated, we note, to third place), 'Preparation for Home-Making and Parenthood', 'Preparation for Citizenship' and 'Preparation for Employment (CHESHIRE COUNTY COUNCIL EDUCATION COMMITTEE (1958) *The Secondary Modern School*, London, University of London Press).

12 The 'Cambridge' position has been recognized in several accounts of the history of English, including Shayer (1972) *op. cit.*, Mathieson (1973) *op. cit.*, Hodgson (1975) *op. cit.*, Hamley (1979) *op. cit.*, and Ball (1983) *op. cit.*

13 *The Use of English* began publication as *English in Schools* in 1939. The title was changed when Denys Thompson became editor in 1949. Thompson was succeeded as editor in 1969 by Frank Whitehead.

14 See e.g. KNIGHTS, L.C. (1958) 'The place of English literature in a liberal education', *UE*, Vol. 9, No. 3, pp. 155–66; p. 165.

15 Percival Gurrey was born in 1890, taught in grammar schools before and after
    World War I and in 1926 joined the London Day Training College (later to
    become the University of London Institute of Education) to develop the training
    of teachers of English in secondary schools. In 1937 he became head of the new
    department for the teaching of English to overseas students. In 1947 he was a
    founder, with James Britton, of the London Association for the Teaching of
    English. He left the Institute in 1948 to become Professor of English as a Foreign
    Language in the new University of the Gold Coast. He retired in 1951. His books
    (mostly written after his retirement) deal with the teaching of grammar, of poetry,
    of writing, of English as a mother tongue and as a foreign language, and with the
    education of teachers. He died in 1980. (Obituary, *The Times*, 19 March 1980
    (written by Nancy Martin — personal communication); BRITTON, J.N. (1973)
    'How we got here', in BAGNALL, N. (Ed.) *op. cit.*, pp. 13–14.)

16 Occasionally, however, there is artwork of quality — the woodcuts, for instance,
    in BURGESS, C.V. (1958) *Verse in Action*, four books: book 2, and teacher's book,
    London, University of London Press.

17 PATERSON, R. (1957–1959) *English with a Purpose*, four books: book 2 (1957),
    London, Nelson.

18 For a full account of these see Medway (1986b) *op. cit.*

19 *op. cit.*, p. 69.

20 *op. cit.*, p. 68.

21 *op. cit.*, pp. 120, 187.

22 The key Leavis statement, in which he speaks of 'a small minority' capable of
    'appreciating Dante, Shakespeare, Donne, Baudelaire, Conrad', who 'constitute
    the consciousness of the race' and 'keep alive the subtlest and most perishable
    parts of the tradition', is the 1930 essay 'Mass civilisation and minority culture',
    reprinted as Appendix III to F.R. LEAVIS (1943) *Education and the University*,
    London, Chatto and Windus.

23 SPENCER, M. 'Three year training — a personal view', *UE*, Vol. 10, No. 1, pp.
    10–13; p. 12. 'Meg Merrilies' is by Keats, 'The Pied Piper of Hamelin' by
    Browning and 'Sea Fever' by John Masefield.

24 GOLDING, W. (1954) *The Lord of the Flies: A Novel*, London, Faber. Douglas
    Barnes tells me that it was 'heavily backed by LATE'.

25 JACKSON, B. (1958) 'A primary anthology: [review of] *The Oxford Book of Verse
    for Juniors*, by James Britton', *UE*, Vol. 9, No. 4, pp. 280–2; p. 280.

26 THOMPSON, K.P. (1958) 'The destruction of Sennacherib', *UE*, Vol. 10, No. 1,
    pp. 35–6.

27 CHAPMAN, J.V. (1959) *Your Secondary Modern Schools*, London, College of
    Preceptors.

28 Only one book, BURTON, S.H. (1958) *A First English Course*, London, Longmans,
    Green, has a substantial representation of twentieth-century poetry, and most of
    that is from the earlier part of the century. According to Tony Davies (1978, *op.
    cit.*) 250 editions of *The Golden Treasury* by Francis T. Palgrave are recorded in the
    National Union Catalogue, and it was the major instrument by which the
    category of 'literature' was constructed as a vehicle for popular education.

29 MONSERRAT, N. (1951) *The Cruel Sea*.

30 CHAPMAN, *op. cit.*, pp. 240–50.

31 *op. cit.*, p. 87.

32 E.g. BURTON, *op. cit.*; WALSH, J.H. (1958, 1959) *Graded Exercises in English*, two

books: book 2, London, Longmans, Green; ROCHE, J.W. (1958) *Background English*, book 1, Leeds, E.J. Arnold.

33 An example: 'Cinema fire. Discovered by night watchman. High wind hinders brigade. Three injured as wall collapses. Daring rescue of cat' (SCOTT, T. (1958, 1959) *English at Work*, two books, book 2 (1959), London, Brodie, p. 58).

34 ROSEN, H., in consultation with Nancy Martin (1958) 'What shall I set?' *UE*, Vol. 10, No. 2, pp. 90–7; pp. 91, 93. Harold Rosen was writing as a teacher from Walworth comprehensive school in London (where John Dixon succeeded him). He had until recently taught in a grammar school and was later lecturer and professor at the University of London Institute of Education.

35 One of his own assignments is: 'Jazz Band. Its arrival at a dance hall; the business of getting ready to play. Your observations of them in action. The leader or one of the performers might come in for special attention, but don't think you've got to work your way through the band one by one' (*ibid.*, pp. 93–4).

36 BARNES, D. and SEED, J. (1981) *Seals of Approval: An Analysis of English Examinations At Sixteen Plus*, Leeds, University of Leeds School of Education, reprinted in: GOODSON, I. and BALL, S. (Eds) (1984) *Defining the Curriculum: Histories And Ethnographies Of School Subjects*, Lewes, Falmer Press, pp. 263–98.

37 In 1958, Pym's book was reviewed by Douglas Brown (PYM, D. (1956) *Free Writing*, with a chapter by Lorna V. Southwell, University of Bristol Institute of Education Publication Number 10, London, University of London Press). Michael Paffard reported in a two-part article on his own experiments in 'free writing' with junior grammar school forms (PAFFARD, M.K. (1957) 'Free writing: I', *UE*, Vol. 9, No. 2, pp. 110–15; (1958) 'Free writing: II', *UE*, Vol. 9, No. 3, pp. 182–9); and Reeves, *op. cit.*, promoted 'free verse' on the same principles.

38 BROWN, D. (1958) 'Writing English: *Free Writing* by Dora Pym', [review] *UE*, Vol. 10, No. 1, pp. 52–4. See the elaborate and abstruse sentence Paffard uses as a stimulus (PAFFARD, (1958), *op. cit.*, p. 184). Pym explains that 'free writing' means 'writing from a starting-point, not with a free choice of subject' (*op. cit.*, p. 122).

39 'It seems to me likely that a majority of the teachers who read this note will already have in hand some forms of "free writing"' (BROWN, *op. cit.*, p. 52).

40 ROSEN, *op. cit.*, pp. 90–2.

41 CHESHIRE COUNTY COUNCIL, *op. cit.*, p. 87.

42 BURTON, *op. cit.*

43 PENDLEBURY, B.J. (1956–1958) *A Grammar School English Course*, four books: book 1 (1956), London, Nelson.

44 BARNES, W. (1958) *English Explained*, four books: book II, Huddersfield, Schofield and Sims.

45 WEBBER, J. (1958) *Let's Write an Article*, two books, London, Chatto and Windus; SCOTT, *op. cit.*

46 ROCHE, *op. cit.*

47 BURTON, *op. cit.*, DAVIES, E. and TREVASKIS, J. (1954) *Visual English*, secondary series, book 2 (1959), London, Evans.

48 TOWERS, B.E. (1958) 'Form newspaper', *UE*, Vol. 9, No. 4, pp. 247–9, GURREY, *op. cit.*, p. 87.

49 BURTON, *op. cit.*; PATERSON, *op. cit.*, p. 5.

50 STEVENS, F. (1958) 'The uses of literacy and the use of English', *UE*, Vol. 9, No. 4, pp. 227–32; pp. 231–2; HOGGART, R. (1957) *The Uses of Literacy: Aspects Of*

Working-Class Life, With Special Reference To Publications And Entertainments, London, Chatto and Windus.

51 Holbrook is one of the key figures in the reconstruction of English in the 1950s and 1960s. An ex-pupil of Leavis at Downing College, Cambridge, in 1958 Holbrook was tutor at Bassingbourn Village College and a prolific contributor to *Use of English*. He was later to be best known for his books *English for Maturity: English in the Secondary School* (London, Cambridge University Press, 1961) and *English for the Rejected* (Cambridge, Cambridge University Press, 1964). An excellent study of Holbrook is that of PRADL, G.M. (1971) 'Toward a moral approach to English: a study of the writings of F.R. Leavis and David Holbrook', unpublished Ph.D. thesis, University of Harvard.

52 HOLBROOK, D. (1958) 'Something they call a play ...', *UE*, Vol. 10, No. 1, pp. 3–9. Emphasis in original.

53 ROSEN, *op. cit.*, p. 92.

54 BROWN, *op. cit.*; ROSEN, *op. cit.*, pp. 90 and 93.

55 EVANS, J.T. (1958) 'The teaching of verse-writing in class', *UE*, Vol. 10, No. 2, pp. 98–104; p. 100.

56 KNIGHTS, *op. cit.*, p. 165.

57 WHYTE, W.H. (1957) *The Organization Man*, London, Jonathan Cape. (New York, Simon and Schuster, 1956); PACKARD, V. (1957) *The Hidden Persuaders*, London, Longmans.

58 WHITEHEAD, F. (1959) '*Teaching the Mother Tongue in Secondary Schools*, by P. Gurrey' [review], *UE*, Vol. 10, No. 4, pp. 265–8; p. 266.

59 GURREY, *op. cit.*, p. 12. Gurrey had certainly read Piaget and Firth, and possibly Sapir.

60 BLACKBURN, T. and CUNNINGHAM, W.T. (1968–1969) *Reach Out: An Anthology Of Poems for Schools*, three books: book 2, 1969, London, Nelson, p. ix.

61 Inglis and Inglis provide a ranting variant of the same phenomenon: INGLIS, F. and INGLIS, E. '"Your England". Notes on the *Use of English* pamphlet "Your England" by the authors', *UE*, Vol. 20, No. 2, pp. 148–50. The mystical strain still runs strong today, notably in the works of David Holbrook and Bernard Harrison, if not in school practice.

62 See e.g. DIXON, J. (1969) 'Conference report: the Dartmouth seminar', *Harvard Educational Review*, Vol. 39, No. 1, pp. 366–72.

63 BUTTS, D. and WATKINS, R. (1968) 'Raising the school-leaving age: an experiment with films and English', *UE*, Vol. 19, No. 4, pp. 315–20; p. 315.

64 '... we find that imaginative writing is the centre-piece, the main object of the English lesson.' '... the stuff of the new style English lesson, even though it does not itself look at literature all the time, is, I would like to say, pervaded by the approach and focus of the literary trained mind ... The categories, the concerns the techniques, come from the study of literature.' SINCLAIR, J. McH. (1968) 'English language in English students', *Educational Review*, 20, pp. 82–94.

65 Doughty argues that one effect of making literature the standard is that 'it effectively determines what a teacher will accept as successful "creative", or "personal", writing'. DOUGHTY, P.S. (1968a) *The Relevance of Linguistics for the Teacher of English*, Programme in Linguistics and English Teaching, series 1, paper 1, London, Longmans [for] University College, London, p. 65.

66 BUTTS and WATKINS, *op. cit.*, p. 316.

67 Directed by M.A.K. Halliday, based at University College, London, funded

originally by the Nuffield Foundation and later by the Schools Council. The best-known outcomes of the project were the source book for secondary schools and colleges, DOUGHTY, P.S., PEARCE, J. and THORNTON, G. (1971) *Language in Use*, London, Edward Arnold [for] Schools Council Programme in Linguistics and English Teaching, and MACKAY, D., THOMPSON, B. and SCHAUB, B. (1970) *Breakthrough to Literacy*, London, Longmans [for] Schools Council Programme in Linguistics and English Teaching.

68 DOUGHTY, P.S. (1968c) *Linguistics and the Teaching of Literature*, Programme in Linguistics and English Teaching, series 1, paper 5, London, Longmans [for] University College, London, p. 63.

69 PEEL, M. (1967) *Seeing to the Heart: English And Imagination In The Junior School*, London, Chatto and Windus; reviewed in 1968 by MULFORD, J., *UE*, Vol. 19, No. 4, pp. 336–9. CREBER, J.W.P. (1965) *Sense and Sensitivity: The Philosophy And Practice of English Teaching*, London, University of London Press.

70 DIXON, J. (1967) *Growth through English: A report based on the Dartmouth seminar 1966*, Reading, National Association for the Teaching of English. HOLLINS, T.H.B. (1968) 'The three-year course and the training of teachers of English', *EE*, Vol. 2, No. 2, pp. 16–22; p. 20. DOUGHTY, P.S. (1968d) 'What remains to do', *EE*, Vol. 2, No. 3, pp. 60–8; p. 62.

71 BRITTON, J. and NEWSOME, B. 'What is learnt in English lessons?' *Journal of Curriculum Studies*, 1, pp. 68–78; p. 73. Or, as Britton put it in 1967, '... what is to be achieved through language in English lessons is the organising and interpretation of the child's personal experiences and their extension in an organised way.' Quoted from BRITTON, J. (Ed.) (1967) *Talking and Writing, a Handbook for English Teachers*, London, Methuen, in a review by Michael TUCKER, (1968b) *UE*, Vol. 19, No. 4, p. 366.

72 SCHOOLS COUNCIL (1968) *An Approach through English*, Humanities for the Young School Leaver series, London, HMSO, p. 5. James Britton and John Dixon tell me that they were the authors of this pamphlet, with help from Geoffrey Summerfield. Douglas Barnes held the same view of the function of English: BARNES, D. 'English with an examination fifth form', *UE*, Vol. 20, No. 2, pp. 130–8.

73 DOUGHTY (1968d) 'What remains to do', pp. 62–4.

74 DRUCE, R. and TUCKER, M. (1968) *Structural English*, five volumes, each with two parts: vol. 1, part 2, *Around and About*; vol. 2, part 1, *Project Survival*, London, English Universities Press.

75 E.g. THOMPSON, A., JEFFERSON, P. and DERBYSHIRE, B. (1968) *English First*, five books: book 2, Cambridge, University Tutorial Press.

76 DRUCE and TUCKER, *op. cit.*, p. vi. The same is true of Nancy Martin's series, MARTIN, N.C. (1968) *Oxford English Source Books*, three books: book 2, *Truth to Tell*, London, Oxford University Press.

77 FLOWER, F.D. (1966) *Language and Education*, London, Longman.

78 The disappearance of competence in English from the aims of the subject is noted by SHARPLES, D. (1968) 'Literacy and curriculum', *Higher Education Journal*, Vol. 16, No. 6, pp. 29–32, and by SINCLAIR, *op. cit.*, p. 90. Butts and Watkins state: 'Our main educational aim ... was to try and persuade these children to consider the implications of violence: to consider the different ways people can inflict mental as well as physical suffering; to examine the effects of violence upon the victim and the agent: and to probe some of the reasons for violence in crime,

sport and even space-travel, for one of our lessons coincided with the news of the violent death of a Russian astronaut' (*op. cit.*, p. 317).

79   DOUGHTY, P.S. (1968b) *Current Attitudes to Written English, And Their Implications For the Teacher of English*, Programme in Linguistics and English Teaching, series 1, paper 4, London, Longmans [for] University College, London, p. 36.

80   E.g. DRUCE, and TUCKER, *op. cit.*, pp. v–vii. LATE produced a report on a meeting about 'Group work and group teaching': BRYAN, B. (1968) 'Note by secretary of studies', *EE*, Vol. 2, No. 1, pp. 36–40. George Robertson, whose work was described in that meeting, has an article on 'Group methods in English', *Forum for the Discussion of New Trends in Education*, 10, 1968, pp. 76–8. Shaw's textbook calls for activities 'in groups of about four': SHAW, W.H. (1968-1969) *Look, Discuss and Write*, two books: book 1, Oxford, Blackwell, p. 4.

81   MARLAND, M. (1968) 'English in the classroom', *Trends in Education*, 12, pp. 33–7; p. 33.

82   E.g. UNIVERSITY OF NEWCASTLE-UPON-TYNE (1968) *No Master's Voice*: a description and evaluation by the teacher concerned of free expression work in prose and verse done by boys failing academically in a selective school, Achievements in teaching, no. 2, Newcastle-upon-Tyne, University of Newcastle-upon-Tyne (Research Committee of the Institute and Faculty of Education).

83   See e.g. RALPH, W. and BARLOW, D. (1967–1968) *Creative Writing for Secondary Schools*, two books: book 1, London, Edward Arnold, and THOMPSON, *et al.*, *op. cit.* The art department of Penguin Education went to previously untapped sources to find photographs of a new kind and quality for the poetry anthology: SUMMERFIELD, G. (1968b) *Voices*, three books and teachers' handbook: first book, Harmondsworth, Penguin.

84   DOUGHTY, (1968a) *The Relevance of Linguistics*, p. 3.

85   DOUGHTY, *op. cit.*, p. 25. SUMMERFIELD, G. (1966) 'Great expectations', *New Education*, Vol. 2, No. 3, pp. 8–11.

86   E.g. MARLAND, *op. cit.*, ROBERTSON, *op. cit.*

87   MARLAND, *op. cit.*, p. 29.

88   The newer style textbooks attest to the reduction in language work; the CSE exam had in some regions abandoned grammar questions and 'The irrelevance of such analysis is now generally recognised': SUMMERFIELD, 1966, *op. cit.*, p. 9.

89   English teachers in the London school I worked in, and others I knew through the London and National Associations for the Teaching of English, constantly filleted their own latest reading for extracts and ideas for creative activity; the aspiration was now that there should be the minimum of disjunction between the reading one selected for oneself and that which one provided for students.

90   See, for instance, BUTTS and WATKINS, *op. cit.*, ROBERTSON, *op. cit.*, CHILVER, P. (1968) *Talking: Discussion, Improvisation and Debate in Schools*, London, Batsford, and DAVIS, V. (1968) 'Prose anthologies: [review of] *Things Being Various* by Simon Clements, John Dixon and Leslie Stratta, and *Impact One, Impact Two*, and *teacher's book*, by R.H. Poole and P.J. Shepherd, *UE*, Vol. 20, No. 1, pp. 80–4.

91   DOUGHTY (1968a) *The Relevance of Linguistics*, p. 4.

92   SCHOOLS COUNCIL, *op. cit.*, p. 1.

93   *Ibid.*, p. 5.

94   'Many grammar school libraries exclude [junior fiction] as insufficiently academic' (TUCKER, Michael, 1968a, '"Readers" or literature?' *UE*, Vol. 19, No. 3, pp. 207–13; p. 211). Garnett, in a survey of educational publishers' catalogues,

lists books currently published in five or more editions. 'Top-of-the-pops' (her phrase) are *Treasure Island* (1883) (29 editions) and *Kidnapped* (1886) (21); amongst those most heavily represented are *The Black Arrow* (1888), *The Water Babies* (1863), and *Quentin Durward* (1823). (As she points out, however, an unknown proportion of sales would be to overseas markets.) (GARNETT, *op. cit.*)

95   BUTTS and WATKINS, *op. cit.*, p. 316.

96   E.g. RALPH and BARLOW, *op. cit.*, p. 3.

97   E.g. UNIVERSITY OF NEWCASTLE, *op. cit.*; POWELL, B. (1968) *English through Poetry Writing: a creative approach for schools*, London, Heinemann, p. 2.

98   SCHOOLS COUNCIL, *op. cit.*

99   The view that writing may serve as therapy is by now firmly associated with the name of David Holbrook — e.g. by William Walsh, who has reservations about Holbrook's enthusiasm for psychoanalysis: WALSH, W. (1968) '[Review of] *The Exploring Word*, by D. Holbrook, *UE*, Vol. 19, No. 3, pp. 243–4.

100   GARNETT, E. (1968b) 'What sort of English teaching for your child? *Where: Information on Education*, 38, pp. 19–21.

101   DEAN, P. (1968) '[Review of] *Creative Writing for Juniors*, by Barry Maybury, and *An Approach to Creative Writing in the Primary School*, by S.M. Lane', *UE*, Vol. 19, No. 3, pp. 254–6; p. 254. A preparatory school teacher mentions, as if it were a normal phrase in the English teacher's biography, the time 'When I turned over from traditional English teaching to creative work ...': McWHINNIE, I. (1968) 'English in the prep. school', *EE*, Vol. 2, No. 2, pp. 37–42; p. 38.

102   The source of the bubble-blowing example was a film by the National Union of Teachers (HOLLINS, *op. cit.*, pp. 20–1). The paper-burning is mentioned by SMITH, D. (1968) 'The best of practice, 11,–14', *EE*, Vol. 2, No. 2, pp. 43–50; p. 49. The approach was classically exemplified by Rowe's earlier (1963) text-book series, ROWE, A.W. (1963) *English through Experience*, five books, London, Blond Educational.

103   SHAW, *op. cit.*, p. 15.

104   HOLLINS, McWHINNIE, SHARPLES, DOUGHTY (1968a) all *op. cit.*; CONQUEST, R. (1968) 'Undotheboys Hall', in COX, C.B. and DYSON, A.E. (Eds) *Fight for Education*, A Black Paper, London, Critical Quarterly Society, pp. 17–20; CHANAN, G. 'The limits of spontaneity — creative writing for older children', *Educational Development*,. Vol. 8, No. 1, pp. 8–13.

105   DOUGHTY, (1968a) *op. cit.*, p. 65.

106   *Ibid.*, p. 63.

107   GARNETT, (1968b) UNIVERSITY OF NEWCASTLE, *op. cit.*

108   CLARK, L. (1968) 'Children's poetry', *Trends in Education*, 12, pp. 26–32; pp. 27, 29.

109   MARTIN, *op. cit.*, p. 69.

110   BENTON, M.G. and BENTON, P. (1968-1969) *Touchstones: A Teaching Anthology*, three books: book 2, 1969, London, Hodder and Stoughton, p. 184.

111   SUMMERFIELD (1968b) *op. cit.*, p. 76.

112   A phrase from a C. Day Lewis poem, taken as the title of the 1967 anthology: CLEMENTS, S., DIXON, J. and STRATTA, L. (1967) *Things Being Various*, London, Oxford University Press. Reviewed in 1968 by Davis, *op. cit.*

113   The quotation is from the end of Act Two of Arnold Wesker's *I'm Talking About Jerusalem*. See also the interesting experiment by GARNETT (1968b) *op. cit.*: confronted with the same pictures, secondary modern pupils describe real or

imagined specific incidents or occasions, while the grammar school productions are essays at a generalizing level.

114 The activities illustrated in the Schools Council booklet are a good example.

115 SHAW, *op. cit.*, p. 17.

116 As Summerfield comments: SUMMERFIELD, G. (1968a) 'A few exploring words on the training of the English teacher', *EE* Vol. 2, No. 1, pp. 4–8. Various writers list the books they find significant. Doughty singles out three which have been published within the last three years: CREBER, (1965) *op. cit.*; FLOWER, (1966) *op. cit.*, and WHITEHEAD, F. (1966) *The Disappearing Dais: A Study Of The Principles And Practice of English Teaching*, London, Chatto and Windus. Michael Tucker (1968b, *op. cit.*, p. 348), lists Flower, Holbrook, Summerfield, Britton, Whitehead and Dixon as those who give most help in 'understanding good English teaching'.

117 LAWTON, D. (1968) *Social Class, Language and Education*, London, Routledge and Kegan Paul. In writers other than Lawton (in whose book sociolinguistics is the main strand) I noted seven references to Bernstein.

118 E.g. HASAN, R. and LUSHINGTON, S. (1968) *The Subject-matter of English*, Programme in Linguistics and English Teaching, series 1, paper 2, London, Longmans [for] University College, London, p. 21.

119 BRITTON and NEWSOME, *op. cit.*

120 Key texts were BARNES, D., BRITTON, J.N. and ROSEN, H. (1969) *Language, the Learner and the School*, a research report by Douglas Barnes, with contribution by James Britton and a discussion document prepared by the London Association for the Teaching of English, introduced by Harold Rosen, Harmondswoth, Penguin; and (later) Chapter 12 of the Bullock Report (DEPARTMENT OF EDUCATION AND SCIENCE, 1975, *op. cit.*) and MARTIN, N., D'ARCY, P., NEWTON, B. and PARKER, R. (1976) *Writing and Learning across the Curriculum, 11–16*, London, Ward Lock Educational for the Schools Council.

121 BANTOCK, G.H. (1968) *Culture, Industrialisation and Education*, London, Routledge and Kegan Paul, p. 8. How extreme was Lawrence's position on the education of the working class, and how decisively he associated folk culture with feeling, is shown in a number of statements quoted with approval by Bantock: 'The great mass of humanity should never learn to read and write — never'. (LAWRENCE, D.H., 1971, *Fantasia of the Unconscious*, in *Fantasia of the Unconscious and Psychoanalysis and the Unconscious*, Harmondsworth, Penguin, p. 87; first published New York, Seltzer, 1922; London, Heinemann, 1923); 'The people lived almost entirely by instinct; men of my father's age could not really read' (1973a, 'Nottingham and the mining countryside', in Williams, J. and Williams R. (Eds) (1973) *D. H. Lawrence on Education*, Harmondsworth, Penguin, pp. 229–36; p. 232; first published in *Adelphi*, June–August 1930, reprinted in Phoenix I, 1936); 'Is not radical unlearnedness just as true a form of self-expression and just as desirable a state, for many natures (even the bulk) as learnedness?' (1973b, 'Education of the people', in WILLIAMS, J. and WILLIAMS, R., *op. cit.*, pp. 120–94; p. 128; first published in *Phoenix I*, 1936); [For the majority] '... much mental consciousness is simply a catastrophe, a blight' (1971, *op. cit.*, p. 69): For such, 'knowledge must be symbolical, mythical, dynamic' (*ibid.*, p. 77). Quotations by Bantock are on pages 20, 20, 14, 21 and 21. Elsewhere the ideology finds full expression in the preface of Blackburn and Cunnignham to their poetry anthology (*op. cit.*) and especially in the work of David Holbrook, e.g.

HOLBROOK, D. (1966) *I've Got to Use Words*, four books, London, Cambridge University Press.

122 Indeed, rational understanding might be seen as a potential curse for those not capable of the highest intellectual insights. Bantock approvingly cites Nietzsche's opinion on 'the perversion of direct sensuous awareness by mind-knowledge and "ideas" (*op. cit.*, p. 20).

123 See note 4 above.

124 In his earlier version Ball calls this paradigm 'sociolinguistic' (1982, *op. cit.*, p. 17). The later term is certainly an improvement, though still somewhat misleading.

125 Although Hamley's thesis is specifically about the treatment of fiction within English teaching, he has much to say about the history of the subject generally and provides a more subtle and convincing account than either Hodgson or Ball. Hamley refers to Mullins, Shayer and Mathieson but not to Hodgson. His thesis was supervised by Mathieson.

126 The position of *Scrutiny* in the early 1930s had, however, been that 'the distinctive innovations of the progressive school were not themselves sufficient' and that the progressives were excessively rationalistic (MULHERN, *op. cit.*, pp. 106–7).

127 HAMLEY, *op. cit.*, p. 24. Amongst his 'literature-based progressives' are Ford, Creber, Holbrook, Whitehead, Inglis and Abbs.

128 HAMLEY, *op. cit.*, p. 337. FORD, B. (1960) *Young Writers, Young Readers*, London, Hutchinson.

129 PRADL, *op. cit.*, p. 197; quotation from WINNICOTT, D.W. (1965) *The Maturational Process and the Facilitating Environment: Studies In The Theory Of Emotional Development*, London, Hogarth Press and the Institute of Psycho-Analysis, p. 105.

130 For Britton, as for Holbrook, the work of Susanne Langer was especially important here.

131 PRADL, *op. cit.*, pp. 175–85.

132 James Britton, personal communication.

133 SQUIRE, J.R. and APPLEBEE, R.K. (1969) *Teaching English in the United Kingdom*, Champaign, I1, National Council of Teachers of English, p. 218. Whitehead recalls 'Leavis questioning me about my London tutor, Dr. P. Gurrey', but doubts whether Leavis would even have understood what Gurrey deeply knew about pupils' ability 'to read, respond, write and act out of their own power and volition'. WHITEHEAD, D. (1984) 'Leavis and the schools', in THOMPSON, D. (Ed.) (1984) *The Leavises: Recollections And Impressions*, Cambridge, Cambridge University Press, pp. 140–52; pp. 144–5.

134 Occupying between a quarter and a third of the time in years one to four. SQUIRE and APPLEBEE, *op. cit.*, p. 56, Table 4.

135 *Ibid.*, p. 43.

136 *Ibid.*, p. 87.

137 *Ibid.*, p. 72, footnote 2.

138 As Britton himself says (1973) *op. cit.*, p. 18); quoted by Ball, 1985, *op. cit.*, p. 67.

139 Frances Stevens noted amongst grammar school teachers 'an emphasis on clear and independent thinking, which is also associated by some with the development of precise expression in speech and writing. The acquisition of powers of criticism and judgement is felt to be important. The practice of intellectual discipline is widely praised ...' STEVENS, F. (1960) *The Living Tradition: The Social And Educational Assumptions Of The Grammar School*, London, Hutchinson, p. 104.

140   In the textbooks in use in 1958 this tradition manifested itself in those of Sussams and Austin. (SUSSAMS, T.W. (1938) *Everyday English*, second series, two books: book 2, London, OUP; AUSTIN, C., (1954) *Read to Write*, London, Ginn.) Guy Pocock's (1924) *Exercises in English*, London, Dent, and R.T. Lewis's (1927) *Composition through Story Writing*, London, Harrap, appear to be authentic predecessors (SHAYER, *op. cit.*, p. 81).

141   VYGOTSKY, L.S. (1962) *Thought and Language*, translated by Haufmann, E. and Vakar, G., Cambridge, Mass., MIT Press. LURIA, A.R. (1961) *The Role of Speech in the Regulation of Normal and Abnormal Behaviour*, Oxford, Pergamon. BRUNER, J.S. (1964) 'The course of cognitive growth', *American Psychologist*, 19, pp. 1–15, reprinted in: CASHDAN, A. and GRUGEON, E. (Eds) (1972) *Language in Education: a source book*, London, Open University Press, Routledge, pp. 161–6. CHOMSKY, N. (1957) *Syntactic Structures*, The Hague, Mouton; (1959) Review of B.F. Skinner's *Verbal Behaviour, Language*, Vol. 35, No. 1, pp. 26–58.

142   See, e.g., CLEGG, A.B. (1964) *The Excitement of Writing*, London, Chatto and Windus.

143   MULHERN, *op. cit.*, p. 289.

144   SQUIRE and APPLEBEE, *op. cit.*, p. 87.

145   The question why change occurred particularly in the 1960s must, of course, be asked not only about English but about the curriculum in general, and about the United States as well as Great Britain. In both countries a widespread recognition that the existing curriculum was poorly adapted to national needs, in terms of economic and military survival in the face of world competition, led to a policy of curriculum development. In England and Wales, the setting up in 1964 of the Schools Council for the Curriculum and Examinations was one response; associated with this innovation were programmes for the development of the key school subjects, including English, and the new Certificate of Secondary Education examination.

146   JONES, R. (1971) 'Going comprehensive', *UE*, Vol. 22, No. 3, pp. 212–17. Quoted by D. ALLEN, (*op. cit.*, p. 70) who gives the author as Esmor Jones.

147   HARRIS, R.J. (1966) 'The education of the teacher of English: an enquiry into the need for a study of the role and status of the English teacher as seen by himself, by his colleagues in other disciplines, by parents and by pupils', *UE*, Vol. 18, No. 2, pp. 114–21; p. 118.

148   'In the subsequent development of a [criticism] based on distinctions between reason and emotion, sensibility was a preferred general word for an area of human response and judgement which could not be reduced to the emotional or emotive'. WILLIAMS, R. (1976) *Keywords: A Vocabulary of Culture And Society*, Glasgow, Fontana, pp. 237–8.

149   '... though pupils in the secondary modern schools were not of superior intellectual ability, they were capable of development in emotional and moral areas ...' (MULLINS, *op. cit.*, p. 286).

150   SQUIRE and APPLEBEE, *op. cit.*, pp. 42–3. The 'radical, almost evangelical, philosophy of reform' (p. vii) which the team found suggests strongly that, however unlike the Leavisite grammar school literature curriculum the comprehensive school 'growth' version appears, and although *Scrutiny* had been opposed even to the 'levelling' implied by the 1944 Education Act (MULHERN, *op. cit.*, p. 220), it is still the moral fervour of Cambridge that is providing the dynamism.

151 '[My mother] used to roll out the pastry and then she took a glass and cut out a jam tart, then cut out another jam tart. Well we have cut out geography, and we have cut out history, and we have cut out science. What do we cut out for English? I suggest we don't. I suggest that is what is left. That is the rest of it.' BRITTON, J.N. (1966) Response to Working Party Paper No. I — "What is English?" Paper A1 in the unpublished papers from the Anglo-American Seminar on the Teaching and Learning of English, Dartmouth College, August 20–September 16, 1966, mimeo, p. 12.

152 Bernice Martin also uses Talcott Parsons' term, 'the Expressive Revolution'. MARTIN, B. (1981) *A Sociology of Contemporary Cultural Change*, Oxford, Basil Blackwell, p. 17.

153 Accounts of the Counterculture are mainly American and deal with its manifestations in the United States. (Bernice Martin, *op. cit.*, and ROSE, M. (1985) *Re-working the Work Ethic: economic values and socio-cultural politics*, London, Batsford, are exceptions.) I am taking it that essential features of the phenomenon were similar in Great Britain.

154 ZICKLIN, G. (1983) *Countercultural Communes: a sociological perspective*, Westport, CT, Greenwood Press, p. 157.

155 Quoted from the manifesto of a rural commune, *Home Comfort: life on Total Loss Farm*, by Zicklin, *op. cit.*, p. 53.

156 GUSSNER, R. (1972) 'Youth: deauthorization and the new individualism', *Youth and Society*, Vol. 4, No. 1, pp. 103–25; p. 119.

157 MARTIN, B. *op. cit.*, pp. 185–7.

158 *Ibid.*, p. 208.

159 *Ibid.*, p. 201.

160 Holbrook is an example of a teacher anxious to divest English of instrumental functions: 'Most of these [practical aims] ... should be given to the secondary modern child by the teachers of other subjects than English', leaving for English the task of 'the development of "whole" men and women' (HOLBROOK, 1961, *English for Maturity*, pp. 26–7).

161 MARTIN, B., *op. cit.*, p. 16.

162 ZICKLIN, *op. cit.*, p. 156.

163 *Ibid.*, p. 155, describing the views of Kelly: KELLY, K.P. (1972) *Youth, Humanism and Technology*, New York, Basic Books.

164 GUSSNER, *op. cit.*, p. 104.

165 SHILS, E. (1962) 'The theory of mass society', *Diogenes*, 39 (Fall), pp. 45–66; pp. 58–9. TURNER, R.H. (1976) 'The real self: from institution to impulse', *American Journal of Sociology*, Vol. 81, No. 5, pp. 989–1016; pp. 1005–6.

166 BERGER, P., BERGER, B. and KELLNER, H. (1974) *The Homeless Mind*, Harmondsworth, Penguin, p. 74; first published USA, Random House, 1973.

167 MARTIN, B., *op. cit.*, p. 16.

168 TURNER, *op. cit.*, pp. 1002–3.

169 ROSE, *op. cit.*, p. 19.

170 BERGER, *et al.*, *op. cit.*, p. 87.

171 COHEN, S. and TAYLOR, L. (1976) *Escape Attempts: The Theory And Practice Of Resistance To Everyday Life*, London, Allen Lane, p. 20.

172 BERGER, *et al.*, *op. cit.*, p. 87.

173 MARTIN, B., *op. cit.*, pp. 16–17.

174 TURNER, *op. cit.*, pp. 989–90.

175 BAUMAN, Z. (1967) 'Some problems in contemporary education', *International Social Science Journal*, 19, pp. 325–37; pp. 326–7.

176 GUSSNER, *op. cit.*, p. 118.

177 *Ibid.*, p. 105–6.

178 *Ibid.*, p. 110.

179 *Ibid.*, p. 112.

180 *Ibid.*, p. 114 — emphasis in original.

181 Lacey shows how usefully this concept of Becker's may be applied to the teaching profession. LACEY, C. (1977) *The Socialization of Teachers*, London, Methuen, p. 70.

182 Over a far longer period than the sociologists I have been citing have in mind, Foucault sees a secular shift in the 'axis of individualization' over the whole modern period, from highly individualized ruler and an anonymous mass of subjects to anonymous, faceless rulers and a population whose unique individualities are tirelessly fostered, supervised and documented. FOUCAULT, M. (1979) *Discipline and Punish: the birth of the prison*, translated from the French by Alan Sheridan, Harmondsworth, Penguin, pp. 192–3.

Chapter 2

Literacy, Politics and the Teaching of English

Stephen Ball, Alex Kenny and David Gardiner

There is no cultural document, which is not at the same time a record of barbarism (Walter Benjamin)

In this paper we present two simple arguments. First, that since the beginnings of mass public education in England and Wales, the teaching of English has been a focus of keen political interest and political control. English has been regarded as a key subject in the 'political education' of the masses. Second, and concomitantly, English teaching, the definition of what is to count as English, has been a matter of struggle and conflict between contending interests. In particular, at various points, governments have attempted to intervene in the field of English teaching in order to discipline practitioners and rectify 'unacceptable' deviations from that version of English which best suits the interests of dominant political elites. We must be absolutely clear that we are concerned here with the public rhetorics and discourses *about* English teaching. We are not attempting to portray either the classroom teaching of English directly or the mediations which are interposed between rhetorics and practice. However, we are interested in the politics of English as a constraint upon the possibilities of practice. Literacy is employed in its broadest sense here, in terms of what Street[1] calls an 'ideological model'. According to such a model reading and writing evolve and exist within power structures and reflect the tensions between competing power and interest groups. The views people have of what literacy involves, of what counts as being literate, what they see as 'real' or appropriate uses of teaching and writing skills determine, directly or indirectly, the realities of practice.[2]

The paper is divided into two main sections. In the first we will describe and analyse the political history of English teaching from the late nineteenth century up to the present day. We will be emphasizing both the conflicts over definition which have beset English since its emergence as a separate school subject and the views of various commentators as to its broader political and economic significance.

In the second we shall be subjecting the debate about English teaching to a more theoretical analysis. We will consider the relationship of the various contesting definitions of English to patterns of inequality and processes of ideological domination, and examine the forms of literacy embedded in each definition.

Establishing a Literary Heritage

Origins

The most immediate and striking fact in the history of English as a school subject is that it is a relatively new subject; even newer is its present position of high status in the school curriculum. The first recognizable university chairs in the subject were established in Cambridge and Oxford in 1878 and 1883 respectively, but English did not exist as a separately identifiable subject lesson in elementary or secondary schools before the turn of the century. Prior to that it was the subject matter and pedagogy of the teaching of Classics which informed the work done by most school children in secondary schools: hence the prominence of the term grammar. In elementary schools pupils studied English in the form of the separate elements of orthography, etymology and syntax, and were subjected to systematic instruction in the principles of English grammar by analogy with the grammars of the classics.

Even this form of English was seen as a subject vastly inferior to Classics: a status distinction which was to remain for many years. Throughout the early stages of its development as a separate discipline English was literally seen as a vulgar, poor person's equivalent of Classics, a subject which was fit for workers whilst Classics remained as the staple diet of the upper classes. At best, English would do for the second- or third-rate university student and, of course, women. [3]

Recognition of these humble beginnings immediately throws up a simple but important question: How is it that English now holds a key position in the political construction of what is to count as education within advanced capitalist British society? The simple answer lies in the vital role played by literacy, or a certain form of literacy, in the development of a mass schooling system in England in the late nineteenth century.

English as a *school subject* originated out of the fears and panics surrounding the development of the city and the emergence of an urban working class mass population. The phenomenal growth of urban society in the nineteenth century profoundly disturbed the moral fabric of the existing social order. In the experiences and imagination of the landed ruling class and the newly emerging industrial middle class the city was a focus and a source of political unrest, social disorder, crime and disease. In 'darkest' London (or Manchester, Birmingham, Liverpool) the rule of law and the influence of the Christian religion were tenuous.

For some commentators anxious to re-establish traditional patterns of authority and compliance the answer to this crisis of morals and order lay in the building of churches and setting up of city missions. For others the solution lay in the building of schools and the secular teaching of subjects 'embodying spiritual and aesthetic values'.[4] The working class would be taught to behave by being taught to read and write.

> The prominence accorded formal schooling and instruction in literacy for the masses as social insurance against criminality and disorder forms one significant example of the broad new consensus about education which emerged throughout Anglo-America by mid-century. In a period of massive social change, of urban-industrial modernisation, education increasingly was seen as the dominant tool for social stability.[5]

But the school-builders of the nineteenth century were well aware of the dangers of untrammelled literacy. 'Morality without literacy was more than ever seen as impossible and literacy alone was politically dangerous. The 19th century education consensus was therefore founded upon the "moral economy" of literacy.'[6] In time reading and writing, literacy, would become the subject English.

Writing in 1868 the Reverend G.C. Bradley urged that English be taught in lower schools 'in an attempt to humanise and refine a boy's mind'.[7] Increasingly the skills of literacy became identified not simply with the mechanisms of language but also with the values and morality of 'literature'. Nearly twenty years after Bradley the liberal politician John Morely urged that literature be taught in schools as an 'instrument for a systematic training of the imagination and sympathies and of a genial and varied moral sensibility'.[8] From the earliest days of state education writers and authorities on English teaching began to blur the distinction between literacy as a technical skill and as a moral technology. The purposes of the subject stretched from meeting the demands of industrial competition to reinforcing national solidarity.

It was becoming clear by the turn of the century that English literature was to be the subject that unified the nation and which would provide an effective vehicle to replace the traditional roles of moral training held by family and church. Speaking at the beginning of the twentieth century George Gordon, Professor of English Literature at Oxford, claimed:

> England is sick and ... English literature must save it. The churches (as I understand) having failed, and social remedies being slow, English literature now has a triple function; still, I suppose, to delight and instruct us, but also, and above all, to save our souls and heal the state.[9]

This lofty claim for the subject and the combative tone of its delivery is a form to be found in much of the discourse regarding English in the curriculum throughout its history right up to the speech of the current Secretary of State for Education, Kenneth Baker, which is referred to below.

The rationale behind the promotion of English as the subject most likely to 'save our souls and heal the state' lies in the remarkable similarity between its discourse and that of religion, Terry Eagleton[10] argues. Perhaps the most important parallel is that both discourses are adaptable to every social level: 'If there is a doctrinal inflection of it for the intellectual elite', writes Eagleton comparing religion to English, 'there is also a pietistic brand of it for the masses.' In providing a unifying bond between the classes, each discourse 'encompasses pious peasant, enlightened middle class liberal, and theological intellectual' in a single organization. Another poignant similarity between the respective discourses of English literature and religion is the manner in which they operate and disseminate their respective ideologies. Apparently dealing in Universal Truths each discourse operates as a pacifying influence, encouraging meekness and the contemplative inner life: both work in a similar fashion through image, habit, symbol, ritual and mythology. Once the work of the advocates of English was completed the Transcendental Signifier would no longer be God but the Author.

Arnold

These then are the roots of the establishment of a 'civilized aesthetic heritage' that was to become increasingly dominant in the course of this century. One of the key figures in this construction of the subject was Matthew Arnold, to whom Henry Newbolt would later refer as 'an apostle of culture'. Arnold's concern was with civilizing the new middle class, thus providing the proletariat with something they could idealize. Underpinning Arnold's work in the development of English as a major subject in the curriculum was the fear that unless this new discourse was firmly established, the social fabric would be torn apart by a restless proletariat. It was with this concern in mind that Arnold justified the efficacy of culture: 'It is of use because, like religion — that other effort after perfection — it testifies that where bitter envying and strike are there is confusion and every evil at work.'[11]

Culture therefore would be imported to the masses, its driving force the moral and social passion for doing good. It would be instrumental in ensuring that Reason and the Will of God prevailed, whilst nurturing a spirit of tolerance and generosity. The schooling of the working class would ensure the preservation of internal peace, it was argued. Matthew Arnold's vision was of a classless society brought about by the 'civilization'

of the new middle class — whom he saw   ‍ling power.
Economic power would be underpinned wit   y:

> The bourgeoisie, then, must appropriate the civilised aesthetic
> heritage of a failing aristocracy in order to equip itself with an
> ideology capable of penetrating the masses. In a 'cultured, liber-
> alised, ennobled, transformed, middle class' the proletariat will
> have a point towards which it may with joy direct its aspirations. [12]

At a time of growing industrial disquiet in the late nineteenth century
the emphasis in English teaching was to be on the installation of national
pride and the transmission of moral values. Contradictions could be
smoothed over rather than exposed, by promoting universal values and
solidarity between classes. An early report on the teaching of English in
schools argues that

> the people need political culture, instruction, that is to say, in what
> pertains to their relation to the State, to their duties as citizens, and
> they need also to be impressed sentimentally by having the
> presentation in legend and history of heroic and patriotic examples
> brought vividly and attractively before them. [13]

We should note that Hunter, for one, challenges Arnold's seminal role
in the making of English: he 'simply did not conceive of a popular literary
education'. [14] Hunter argues instead that Kay-Shuttleworth should be seen
as the founder of the nineteenth-century popular school as a 'purpose-built
moralising environment'. There is certainly room for doubt about whether
Arnold's theoretical statements bore significantly on his work as an
Inspector of Schools.

Sampson and Newbolt

If Matthew Arnold played a major part in the establishment of a nascent
cultural heritage, it was George Sampson's *English for the English* [15] and
more particularly the report of the Newbolt Committee of the same
year which finally moulded it into shape. These two works, Margaret
Mathieson suggests, are landmarks of any survey of the history of English.
Victory over Germany in the First World War heralded a restoration of
national pride and an upsurge of patriotic feeling; a sense of national
mission and identity, which had been lacking as the capitalist crises
deepened in the build up to the Great War, was evident once again. The
goal, as the new educators saw it, was to force home the advantage and
promote English as the subject which could lock onto, and act as a focus
for, this new national pride. The fear of strife and political restlessness
expressed by Matthew Arnold is echoed in Sampson's work; the task of
literature would be to circumvent any possibility of insurgence, such as

that witnesse... eny to working class children any common share in the ... presently they will grow into men who demand, with ...mmunism of the material.'[16]

This period immediately following the First World War could be said to be the one during which English became firmly established as a, if not yet the, major subject on the school curriculum; and it was increasingly considered as a subject suitable for study by the enlightened intellectual. Not only would it act as a basis for national unity, but it would serve also as a source of spiritual comfort for those sections of the community whose good faith and morale had been shaken and scarred by the war, leaving them with feelings of hollowness and desolation. As Eagleton comments: 'Literature would be at once solace and reaffirmation, a familiar ground on which Englishmen could regroup both to explore, and to find some alternatives to, the nightmare of history.'[17]

The thesis of both Sampson's work and the Newbolt report especially, is that a new patriotism could be fostered through a knowledge of a 'cultural heritage' and a disinterested pursuit of literary culture. National unity therefore was to be restored based not on social equality but on 'everyone forgetting that classes existed'. The aim of education, says Newbolt, should 'be the guidance in the acquiring of experience' and the 'development of the whole man to attain fullness of life'. This is best achieved through literature which, says the report, is the 'only basis for a national education'.

In this respect literature must be considered as a 'record of the experiences of the greatest minds' and books are to be seen as 'instruments through which we hear the voices of those who have known life better than ourselves'. The study of the 'self expression of great natures' is seen by the Committee as having an historical dimension, but their primary interest is in the timeless and universal:

All great literature has in it two elements, the contemporary and the eternal. On the one hand, Shakespeare and Pope can tell us what Englishmen were like at the beginning of the 17th and the beginning of the 18th centuries. On the other hand they tell us what all men are like in all countries and at all times. To concentrate the study of literature mainly on the first aspect, to study it mainly as history, is to ignore its nobler more eternal and universal element.[18]

Viewed in this light, literature will provide the pupil with a 'source of delight, a personal intimacy and the gaining of personal experience ... an equipment for the understanding of life'. The irony is that although the report claims that 'great literature can never depend for its importance upon historical considerations', this faith, argues Malcolm Evans, 'is stated in the context of a historical mission to make literature itself a central bond in the national culture'.[19]

The Newbolt report's analysis of literature, pedagogy and their relation to English society is formed by what the committee consider to be the overriding historical and political concerns of the period. Thus, promoting English literature in education as a basis of 'humane culture' a 'great source of national pride' and potential bond of national unity, the report concludes 'the nation of which a considerable portion rejects this means of grace, and despises this great spiritual influence, must assuredly be heading to disaster'. There can be little doubt now that the report of the Newbolt Committee was one of the first attempts to discipline and police the development of English teaching. Mindful that some sections of society, 'especially those belonging to organised labour movements', are 'antagonistic to and contemptuous of literature', viewing it as an attempt 'to sidetrack the labour movement', the report represents the language and culture of the new ruling class as Language and Culture themselves. In stripping literary study, for example Shakespeare, of its philological apparatus, Newbolt sought to deploy the text in a new way — as a source of characters and experience, to which students could 'immediately' respond. Control and preservation of the discourse of English teaching were firmly established in the Newbolt era, an era which Malcolm Evans claims finally saw the construction of a national language and culture.

F.R. Leavis

The missionary passion called for in Sampson and Newbolt was to be echoed, and amplified, by F.R. Leavis and his Cambridge School in the 1930s and 1940s. Again, this reformulation of English emerged against a background of social and political unrest among the working classes — particularly the General Strike of 1926. In the post-war context, Leavis saw a profound cultural impoverishment and historical displacement in an ever more fragmented society. Against what was seen as a worsening moral and cultural crisis, Leavis called for 'warriors, men and women who would fight to overcome the severe threats to quality of life at every level'.[20]

Leavis was again and again to advocate literature — and in particular the reading of it by the invigorated discipline of English — as a potent basis for social harmony. Believing, as Mathieson says, 'in the central value of great literature and in the need for critical discrimination in our debased cultural environment'.[21] Leavis used a particularly combative tone and adversarial manner in his struggles against the 'complacent debility'[22] of the literary establishment and of the culture.

One theme of the Newbolt report, and of the work of others, that Leavis was not only to expand, but to make a central tenet of his prescription, was the call for a reawakening of an organic cultural life. He looked back at significant moments when 'the traditional culture of the people'[23] bore an intimate and informing relation to literary culture (for example in the seventeenth-century England of Bunyan). The possibilities for unifying society suggested by this analysis were put by Leavis at the core of what he saw as 'English', with such organic metaphors as 'life' and 'health' central in his vocabulary.

His essentially liberal individualist stance presupposed a moral and intellectual elite to promulgate it. As late as the 1970s, he would write: 'The humanely perceptive, actual and potential, are those that matter; they may be a minority, but it isn't from majorities that the creative stimulus comes. A minority can change the spiritual climate.'[24] Hence Leavis's belief in the university English School: his moralism was to be transmitted by followers, such as Denys Thompson and David Holbrook, going out into the schools and influencing by their writing and teaching the rising generation of English teachers, and thence their pupils.

Leavis and the Cambridge School were to be instrumental in removing any lingering doubts about the seriousness of English as an academic discipline (though Leavis himself continued to see his position as an embattled minority view). His realignment of the 'Great Tradition' of English literature, and resolute purging of this canon, had a profound influence, embodying in specific readings of chosen texts the literature-centred, value-laden ideology of English as he saw it. The English teacher could be equipped with a moral vision, a canon of texts which embodied it, a technique for discrimination with which to fight against the evils of cultural impoverishment brought about by mass industrial society.

In many ways, Leavis's rewriting of English was an extremely radical stand against modern mechanized society; a project which, Terry Eagleton claims, 'has yet to be surpassed in its tenacious devotion to the moral centrality of English studies'.[26] The emergence of Cambridge English was a direct response to the triviality of the contemporary formulations of English, and to the perceived evils of the age. It coupled the advocacy of certain aesthetic and literary judgments, with a particular set of social, moral and political issues. The analysis and assessment of art was bound up with evaluations of the nature of history and society as a whole. However, in its focus on the individual response, and in its moralism, as well as in its prescriptions about society, Leavis's stance was a rejection of political involvement and of the rationalist and progressive aspects of liberalism.

Study of the Great Tradition of English Literature would educate the reader, Leavis believed, to discriminate between the rich sensitivity of one work and the gross banality of another. The writers to whom Leavis turned were those who he saw as celebrating life and organic spontaneity, valuing the uniqueness of the individual and the creative realm of the interpersonal. Exposure to, and a close reading of, all these values through English literature would equip the reader to withstand such evils as 'bad art', 'bad literature', 'the cinema', 'advertising' and 'the popular press'. Subsequently work evincing the qualities mentioned above would train the reader to be, and here we list some of Leavis' catchphrases, sensitive, imaginative, perceptive, sympathetic, creative, reflective and responsive. Leavis' vision was essentially one of ethical development. Its heyday coincided with the period of post-war political consensus; in fact the Cambridge School had its apotheosis in the post Second World War Grammar School sixth form. Of the Cambridge School's attempts to restructure the teaching of English, Peter Abbs comments 'in the context of English teaching this school provided a critical method of reading, a method for the analysis of mass culture and an informed awareness as to the place of literature in society'.[27] Referring to the radicalism and personal contribution of Leavis, he says, 'in new and worsening cultural circumstances he gave a powerful currency to the notion that the teacher, critic and artist had no choice but to oppose the destructive and seemingly inexorable drift of industrial civilisation'.[28]

As to appropriate pedagogic strategies, for Leavis teachers remained at the centre of the equation, instilling sensitivity and responsiveness into their students. He set an essentially individualistic, organic conservatism over and against the mechanical, utilitarian tradition. A vision of complete, humane, human development based on access to a culture lay at the core of Leavis' ethico-political system.

Leavis' lofty aims were built on his faith in the transformative power of education in general and literature in particular. The battle would be hard, but it could be won. The Cambridge School set about implanting themselves in educational institutions with missionary zeal. During the period of growth and change in education following the 1944 Education Act, many of Leavis's acolytes attained prominence in education, including a major role in the early history of the National Association for the Teaching of English (NATE) and influential positions in university English departments, colleges and schools of education. A definite movement had emerged — though major challenges to it soon developed.

It is testimony to this resolve and conviction that Leavis' voice became the dominant one in English teaching throughout the period of post-war consensus. In fact the Cambridge movement was so 'impassioned in its evangelism and its conviction of the importance of its message' that, with some truth, it could be said still to be the established voice in secondary schools today. It remains the most powerful philosophy of English teaching 'not because of the coherence of truths of its underlying philosophy but because what Scrutiny proposed was a practical cultural-educational project, concern with what should be taught and how it should be taught'.[29]

It was in the drawing up of the literary heritage, and the pedagogic strategies that accompanied it, that Leavis through his compelling combination of energy, sensitivity and rigour, effectively rounded off the policing of the language begun by Arnold and Newbolt; and ensured that its adherent teachers were to become custodians of a discourse of orthodoxy.

However, Leavis's detractors claim that it was in the apparently apolitical nature of its focus on Quality of Life that *Scrutiny* was ultimately defeatist and elitist. Admittedly *Scrutiny's* focus was social and cultural, but its historical and political analysis was based in the context of England's organic tradition. The key of Scrutiny's doctrine was that people should be educated to withstand and survive technological society; thus there was never any serious consideration of actually trying to change politically or structurally the society which brought forth the triviality and vulgarity that were anathema to Leavis and his cohorts. In consequence, by harking back to a golden past of organic social unity the Cambridge School was seen to address, and aimed its writing at, an ever decreasing 'cultured' minority. Given that Leavis's missionaries, or 'preachers of culture', were bound to be few and far between, Eagleton argues that 'the only hope was that an embattled cultivated minority might keep the torch burning in the contemporary cultural wasteland, and pass it on via their pupils, to posterity'.[30]

This then was the ideological situation of English in the 40s and 50s; less than three quarters of a century of English teaching had seen changes and shifts in emphasis, but the outcome of these was a more or less fixed notion of what culture and language meant. There had been a series of moral panics and political crises for the British Establishment which were followed or accompanied in each case by the emergence of new paradigms of English teaching. Each new paradigm was a development of the already existing ones. These emergent paradigms were usually followed by 'official' responses, reports, etc., which attempted to frame policy for schools. As we shall see this pattern continues. Thus, we suggest discourses about English are essentially political discourses.

In the 1960s and 1970s new versions were to emerge which would challenge profoundly the recently established, if precarious, Leavisite consensus on English teaching by reworking and adapting particular aspects of Leavisism — its individualism and concerns with authentic culture and 'growth'. In these developments of rhetorics and discourse one motivation at least was to eradicate the cultural politics of the literary canon and the Great Tradition; literature was no longer to be seen as an unproblematic medium for social integration.

1960s

In the 1960s and 1970s English was in a state of almost continual ferment and contestation. This situation was produced and encouraged by developments in the 'theory' of English teaching, changes in the balance of power within the organization of the subject (subject associations, professional journals, institutions of teacher training, key positions on key committees, etc.), and changes in the structure and constitution of the education system (the beginnings of comprehensive education, and progressive primary education, the raising of the school-leaving age, etc.). The variety of influences and conditions for change can, for purposes of explication, be presented in terms of a series of useful, if somewhat crude, contending polarities and the shift of opinion between these polarities:

grammar schooling—comprehensive schooling
literature—language
elite—mass
cultural heritage—cultural relevance
transmission—participation
Cambridge—London

The direction of the shift, initially, is from the left side to the right. (And, latterly, from the right back to the left.) In general terms during the 60s and 70s there was a decline in the overall influence of the Leavisite literary critical tradition; although it is important to record that this decline was relative rather than absolute. Leavisite English was to remain strongly entrenched (but not unchallenged) in the universities, where many English teachers are trained, and in the elite highlands of the school system, particularly A level courses (pre-University examination courses for 17–18 year olds), the most obvious vestige of grammar schooling in the piecemeal comprehensive system. Nonetheless the development of comprehensive education (formally initiated in 1965 by the Labour government of Harold Wilson, and never fully completed) provided a powerful new modality for the expression and definition of an alternative (or several alternative) versions of school English.

The Leavisite vision of English teaching, with its almost exclusive concern with a highly selective and partial literary canon, provided its supporters with a complete dogma of political, moral and psychological rationales which fitted in many significant ways with the rarified, and single-minded, academic orientation of the grammar school. As bastions of middle class privilege and conduits for the social mobility and re-socialization of 'bright' working class children they both embodied and required that emphasis on certainty, tradition and 'quality' which Leavisite English provided. Their keynote was 'heritage', 'literature itself tended to be treated as a given, a ready-made structure that we imitate and a content that is handed over to us'.[31] The past was fixed in a strict hierarchy of worth, of values, of morality; that hierarchy was seen as being embodied in 'literature'. As Holbrook argues, 'Any culture worth having depends, at its best on words. Everything of importance, from the techniques whereby we exist to our attitudes towards life, is shared and handed on in words ...'[31] Holbrook's personal mission was to extend Leavisism into the secondary modern school and to the 'less able'.

In contrast what the comprehensive school offered was uncertainty and, in rhetoric at least, it marked a break with the past. While the discourse of comprehensive education was incoherent and disorganized, while the 'noise' of change was more apparent than actual change, in

English, perhaps more than any other subject, the need for change was clearly articulated and the direction of change clearly argued for. The critique of the Cambridge Leavis position was based upon an alternative conception of experience and its relation to meaning, rooted in the immediacy of language rather than the traditions of literature. This critique was fueled by the theories and research of James Britton and his colleagues at the London Institute of Education, and by the school experiences and classroom practice of members of LATE (the London Association of Teachers of English), people such as Douglas Barnes, Harold Rosen and John Dixon. The 'English as language' lobby sought to shift the canonical tradition from the centre of the English stage and replace it with the pupil, the learner. In other words to replace the emphasis on second-hand meaning, in the text, with first-hand meaning, in the daily life and authentic culture of the child.

> The fact is that in sharing experience with others man [*sic*] is using language to make the experience real to himself. The alternative expressions so that language shall fit the experience and bring it to life 'as it really was' — these activities imply imaginative work.[33]

Here the English teacher was no longer to be a missionary disseminating the values of civilization but an anthropologist mapping and collecting the values and culture of subordinate groups, initially the working class (later girls and blacks). The notion of 'literature' is profoundly expanded here to encompass all that can be said or written, to encompass language.

Responses in the enactment of English varied and it is easy to stereotype, but certain trends in this new English movement are discernible (some of which remain in evidence, others of which have faded, or been pushed, from view): (i) A de-emphasis of 'standard' or 'correct' forms of expression (or punctuation and spelling in some cases), a concomitant recognition of the importance of 'street languages'. This was to lead the way towards an acceptance of West Indian dialects and patois, and of Black English, as valid linguistic and literary forms. Imagination and expression were given precedence over 'correctness'. (ii) Pluralism in terms of values and morals, and worth. Teachers became less comfortable with their role in validating a version of morality embedded in a literary canon increasingly under criticism as representing a middle class, white and male perspective. (iii) A redefinition of literature to include a broader range of media and sources. The pupils' own work, popular literature, the poetry and literature of the West Indies, Africa and Asia, television, newspaper and comics all began to make their appearance in the English classroom, to be studied, discussed and written about rather than derided. (iv) A set of teaching methods giving greater autonomy and freedom to the pupils. The use of project work, worksheets and group work where the teachers' role would be to facilitate and guide rather than to transmit knowledge. Streaming was abandoned in favour of mixed-ability groups. Talk, oracy as it was to become, was also given greater emphasis over and against written work. Writing about the period after 1966 Dixon suggests that 'dialogue among teachers of English has been marked by growing concern with student-centred education — with "learning" rather than "teaching"'.[34] (v) An explicit engagement with social issues 'relevant' to the pupils' lives and experiences outside school, particularly the use of projects and themes — war, poverty, old age, pollution, the family. In some schools this was part of a move to 'integrated studies', English being taught in relation to history, geography, social studies and religious education. In many schools these trends were given greater opportunity by new forms of examining, especially the introduction of Mode 3 CSEs (Certificate of Secondary Education); courses designed and assessed by teachers themselves, intended to reflect directly the interests and needs of pupils.

In practical terms the 'English as Language' movement was supported by a series of curriculum development projects funded by the Schools Council. Furthermore, the newly established subject association of English teachers NATE (the National Association of Teachers of English), set up initially on the initiative of a small group of Leavisite teacher educators, was quickly captured by grassroots advocates of the 'English as Language' movement and became, with its new journal, *English in Education*, a powerful voice in support of change.

At the heart of the dispute between Cambridge and London, literature and language, there are not simply two views of the subject, but more profoundly, and politically of importance, two conceptions of the 'good society', and of the nature of civilization and citizenship. In crude terms the positions rest upon commitment to two opposed knowledge bases, one elite knowledge and the other the knowledge of the masses. In the Cambridge vision the English teacher and the great literary heritage, with which they are entrusted, are to stand against the depredations of the machine age. The Leavisites hark back to a better time before the coming of the mass industrial society, when social order and morality were invested in and maintained by the community. In contrast the London vision celebrates the immediate life, culture and language of the school student. And for many teachers, especially those in the urban centres, that has meant primarily the lives, culture and language of the working class. While one position might be said to embody the subordination of the pupils to a romanticized view of the past, the other was always in danger of subordinating pupils to a romanticized view of the present, an attempt to celebrate working class experience rather than to change it.

While the polarization of the English subject community between the London and Cambridge positions certainly captures the broad outlines of the disputes within English teaching in the period 1966 to 1975 it does not provide an exhaustive analysis. In particular it is important to recognize a further separation of emphasis and development taking place within the London position, a separation between what can be termed *progressive* and *radical* versions of English. But a word of caution here. If the London school represents a minority, assertive position among English teachers as a whole, and one with a distinct urban bias, then the radical version in particular is representative of an even smaller minority.

In various ways it seemed that for many English teachers attitudes and commitments embedded within their teaching and their view of their subject, the political vision noted above, were being translated into general concerns about education and schooling. English teachers were thus frequently in the forefront of progressive change in schools. *The English Magazine*, published by the ILEA English Centre, reviewing the development of English teaching, captures this period in the following terms and gives a sense of the relationship between the conception of the subject in the classroom and broader social issues and concerns.

> The growing sense of confidence among English teachers which NATE both drew on and inspired, was to deliver an addition to the three main strands of English teaching: English for critical consciousness and change. The events of 1968 in Paris, California and, more modestly, in Britain, had a powerful effect on the thinking of many teachers. One half of the counter-culture veered off into drugs, mysticism and utopian life styles; the other half developed a more political perspective. It was not an illogical progression. While the counter-culture was not subversive in itself, it did have built-in oppositional ingredients: 'The cult of being true to your own feelings becomes dangerous when those feelings are not the ones that society would like you to feel' (Juliet Mitchell). That disjunction was especially pertinent for English teachers, who by the nature of their subject, were in close contact with the experiences of working class children; it offered them a microcosmic view of the contradictions of schooling in a capitalist society. Such teachers were doing no more than focussing on a range of social injustices endemic in our society and asking questions about the value and relevance of a pedagogy and content which did not acknowledge these facts. They felt the need to incorporate an extra dimension in their practice which faced the conflicts at the heart of a model of personal development which the rest of the school and society at large had no time for except in the case of a very small minority of pupils. It went beyond the reflections-style interest in social issues; it tried to inject into the English curriculum the kinds of knowledge and experience which would give working class pupils an understanding of inequality and its causes; the emphasis would be on solidarity rather than upward mobility. [35]

The progressive and radical versions of English are articulated here. The first focuses upon personal aspects of experience, stressing the relevance and validity of each child's culture, language and self-expression.

This has tended towards an emphasis upon the needs and interests of individual pupils, usually via a form of mixed-ability pedagogy and using worksheets. Working class family and neighbourhood culture is explored via the pupils' own creative writing and through 'themes' and projects. To some extent this version of English was based on a rejection of the conception of the working class home as a deficit system and of the elitism of the great literary tradition. Working class culture was taken to be a vital, meaningful and valid alternative. The second moves beyond a celebration of working class culture into an analysis of the political and economic conditions that produce inequality; it is a critical rather than a celebratory stance. It involves the construction of a working class curriculum, often taught in a traditional authoritarian manner. It is a version of English which takes seriously both the lives and culture, and alienation and lack of opportunity, of working class pupils. This amounts to what Aronowitz and Giroux call 'critical literacy'.

> Critical literacy responds to the cultural capital of a specific group or class and looks at the way in which it can be confirmed, and also at the ways in which the dominant society disconfirms students by either ignoring or denigrating the knowledge and experiences that characterise their everyday lives. The unit of analysis here is social, and the key concern is not individual interests but with the individual and collective empowerment. [36]

Such a form of practice is certainly less romantic in its conception of working class culture; it also appears deeply subversive and threatening. It challenges both the established curriculum and the cultural selection that that embodies, and the patterns of advantages and privilege which that selection gives rise to and perpetuates. What was being attempted here by English teachers, in both cases, may be seen as a positive response to the establishment of comprehensive education. But while the progressives were working to establish an *alternative* to the dominant versions of 'culture', the radical's position was *oppositional*. It represents an attempt to radicalize profoundly the practical ideology of schooling, 'what to be taught entails', by the 'teaching' of and empowering of a counter-hegemony. Pupils were encouraged to develop a critical relationship to their own knowledge, to recognize common experiences of oppression and the possibility of concerted action for change. The journal *Teaching London Kids* might be identified with this position as would the work of Chris Searle. Reaction from those whose interests were thus threatened was inevitable. And in real terms, the gap, the moment within which these radical versions of English were able to flourish, was short-lived. Thus while these attempts at radical practice demonstrate again the crucial position of English as a medium of liberation that was recognized in the nineteenth century, they also highlight the 'necessities' of control also in exactly the same way.

However, since the mid-70s in London and other metropolitan areas, both versions of English, progressive and radical, have tended to become less preoccupied with social class as the main focus of inequality in society, and more attention is given to racial and sexual oppressions. The progressive impetus emerges as multi-culturalism, again centred upon a celebration of cultural differences; often via the examination of black and women's literature. The radical position again involves a pro-active examination of the root causes of inequality. For some teachers anti-sexism and anti-racism now constitute the basic political concerns of mother-tongue teaching (the automatic preoccupation with the English language as such is also sometimes called into question). Multiculturalism is seen as flawed and limited.

> While policies associated with a 'concern for diversity, particularly those which involve acknowledging and valuing black people's cultural identities and bi-lingual competence, and promoting mutual respect between cultures' would be included, the central emphasis would now be the pervasive influence of fascism: the need for all children to be able to identify, resist and combat racism in their own sphere of influence; the experience of black communities in Britain; and the need for schools and other educational institutions to ensure that none of their practices was racist in intent or result.[37]

To be sure, multi-culturalism with its primary concern with changing attitudes and increasing tolerance between groups and improving the supposedly poor self concepts of ethnic minority children receives considerable lip-service support from government agencies and politicians. Anti-racism however with its critical thrust and its emphasis on the structural and institutional bases of inequality and oppression is regarded with suspicion and hostility. Particularly during Keith Joseph's period as secretary of state for education there were several attempts to exclude anti-racist initiatives from the activities of agencies like the CNAA (Council for National Academic Awards) and the FEU (Further Education Unit). Even Local Authorities like ILEA (the Inner London Education Authority) have recently begun to distance themselves from their initial commitments to anti-racism in schools.

It could perhaps be argued that, in the absence of coherent and committed political support for educational change, a reaction against the 'progressive consensus', so-called, of the 1960s was inevitable. But there was nothing in the history of the politics of education in England and Wales to prepare even the most far-sighted commentators for the scale and organization of the right-wing attack upon comprehensivism and progressivism. Furthermore, in retrospect the scale of the attack seems out of all proportion to the nature of the changes being attempted and the overall extent of participation in change. The CCCS review of educational policy in the 1960s makes it clear that the 'noise' of educational reform in the emergence of comprehensive schooling was often not necessarily matched by real changes in educational practices. They also argue that while 'There was a distinctive social democratic "moment" in the formulation of policy' in the 1960s, 'it was always caught within sharp limits'.[38] It is important to bear in mind that reforms in English teaching are no exception to this general pattern; although in many schools English departments did take a leading role in the advocacy of change. Nonetheless, English teaching was to be implicated as a major factor in the 'crisis in comprehensive education' skilfully constructed by Conservative critics during the 1970s. The first stage of the Conservative critique of comprehensivism is marked by the publication of the first of the *Black Papers* on education in 1969. Its basis is within the tradition of what Williams[39] calls 'old humanism' with which we were concerned previously. It contains both a defence of elitist, liberal curriculum and an attack on the destabilizing effects of 'progressivism'. Indeed much of the first volume of the *Black Papers* was addressed to the student unrest of the year 1968. The discourse being generated here links education with traditional values and to social order. This discourse and its antecedents were to provide the groundwork for two key aspects of what has come to be called Thatcherism. First, in the sphere of cultural politics, an intellectual basis for and legitimacy of anti-progressivism (not only in education but also in art, music and the theatre). Progressivism is identified unequivocally (but mistakenly) with egalitarianism. It is also linked to the decline of traditional values and moral decay and to the devaluation of the family, and the family writ large, the nation. Here a set of objects, modes of statement, concepts and thematic choices are welded into a powerful regularity. Racial politics (and immigration laws), are bound with a rediscovery of Nation (underpinned by the Falklands War). These in turn are articulated with attacks on trade unionism ('the enemy within') and student radicalism. The whole package is tied in turn to the virtues of the traditional family which are set over and against the 'rise' in sexual permissiveness, pornography, abortion, child abuse and homosexuality. These affinities within the discourse capture and evoke a whole range of commonsense fears and concerns. A great deal of the popularism of Thatcherism has its basis in this corpus. The discourse is realized in the style and practice of Thatcherism.

As regards education specifically the *Black Papers* reiterate three major themes, each of which involves direct criticism of comprehensive education. First, that academic standards are in decline, particularly standards of literacy and numeracy. For many commentators the nation had to look no further to explain Britain's economic decline. The oil price rises and the decline in world trade aside, Britain's recession could be blamed on comprehensive schools, progressive primary education and particularly poor and/or politically motivated English teachers. All this despite the absence of clear evidence of decline in standards and indeed counter evidence of no decline in standards,[40] and more pupils than ever before leaving school with examination passes.

Crucially as part of a complex, interrelated discourse this refrain remained largely impervious to disconfirmation. The second and third themes have the same dubious empirical status but taken together they 'do' powerful political and ideological work, effectively deconstructing the fragile democratic possibilities of the comprehensive school. The second theme is that of dangerous, politically motivated teachers preaching revolution, socialism, egalitarianism, feminism and sexual deviation. Here the link is between comprehensive schools and social disorder. Teachers of English were in particular indicted on this count. Attempts by a painfully small number of teachers to bring aspects of working class culture into the school curriculum and to develop forms of critical literacy were regarded as subversive. Thornbury captures the mood in his description of English teachers in London.

> Young English teachers in the 1960s revived the romantic nineteenth century notion of 'enthusiasm', encouraging the working class child to remain a literary primitive ... Many of the new English teachers indoctrinated themselves and their classes in attitudes critical to the police, local government bureaucracy, industry and employers. They did not hesitate to encourage this ideology in the children's writing, or classroom discussion. The new wave of English teachers was committed to the comprehensive school, to unstreaming, subject integration and team teaching.[41]

The general analysis of the 'ills' of education can clearly be situated within the context of the general Conservative Party attack on socialism, trade unionism and egalitarianism which was being formulated to the early 1970s. The shadow cabinet conclave at Selsdon Park in 1970 produced an election strategy which centred on the issue of law and order and which was aimed to fuel a national moral panic based on the idea of 'a nation under threat'. Hall *et al.* describes one phase in the social construction of this panic in the following way.

> In this atmosphere, which the most measured commentators could only describe as one of mounting, often carefully organised, public hysteria, the students at Warwick University occupied the administration buildings and began to consult the personal and political files which this 'community of scholars' had been keeping on them; and a group of Cambridge students noisily interrupted a private dinner being held to celebrate the success of the Greek colonels at the Garden House Hotel. This renewal of student protest moved Mr. Heath to contribute another brick or two to the construction of the populist crusade. He traversed in his

speech the whole terrain of authority (unions, universities, government) versus disorder (strikes, sit-ins) in a powerful coupling of the two great thematics of Selsdon Man: 'Great factories, railways, airports are being brought to a standstill by strike action ... Great seats of learning ... are disrupted by rebellious students.' Both, however, descanted towards a political, indeed, an electoral conclusion: 'We [i.e. the Conservatives] are not going to become a nation of pushovers.' It was a threat he intended to honour.[42]

This leads directly to the third education theme of the *Black Papers*, that of discipline. Again the comprehensive schools were identified with a decline in standards, this time standards of behaviour. The comprehensive classroom was portrayed as unruly and ill-disciplined, with the teachers unable or unwilling to assert their control. The schools were subject, it was argued, to vandalism and disfiguring graffiti. Lack of classroom control spilled over into the rest of the school and thence onto the streets. The rising level of juvenile crime, particularly street crimes, could then be laid at the door of the comprehensive school. Teachers proved to be a relatively unpopular and susceptible group who could be constructed as scapegoats for general social problems. The streets and classrooms were no longer safe places to be. Teachers could no longer be trusted with the education of the nation's children. The progressivism of the comprehensive school — curriculum, teaching methods and social relationships — was thoroughly debunked in the critical discourse of the *Black Papers*. However, this would hardly have been feasible without the ideological support of the greater part of the media for the educational project of the 'Old Humanists'. The *Daily Mail* and more recently the *Sun* and the *Daily Star* have played a particularly important role in a sustained campaign of 'teacher-bashing'. (The CCCS[43] offer a detailed content analysis of the anti-comprehensive stance of the *Daily Mail* during the 1970s.) Furthermore, a number of key events provided particular focus for the elaboration of the discourse of critique. The events at William Tyndale primary school brought the possibility of linking all three of the *Black Papers* themes. Here were politically motivated teachers, making no attempt to teach traditional basic skills, who were deliberately abdicating from their responsibility to discipline and control their pupils. It revealed teachers to be unaccountable to their community and their employers. It 'showed that teachers could run the schools in ways that clearly contradicted many of the shared assumptions on which the education system rested. Teachers could be in effective day to day control of the schools, and they could use that control in ways not welcome to the school managers or its funding authority.'[44] Here indeed the managers had deliberately encouraged press coverage to put pressure on the teachers. Within the emerging rightist education discourse the lessons of Tyndale were obvious; teachers needed to be made more accountable, they needed to be more closely monitored and controlled. A similar message could be constructed out of Neville Bennett's much publicized report *Teaching Styles and Pupil Progress.*[45] The analysis of data from different primary classrooms purported to show that children did notably better on a whole range of measures in formal rather than informal regimes. Indeed, significantly, the BBC *Horizon* programme based on the book was entitled *Lesson for the Teacher.* Teachers were being told again they had got it wrong.

This is the general context in which the specific reaction against English teaching was constructed. Both the Leavisite 'old humanists' and the skill-oriented 'industrial trainers' represented in the Conservative Party focused attention on what they perceived as a decline in standards of literacy and decency. This clearly struck a note of major political and ideological significance. The very future of the nation was at stake. Something had to be done. In response to this 'climate of public concern', Mrs Margaret Thatcher, the then Secretary of State for Education, was moved to set up an inquiry under Sir Alan Bullock, 'to consider in relation to schools, all aspects of teaching the use of English, including reading, writing and speech'.

The report *A Language for Life*, published in 1975, attempts to review the state of English teaching from the earliest development of pre-school language skills through to the teaching of English literature to 16–19 year olds studying for A levels. But as the title indicates the emphasis of the report is on the development of language as a high priority 'in the complex life of the secondary school'. However, in response to the critics of 'progressivism' the committee's detailed research provided no evidence that formal work in English was decaying 'in a climate of unchecked creativity'. The report *is* critical of 'the notion of English in the secondary school as almost exclusively a source of material for personal response to social issues',[46] which was regarded as often lacking in direction and tending to produce clichés in pupils' work. This approach was seen by the Committee to be diminishing the pupils' experience of English work. Alongside this, literature is strongly defended against the inroads of 'thematic' work. The undue emphasis on 'creativity' in the primary classroom was also seen as worrying when other types of work were 'neglected': 'We have equal lack of sympathy with the notion that the forms of language can be left to look after themselves. On the contrary, we believe that the teacher should intervene, should constantly be looking to improve the quality of the utterance.'[47] Strong encouragement was given for the need for teacher intervention in pupils' work. (Here, then, the traditional teacher role is reinforced over and against attempts to develop less hierarchical forms of classroom relationship.) In many respects the report attempts to steer a middle course and to establish a 'coherent' basis for English teaching which draws together some of the diverse and competing versions of school English that had been in contest during the period 1960 to 1975. Thus alongside the criticisms of 'unchecked creativity', the teaching of 'grammar' as an isolated topic is roundly condemned; 'Competence in language comes above all through its purposeful use, not through the working of exercises divorced from content.'[48]

In fact both of the major contesting paradigms outlined earlier, 'English as language' and 'English as literature', receive positive reinforcement in Bullock. Support was given to the teaching of literature 'which aims at personal and moral growth' and stresses 'the "civilising" power of literature'.[49] 'Literature brings the child into an encounter with language in its most complex and varied forms and is a valuable source of imaginative insight. It should be recognised as a powerful force in English teaching at all levels.'[50] The ideas in the report about 'English as language' clearly draw on the work of James Britton and NATE. And considerable attention is given to *oracy*: the report argues that 'a priority objective for all students is a commitment to the speech needs of their pupils and a serious study of the role of oral language in learning'. Also support is given to the role of linguistics in English teaching and teachers are encouraged to acquire 'an explicit understanding of the operation of language'.

Two central themes — language and learning, and teaching — lie at the heart of the report. A continuing programme, aimed at the development of pupils' language from pre-school to school leaving is the main recommendation, with the 'reading curriculum' seen as an integral part of the total 'language curriculum'. Two keywords widely taken up from the report into general educational discourse reflect these primary concerns. First, the notion of 'basic skills', which in the report refer not simply to the starting point of language development but to a concern with language competence throughout the pupils' school career. Second, the concept of 'language across the curriculum'. The need, that is, for schools to have a language policy which addresses the problem of language development across all the subjects of the curriculum.

> ... we must convince the teacher of history or of science, for example, that he [*sic*] has to understand the process by which his pupils take possession of the historical or scientific information that is offered them; and that such an understanding involves his paying particular attention to the part that language plays in learning.[51]

Both of these keywords sparked off a considerable barrage of 'noise' in schools, local education authorities and the media. Following the publication of the report, hundreds of schools, both primary and secondary, established working parties to examine and devise a policy for 'language across the curriculum'. Equally, in many schools teachers were given posts of responsibility for 'language across the curriculum' and numerous in-service education courses were soon being offered under this title. However, one cannot take for granted that this public 'noise' and activity was translated into widespread changes in the classroom practices of teachers. More generally the symbolic and political functions of the Bullock report are probably in the long run of greater significance than its specific findings. In one sense it demonstrated the power of 'public opinion' and the mass media to stimulate government action to intervene in teachers' classroom decision-making. In terms of a more 'political' reading the significance of the Bullock report is twofold. First, in a fairly arcane fashion it is one form of official response to the 'moral panic' about English teaching. It is an attempt at social control, a curriculum policing action aimed at controlling the unacceptable aspects of 'progressive' teaching, and redefining the boundaries of acceptable practice. The role of monitoring the response of English teachers was to be taken on by the APU (Assessment of Performance Unit), set up in 1976 with a brief to devise reading and language tests. At first sight this appeared to be a step towards the establishment of and testing for national standards of literacy and was received by the teaching profession with some scepticism. Indeed it seemed like one further attack on their already fast-fading classroom autonomy. And writing in 1980, Lawton saw the development of the APU as both anachronistic and dangerous and the establishment of testing on a national basis as likely to have massive and untoward 'backwash effects' in the classroom.

> ... having moved away from the Scylla of laissez-faire the DES show no signs of possessing an adequate theoretical base for curriculum change and is in danger of getting too close to the Charybdis of behaviouristic, mechanistic approaches to curriculum and evaluation.[52]

In fact the Bullock Report and the role given to the APU were to be only the first in a steady stream of increasingly direct interventions into the school curriculum. At the time of writing in 1988 the national testing for all children at ages 7, 11 and 14 is in the process of being introduced.

The second significant aspect of Bullock is that it specifically reasserted the economic and political role of English teaching in relation to capitalist society. The emphasis given to 'basic skills' and 'language across the curriculum' underlined the role of English in preparing pupils for work and the need for a literate labour force. The repositioning of literature attempted by Bullock, the *Black Papers* and writers like Marenbon (see below) — that is, the literature of the great tradition, as having a central role in English teaching — underlined the role of English in the moral education of youth, the civilizing process. National efficiency and social order were at stake. As we have seen, declining 'standards' and the 'politicization' of English were seen by critics as being linked to, if not posited as causes of, the failings of the British economy and increases in crime and social disorder. If this rhetoric of debilitation is taken seriously we have in microcosm a representation of the classic relationship between education and the economy, the reproductive functions of the technical and attitudinal preparation of the workforce and the maintenance of social control. And in particular the emphasis given in the report to *skills* marked a significant shift in the discourse of English teaching; excised of its 'social realism' and political criticism 'English as language' emerged as a 'form without content'. This vacuum was quickly filled. Reading and writing as bare skills, as tasks, were to be increasingly oriented towards 'the world of work'. Under the influence of models drawn from Technical Colleges and Further Education, areas which might previously have been designated as within English are being colonized and reconceptualized as 'communication'. TVEI (the Technical and Vocational Education Initiative) and CPVE (the Certificate of Pre-vocational Education) are attempting to link literacy 'skills' directly to the needs and demands of employment. At its most extreme literacy is reduced to form–filling and letter writing, oracy to answering the telephone. Discursively at least, vocational realism has replaced social realism. The world of work, or rather employment, is the dominant reference point. 'This represents little more than a particular form of mass vocational literacy that shifts the responsibility for the reproduction of workers back onto themselves.'[53]

What we are suggesting here is that the Bullock Report served as a vehicle for restructuring English. Its role was symbolic in giving public censure to significant aspects of the 'new wave' English and in creating space for the insertion of alternative concepts of the role and purpose, and form and content, of English teaching. It gave credibility to those voices which said 'things have gone too far'. But it would be crude indeed to suggest that the Bullock report was simply a mouthpiece for the voices of reaction. Certainly, for instance, Bullock had little that was positive to say about the teaching of grammar. It is clear that the educationalists of the 'new right' found the report unsatisfactory. The *Daily Mail* summed up its view of the report in the following ironic headline:

> WHITEWASH spells whitewash. Sir Alan Bullock's report on the teaching of English shrouds the reality in trendy pieties (19 February 1975).

Clearly, from the *Mail's* point of view, the report had failed to come to grips with the 'realities' (to which the *Mail* itself had privileged access). And a great deal of the press attention centred not on the main findings of the report itself — which included the refutation of the suggestion that reading scores were declining — but on the minority report of the one dissenting member, Stuart Frome, a *Black Paper* contributor, who argued for a return to the traditional forms of teaching English in the primary school. This is where the re-emphasis upon grammatical skills emerges.

> My own observation in a number of schools leads me to the belief that in the zeal for 'creativity' by teachers today, there is not the rigorous critical marking of spelling, punctuation and grammatical

errors which there used to be, while the traditional systematic 'doing of corrections' is fast disappearing. This has led, in my view, to the wretched solecisms exhibited in students' written work, and I believe that the Committee should have made even more of the unfortunate side effects that the policy of free, uninhibited creativity has engendered. And I believe the Committee is in error in putting undue emphasis upon talking as a means of learning language. It has its place, but in my view, one of the causes of the decline in English standards today is the recent drift in schools away from the written to the spoken word. [54]

1980s

To a great extent it is this minority view, articulated via both vocationalist and 'standards' arguments, that has emerged as the dominant conception of the role of English teaching in the 1980s. The new emphasis of 'skills' continues and as has been the case in previous periods of crisis the notions of standards and functional English (functional for industry, for the economy) have become linked to grammar, 'correct' English. The 1984 HMI (Her Majesty's Inspectorate) consultative document *English from 5 to 16* urged that grammar, spelling and punctuation should be brought back to the forefront in English teaching and attempted for the first time (since the revised code of the nineteenth century) to set specific objectives for English teaching. *The Times* (3 October 1984) commented:

> The paper puts parental concern about literacy, and ability to communicate intelligently and accurately, back in the forefront of educational aims. The proposals are certain, however, to lead to criticism by some teachers, who will view its emphasis on learning grammer [*sic*] as a reversion to traditional teaching methods.

Here crucially, and typically, the interests of parents are counterposed to those of teachers. The image of the subversive teacher (needing to be controlled) is sustained. The fact of a widespread continuing adherence to grammar teaching by English teachers is irrelevant to the discursive work attempted by these public, official documents. [55]

To a great extent the discourse of critique mounted by the *Black Paper* ideologies in the 1970s is now government policy. The educational clock is being wound firmly backwards. The dual orthodoxies of English teaching in the 1920s, of the Newbolt report and the Classical tradition are being re-established: on the one hand, a standard canon of literature, the great works that must be read, linked to the literary and cultural heritage of *Great Britain*; on the other hand, a standard language, fixed in grammatical structure, spelling and punctuation, defined from above and ignoring all cultural variations and widely used non-standard forms. Thus, alongside the emphasis on 'skills', and sometimes over and against it, 'old humanism' is being vociferously re-articulated. The message is of 'culture in decline'. This was the argument put by George Walden, speaking to the Tory Reform Group in 1986 and then Parliamentary Under Secretary of State at the Department of Education and Science:

> We need more emphasis on intellectual achievement in the humanities not less, both for itself, and for sound vocational reasons too. Latinists make good in the City, philosophers move easily from Kant to the computer keyboard, and the arts as a whole — exactingly taught — train the mind in rigour and adaptability. At every level, from the all-important technician to the research scientist, there is no conflict between thinking and doing, least of all in the intellectually demanding new technologies. Numeracy and pragmatism do not exclude literacy ... The "liberal tradition", neatly distilled in the 1975 Bullock Report on English, has been quietly disintegrating too. The Report is worth re-reading today: its august equivocations accurately mirror the passive accommodation to decline which was the hall-mark of the era. The belief in literature as a civilising experience for all pupils of all abilities is described, with deft condescension, as a 'spirited credo'. 'Discernment' is gently derided too. Only *Billy Liar* aroused the committee's enthusiasm. Conservatives want change within continuity, and to enrich the present with a knowledge of the past, we would do well to encourage a little more familiarity with it. There is a spark of revolt against the inculcation of ordinariness, the beginning of a new spirit of educational idealism which the Tory party must capture.[56]

A variation on this theme is provided by a recent publication from the Centre for Policy Studies, one of the many pseudonyms of the group of right wing educational critics who have taken up the cudgels of the *Black Papers*. John Marenbon, of Trinity College, Cambridge, in a pamphlet titled *English our English*[57] argues that the emphasis on practical criticism in the school teaching of English has undermined children's knowledge of their literary heritage. The 'skills' of criticism are emphasized to the detriment of reading itself. Children need to read a variety of outstanding works, he says, rather than learn the techniques of academic criticism.

However, against all this the common examination at 16 plus, the General Certificate of Secondary Education, awarded for the first time in 1988, has allowed and in some senses enhanced many aspects of practice identified previously with the apparently beleaguered progressive paradigm. At present GCSE seems a solid gain for this paradigm, though it remains to be seen whether its progressive features can survive a renewed pro-elitist push on the standards issue. But perhaps the most significant recent intervention into the public discourse about English teaching has come from Kenneth Baker, Secretary of State for Education. In a speech delivered on 7 November 1986 he announced the setting up of a new committee of enquiry. Following Newbolt and Bullock the 'crisis' in English teaching was again to be the subject of high level pronouncement. In a sense the new committee indicates the perceived failure of the Bullock 'police action' — stronger measures are evidently called for.

> ... like a garden a language needs care and attention, it needs cultivation and I am not at all happy that this is happening. Two years ago my predecessor, Sir Keith Joseph, authorised Her Majesty's Inspectorate to publish a discussion paper on the HMI curriculum in English from 5 to 16. The paper invited comments. HMI received 931 formal representations. It was quite obvious that, while there was widespread agreement about the purposes of English teaching, the importance of dealing with language in use, spoken and written, and about the centrality of literature in English teaching, there was no agreement or consistency about what children of various abilities should be expected to achieve at different ages. In particular there was widespread disagreement and confusion about what should be taught about how our language works. For example, in a few schools there is still an attempt to teach grammar in the way that my generation understood that term. In other schools pupils are no longer taught about their own language. [58]

He went on:

> I would like to see bench marks for progress in English which actually set out lists of the sort of books or authors which children should be able to read and understand at particular ages and levels of achievement. [59] ... the proper emphasis on the application and practical aspects of subjects as exemplified in the Technical and Vocational Education Initiative, in the GCSE and in the new City Colleges, should not lead to any diminution of the appreciation of the magic and potency of literature. [60]

And:

> It must be right for any worthwhile system of education to have as one of its central purposes to make its pupils reflective users of our language: able to understand it as well as to use it; to be in control of it rather than at its mercy. [61]

The result was the Kingman Committee, chaired by Sir John Kingman, an eminent scientist. The terms of reference of the Inquiry are as follows:

1 To recommend a model of the English language, whether spoken or written, which would:

(1) serve as the basis of how teachers are trained to understand how the English language works;

(2) inform professional discussion of all aspects of English teaching.

2 To recommend the principles which should guide teachers on how far and in what ways the model should be made explicit to pupils, to make them conscious of how language is used in a range of contexts.

3 To recommend what, in general terms, pupils need to know about how the English language works and in consequence what they should have been taught, and be expected to understand, on this score, at age 7, 11, and 16.

In contrast to Bullock the membership of this committee contains no representation from the comprehensive/progressive camp — no liberal academics or practitioners here. But the published report contains many of the ambivalences of Bullock, the Secretary of State found it no more than "interesting" and proceeded quickly to establish his English working party, anticipating the provisions of 1988 Education Reform Act, and the requirement to test children at 7, 11 and 14. Professor Brian Cox, founder of the *Black Papers*, will chair the working party.

The Secretary of State's lack of enthusiasm for the Kingman Report seems to stem from the report's lack of enthusiasm for a return to formal grammar teaching and its support for a model of language we use rather than a standard form. The report also urges that teachers be left to make their own decisions about how and when knowledge about language should be made explicit to students. And the use of textbooks is regarded as against the spirit of the recommendations. But, most of the time, the Kingman Committee do assert the existence of a relationship between explicit knowledge of the structure of the language and mastery of language in use. Also Standard English is suggested as an attainment target for all 16-year-olds — social class, regional and ethnic variations are set aside. The issue of community languages is dismissed in one paragraph as outside of the brief of the committee.

The report is clearly somewhat gnomic and confusing in its fence sitting stance. Most of the newspaper responses however seem to read into the report a hard line attack on progressive English and a thorough-going defence of standard English. At the extreme Ferdinand Mount (right wing) in the *Spectator* of 18 March 1988, in an article headed 'The Grammarian's Resurrection', declares:

When scenting success, one is supposed to wipe the smirk off one's face and talk of 'a victory for common sense'. In welcoming the report from Sir John Kingman's Committee on the Teaching of English Language I can contrive no such imperturbability. I read it with a song in my heart and smile on my lips. For the report rehabilitates and revives, in most uncompromising and irrefutable fashion, the rigorous study of formal, correct, standard English. It is the grammarian's resurrection.

The ILEA teachers' journal *The English Magazine* (Summer 1988) shares Mount's analysis but not his glee, as might be expected. The editorial states:

> The Kingman Report slots into a pattern that has attended all government reports on English teaching over the last 13 years. Behind each one there has been a set of simple-minded and reactionary intentions and each one has been 'rescued' by the mobilization of enlightened opinion. With each report ground gets lost and valuable energy diverted.

The setting up of the Kingman Committee does underline the key position held by English teaching in the political imagination of the Conservative Party but its work should not be isolated from the broader scenarios of the cultural politics and authoritarianism of Thatcherism. The taming of English and the establishing of national criteria for a programme of testing at 7, 11, 14 and 16 are part of a general process of increasing centralization of control over education. The administrative centralism of the British state is now perhaps the greatest in Western Europe. [62] Within this English teaching, potentially, has a major role to play in the ideological re-creation of nation and 'greatness', one of the major preoccupations of Thatcherism.

English and the Forms of Literacy

It should be clear from the analyses of movements in English teaching that we view English and the forms of literacy it embodies as pre-eminently a subject of major political significance. The versions of English outlined above are 'political' in different ways and are involved in or related to the social reproduction of inequality and political hegemony in different ways. And as Graff asserts: 'Despite traditions of positing literacy as "neutral", as a "variable", this can no longer be tolerated.' [63] In his wide-ranging work on the history of literacy he goes on to make the point that:

> It remains nevertheless important to stress the integrating and hegemony creating functions of literacy promoted through formal schooling. Especially with the transition from pre-industrial social orders based on rank and deference to class societies of commercial and then factory capitalism, schooling became more and more a vital aspect of the maintenance of social stability, particularly during periods of massive but often confusing social and economic changes, and a regular feature of the life course. Many persons, most prominently social and economic leaders and social refor-

mers, grasped the uses of schooling and the vehicle of literacy for the promotion of values, attitudes and habits considered essential to the maintenance of social order and the persistence of integration and cohesion. The people's acceptance of literacy's import forms the other dimension of this history. [64]

During the current period of massive and confusing social and economic changes we see the terrain outlined by Graff as continuing to be the main battleground over which contests concerning the role of English teaching in school is fought out, the only difference being that in the contemporary context 'the vehicle of literacy' takes different forms, with different implications for 'the persistence of integration and cohesion'. This is the arena which Lankshear and Lawler designate as the 'politics of literacy': 'As a specific field of inquiry, politics of literacy focus upon the form or forms literacy takes and the role it plays within this process of humans pursuing interests, goals and aspirations under conditions of unequal power.' [65]

Indeed Lankshear and Lawler share our own conception of literacy, in this case English as a subject, as an object of struggle. 'The actual form (or forms) literacy takes in daily life is/are shaped and defined with the process of competing interest groups struggling to meet their respective interests.' [66]

In relation to the processes of struggle outlined above we identify four forms of English and thus four embedded forms of literacy at stake. We now intend to relate these together and analyse them within a single model: this is a systematic version of the differentiations established thus far. The model is basically a simple one based on a two-by-two matrix.

Figure 2.1

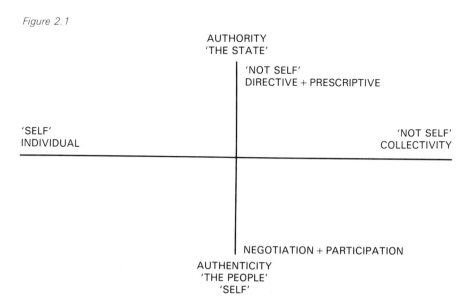

The bases of the bi-polar axes of the model lie in the structuralist work of Bernstein, Mary Douglas and Bachelard[67] and are presented here, for the purpose of simple exposition, in composite form. The lateral dimension stretches from a focus upon the individual on the left, to a focus upon societal or collective forms on the right. The emphasis on the individual suggests atomistic, home-centred social relationships, private social lives and formal, contractual relationships between people. The individual actor, the 'self', is paramount, group orientation is low, social encounters may take the form of individual, face-to-face exchanges, as client or consumer, or applicant or functionary. The needs of the individual, material or personal *and* psychological take precedence. The emphasis on collectivity on the other hand emphasizes the subordination of individual needs to the interests of the group. The individual is regarded primarily as a member, their position, their rights and their needs are interpreted in terms of their ascribed role in the collective. Abstract rules and social institutions constrain and define the 'self'. And the boundaries between members and non-members are carefully defined and frequently reiterated.

The vertical dimension cross-cuts and modifies the lateral. Where the lateral is concerned with relationships between people, the vertical is concerned with relationships between authorities (the state, the management or the leadership) *and* the people. It extends from an emphasis on authoritative, directive and prescriptive forms, relationships and modes of activity, at the top, to an emphasis on negotiation, local and authentic knowledge and participative modes of activity, at the bottom. Social activity and control may be initiated from either direction, that is, top-down, where needs (individual or communal) *and* the solution to needs are defined by the state, or bottom-up where needs (individual or communal) *and* the solution to needs are defined locally, at the grassroots,

Figure 2.2

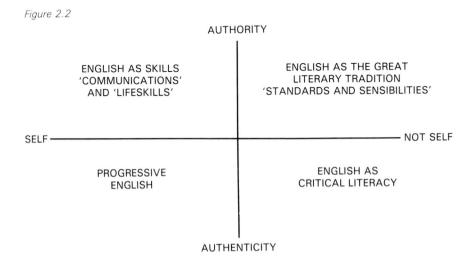

and in relation to perceptions of immediate experience. The rules of discourse here are contrasting, abstract as against immediate, prescriptive as against negotiable, positivist, objective and reified as against interpretive, subjective and authentic.

How, then, can this analytical structure be usefully applied to English teaching? We want to suggest that the four major versions of English identified previously can be mapped directly onto this structure. Such an exercise serves two purposes; first, it highlights the fundamental differences in the definition of 'what counts as literacy' embedded in each of these versions; second, and relatedly, it enables these different forms of literacy to be identified with different kinds of relationships between 'the subject' (English) and the state, and the citizen (the student) and the state.

To a great extent the placing of the versions is fairly straightforward. Beginning with the top left-hand sector — English as skills. Here the primary emphasis is upon competitive individuals acquiring skills and competencies required by the market and the economy. Correct forms of expression and presentations of self are of prime importance; the standards and criteria for which are determined by agencies of the educational state acting on behalf of 'industry'. The relationship of education to the state is exercised in terms of the state's role in providing the social and technical conditions for the reproduction of capitalism. According to Lankshear and Lawler the very logic of such a version of English is ideological, 'it operates on the model of donating 'competencies'' to passive recipients'.[68] The literacy *of* skills serves to provide docile and effective workers and acquisitive consumers. The curriculum becomes carefully pre-specified in terms of grade-criteria, assessment items and levels of achievement. 'Such items become "targets" which, on the one hand, treat language development as the serial progression of atomic units or, on the other hand, set up "goals" of narrow performances which are thought to be achievable by "task-analysis"'.[69] The attendant pedagogy rests on a strongly behaviourist notion of motivation by reward. There is little room here for the consideration of feelings or emotions, or social or moral issues. Counselling and negotiation of assessments are employed, but as a result of these, failure is turned back upon the student and identified in terms of individual inadequacies. The learner's *sense* of self is of little concern, their *presentation* of self is all important. The students will learn how best to 'sell' themselves to prospective employers or clients, the values to be learned draw upon the world of advertising and the competitive market place, image and hype are to the fore.

> The effect if not the object of this vocabulary is to convey to pupils and teachers the view that human relationships and most human activities consist of strategies and stratagems, knacks and techniques, execution of roles and a mechanistic repertoire of behavioural signals and responses.[70]

Individual relations take the form of role incumbency and formal contract. The competition is all against all with each seeking advantage over the others. This carries with it a latter-day ideology of meritocracy, the idea that anyone can succeed, if they are skilful enough; everyone starts out equal. Note skills here should not be confused with grammar teaching as such, although an emphasis on correctness might be linked with aspects of grammatical analysis.

Moving to the top right-hand sector, English as 'great literature', the primary emphasis is upon the creation of a sense of shared culture and thus common values. Literature is employed as the great heritage to reproduce a moral community based upon schooled sensibility and acquired appreciation. The works of the 'great writers', selected by trusted arbiters of judgment, are passed down. A particular view of history, society and what is valuable is fiercely argued and dogmatically disseminated to the uncultured masses. 'It provide(s) a civilising and socially unifying content through great literature which would transmit all that was best in thought and feeling.'[71] The authority of the text is paramount, the tradition unassailable. The questions of what is culture, what is history, are closed. For example, the recent Centre for Policy Studies (right-wing think tank) publication *English our English* argues that: 'Children learn to read literature as literature only by reading the literary works which are recognized as outstanding, and talking to those who are already competent readers of literature.'[72] The matter of what is recognized as literature is simply regarded as obvious.

Teaching and examining within this form thus faithfully reproduces the familiar themes and preoccupations of liberal humanist literary culture — interpersonal morality, the unique value of the individual, the privileging of intuition and immediacy over 'abstraction' and systemized thinking, the past as a source of timeless values, a nostalgic ruralism.[73] Values and morality are taken to transcend differences of race, class and gender. The heritage is embodied in and reproduces an inherently racist conception of the nation and the nation-state. As Barker argues, the construction of a new idea of nation — feelings of belonging, of sharing traditions, customs, beliefs, language — with its arguments that it is 'natural' for a 'nation' to wish to exclude outsiders, *effectively constitutes a new form of racism.*[74] This unifying idea of the nation is, Barker suggests, rooted in the economic and legitimation crises of the early 1970s. Such a conception and such a role for the school curriculum is strongly represented in recent Conservative Party discourse on the purposes of education. The right-wing conservative Monday Club in its paper on 'Education and the Multi-racial Society' epitomizes this view.

> To say that British History, English literature, the civilization of Western Europe should have pride of place in our schools is not to argue from a sense of superiority. It is to argue for relevance. Black

and white children need to learn, and they can, of the nation in which they live and the forces that have shaped it. Britain has had a great and inspiring heritage. Our children need to be fed on it, to be encouraged to make its values their own. Such an approach to education will unify, not divide; nurture shared pride and common loyalties, not cynicism and racial hatred. [75]

This, then, is the literacy of morality: English teaches the inevitability of the state, the virtues and duties of citizenship, the demarcation of power. It is here that we place grammar teaching with its concern for a fixed, standard English. The standard form is identified with cultivation and national identity and acts as a form of social closure and social exclusion.

It is not difficult to find support *within the educational state* and in the Conservative Party *in particular* for both of these positions: English as 'skills', and English as great 'literature'. While the Cambridge liberal humanist tradition finds its natural supporters among the civil service of the DES (Department of Education and Science), the Oxbridge High Tories and right-wing philosophers, and advisers to the Prime Minister on matters of education, like Scruton, Flew and Quinton, the cult of skills is sponsored by the MSC (Manpower Services Commission) specifically, the industrial training lobby in general and the Tory free-marketeers who follow Hayek and Friedman. Where the former stress nation, heritage and traditional values, the latter urge legitimation of educational forms through 'the bourgeois ideal of the market', where social relations are not so much based upon common values as individual calculation and the pursuit of self-interest — discipline via competition. While the former push for closer, more authoritarian state control over the everyday running of schools and the curriculum, with schools pursuing predetermined cultural and moral objectives, the latter advocate the privatization of schooling, either directly by setting up Company Schools or indirectly by introducing Vouchers which would allow parents to 'purchase' education from the school of their choice. Curriculum and pedagogy would be determined by the effects of market forces.

In the bottom left-hand sector I have placed 'progressive' English; the English of individual creativity and self-expression. Teaching and the definition of English is child-centred. Each child is treated as a unique individual and their work and their talents are viewed in these terms. Self-discovery and personal growth are at the centre of the enterprise. Comparisons between children or the stereotyping of them by group identity or ability is avoided. The expression of feeling and individual responses to stimuli are valued, rules of taste and absolute criteria of judgment are eschewed. Participation and interaction are encouraged and diversity celebrated, as in the use of multi-cultural literature. Curricula selection relies heavily on interest: the mass media and youth cultures are as valid as the literary tradition, talk as good as writing, one opinion as acceptable as the next. 'Civilization begins anew in every child.' The children are encouraged to explore their own agendas and concerns and to share these with their teachers. Paradoxically this kind of freedom and relativism, what Bernstein calls the invisible pedagogy, opens up more of the child, more of the self, to surveillance and judgment than previously.[76] The whole person is now a pedagogical subject, whole lives are examined and assessed. This is the literacy of personal discovery; freedom and control are learned through exploration and infinite differentiation. Again differences are taken to reside in the child, but here failure becomes plurality, the children learn to take pride in their individual qualities whatever they may be, to follow their own route of learning, to fulfil themselves as a person.

Finally, the bottom right-hand sector. Here I place 'radical' English. This version of English is assertive, class-conscious and political in content. Social issues are addressed head on. The stance is oppositional, collective aspirations and criticisms become a basis for action. Campaigns and struggles in the community become vehicles for learning social and literacy skills. Children are taught how to 'read the world',[77] to question the grounds and origins of knowledge. In this form 'Literacy has a potential role within attempts by subordinate groups to engage in political action aimed at resisting existing inequalities of structural power (and their human consequences) and bringing about structural change'.[78] This critical gaze is turned upon the school itself and the processes of schooling. Education and schooling are separated. Attempt is made to confirm the voices of the oppressed: anti-sexism and anti-racism become a crucial part of this. And the emphasis is upon shared experience and collective struggle: the state is challenged. Not surprisingly the response to such attempts at English teaching as a form of critical literacy is sometimes hostile, hysterical and repressive. The state is threatened and reacts.

Each version of English contains and informs a particular political epistemology, the learner is placed differently in relation to subject knowledge, their teachers and the state. Each produces different kinds of students (and citizens) with different kinds of abilities and relationships with peers. In each version the root paradigm of meanings *within* and *about* English differs and conflicts.

Since the mid-seventies English teaching has been brought firmly and overtly into the political arena. As a result the conception of what it is to be literate has been significantly reworked in a sustained process of state and political intervention into the subject arena of English teaching. As Raymond Williams argues, 'The content of education, which is subject to great historical variation, again expresses, again both consciously and unconsciously, certain basic elements of culture, what is thought of as "an education" being in fact a particular selection, a set of emphases and omissions.'[79] The limit of the possible and the zone of tolerance — that is the conditions of change, the selection of culture — within which the English teacher works have been redefined as the purposes and concerns of

English teaching have come under pressure from opposing lobbies and interest groups both within and outside of the organic subject community.

Culture, Ideology and Change: Some Elaborations and Conclusions

Our analysis of the history of disputation in the field of English teaching indicates how, in the 1970s and previously, teachers, and teachers of English in particular, had found themselves positioned as scapegoats for the social and economic problems evident in the society at large. Under Thatcherism a particular technique, the notion of an 'enemy within', has been employed in this positioning process. Margaret Thatcher's key-note speech to the Conservative Party Conference on 12 October 1984 linked the striking miners with the IRA to create an image of singleness of enmity. This speech echoed the very first *Sun* newspaper editorial of that year in calling for vigilance. Under the headline 'What we must do to keep Big Brother at bay', the *Sun* targeted 'subversive' teaching as one area for concern and declared:

> As 1984 opens we have been spared the Orwell nightmare. We have liberty under Margaret Thatcher. We have hope of a better tomorrow.
>
> Yet all these things are not automatic. We have to deserve them. We have to earn them. We must be vigilant every day in 1984 and beyond to preserve them from any assault.

In several respects the counterpointing of Orwell's 'big brother' to 'liberty under Margaret Thatcher' seems ironic in the current context of the Conservative government's push to assert a direct, centralized control over the school curriculum. But the ensemble of political rhetoric, political control and moral panic embedded in this positioning work also serves to illustrate our contention that English teaching occupies a special and critical role in education and that control of the subject of English, and thus of 'acceptable' versions of literacy, is central to the ideological maintenance of political and social order and national culture. Such an analysis moves beyond the arenas of academic debate concerning methods, theories, techniques and the syllabus and involves a broader consideration of those processes involved in 'winning and shaping consent so that the power of the dominant classes appears both legitimate and natural'.[80] English as a school subject, more than any other, represents particular understandings of personal relations and processes, and excludes others, rendering them unsayable. It has become in Eagleton's terms a 'moral technology': 'a specific set of techniques for the instilling of specific kinds of value, discipline, behaviour and response in human objects'.[81] Systematic induction into a particular form of subjectivity — in the case of Leavisite English a subjectivity that is reflective and sensitive — is, according to Batsleer, O'Rourke, Weedon and Davis 'one of the most effective ways in which the exploited classes have been induced into the conditions of their own cultural subordination'.[82] Furthermore, the defence of a standard language and a unified national culture, as the Kingman Committee appears to be charged with mounting, places English teaching back into the position of arbitrating and differentiating between students according to fixed cultural standards. A process which 'includes not only access to the riches of culture', for the 'successful' minority, but also the perpetuation, within the dominant ideology, of a class ejected from the education system at an early stage which can experience 'the "natural" language and culture only in terms of an exclusion and a state of being tongue tied to a basic fragment'.[83] Bourgeois values are presented as timeless and inevitable. The establishment of a single standard of expression and a universal heritage thus serves both to exclude the possibility of alternatives and by definition to limit access to 'valued' knowledge. The dominance which is achieved is at once cultural *and* structural in form.

As suggested earlier, the liberal humanist version of English, advocated by the Cambridge school, and staunchly defended by Bullock, *par excellence*, presents life, culture and subjectivity as intransmutable givens, independent of politics and history. Through a series of innocent readings and 'natural', common-sense approaches to literature, the Cambridge school sought to enrich the student's mind without questioning the 'natural order of things'. The notion was not to eradicate class distinctions and inequality but to gloss over them — thus a reading of George Eliot could vicariously compensate for material impoverishment, a rich inner life making up for an impoverished material existence. The shared assumptions of the Leavisite discourse — intelligence, distinction, discrimination, evaluation and judgment — are rigorously purified and drained of political content.

> If we allow some of their own meanings and contexts to creep back in, however, it becomes possible to see literary criticism as a discourse and a practice in which certain words with a very powerful charge of social meaning are doing something other than they appear to be.[84]

In this way, the literary canon emerges not merely as an arbitrary set of works selected in a vacuum, but as a system of 'hierarchies' whose value exists not in any inherent properties, but from the fact that the 'canon' presupposes an on-going process of evaluation, placement and opposition. This work is worth more than that, but is not as valuable as this.

This then appears as essentially 'disinterested' or 'non-political' teaching, a discourse which by offering itself as a totalizing explanation — the exploration of timeless truths — is able to displace and supplant historical, social and, above all, political analysis of cultural activity as too narrow, parochial or partisan and thereby marginalize or neutralize whole sections of the population, effectively robbing them of their own histories, culture and politics.

Eagleton in his keynote speech to the 1985 NATE conference mounted this challenge to the liberal versions of English teaching:

> Why does it insist so dogmatically on abstracting personal values and qualities from the whole concrete context — political society — in which they are embedded? Why does it continually offer us the cerebral abstraction of something called 'interpersonal relationships' or 'personal growth' or 'immediate experience', when a moment's thought is enough to reveal that such things gain their fully concrete significance only in the whole political and historical context which shapes them?[85]

It was precisely this 'disinterested' way of looking at and presenting the world that enabled Leavis and his cohorts — his 'preachers of culture' — to champion the spontaneous, creative, inner life evinced by D.H. Lawrence whilst at the same time ignoring his virulent sexism, racism and rigid authoritarianism. In order to address issues of class, gender and race the assertive versions of English teaching that emerged in the 1960s and 70s needed to pose a direct challenge to the very notions of cultural heritage and literary canon, and also, by implication, the critical discourse in which they are embedded. Thus, they were engaged, as we have outlined, in what Hebdige calls a 'struggle within signification'. The reactions to and attacks upon these assertive versions in the 1970s and 80s have been relatively successful in displacing them; Bullock, Kingman, the Cox working party, a national curriculum and student tests will no doubt serve to reduce their presence even further given the possibilities of GCSE. The assertive versions were always represented and disseminated in practice in a fragmentary, situationist manner, often with limited ambition, scope or support. However, the degree to which the conservative reaction is successful in eradicating these counter-critical practices from English altogether, and establishing the total, social authority of a standard language and national literary heritage, will depend upon the outcome of struggles in various educational arenas in the educational state, institutions of teacher training, publishing houses, subject associations and schools and classrooms. The control of the subject is at stake, and more.

> Together with the problem of gaining political power, the proletariat must also face the problem of winning intellectual power. Just as it has to organise itself politically and economically, it must also organise itself culturally.[86]

Notes

1   STREET, B. (1984) *Literacy in Theory and Practice*, Cambridge, Cambridge University Press.
2   LANKSHEAR, C. and LAWLER, M. (1988) *Literacy, Schooling and Revolution*, Lewes, Falmer.
3   MATHIESON, M. (1975) *Preachers of Culture*, London, Allen and Unwin, p. 125.
4   *Ibid.*, p. 79.
5   GRAFF, H.J. (1987) *The Labyrinths of Literacy*, Lewes, Falmer, p. 187.
6   *Ibid.*
7   BALDICK, G.C. (1983) *The Social Mission of English Studies*, Oxford, Blackwell, p. 156.
8   BATSLEER, C. *et al.* (1985) *Rewriting English: Cultural Politics of Gender and Class*, London, Methuen, p. 22.
9   BALDICK, *op. cit.*, p. 156.
10 EAGLETON, T. (1985) *Literary Theory*, Oxford, Blackwell, p. 23.
11 ARNOLD, M. (1984) *Culture and Anarchy*, J. Dover Wilson (Ed.), Cambridge, Cambridge University Press.
12 EAGLETON, T. (1986) *Criticism and Ideology*, London, Verso.
13 BALDICK, *op. cit.*, p. 100.
14 HUNTER, I. (1987) 'Culture, Education and English', *Economy and Society*, Vol. 16, No. 4. p. 573.
15 SAMPSON, G. (1921) *English for the English*, Cambridge, Cambridge University Press.
16 BALDICK, *op. cit.*, p. 153.
17 EAGLETON (1985), p. 30.
18 NEWBOLT, p. 205 quoted in EVANS, M. (1984) 'Text Theory Criticism', in NORRIS, C. (Ed.) *Inside the Orwell Myth: Views From the Left*, London, Verso.
19 *Ibid.*, p. 87.
20 MATHIESON, *op. cit.*, p. 123.
21 *Ibid.*, p. 122.
22 LEAVIS, F.R. (1932) *New Beginnings in English Poetry*, p. 22.
23 LEAVIS, F.R. (1952) *The Common Pursuit*, p. 192.
24 LEAVIS, F.R. (1972) *Nor Shall My Sword*, p. 204.
25 BALL, S.J. (1982) 'Competition and Conflict in the Teaching of English', *Journal of Curriculum Studies*, Vol. 13, No. 4.
26 EAGLETON (1985) *op. cit.*, p. 31.
27 ABBS, P. (1982) *English Within the Arts*, Sevenoaks, Hodder and Stoughton, p. 1.
28 *Ibid.*, p. 2.
29 BATSLEER, *op. cit.*, p. 164.
30 EAGLETON (1985) *op. cit.*, p. 34.
31 DIXON, J. (1975) (3rd edn) *Growth Through English*, Oxford, Oxford University Press.
32 HOLBROOK, D. (1981) *English for Meaning*, Windsor, NFER, p. vii.
33 DIXON, *op. cit.*, p. 6.
34 *Ibid.*, p. xv.
35 SIMONS, M. and RALEIGH, M. (1982) 'Where We've Been', *The English Magazine*, No. 1, pp. 23–8.

36 ARONOWITZ, S. and GIROUX, H. (1985) *Education Under Siege: The Conservative, Liberal and Radical Debate Over Schooling*, Mass, Bergin and Harvey, p. 133.

37 GOODY, J. and KNIGHT, H. (1985) 'Multicultural Education and Anti-Racist Teaching', *English in Education*, Vol. 19, No. 2, p. 6.

38 C.C.C.S. (1981) *Unpopular Education*, London, Hutchinson, p. 111.

39 WILLIAMS, R. (1982) *The Long Revolution*, Harmondsworth, Penguin.

40 THE BULLOCK REPORT (1975) *A Language for Life*, London, HMSO.

41 THORNBURY, R. (1978) *The Changing Urban School*, London, Methuen, p. 136–7.

42 HALL, S. *et al.* (1978) *Policing the Crisis*, London, Macmillan, p. 275.

43 C.C.C.S. *op. cit.*

44 DALE, R. (1979) 'The Politicisation of School Deviance: the case of William Tynale', in BARTON, L. and MEIGHAN, R. (Eds) *Schools, Pupils and Deviance*, Nafferton, Driffield, p. 96.

45 BENNETT, N. (1976) *Teaching Styles and Pupil Progress*, London, Open Books.

46 BULLOCK, *op. cit.*, p. 7.

47 *Ibid.*, p. 8.

48 *Ibid.*, p. 528.

49 *Ibid.*, p. 125.

50 *Ibid.*, p. 525.

51 *Ibid.*, p. 108.

52 LAWTON, D. (1980) *The Politics of the School Curriculum*, London, Routledge and Kegan Paul, p. 48.

53 GLEESON, D. (1986) 'Further Education, Free Enterprise and the Curriculum', in WALKER, S. and BARTON, L. (Eds) *Youth, Unemployment and Schooling*, Milton Keynes, Open University Press, p. 57.

54 BULLOCK, *op. cit.*, p. 526.

55 ALLEN, D. (1988) *English, Whose English?*, Sheffield, NATE.

56 WALDEN, G. (1986) 'The Culture of Excellence', *Times Higher Education Supplement*, 21.11.86, p. 14.

57 MARENBON, J. (1987) *English Our English*, London, CPS.

58 BAKER, K. (1986), Speech, pp. 4–5.

59 *Ibid.*, p. 9.

60 *Ibid.*, p. 11.

61 *Ibid.*, p. 11.

62 ANDERSON, P. (1987) 'The Figures of Descent', *New Left Review*, No. 161, pp. 20–77.

63 GRAFF (1987) *op. cit.*, p. 7.

64 *Ibid.*, p. 36.

65 LANKSHEAR and LAWLER, (1988) *op. cit.*, p. 47.

66 *Ibid.*, p. 62.

67 See BEATTIE, A. (1986) 'Community Development for Health: from practice to theory; *Radical Health Promotion*, No. 4, pp. 12–18.

68 LANKSHEAR and LAWLER (1988) *op. cit.*, p. 104.

69 PALMER, F. (1986) 'English: reducing learning to short cut "skills"', in O'KEEFFE, D. (Ed.) *The Wayward Curriculum*, London, Social Affairs Unit, pp. 48–9.

70 *Ibid.*, p. 46.

71 BARCAN, A. (1986) 'English: two decades of attrition', in O'KEEFFE, D. (Ed) *op. cit.*

72 MARENBON, (1987) *op. cit.*, p. 37.

73 GODDARD, R. (1985) 'Beyond the Literary Heritage: meeting the needs in English in 16–19', *English in Education*, Vol. 19, No. 2, pp. 12–22.

74 BARKER, M. (1981) *The New Racism — Conservatives and the Ideology of the Tribe*, London, Junction Books.

75 PEARCE, S. (1985) 'Education and the Multi-racial Society', Monday Club Policy Paper No. IR4, London, The Monday Club, p. 6.

76 BERNSTEIN, B. (1975) *Class, Codes and Control*, Vol. 3, London, Routledge and Kegan Paul.

77 ARONOWITZ and GIROUX (1985) *op. cit.*, p. 132.

78 LANKSHEAR and LAWLER (1988) *op. cit.*, p. 47.

79 WILLIAMS, R. (1962) *op. cit.*, p. 145.

80 HALL, S. quoted in HEBDIGE, D. (1981) *Subculture: The Meaning of Style*, London, Methuen.

81 EAGLETON, T. (1985a) 'The Subject of Literature', *The English Magazine*, No. 15, p. 3.

82 BATSLEER, C. *et al.* (1985) *op. cit.*, pp. 36–7.

83 EVANS, M. (1984) *op. cit.*, p. 30.

84 BATSLEER, C. (1985) *op. cit.*, p. 29.

85 EAGLETON, T. (1985a) *op. cit.*, p. 5.

86 GRAMSCI, A. (1985) 'Questions of Culture', in FORGECS, D. and NOWELL-SMITH, G. (Eds) *Selections from Cultural Writings*, London, Lawrence and Wishart, p. 19.

We would like to thank Ian Hunter, Peter Medway and the MA Urban Education students at King's College London for their comments on earlier drafts of this paper.

Chapter 3

Class, Language and Power in Franklin's Idea of the English School and Other Early Texts of Vernacular Advocacy: A Perspective on the Social Origins of English

Gerald T. Burns
Wesleyan University

In her book *Social Origins of Educational Systems* Margaret Archer writes that the three basic questions about education are, 'Who gets it? What happens to them during it?' and 'Where do they go after it?'[1] Although Archer's reference is to educational systems, the same statement may be made of individual school subjects. Moreover, the practical urgency of those questions is apt to be greatest when the answers to them are most uncertain, that is, when the given educational entity, system or subject, is in the process of being originated. Such is certainly the case for the study of English language and literature during the period of its coming into being as a coherent discipline and successor to Latin and Greek as the principal vehicle for post-elementary linguistic instruction.

Early advocates of vernacular training beyond the level of the ABCs and Bible reading were faced with the task not only of creating an academic subject matter but of providing a *raison d'être* for it. To this end they found it necessary to specify 'who gets', indeed who might want, such novel instruction: in other words to identify what William Reid has termed a social 'constituency' for advanced study in English.[2] These advocates also tried to say what would 'happen' to pupils in the course of pursuing this study, that is, what skills and capacities could be expected to be derived from it. Finally, they sought to link those immediate educational acquisitions to destinations beyond the school — 'desired futures', as Reid, again, with Jane Filby, has characterized them.[3] In attempting to answer these basic questions such writers aided, in greater or lesser measure, the cause of the new subject matter. They also produced texts which reflect, with varying degrees of accuracy, the larger dynamics of collective support and aspiration that propelled that cause: texts which furnish a perspective on the social origins of English.

The present essay examines four early texts of vernacular advocacy, with the aim of elucidating this perspective from them. The one of the four among them arguably most significant in this respect, and which constitutes the focus of the treatment that follows, is Benjamin Franklin's *Idea of the English School*. In this 1751 pamphlet Franklin not only devised a programme of vernacular linguistic and literary instruction which anticipated the subject of 'English' that would fully emerge in American secondary schools only a century and a half later; he also articulated a rationale for that programme that carries us to the heart of the social process by which the modern discipline was originated. The *Idea* answers Archer's questions of constituency, immediate educational result, and extra-educational aim, in terms, respectively, of class, language and power. Moreover, under these heads more specific identifications are made: of a commercially-oriented 'middle class' as the natural constituency for advanced vernacular study; of a type of enhanced linguistic competence, mainly associated with that constituency's social superiors, but also keyed to the technology and culture of print, as the immediate benefit of that study; and of access to positions in a power structure normally closed off to those of middle-class status, as the longer-term advantage. The text thus points, first to the general social parameters, then to the particular social historical dynamic, behind the eventual establishment of 'English' at the secondary level in the United States.

The development of this thesis will of course not be dependent on the *Idea of the English School* alone, the actual analysis of which occupies only one of the main sections (section five) of the essay. The other texts to be examined for their contribution to the overall 'perspective' will, however, be related in one way or another to Franklin's centrally revealing work. Thus sections two and three deal respectively with John Locke's *Some Thoughts Concerning Education* (1693) and an anonymous essay bearing a nearly identical title that appeared in a Philadelphia newspaper in 1735, at once in their own terms for the vernacular 'rationales' they advance and the light these shed on the incipient process of social origination, and as precursors and possible sources of the *Idea*. Likewise, with the subject of section four: what could without unduly stretching the point be construed as an additional 'text' of vernacular advocacy, Franklin's *Autobiography* (together with other information on his life and career), will be treated principally as an aid to interpreting the 1751 pamphlet. Finally, the latest in time of the four principal texts, a rationale collectively and progressively articulated at annual meetings of the National Educational Association in the latter part of the nineteenth century, and discussed in section six, reflects directly on the decisive phase of the origination process; but it will be studied, at least in part, to demonstrate the prescience of Franklin's much earlier intuition of that process.

Having said this much on the score of general aims and organization, several matters of scope and method need to be addressed, and a further feature of the treatment introduced, before proceeding to the body of the essay. First, although this is not signified in my title, preliminary discussion has indicated that this study is concerned with the origins of English in America, and at the level of secondary instruction. The latter specification, in particular, may strike some readers as unduly restrictive, isolating as it seems to this stratum of education from factors affecting the teaching of the vernacular in elementary schools and in colleges and universities. No such isolation existed in historical fact and there is no wish here to argue or to imply that it did. Nonetheless my own previous research on the secondary curriculum in the US, together with similar work by other scholars, convinces me that a measure of distinctness and even independence may be claimed for developments at this level, or at the very least that certain educationally universal developments, such as the emergence of English as a major subject area, manifested themselves first and most characteristically in the secondary context.[4] This conviction, as well as the practical need for limiting the scope of the inquiry, undergirds my selection of this particular focus; at the same time it emboldens the generality of my title.

Second, the notion of 'social origins' deserves to be defined and circumscribed. On the one hand a fairly broad meaning is intended for the first term in this formulation, by including within it factors not only of class but language and power, considering these latter to be fundamentally social realities. On the other hand, this breadth does not extend to ideas, cultural patterns, and even economic considerations (relating to the textbook publishing industry, for example), all of which also entered into the origins of English. Moreover, the meaning of 'social' here does not embrace motives for undertaking vernacular study that might be expected to fall under this heading, e.g., occupational success and class mobility. Instead the emphasis lies with motives, 'desired futures', defined in broadly political (though at bottom social) terms, of leadership, authority, and/or influence in the society.[5] Further, and to bring the second term in the formulation, 'origins', into view, it needs to be said that the depiction of a certain social dynamic — the efforts of an evolving class constituency to realize by linguistic and linguistic educational means its ambitions for (socio)political power — constitutes the limits of this study's explanatory aspirations. Clearly, changes in what Ivor Goodson has described as the 'broader structural milieu',[6] relations of production, large-scale institutional configurations, mentalities, and so on, conditioned this process at every stage. But such changes, even though they too might conceivably be characterized as 'social' in the broad sense, and despite their materiality to the 'origins' of English, will figure in the background when at all in this account.

Finally, there is an issue lurking in the use of 'texts' of vernacular advocacy as focal points for analysis, and the relation of this procedure to the larger objectives that have been proclaimed for the essay. Obviously no direct reconstruction of the social origins of English, which would require a very different body of primary source materials, is contemplated here. The texts individually and together provide 'a perspective' on that larger process, and both words in that phrase deserve to be underscored. Yet even this caution is not sufficient, for verbal and intellectual constructs, such as three of the four documents under consideration advertise themselves by their titles to be, cannot be taken at face value, in the absence of other evidence, as reflections of the social realities to which they refer. No better illustration of the risks of making such an assumption exists than the fact that Franklin's *Idea*, the only one of the three earliest sets of recommend-ations *vis-à-vis* vernacular study intended to be acted upon, failed very nearly completely to achieve implementation.

The answer to this problem lies of course in furnishing that 'other evidence', *context* for these texts. In Franklin's case this will come partly from the sketch of his life and career, which grounds his pamphlet's scenario of middle-class ascent to power by means of a vernacular-derived linguistic mastery in the experience of at least one eighteenth-century American. Moreover, the effort will be made to provide a more general and more genuinely social context, not only for the *Idea*, but for the other texts as well, utilizing some of the same types of sources that might be used in a more direct reconstruction.

This effort begins — it will be continued and expanded as the treatment proceeds — in the following, first section of the essay, which presents a brief sketch of the class and power structure of the social world Franklin shared with his two predecessors in vernacular advocacy.

I. Background: Class and Power

Class stratification and the distribution of political and other forms of power in Franklin's Philadelphia reflected the arrangements prevailing in other colonial urban centres and in the preindustrial but increasingly market-oriented Anglo-American world generally, extending back into the preceding century. Let us examine class first,[7] beginning at the top. Of the wealthiest 10 per cent or so of the population who in economic terms constituted the upper class in this milieu, the core social and occupational grouping was composed of 'gentlemen' and their families. The 'gentleman' was a clearly recognizable type of individual: a man of leisure, his income secure and derived at least in conspicuous part from landed property. If as often happened he pursued one of the 'learned professions' of law, medicine, or divinity this was a matter of choice and did not obscure his more basic occupational identity, that of 'gentleman'. In the cities and especially in colonial seaports like Philadelphia, the gentry were joined in the upper ranks by successful and well-established merchants, men of great wealth but lesser social status, whose sons might nevertheless have expectations of becoming gentlemen. Membership in this class was also open, at least nominally, to persons from modest backgrounds who, taking advantage of an opportunity somehow offered to pursue the traditionally privileged course of classical education, had acquired professions, the duties of which brought them into relation with their betters but also thoroughly defined and limited their social positions. Other kinds of divisions also appeared within the upper class, divisions often fraught with tension and conflict, such as that between gentry and nobility in England, and Quaker versus Anglican or 'Proprietary' factions in Philadelphia. But as this stratum of society did not produce the particular educational constituency with which this study shall be concerned, being important mainly for its function as both a model for and force of resistance to the aspirations of the focal group, no further account of it need now be given.

A significant constituency for English study at what would now be regarded as the secondary level did emerge from within the next tier down in this society. What contemporaries referred to as the 'middling sort' in the population and what may without undue fear of anachronism be described as a 'middle class'[8] occupied a great length of the economic ladder, in Philadelphia from approximately the 30th to the 90th percentile of personal wealth as measured by tax assessments and estate inventories. Occupationally, members of this class were defined by their direct involvement in commercial and productive activity, providing basic goods and services. They included merchants operating on a small scale, and also a large number — arguably, the 'core' group in this category — of 'tradesmen' or 'artisans', small shopkeepers and craftsmen or 'mechanics' of a hundred different types, and persons possessing certain specialized technical skills, surveyors, scriveners, schoolteachers and the like. In the countryside, of course, independent farmers or 'yeomen' would have dominated the 'middling' classification. From some time in the seventeenth century if not before this segment of the population had been becoming an increasingly visible and vigorous presence on the social scene in England and America. In Philadelphia, in particular, over the first half of the eighteenth century, the 'artisan community' appears to have enjoyed a rather remarkable degree of sustained prosperity, and by the middle of the eighteenth century was showing certain signs of cohesion as a class.[9]

A third major division in this social world comprised the poorest third of the population, men and the families of men following the less remunerative trades, unskilled labourers and seamen, indentured servants and slaves. This group will not receive attention here, until it comes time to ask the question, omitted from Archer's list, Who was *not* to get the sophisticated vernacular education proposed in the *Idea* and similarly motivated texts?

What about power in this society? Obviously this is a vast subject, but it may be made more manageable by concentrating on the formal distribution of power to certain well-defined and more or less official positions of leadership, authority and influence. In the seventeenth and eighteenth centuries these included elective and appointive political and legal offices: membership in legislatures, governorships, ministry positions, various high bureaucratic and military posts, judgeships and magistracies. In addition, a number of more purely civil, but functionally important positions should be considered under this head: places on select committees and in prestigious clubs; roles as advisers or directors of ecclesiastical, educational, charitable and other institutions and associations; honorary and ceremonial offices. In a certain light, too, the professions themselves might count as such positions, although ordinarily a lawyer, say, would have to win an election or secure an appointment or assume a seat on some commission or board in order to begin to exercise socially appreciable power. In any case, in view here are what sociologist C. Wright Mills has called the 'strategic command posts of the social structure', positions of consequence in the 'major hierarchies and organizations' of society. Further, to the persons occupying these places as well, Mills' famous formula, while needing to be adjusted for the historical distance from the twentieth century to Franklin's world, is apropos: the 'power élite'.[10]

Even more to the point is the formulation of Mills' concept made by one of his followers, because it provides a link between the exercise of power and the scheme of social division discussed previously. 'The power elite', writes C. William Domhoff, 'is the operating arm of the upper class.'[11] Certainly the upper classes of this earlier period tried to make it that. Various steps were taken to ensure themselves a virtual monopoly of key leadership and decision-making positions. Restriction of the franchise by property and other requirements was one: in Pennsylvania in Franklin's time, according to one estimate, only one in fifty of the inhabitants was eligible to vote.[12] Hegemonic control over social expectations represented another, scarcely less effective. Sponsorship of charitable enterprises, writes another historian of the place and period, was simply presumed by the mass of people to be among the traditional prerogatives (and duties) of gentlemen.[13]

And yet this monopoly was never complete. In extraordinary times, such as the English Revolution had been and the American Revolution would be, 'new men', most often the 'middling sort', came forward to assume (or at least place their hands on) the reins of power.[14] Even in ordinary times a pressure for access from below existed. Individuals of extraordinary wealth, talent, or personal power occasionally found entry even without having first been assimilated to the upper class. Further, such widening of political participation as occurred, usually at the instigation of an upper-class opposition party, similarly raised the prospect of rude newcomers entering the formerly exclusive corridors of power. Whig doctrine, according to a seventeenth-century Tory critic, implied that 'meaner persons must have greater share too in public administration as soon as they grow greater in possessions'; another spokesman portrayed the threat in more apocalyptic terms: 'the very rabble [will become] the sole magistrates and legislators'. [15]

As this testimony indicates, the offices of power represented an area of vital interest for the upper classes of the period and an at least occasional object of ambition for those positioned less advantageously on the social scale. They were, as we shall see, the ultimate prizes held out by those who believed that another measure of capacity and merit than increasing 'possessions' — a linguistic measure that could be cultivated by educational means, and specifically by formal study of the native language — should serve as a leading qualification for such positions. For seeing how language mediated, or was conceived to mediate between these two realms of class and power, no better source is available than the several rationales for vernacular study advanced during this period. Locke's *Thoughts Concerning Education*, in particular, provides a treatment of the relationship which Franklin knew and, arguably, incorporated wholesale into his own rationale. And even if it should prove that rather than any influence, the logic of class, language and power that operated in Franklin's life supplied the decisive pattern for the *Idea*, it is still to the earlier treatise that we should look for the clearest exposition of that logic.

II. Locke's *Thoughts*

Locke's *Thoughts* is perhaps the best-known of all the early texts of vernacular advocacy, and its reputation is certainly well-deserved. Although he wrote in a tradition of academy/private tutorial instruction that had consistently shown favour to the native tongue, at least as a teaching medium, [16] Locke was the first educational thinker (or thinker exploring educational issues — like the other early advocates he was not professionally engaged in the field) to seize fully upon the disparity that had come to exist between linguistic practice and linguistic training.

While by the late seventeenth century English was the language of everyday use for all segments of the population, and for all but a few forms of official discourse, as well, a mastery of Latin and Greek continued to be the principal, indeed almost the obsessive aim, of the grammar school and university instruction which represented the society's most highly developed and valued provision for formal education. Locke, whose own training had been precisely of this sort, railed at the potency of 'Custom' in supporting such illogical arrangements[17], but in fact the matter went deeper than that. The place of Latin in the schools had been preserved and invigorated (and that of Greek initiated) at the time of the Renaissance, when it was still almost universally the language of religion and the learned world. Moreover, the humanist 'revolution' had attached this revivified ancient language curriculum to a robust institutional expansion and to a larger pedagogy and set of educational purposes and ideals that were in many ways bracingly new and that continued to have an appeal even a half century and more after the revolution had run its course.[18] It was this purely educational momentum, above and beyond the claims of the two languages and literatures themselves and beyond the force of habit, as well, that made the establishment of Latin and Greek so formidable — and concomitantly their displacement as centrally educative subjects by an as yet untried (at the secondary school level and above) vernacular subject matter so radical an innovation. Yet this was precisely what Locke wished to propose, and while he does not seem in the *Thoughts* to have been aware of the whole nature of the resistance, he surely sensed that his argument had to be a good one. Accordingly, the argument he developed in the text cut to fundamental interests of the ordinary constituency for classical education, interests defined in terms of the exercise of élite power and linked to a specific type of linguistic competence.

This argument hinges on a distinction Locke draws between two purposes of language use and therefore two types or styles of linguistic performance. The first of these is delineated in the following passage (the question at issue at this point in the treatise is whether as a general thing the formal study of grammar is advisable):

> Men learn language for the ordinary intercourse of Society and Communication of thoughts in Common Life without any farther design in their use of them. And for this purpose, the Original way of Learning a Language by Conversation, not only serves well enough, but is to be prefer'd as the most Expedite, Proper, and Natural. Therefore, to this use of Language one may Answer, That Grammar is not Necessary ... Which I suppose is the case of Incomparably the greatest part of English Men; of whom I have never yet known any one who learnt his Mother Tongue by Rules.

The contrast between this and the second purpose/type, set forth in the immediately succeeding paragraph, is palpable:

> Others there are the greatest part of whose Business in this World, is to be done with their Tongues, and with their Pens, and to those it is convenient if not necessary that they should speak properly and correctly, whereby they may let their Thoughts into other Men's minds, the more easily and with the greater impression. Upon this account it is, that any sort of Speaking, so as will make him understood, is not thought enough for a Gentleman...And to this purpose Grammar is necessary.[19]

It is instantly clear from the passage that class enters largely into the differentiation of these two modes of language use. On the one side we have 'Incomparably the greatest part' of the population, on the other the small minority of the 'Gentleman'; and the linguistic performance, and therefore the linguistic training needs of the two are depicted in starkly divergent terms. Locke was here anticipating the class-based distinction of linguistic 'codes' that the contemporary sociologist Basil Bernstein has observed and intensively explored. In fact, the *Thoughts'* formulation probably has more affinity with Bernstein's early conception of 'public' versus 'formal' language than with the more mature and better-known notion of 'restricted' versus 'elaborated' codes.[20] The Lockean 'ordinary intercourse of Society', on the one hand, and the speech thought appropriate 'for a Gentleman', on the other, correspond respectively with the modern analyst's 'public' and 'formal' usage not only in their generalized class locations but also in the performance characteristics that may be inferred of them. Short, grammatically simple and syntactically loose sentences, limited logical connection and little attempt at qualification, an overall tacit-implicit quality of utterance, these are among the features Bernstein attributed to public language, and it takes little effort to imagine that they were what Locke heard in the 'Communication of Thoughts in common Life without any farther design'. Moreover, the enhanced style of expression that he desiderates for upper-class speakers and writers correlates even more clearly with the 'formal' category: grammatical accuracy and complexity, logical sequence and indication of relations, expressive symbolism, and explicitness of qualification and meaning.[21] Finally, in an effort to bring the parallel theoretically up to date, it might be noted that Bernstein's definition of 'codes' has evolved away from this earlier conception precisely by its departure from 'linguistic indices' *per se* toward a broader apprehension of competence/performance that might without too much distortion be labelled cultural.[22] Locke, too, shows some sense of this larger perspective when he makes provision in his plan of study for the 'young gentleman' to acquire general knowledge and a measure of aesthetic awareness, as a necessary complement to the purely linguistic facility.

In any case, if at least some part of the parallel holds, and Bernstein's work can help us to understand the force of this distinction advanced in the *Thoughts*, it is also true that Locke goes somewhat beyond his theoretical descendant in linking the need for greater than ordinary linguistic competence not only with the standards of a class but the functions of an elite. It is not only with the 'Gentleman' *per se* that the quoted passage is concerned, but with what Locke refers to elsewhere as the 'Gentleman's Calling' and in this passage as the 'Business' to be done with tongue and pen. And there can be little doubt that that calling, this business, was related in his mind to the offices of leadership, authority and influence — power — that male members of the upper class expected to fill.

The linkage is clear first of all from what further Locke has to say about the nature and purpose of the skills he saw it necessary to inculcate. True, in this passage he does go on, perhaps to some extent because he has begun the discussion in context of grammar, to emphasize the values of propriety and correctness and to endorse expression graced with them in terms of social status, as means for the gentleman to win favourable judgment on his breeding from upper-class peers. But as the discussion continues the special competence comes to be associated more decisively with *rhetoric* than grammar. The stress initially placed on efficacious, persuasive communication, entering 'into other Men's minds ... with the greater impression', regains relevance. Instead of the polite addresses that one must imagine being evoked when 'propriety and grammatical exactness' are the issues at hand, the model linguistic performances that now occupy the foreground of attention are 'speeches' and 'Dispatches'.[23]

The choice of these two examples is especially significant because they, together with the letter-writing that he discusses extensively elsewhere in the text, and the political pamphlet, represent the basic forms of discourse that Locke traded in during a long public career. That career included an appointment as a diplomatic aide, long-time service as 'assistant pen' to the prominent Whig politician the Earl of Shaftesbury, a series of government posts ranging from obscure secretaryships to a £1,000 per year seat on the prestigious and powerful Board of Trade, and successful intervention in a number of major policy decisions at the national level.[24] In short, Locke was a member in good standing of the power elite of his day, and one the execution of whose duties and the range of whose influence depended very materially on the linguistic capacities he was now urging on his young gentlemen successors. Just as we shall see in Franklin's case, Locke was importing into his text a good deal of personal experience with language and power.

Of course, that experience was in certain respects unique (as will be able to be said of Franklin, as well): Locke was a man of language, a man of letters, author of brilliant treatises in philosophy and political theory (and education) in addition to ghostwritten speeches, political correspondence and position papers; naturally he would recommend to others what had been his particular strength. Yet he appears to have been convinced of the general applicability of the lessons he had drawn, insisting near the very end of his life that the greatest share of a gentleman's 'business and usefulness in the world is by the influence of what he says or writes to others'.[25] Moreover, it seems clear, again from the pattern of his own career and from suggestions contained in the *Thoughts*, that for Locke this 'business and usefulness' largely involved the exercise of power. And in his treatise he was concerned to argue that that 'influence' could be enhanced by a course of training leading to a command of language that today might be described as 'formal' or 'elaborated' in character. Only then would the young gentleman be qualified to participate fully and effectively in the discourse of power.

Now it should be pointed out that this rationale for linguistic instruction as such was nothing new. The humanists had relied on a version of it to justify their curricular reforms, arguing that the intensive study of

Latin (and Greek) language and literature would prepare young men for high offices of privilege and responsibility, and in particular that it would produce, in contrast to the monotonous stream of clerics that the medieval universities had turned out, a significant number of new men of affairs to meet the needs of the expanding secular states of Europe. What is more, the humanists derived their idea from the practice of Greece and Rome, where youth trained in schools of grammar and rhetoric took up the key positions in law courts, legislative forums, and imperial administrations.[26]

In fine, the radicalism of the *Thoughts* did not lie in the form of this rationale, which had these precedents and was likely to be understood at least intuitively by most readers prior to encountering this clear and forceful articulation of it in the text. Rather, the novelty and the challenge lay in Locke's insistence that the study of English be made the substance of that rationale. For he rejected the presumption that had grown up, reinforced by 'Custom', in the interval since the Renaissance when the actual use of Latin had been withering away, that the intensive study of it nonetheless constituted the best and the only true means to a sophisticated mastery of any language, the native tongue included. Indeed, the *Thoughts* makes the charge than an obsolescent concern with the ancient foreign languages had led to a widespread failure, among those who ought, to speak 'better than the illiterate'. 'If any one of us have a facility or purity more than ordinary in his Mother Tongue, it is owing to chance, or his Genius, or anything rather than his Education ...'.[27] While acknowledging the necessity of Latin, at least, to the future gentleman — and in so doing conceding the insufficiency of English in its contemporary state to serve as the basis for a complete general education — the text in the end comes down emphatically on the side of the native language:

> But whatever foreign languages a man meddles with (and the more he knows the better) that which he should critically study, and labor to get a facility, clearness, and elegance to express himself in, should be his own; and to this purpose he should be daily exercised in it.[28]

This ringing assertion of the general educational importance of the vernacular, linked as it was to a specific linguistic and political argument for its utility, and backed by practical, sophisticated recommendations for teaching English reading, grammar, rhetoric and oratory, logic, and several forms of written composition, is among the most impressive to be found in the history of early vernacular advocacy. The reasons why it can hold no more than a preliminary interest for this study, however, are two. First, the *Thoughts* is manifestly addressed to an upper-class constituency. This is consistent with the academy/private tutorial tradition within which Locke wrote, a tradition standing in oblique opposition to mainstream classical education, but evolved from within the upper reaches of society and clearly still bearing the marks of that origin.[29] The word 'Gentleman' resounds throughout the text, and side-by-side with unprecedented suggestions for instruction in English and other nontraditional subjects may be found discussions of the finer points of dancing, fencing, and 'Riding the Great Horse'.[30] The choice of constituency is consistent with Locke's biography, as well, for he was born into the upper class and relied on this status, at least as much as he did on his own communications skills, for entry into the governing elite.[31]

There may in fact be something more to the text on this score than first meets the eye. Historian Richard Ashcraft has recently argued that Locke's involvement in radical Whig politics suggests a hitherto unappreciated solidarity on his part with the needs and interests of the commercial middle class; and he offers a revisionist reading of Locke's political writings from this perspective.[32] The *Thoughts* is susceptible to such a re-reading, to a limited extent.[33] That limit becomes clear, however, in the one passage where Locke talks directly about the group below his own on the social scale. He takes a predictably superior attitude. 'Can there be anything more ridiculous', he asks, 'than that a Father should waste his own Money, and his Son's time, in setting him to learn the *Roman Language*, when at the same time he designs him for a Trade ...?' Moreover, while the animus of this criticism, later in the passage applied to 'Tradesmen and Farmers' who would send their sons to classical grammar schools,[34] is more strongly directed against the ancient languages than the middle class, and might actually seem to create a common bond of opposition to 'Custom' in such matters, in fact it drives a wedge between the educational interest of Locke's own and the lower status group. For recall that he had acknowledged Latin to be necessary (indeed, 'absolutely necessary')[35] to a gentleman, however much its centrality to the course of study ought to be reduced. And where Latin was not necessary, neither presumably would the advanced regimen of vernacular study outlined in the *Thoughts* and designed to prepare young men for the exercise of social power be meet. Indeed, outside of a brief reference to the strictly vocational subjects of handwriting and casting account, Locke makes no acknowledgement whatever of the positive educational requirements, linguistic or general, of young men 'design[ed] ... for a trade'.

The second reason for according only preliminary attention to Locke's text may be dealt with more briefly. While its recommendations appear to have been taken to heart in some measure by practitioners of the academic and private tutorial tradition, the *Thoughts* did not succeed in creating a significant upper-class constituency for English as opposed to classical study at the grammar school or secondary level on which Locke had particularly set his eye. In any event, *Thoughts* or no *Thoughts*, such a constituency did not come into being. Thus in order to bring ourselves into position to view, from a textual 'perspective', the social origins of English at this level, as well as (and at the same time) to see the linguistic educational needs of the middle class positively addressed, it is necessary to move forward in time to other efforts at vernacular advocacy.

In this movement, though, which of course by stated design also involves crossing the Atlantic, Locke will not be left completely behind. His treatise holds signal relevance stemming both from its general defence of the vernacular as an advanced subject matter and, especially, from its claim for this study as a means to a 'more than ordinary' linguistic competence, and for that competence as a qualification for the exercise of power. Both the texts to be considered next manifest a Lockean influence; and, whether the influence extends to this specific point or not, both in effect transfer — the first only partially and tentatively, the second boldly — the linguistic and political aspect of his rationale to a new class constituency.

III. 'Some Thoughts of Education'

This anonymous letter-essay published in the Philadelphia newspaper the *American Weekly Mercury* in 1735, provides an ideal stepping-stone from Locke to Benjamin Franklin in two respects. First, it relocates the setting of this study's textual perspective not only to America but to the very city in which Franklin was living, beginning to flourish, and presumably reading the pages of his rival printer Andrew Bradford's *Mercury* from time to time. Second, while as its title suggests this piece manifests a strong continuity with Locke's treatise, it also anticipates Franklin's *Idea of the English School* in urging a programme of advanced vernacular and other nonclassical instruction upon a middle-class constituency. At the same time, the author does not go so far as Franklin would in advancing Lockean-style considerations of language and power in support of that programme. To be more precise, the 1735 essay, while choosing to emphasize a 'desired future' drawn from another, middle-class-specific tradition of vernacular advocacy (to which Franklin would also prove responsive) does manage to convey a hint of the politically-oriented rationale spelled out in the *Thoughts* and recast in the *Idea*.

'Some Thoughts' shares with the immediately evident source of its inspiration a willingness to differentiate educational needs on a class basis. 'Compting-House and Counter require different Qualifications from those which [illegible] a man for the Pulpit and Bar.'[36] Like Locke, too, this author does not include Latin among the qualifications for the former set of occupations. Indeed he quotes verbatim the *Thoughts'* rhetorical query, 'Can there be anything more ridiculous ...?' and goes on to give several reasons of his own for 'entirely declar[ing] against' the study of a 'dead language ... unnecessary to most People' by 'those who are designed for Trades'.

Where the writer departs from his predecessor is in declaring *for* a definite programme of study for this constituency: English grammar, spelling, and composition with emphasis on letter-writing; and a range of other nonclassical subjects. While this programme reflects, even while falling short in range and sophistication of the one recommended by Locke, its content derives also from another curricular tradition, that of 'English education'. The so-called 'English school' had been the birthplace of vernacular instruction and long its home on the elementary level of reading, spelling and Bible lessons. Now, in the first half of the eighteenth century, this type of education was being extended upward and 'secondary' English schools — the curriculum of which though still very much in flux, is fairly represented by this 1735 essay's suggestions — were coming into being in England and the American colonies.[37]

More to the purposes of this inquiry, the English tradition also carried with it, in addition to a certain array of academic content, a characteristic rationale. The tradition itself having quite literally grown up with the commercial middle-class — its earliest known champion, in the sixteenth century, having been a 'capper' (capmaker), and its first teachers 'Men and Women of Trade'[38] — this rationale understandably spoke to the most immediate interests of that class, which were economic. Thus 'Some Thoughts' concludes its recitation of studies thought appropriate for future merchants and tradesmen with the observation: '... and these sure are parts of knowledge, which will turn to more Account, than all of Lilly's Rules and Exceptions; and will make [the pupil] more capable of ... Business'. There can be no question here of this last word's having the generic significance we find attached to it in the *Thoughts*, capable of embracing the traditional intellectual and political activities of gentlemen. The associations of the phrase 'turn to ... Account' alone are nearly enough to clinch the meaning: the essayist sees the study of English (and other subjects; like Locke he does not restrict the goals of education to a narrowly linguistic competence) as a means to success in a commercial career. The claim was in fact a common one at the time, Lawrence Cremin noting of conventional educational wisdom in the early eighteenth century that 'the use of the mother tongue [was] acknowledged universally as a necessary qualification in business'.[39] Moreover, it was a claim that may well have had special resonance in Philadelphia, whose tradesmen and ordinary merchants were at this period, as pointed out in the background sketch, meeting with an unusual degree of general success and prosperity.

What about the other, Lockean motive, then, the one that would link such training with the type of 'Business' done with tongue and pen, the traditional 'Gentleman's Calling' of exercising leadership and authority in society? It turns out that this, too, is indicated in the 1735 essay, although not that much more emphatically than the aims and ethos of the middle classes are evoked in the *Thoughts*. One part of the indication comes in that same statement of the benefits to be derived from pursuing the recommended course of study. In the full text of the statement, a goal in addition to the one cited above is declared: '... make him more capable of

Conversation, as well as Business' (emphasis added). 'Conversation' in this context clearly denotes a type of discursive activity not primarily situated in the economic realm. Moreover, it connotes, together with the objectives stated for composition training, i.e., the cultivation of 'a good Narrative Style, or a facility of expressing himself handsomely by Letter', a certain quality of utterance over and above the 'Communication of thoughts in common Life'. Both conversation and writing in these senses may be regarded as 'formal', 'elaborated code' activities. Indeed, both figure expressly in Locke's treatment, as the two types of verbal performance wherein the gentleman would be most likely to have his breeding judged. And it is impossible to read this later text on these points without detecting a subliminal message of encouragement to the potential constituency for this type of education, to think of themselves or their children as one day rising to the circles in which such judgment might be passed.

Of course, if such considerations do not belong strictly to the economic realm of 'Business', neither do they belong to the political realm of power. Facility in conversation and a handsome epistolary style appear to be associated here, as they are also, in part, in the *Thoughts*, with social status, class mobility, but not necessarily with entry into positions of functional significance. Still needed as evidence of the advertised 'hint of the linguistic-political rationale is, at the very least, some reference to more public, official types of discursive performances, such as the 'speeches' and 'Dispatches' instanced by Locke. These might be linked once again with the exercise of power by a governmental and/or civic elite.

In fact, the text of 'Some Thoughts' makes no such reference. But it does after a fashion *constitute* one. For what this essay represents is a public linguistic performance by a likely member of the middle class on whose behalf (and in part to whom) he spoke. While no assurance exists that the author thereby exercised power, or spoke from a position of power, clearly the potential — a relatively new potential for the class, historically speaking — was there. Moreover, in the newspaper that served as the format for this performance — also an essentially new phenomenon since the time of Locke — this segment of the population found an unprecedented channel of linguistic access to public life. If the middle class did not control the new medium of the popular press, as has sometimes been claimed,[40] and if members of the group did not automatically emerge by its means as spokespersons and office-holders, they did become more of a collective force to be reckoned with. As Gary Nash has written of the marked expansion of the newspaper and kindred forms of publication in eighteenth-century American cities, the 'printed word' activated pre-viously 'untapped sources of political energy' and became an 'indispensable part of both campaigning for office and pressuring legislators'.[41] There can be little doubt that the middle class whose linguistic educational needs the 1735 essayist addressed participated largely in this mobilization.

Perhaps the foregoing suggestions will be thought to have stretched the supposed 'hint' of a Lockean rationale embedded in this text rather far. Admittedly, 'Some Thoughts' makes no connection, such as was found in its predecessor, between the type of discursive performance it represents and the programme of vernacular training it set forth — unless it were to be noted that this 'essay' in the *Weekly Mercury* is couched in the form of a letter, to which some attention is given in the curricular description, and which form (i.e., the public letter) Locke also made use of to broadly political ends.[42] However that may be, it is clear that this text does not make the connection explicit. Nor does it suggest with even the amount of force that lies in its hint of a purely social mobility, any general access for the middle class to the discourse of power in which the author himself, by writing and publishing the piece, in some measure participated. Whether it reflects the limits upon the constituency's ambitions at this time or simply his own understanding, this writer appears not to have explicitly entertained the idea that young men bound for the 'Compting-House and Counter' might, by the strength of training in a language by no means 'dead' and 'unnecessary', be qualified to speak with the same social efficacy and weight as those educated by the traditional means to speak from 'Pulpit and Bar'. It would be left to another spokesman for Philadelphia's middle class, and not coincidentally a master of the forms of discourse appropriate to the print medium, to articulate and promote precisely that '*Idea*'.

IV. Franklin, Life and Career

'Some Thoughts of Education' reflects, albeit obliquely, upon the dawning possibility of a social force, a conjunction of specific factors of class, language and power, operating toward the origination of formal vernacular study at the secondary level. Moreover, together with Locke's *Thoughts*, it — or at the very least the larger tradition of vernacular advocacy and educational thought and practice it represented — constituted a source for Franklin's *Idea of the English School*. Another such 'source', also revealing of emergent possibilities relative to English, is to be met with in the life and career of the author of this later text. In his personal experience of class, language and power in the social world of late colonial America, Franklin essentially lived out the rationale for a vigorous programme of training in the native language and literature that he set forth in his 1751 pamphlet.

In reconstructing the relevant aspects of that life and career in this section, it will be advisable to have recourse to a procedure employed earlier in the essay. The discussion will proceed first in terms of class and power, and only then introduce considerations of language. The purpose thus served will be first of all to highlight the linguistic factor, which of course is the one most directly connected with vernacular study *per se*; second to acknowledge what is probably the most common general and even scholarly view of the dynamics of Franklin's career, which focuses upon the two poles of class and power (and upon economic behaviour as the link between them). This view deserves to be reckoned with, for it is one that Franklin himself, in the famous *Autobiography*, took of his achievements. But in that same text — which constitutes the principal but not the exclusive source of this section — he presents another and arguably more penetrating perception in which a facility with language and communication in the broad sense, and therefore the training that encouraged that facility, provided the critical mediation between class and power, threw up the bridge over which he travelled from middle-class beginnings to positions of almost unexampled power and influence in his society. It is this latter perception that the present discussion chiefly seeks to document, and eventually to link up with the vernacular advocacy of the *Idea of the English School*.

That Benjamin Franklin's beginnings lay within the socioeconomic group whose educational needs Locke largely ignored and the 1735 essayist addressed without explicitly attempting to redefine, is undeniable. Born the son of a Boston tallow chandler in 1706, young Ben was in fact marked out for possible ascent out of the middle class by educational means, but his father's plans to have him trained as a clergyman collapsed for want of financial resources, and he had to be withdrawn from the Boston Latin (grammar) School after less than a year's study in it.[43] Later, in a piece written for his brother James's newspaper the *New England Courant* Franklin satirized the pretensions of the traditional education from a middle-class perspective. 'Silence Dogood', the protagonist of an allegorical dream-visit to the 'Temple of Learning' (Harvard College, to which Franklin's studies at Boston Latin would have led him) observes with disgust that the door to the temple is guarded by porters who turn away all but wealthy applicants.[44]

Franklin's own formal education was limited to a short stint in a writing and arithmetic school, receiving the vocationally-oriented training that Locke mentioned in passing (and the anonymous essayist discussed at some length) as desirable for future merchants and artisans. To this might be added the apprenticeship he served to his brother James, in the printing trade. In any case, and whether owing to this training or, more likely, to the self-taught lessons of industry, frugality, temperance, close calculation of profit and loss, and the like, which he held up before readers of *Poor Richard's Almanack* and later the *Autobiography*, Franklin achieved a huge success in his chosen trade. The success needs to be seen in context of the growing prosperity of the commercial middle class generally, and especially in Philadelphia (where the young printer relocated in the 1720s), but it far exceeded the norm. Franklin was able to retire from business in 1748 and to assume the life of the leisured gentleman, with a modest country estate and the title of 'Esquire' after his name in the tax rolls.[45] At around the same time he made his way into the ranks of the local power elite, being elected in 1750 to the Pennsylvania Assembly (where he had previously served for fourteen years as clerk, an office fitting his class status at that time). Shortly thereafter he was appointed to the highly exclusive Philadelphia Common Council, and found himself a member or even the head of various committees and boards. This accession, moreover, represented only a prelude to this remarkable figure's rise to the pinnacle of colonial and then national leadership.[46]

Viewed in these terms Franklin's career has generated a certain amount of controversy among scholars concerned to define the relation between the brilliant and powerful citizen and his one-time peers in the trading community. Biographer Carl Van Doren contends that he 'emerged from his class without deserting it', although more recent historians have uncovered evidence of a good deal of ambivalence in his class loyalties and even class identity.[47] The latter view will have to be taken into account, especially when evaluating the larger educational initiative out of which the plan for the English School emerged. Nevertheless, it is clearly true that Franklin undertook much on behalf of the improvement of his original social group. He was instrumental in creating a series of organizations and institutions which, drawing their primary support from the middle class, in turn contributed to the coalescence of the group and its increasing leverage over public life in the city and colony. Among these entities were the all-purpose philosophical and civic society called the 'Junto', the subscription library, a firefighting company, and a voluntary militia known as the 'Association', which Franklin called into being with an appeal to 'the Middling People, the Tradesmen, Shopkeepers, and Farmers' to assume the responsibility for defending the colony that had been abdicated by the 'wealthy and powerful'.[48] Lying squarely in the line of these institutional initiatives aimed at the empowerment of the 'middling People', too, was the Philadelphia English School, whose curriculum Franklin sought to define and justify in his 1751 pamphlet.

Of course it was its proposed curriculum which made this institution distinctive, and the curriculum, dominated by vernacular linguistic study, which according to the *Idea* was to foster the empowerment. In order to shed biographical light on that intention it is necessary to enter into Franklin's experience of language, the native language in particular. That experience was extensive and profound. If the *Autobiography* is most commonly read as a story of success through the self-acquired virtues of industry, frugality, and so on, it is at least equally possible to read it as a story of success — and particularly of ascent to the ranks of power — through a self-acquired mastery of certain verbal and general communication skills. And the medium of that mastery was first and foremost the vernacular language.

Clues to the spirit and nature of this endeavour on Franklin's part can be found in the 'Silence Dogood' essay referred to earlier. Once Mrs Dogood gets admitted to the 'Temple', as a spectator, she does observe a majestic, goddess-like figure of 'Learning'. But this presiding eminence appears ill-served by the 'handmaidens' Latin, Greek and Hebrew: 'Antique Figures', veiled and uncommunicative. Thus the piece registers a criticism not only of the social exclusiveness of the traditional classical education but of its academic content, as well. Moreover, a positive alternative vision is also suggested. At the right hand of Learning sits 'English', 'handsomely attired' and showing a 'pleasant smiling Countenance'.[49] This representation would seem to imply a higher confidence in the value of the native tongue relative to general scholarship than Locke had been prepared to allow. Furthermore, while the vision itself was a strictly counterfactual one — English at that date having been given a conspicuous place in no institution of advanced learning — it did accurately point to the substance of Franklin's own *self*-education, in which the vernacular constituted not only the means but the principal object of study, and which was already bearing its first public fruits in the 16-year-old apprentice's Silence Dogood series.

For a more specific sense of the content of this self-education we may turn to the *Autobiography*. The text records rather loosely the progress of its author's prodigious general learning in philosophy, science, history and other fields of knowledge, and quite closely his efforts to master the vernacular language. While he learned to read so early he could not remember it, Franklin does frequently note the development of this skill, as it evolved toward a keen technical appreciation of the native literature. He further recalls working through an English grammar textbook on his own. Most significantly, he reconstructs what amounted to a pedagogically formalized course of (self-)instruction — what Locke would have referred to as a 'critical' study — in composition. 'Extremely ambitious' to become a 'tolerable English Writer', in his early days in the print shop he devised an ingenious series of writing exercises utilizing back numbers of the popular periodical the *Spectator*, and repeatedly executed them. The method produced results. Franklin himself writes of these exercises that 'I sometimes had the Pleasure of Fancying that in certain Particular ... I had been lucky enough to improve the Method of Language [i.e., of the essay being used as a model] ...'[50] Indeed, if the Dogood series offers any indication, the young man was soon expressing himself with what Locke, again, might well have called a 'facility [and] purity more than ordinary in his Mother Tongue'.

What is more, it is apparent, again from the *Autobiography*, that Franklin was far readier than the 1735 essayist to link the achievement of this level of linguistic competence with mobility in his society. 'Prose writing', he reflects, 'has been of great Use to me in the Course of my Life, and was a principal Means of my Advancement.'[51] Now what still needs to be determined, as in the case of that earlier text, is the precise nature of that 'Advancement'. In fact it had multiple dimensions, but one happens to have been more directly and spectacularly connected with what Franklin here calls his 'writing'. But before going on to sort these out it will be well first to specify and flesh out the capacity that he tended to identify rather too simply with this one skill.

There can be little doubt that that capacity was intimately bound up with the medium of print. As noted at the close of the preceding section, the expansion of the press constituted one of the most salient facts of public and political life in eighteenth-century American cities. Franklin appears to have had an intimation of this development, and perhaps also of the deep connection between it and the ongoing triumph of the vernacular that has been remarked by one modern media theorist.[52] In that same Silence Dogood piece he portrays 'Learning', assisted by 'English', composing on a half-sheet which turns out on inspection to be the *New England Courant*.[53] Moreover, his own earlier vernacular pedagogy seems tailored, whether consciously or unconsciously, to produce a competence suited to the demands of print. Unlike Locke, for example, who in the *Thoughts* dilates on polite speech and formal oratory, the young Franklin put himself through the paces only with visual forms of language, and strove in particular to master the style of the short essay that the *Spectator* and kindred publications succeeded in establishing as a sort of paradigm of expression in the periodical press.[54]

But it was more than mastery of a type of discursive performance characteristic to it that made Franklin an effective communicator in and with print. Also at work was what Lewis Simpson has called 'his unfolding vision of the intellectual resources of the printer's product and commodity'.[55] The *Autobiography* records this 'unfolding vision', a growing awareness on the part of this printer — and promoter/propagandist — of the total informational and rhetorical potential of his medium, and a growing ability to exploit that potential. Franklin tells of learning the advantages of anonymous authorship, the value of a nonpolemical tone, and the crucial importance of delivering a given message to the public from apparently different sources and repeatedly over a period of time.[56] It appears that he might lay claim to being the inventor of, among many other things, the 'publicity campaign'.

In short, both Franklin's mastery of language *per se* and written expression in particular, and his equally self-taught command of the print medium, reinforced each other and undoubtedly blended together at any number of points. Both combined to define what one commentator has called Franklin's 'art of benevolent persuasion'[57] and what he himself characterized more than once as 'preparing the Minds of the People' (i.e., to accept the position or plan he happened to be championing at that moment).[58] Indeed, few persons in history have succeeded so well in achieving the Lockean desideratum of 'let[ting] their Thoughts into other Men's minds ... easily, and with ... impression' — except of course that where Locke's gentlemen were to accomplish this part of their 'Business in this World' with tongues and pens, the Philadelphia printer employed the newly potent instrument of the press.

Further, it was this larger persuasive capacity, to return the point at issue before the discussion paused to define it, which constituted the 'principal Means of...Advancement' to which Franklin referred. Still needed, though, is to identify the particular kind of advancement, of the several he experienced, to which this capacity contributed most directly. He himself could think of the matter in economic terms: at one point in the *Autobiography* he exults over a 1729 episode in which a pamphlet he had authored urging the need for a paper currency in Pennsylvania ultimately brought him the lucrative contract for printing the bills.[59] It is also evident from certain indications in the text, that a basic linguistic facility, including the 'Conversation' and letter-writing mentioned by the author of 'Some Thoughts', but not necessarily the added dimension of print mastery, eased his way up the ladder of social status.

And yet neither of these two represented the most crucial aspect of the mobility Franklin was able to achieve by means of his mastery of social communication. The direction of that advance was a broadly political one; it had to do with the acquisition and exercise of power. The 1729 currency episode, for example, not only produced a financial coup for the young businessman, it also marked, as the *Autobiography* is well-aware, Franklin's first significant intervention in the public affairs of the colony. The issue was a charged one, and in swinging, with his pamphlet, the tide of opinion on it in favour of the 'common People', and against the position of the 'Rich men' (who happened to have 'no Writers among them that were able to answer' his argument), he showed himself a force to be reckoned with in such matters.[60] Similar interventions followed, at decreasing intervals as prosperity began to free the printer from the daily demands of his shop. Franklin spoke — or rather wrote — out, either in pamphlets or in the pages of his newspaper the *Pennsylvania Gazette*, on such subjects as the need for a constabulary, clean streets, fire protection, and of course education, ecclesiastical controversies, and imperial policies. His most dramatic success in this respect came within context of the crisis over defence of the colony, referred to above, when his pamphlet *Plain Truth* resulted in the nearly overnight creation of a 1,200 member voluntary militia.[61]

It will be readily apparent from these examples that the power which accrued to Franklin as a result of his communications mastery was a power over public opinion. He was able to bring to bear on selected issues, and the affairs of the city and colony more generally, those previously 'untapped sources' of political energy being made accessible by the expansion of literacy and print. While Franklin tended in his own remarks on the matter to define 'public' too broadly, referring to 'the People' when the operative audience for his performances likely extended no further than the middle class,[62] its size was nonetheless considerable and its influence upon political and other decision-making newly significant. Moreover, his ability to channel and direct this influence gave him what was in some respects a novel position of power in the society, one independent of the positions traditionally monopolized by the upper class elite. Most important, if independent, this was a position that nonetheless had to be reckoned with by that elite. Thus Thomas Penn, the hereditary proprietor of the colony, wrote from England to one of his local agents in the wake of *Plain Truth* and the results it produced: 'Franklin is a dangerous Man and I should be very Glad [*sic*] he inhabited any other Country ... However as he is a Sort of Tribune of the People, he must be treated with regard.'[63]

To conclude this line of argument, it was as a 'Sort of Tribune of the People', that is, by virtue of the power base he had created for himself through expert use of language in its printed form, that Franklin entered the power structure of colonial Philadelphia and Pennsylvania. For it was no long time before leaders on the local scene were effectively following the proprietor's advice, accommodating to the upstart printer's influence where they could not resist it. His invitation to stand for election to the Pennsylvania Assembly in 1750 came from one faction of the ruling elite who hoped to make use of his sway over 'the people' to further their interests. A magistracy soon followed from the same quarter. The opposing faction responded to these moves with the appointment to the city council and by throwing his way the highly prestigious post of Deputy Postmaster of North America.[64] The gentlemen also came round to him in the realm of civic affairs. In perhaps the most revealing instance of this, a local physician attempting to promote the idea of a charitable hospital for the city found himself stymied for donations until he at last approached Franklin, who solved the problem 'by writing on the subject in the Newspapers, which was my usual Custom in such Cases, but which [the physician] had omitted'.[65] He was also elected president of the board of trustees of the Philadelphia Academy (the educational institution, founded in 1749, in conjunction with which the English School would be established), in recognition of his having initiated the undertaking and generated widespread support for it through a skilfully executed publicity campaign.[66]

For good measure, it should probably be stated that Franklin was aware of this entry into the power structure as a distinct dimension of his 'Advancement'. In the section of the *Autobiography* where he discusses his assumption of many of the positions just described, we find him acknowledging that his 'Ambition was ... flatter'd by all these Promotions. For considering my low Beginning they were great Things to me.'[67] Moreover, it is important to emphasize that the 'Promotions' were not in any decisive way a function of the success in business that enabled him to live the life of a leisured gentleman. Upper class status did not automatically entail access to prized offices of leadership and authority; in fact, had his success been only economic and social, an *arriviste* such as Franklin might well have been shut out from these. Instead, he created a power base for himself not only independent of the existing power structure but to an extent independent of conventional socioeconomic divisions as well. And it was this base, resting, again, upon a certain capacity with language, that capacity in turn established upon a certain broadly linguistic self-education, that most crucially mediated in Franklin's case between class and power, that formed the indispensable bridge between 'low Beginning' and 'great Things'.

At this point, however, a question must arise concerning the typicality, the relevance of this position and the linguistic/communications competence upon which it was built to the constituency that Franklin ostensibly represented. For his was not only a 'more than ordinary', it was a truly extraordinary educational experience with language and print, and it led to a newly prominent, but yet rare and unique occupational/social role. Indeed, viewed from yet another perspective, the *Autobiography* tells the story of the making of a *writer*, a publicist, or perhaps best a 'man of letters', which is how David Hume among other contemporaries regarded Franklin first and foremost.[68] How many middle class youths could expect to follow such a path to success and recognition?

Of course, this question also came up with regard to Locke *vis-à-vis* the 'ordinary Gentleman's son' on whose behalf he avowedly wrote, and the answer here is much the same. Franklin does not appear to have expected every son of a merchant or tradesman whom he sought to bring along with him from 'lowly Beginning' to 'great Things' to follow in his exact footsteps. Surely other aspects of the changing eighteenth-century world, that is, besides the expanding force of print culture, would provide ready youths from this background opportunities to forge their own nontraditional bases of power. Moreover, some semblance of the education he had acquired for himself, if nothing quite as intensive and profound, would likely assist in that process. This premise is evident in a general way in plans for the subscription library, one of the many institutional vehicles of middle class empowerment that Franklin set on foot in Philadelphia. Its collection pointedly limited to 'only ... English books',[69] the library embodied the connection between the vernacular language and 'Learning' whose possibility Silence Dogood had glimpsed earlier and whose validity Franklin's lifelong experience would seem to have borne out. And the premise is evident quite specifically in plans for that further middle class institution, the English School. In his *Idea* for this school Franklin sought at once to articulate, to generalize and to translate into formal curricular terms his own linguistic (and general) self-education, and in so doing to serve the needs and aspirations — perhaps to extend the aspirations — of the broad social constituency from which he had sprung.

V. The Idea of the English School

The *Idea of the English School* is, as stated at the outset of the essay, the most

significant of the early texts of vernacular advocacy from the standpoint of
the thesis being pursued here. In it Franklin proposed a thoroughgoing
programme of advanced vernacular instruction and gave answers to the
three fundamental questions relating to it, of constituency, skill development, and extra-educational destination or 'desired future', that shed
revealing light on the actual social origins of English at the secondary level
in the US. Moreover, having examined in the preceding sections the
principal intellectual and biographical sources, or at least precedents for this
text, we are in a position to identify those answers in what turns out to be,
for all its significance, a rather compressed statement of rationale. However, before preceding to an analysis of the *Idea*, some further background
is requisite.

It happens that this 1751 pamphlet was not Franklin's first attempt to
conceive a programme of and rationale for advanced vernacular instruction. That earlier conception and the process by which it rather quickly
metamorphosed into the *Idea* are of importance primarily because of what
they reveal of the influence on Franklin's thinking of the two previously
discussed textual and/or traditional 'sources', and also of the likely manner
in which his own experience came to enter into the ultimate conception.
Secondarily, if these immediately prior developments may be taken as
'background', they also constitute an integral part of the story of Franklin's
exemplary text, part of the overall reflection that this story casts on the
social origins of English. As such they introduce a complication, an element
of refraction, as it were, into the textual perspective available from this
source on the larger phenomenon. While not warranting major emphasis,
this element does deserve to be taken into account.

Background: the Proposals

Franklin's initial scheme for vernacular (and general nonclassical) study is
to be found in his *Proposals Relating to the Education of Youth in Pennsylvania*, a
1749 pamphlet outlining a plan for a 'publick Academy' in Philadelphia. The
plan drew many of its features from the academy/private tutorial tradition
within which *Some Thoughts Concerning Education* was also composed.
Indeed the 'great Mr. Locke' is manifestly the most important of the half
dozen or so educational authorities — a veritable who's who of the
academy tradition — cited at the outset of the piece.[70] Locke's influence
makes itself felt especially in the vernacular portion of the overall
curriculum. Several of the disciplines mentioned — English grammar,
oratory, composition — recall the suggestions of the *Thoughts*, and in fact
copious footnotes to the text reproduce Locke's remarks on each of them.
What is more, those footnotes contain verbatim the core rationale for
vernacular study found in the earlier work: the singling out of that portion
of the population whose main business was to be done with 'Tongues' and

'Pens', the need for an enhanced linguistic competence on the part of such 'Gentlemen', the appropriateness of the study of the native tongue to this end.[71] It is true that the *Proposals* itself does not make the implicit linkage between this type of verbal facility and the traditional exercise of power that can be discerned in Locke's text. But in a slightly later paper on the Academy presented to the Philadelphia City Council Franklin made the point that graduates of the proposed institution would be 'qualified to bear Magistracies, and execute other public Offices of Trust ...'.[72]

Surely it will seem incongruous to find such a plan and such a rationale, even if borrowed, issuing from the press of the figure this study has sought generally to present as the champion *par excellence* of middle class interests in education. In pausing for a moment to consider this, it does need to be reiterated that the academy tradition was an oppositional one, with respect to the orthodox classical system. Moreover, the *Proposals* took liberties even with it, naming future 'Merchants' and 'Handi-crafts[men]', as well as future 'Divines' among the Academy's likely clientele, and insisting upon Latin and Greek as purely optional elements of the curriculum, not to be allowed to interfere with the teaching of 'English, Arithmetick, and other Studies absolutely necessary'.[73] Nevertheless, the academy/private tradition had grown up under upper class, if dissident, sponsorship, designed to serve the needs of constituencies located within that social stratum. What prompted Franklin, with his avowed 'low Beginning', to advance his initial proposal under such colours? Two reasons may be offered. First, having received almost no formal education he ranked as an outsider in such matters and may well have been eager for the intellectual support and the credibility that this most articulate body of heterodox educational opinion — that is, the tradition anchored by Locke — gave to what was in fact an innovative proposal ('differ[ing] a little', as he wrote, 'from the Forms of Education in common use').[74] Second, the ambivalence in Franklin's class identity, alluded to in the preceding section, appears to have swung fairly markedly toward the gentlemanly end of the spectrum, as he collaborated with 'Persons of Wealth and Learning' on a number of ventures at this period, the proposed Academy chief among them.[75]

Now the implications of this, Franklin's first venture into vernacular advocacy, and the associations it had, cannot be dismissed. But, whether by accident or as the consequence of contemporary social and educational circumstances and the coming to the fore of his own deepest loyalties, the *Proposals* was not his last word on the subject. What initially set him on his way toward the very different *Idea* was the rejection of the curricular heart of the Academy plan. This proved too unconventional for upper class backers of the general initiative, for whom optional status for the ancient languages was not enough. They insisted upon a traditional grammar school to house the classics and to serve the purposes (among them preparatory training for college and the learned professions) of a traditional upper class constituency. One immediate result of this demand was a compromise whereby a secondary-level 'English School' came into the plans as a counterweight within the Academy (now effectively reduced to an administrative unit) to the 'Latin and Greek School' and as a preserve for Franklin's initial vision of an essentially nonclassical education featuring advanced vernacular instruction[76]. This development of course ushered 'English education' onto the scene. Moreover, Franklin made that entry more than a nominal one. He knew this generally less than explicitly formulated tradition from various textbooks his printing firm had marketed, and in all likelihood also from miscellaneous writings such as his fellow Philadelphian's 1735 essay, if he was not aware of it specifically. And, while retaining certain features of the Lockean/academy-inspired *Proposals*, he unmistakably drew from the English tradition for the content and the rationale of the plan of study he was tasked to prepare for the new facility.

The setback to the Academy plan appears to have had other, deeper consequences for the subsequent conception. What Franklin can only have perceived as a rebuff from the important men he had courted in this matter[77] may well have propelled him toward the other pole of his social identity. Requested in a sceptical challenging manner by the other trustees of the overall institution to outline the curriculum and purpose of the English School, he complained in a letter of his 'unfitness' as an uneducated 'Tradesman', for the task:[78] a sense of himself hardly in evidence in the authorship of the *Proposals* and other papers on the Academy. By this indication Franklin may have had the class of his origins more nearly and sympathetically in mind as he wrote than the simple fact of having to work with the English tradition would have encouraged. Then, too, the unexpected necessity of having to draft a second curricular plan clearly provided him with an opportunity to deepen and mature his understanding of the entire matter. It was an opportunity Franklin took, apparently relinquishing in the process a large measure of his dependence on the academy tradition and not making up the deficit entirely out of the English. A significant dimension of the emergent conception consisted in an articulation of his own experience: both the anything but inferior education he had created for himself, in the vernacular language and more general learning, which found its way into the programme of study proposed for the English School; and his larger experience of class, language and power, which became incorporated into the rationale for that programme. Moreover, this turn to personal experience also represented, bearing in mind the qualifications previously stated in regard to his 'ambivalence' on this score, a turn to the experience and aspirations of the middle class. Thus the correspondent to whom Franklin had complained, and also sent a draft of what was to become the *Idea of the English School*, may have been right to proclaim it a work of 'True Genius'; but he was wrong to say, in an attempt to be reassuring, 'Nobody would imagine that ... [it] was done by a

Tradesman.'[79] For to the eye prepared to read it that personal and social signature is all over the *Idea*, which was composed under different auspices, and to appreciably different ends, than the *Proposals*.

The Idea

Let us look, then, at the *Idea*, seeking to identify the answers it gives to Archer's three basic questions, and beginning with the one of constituency. The text, most of whose length is devoted to the details of the recommended programme of study rather than a rationale for it, does not answer this question directly. But reference is made in the context of the curricular discussion to the purposes of the 'Merchant' and the 'Handicraftsman';[80] significantly, no mention can be found here, as in the *Proposals*, of the future 'Divine'. This evidence for the presumption of a specifically middle class constituency receives confirmation in the one paragraph of summary and rationale that closes the pamphlet: 'Thus instructed, Youth will come out of this school fitted for learning any Business, Calling, or Profession, except such wherein [ancient] Languages are required.'[81] In earlier correspondence Franklin had instanced the 'Professions' toward which the new school's training would be directed with the examples of 'Merchandizing' and 'Husbandry'.[82] Furthermore, actual enrolment at the facility as of the mid-1750s bears out these expectations: ten of the thirteen identifiable fathers of boys in the English School were either artisans or merchants of modest wealth; by contrast twenty-six of thirty-six pupils in the Latin and Greek School were the sons of upper-class parents.[83]

With what sort of intellectual equipment, and specifically what sort of linguistic competence, could middle class 'Youth' expect to emerge from the course of training Franklin envisioned? Again, the *Idea* does not elaborate on this point to the extent that Locke's treatise does, perhaps not even to the extent of the 1735 essay. However, the gist of what was intended may be inferred from the programme of vernacular study itself. This was quite extensive, occupying very nearly three-quarters of the entire space given to curricular discussion. It was also, as Franklin's correspondent proclaimed it, a work of 'True Genius': marking a quantum leap over contemporary practice in this area and foreshadowing in much of its content and some of its methods the modern secondary subject of English. The programme provides for much vigorous work in reading, especially reading of a critical kind, begun with fables and stories, continued with periodical essays, and carried over into the study of actual works of English literature. Spelling and English grammar are included, and also rhetoric, with attention to polite speaking and formal declamation. Further, two full years of vernacular study are earmarked for composition, first of letters, then of essays, with an ingenious series of exercises involving the *Spectator* recommended for developing ability with the latter form.[84]

Clearly the outlines of Franklin's own experience are evident here and throughout the programme, interwoven with features from Locke's *Thoughts* and the academy tradition carried over from their initial appearance in the *Proposals*. Close inspection, which I have undertaken elsewhere, would also reveal a debt to the English tradition and a decided bent toward forms of language and types of discursive performance associated with print.[85] More to the purpose here, there can be no doubt that if conscientiously pursued this regimen would have produced the kind of facility in communication expressly called for by Locke and *de facto* achieved by Franklin himself. 'Thus instructed', runs the *Idea's* only explicit statement on this score, graduates of the English School will, 'tho' unaquainted [*sic*] with any ancient or foreign Tongue ... be Masters of their own',[86] and it is evident from the thoroughness and sophistication of the projected instruction that this mastery would have been of the 'more than ordinary' variety.

Indeed, the only question that may arise here is the same one that came up when considering the nature of Franklin's broadly linguistic competence and the power base it furnished him, and that is whether the 'mastery' looked forward to here might be *too* exceptional. One commentator has made the remark, apropos of the curricular plan of the *Proposals*, that it seems 'geared to turn out the maximum number of young Franklins'.[87] Of the *Idea*, likewise, could it be said that it was effectively designed to turn out the maximum number of young men of letters? Certainly it does appear, in retrospect, that this regimen lay beyond the reach of most middle class youth in Philadelphia at the middle of the eighteenth century, and beyond the expectations of their parents and the capacities of any available English master, as well. This is a point that will be touched upon in the next section. However, as to reproducing educationally an idiosyncratic experience with language, this does not appear to have been Franklin's intention. It may be that he adopted a 'man of letters' persona as well as that of the 'Tradesman' as he composed the *Idea*, but the aims of the latter were not totally eclipsed. This is reflected first of all in the programme of vernacular study, which does reach beyond the emphasis of Franklin's self-education to include not only Lockean-style oral and oratorical training but also the spelling and elocutionary reading that middle class parents would have come to expect from a conventional English education. More directly, the brief peroration to the text explains the expected benefits of study at the school in terms of 'desired futures' to which the 'middling People' of Philadelphia could, certainly if they were willing to raise their sights in some respects, very plainly relate.

The first two elements of the rationale set forth in this peroration, which was manifestly written to justify the novel programme of study in the eyes of upper class skeptics and potential middle class supporters, may be briefly dealt with. One consisted in the very general endorsement, found also in Locke and the 1735 essay, of the practical value of a mastery of the vernacular, here touted as 'of more immediate and general Use' than the ancient languages.[88] Franklin had not yet come to the position he would embrace some years hence, of Latin and Greek as 'absolutely unnecessary' and the 'quackery of literature',[89] yet his challenge in the *Idea* was more aggressive than either of the two preceding it, containing as it did the implication, adumbrated in the Silence Dogood piece, that an education centred on English might well prove superior to the traditional classical regimen. A second argument on behalf of vernacular training has already been presented: it would fit pupils for any 'Business, Calling, or Profession' (except the learned professions). This consideration is the economic one that has been associated with the English tradition of vernacular advocacy, and which Franklin also lived out, this being one dimension of the 'Advancement' he attributed in principal part to linguistic means. No promise of outstanding success or wealth is made, just preparation to 'learn' an occupation, but the facts of his business career must have supplied a certain lustre to this goal, both in Franklin's and his readers' minds.

The third element of the rationale is invoked in the closing sentence of the peroration and the pamphlet. It is the broadly political one that this essay has followed from its articulation in Locke's *Thoughts* through the oblique manifestation in the 1735 essay and through its enactment in Franklin's life. The proposed programme of study would, in addition to giving those who pursued it the tools to succeed in commercial occupations, 'qualify them to pass thro' and execute the several Offices of civil Life, with Advantage and Reputation to themselves and Country'.[90] In short, the mastery of the vernacular language, together with the 'other valuable Accomplishments' predicated of the wider reach the English School curriculum (ranging from history and geography to mathematics, logic and ethics), was here being held out as the educational key of access for middle class Philadelphia youth to positions of power hitherto considered to lie out of their reach. Should there be any doubt that this rather brief closing flourish does indicate just that, i.e., new access to positions occupied by the traditional power elite, consider its apparent source, the statement from the 1750 'Paper on the Academy' that has already been quoted in context of the discussion of the *Proposals*. The full text of this statement not only identifies the 'Offices' a bit more specifically, it also argues the need for additional recruitment to fill them:

That a number of our Natives will hereby be qualified to bear Magistracies, and execute other public Offices of Trust, with Reputation to themselves and Country; there being at present great Want of Persons so qualified in the several Counties of this Province. And this is the more necessary now to be provided by the English here, as vast Numbers of Foreigners are yearly imported among us, totally ignorant of our Laws, Customs, and Language.[91]

Now it cannot but be remarked here that the supplemental reasoning contained in this statement reveals Franklin's answer to a question that fails to find inclusion in Archer's list: Who does *not* get a given type of educational experience, in this case that envisioned for the Academy, and by extension that projected in the *Idea*? One constituency not likely to be included in the pamphlet's scenario of 'advancement' via linguistic mastery is that composed of the 'vast Numbers of Foreigners'. Franklin's fears concerning the tide of mainly German immigrants flowing into Pennsylvania at that period, and the threat it seemed to pose to 'Native' political control, customs, and the English language itself, have been well documented.[92] Moreover, the exclusion was repeated, on an implicit basis, in the case of Philadelphia's lower class generally. Just as Locke's *Thoughts* had next to nothing to say about the positive educational needs of merchants and tradesmen, so the *Idea* makes no mention of the labourers and seamen and others (indentured servants and slaves) who made up the next group down on the socioeconomic ladder, the poorest 30 per cent of the city's population.[93]

The fact of these exclusions (and the observation might be extended to gender; the English School was to admit boys only) must enter into any evaluation of Franklin's achievements *vis-à-vis* vernacular study, and will in fact be touched upon again in the essay's final section. But for now the chief interest of the reasoning behind this statement lies in the indication it gives of a need for the infusion of new blood into the colonial elite, new blood that most logically would have been furnished by the middle class. Indeed the situation Franklin evokes here bears an instructive similarity to the one discussed by Reid and Filby in their study of the British public school 'sixth form', where an increase in population together with other factors in the Victorian period created the need for 'an extended ruling and administrative class' and opened the door to participation in these functions by previously excluded elements of the middle class.[94] It is true that the statement itself pertained to the Academy, which as we have seen was to have offered training to upper class youth, but even in the original conception a mixed clientele was envisioned for that institution, and the 'Paper' dated from a time when the English School had become part of the plan. In any case, it seems evident from the almost literal recurrence of the basic statement in the *Idea* that Franklin intended to carry forward this reasoning to the mission of the expressly middle class institution.

Moreover, with this closing vision of elite access as an advertisement for the English School's curriculum, he succeeded in fully appropriating the Lockean linguistic-political rationale found in the *Proposals* to the presumed purposes of a middle class constituency. Or, if this way of putting it overstates the extent to which Franklin depended on Locke's treatise for a sense of that rationale, it may be said that the *Idea* represents the conversion into formal, educational terms of its author's own experience of accession, largely via his prowess in language and communication, to those 'public Offices of Trust' that he had just begun to assume even as he wrote. But however the balance between intellectual influence and biographical experience is to be struck in accounting for this text, and whatever construction might be placed on its immediate predecessor, the *Proposals*, the gist of the *Idea of the English School* is clear. The sons of Philadelphia's 'middling People' were to be enabled, through systematic study of their own language and other nontraditional subjects in that language, to progress from relatively 'lowly Beginnings' to 'great Things': positions of leadership, responsibility and power in their society.

VI. The *Idea* and the Social Origins of English: a Nineteenth-century Rationale and its Context

Franklin's 1751 pamphlet presented a stirring case for secondary-level vernacular study on the part of pupils drawn from eighteenth-century Philadelphia's middle class. It was not, evidently, a compelling case. For all its brilliance — and perhaps, as we shall see, in part on account of it — the *Idea* proved a practical failure. Indeed, the English School episode constitutes one of the better-known failures in American educational history.[95] This fact, however, does not diminish the significance of the reflection Franklin's text casts on the social origins of English, except that its answers to the questions of constituency, skill and destination need to be taken as a kind of pre-reflection, an anticipation of the decisive stages of that larger process. Just as the programme of vernacular instruction set forth in the *Idea* foreshadowed with remarkable accuracy the content and to some extent the methods of the subject of secondary English that would definitively come into being only late in the nineteenth century, so would the terms of its rationale be repeated, and realized, in that subsequent period.

This section first relates the circumstances and analyses the causes of the nonimplementation of Franklin's plan. It then jumps forward in time to the late nineteenth century to consider, actually to assemble from a number of individual pronouncements, a composite 'text' of vernacular advocacy, continuous in its main features with the 1751 rationale. Further, in order to interpret this text it will be necessary to construct a context for it, that is, a social historical description of factors of class, language and power in this later period, more or less equivalent to the background provided in section I for the earlier texts. This description, together with the analysis of the collectively articulated rationale, will constitute a hypothesis about the social origins of 'English' *per se* (a 'hypothesis' because based on research that is still preliminary) and, again, a demonstration of the relevance of Franklin's thinking to these decisive developments.

Failure

In spite of the enthusiasm that Franklin reports it generated,[96] his *Idea* never received full implementation, and in time both the sophisticated programme of vernacular/nonclassical instruction and the vision of class empowerment that the text embodied were wholly degraded. From the outset the English School took a back seat to its classical counterpart the Latin and Greek School in the apportionment of financial and other resources available to the overall institution. Partly for this reason and partly owing to the limitations of his training and experience, the first English master did not follow the elaborate recommendations Franklin had set forth in the pamphlet, offering instead a version of the conventional secondary English curriculum, not too far different from the regimen advocated by the anonymous author of 'Some Thoughts' in 1735. While this instruction proved popular, and early enrolment at the school was high, the replacement of the first master by one less competent, together with the effects of continued partiality shown to the classical side of the institution (which flourished, a traditional college being erected on the base of the grammar school in 1755, the two together becoming known as the 'College of Philadelphia'), brought about a further deterioration of the original ideal. In 1763 Franklin charged that the English School had effectively sunk to the level of a contemporary (English) elementary school, 'teaching little boys the Elements of the English Language'.[97] At this point, too, parents began to complain and to remove their youngsters from the rolls. The only response these protests brought from the majority of trustees was a move to discontinue the facility. While this action was rescinded, from that point on the English School and its curriculum for the most part lived out an undistinguished existence in the shadow of the College of Philadelphia, subsequently to become the University of Pennsylvania. Franklin tried one more time to rescue his conception from oblivion, writing in 1789 near the end of his life an impassioned appeal for the restoration of the English School to its intended educational status and purpose; but the plea went unheeded.[98]

A number of reasons might be advanced to account for this failure. Evidently, the curricular content of the *Idea* far exceeded the capacities of practitioners of English education in that day to administer it. Add to this the manifestly high degree of development and even the vitality of the opposing classical tradition, and it is clear that purely educational factors played a role. More to the purposes here, however, the social premises of Franklin's vernacular advocacy appear to have lain similarly in advance of contemporary realities of class, language and power.

Take first the intended constituency for the programme. While Philadelphia's middle class did experience growing prosperity and coalescence during this period, neither gain was of sufficient magnitude to allow the group to sustain a venture of the scope and innovative quality that Franklin envisioned in his text. The inability became manifest in the face of what amounted to direct competition from the local upper class, which formed the constituency for the Latin-Greek School, then the College. The 'middling People' could not hope to contribute start-up funds to the overall institution, and thereby to gain a say in the initial priorities set within it, in anything like the proportions managed by those to whom Franklin referred as 'Persons of Wealth and Learning'. Nor, even when direct financial contributions had ceased to be a factor in determining policy, did the group have the means of focusing its will (beyond verbal protest and the expedient of withdrawing pupils) on the internal affairs of the institution — again unlike the upper class, which determinedly forged the grammar school/college into both an instrument and ornament of its transformation, by 1770, into what one observer has called a true urban 'aristocracy'.[99]

The contemporary state of the various aspects of what this study has been referring to as 'language' is more difficult to pin down. Evidence exists, however, to suggest that the assumptions of the *Idea* on this score, as well, may have been in the lead of actual conditions. It has, for example, been argued by recent scholars that the decisive advent of a print culture did not take place until well after the Revolution in the United States,[100] and while that contention may underrate development in colonial cities earlier in the eighteenth century, it is certainly true that Franklin helped to lead and his fellow Philadelphians experienced only the first stages of the great expansion of the medium and the transformation of social communication by its means. Perhaps, too, the vernacular itself had not outgrown certain of the weaknesses that prevented Locke from recommending it as the sole matter of linguistic instruction. One modern commentator can be found who makes this point.[101] Closer to the nub of the matter, the enhanced facility with language recommended by Locke and implied in the programme of the *Idea* may simply have been no more than marginally relevant to the great run of merchants and tradesmen at this time, or have been perceived by them as such. Indeed, the enthusiastic response to the first English School master's regimen of English grammar and declamation could perhaps be taken as a measure of the extent of middle class linguistic ambitions as of the middle of the eighteenth century: ambitions perhaps, then, more accurately reflected by the 1735 essay than by Franklin's pamphlet.

Of course, since this constituency did not have the option of choosing the more exacting programme, no substantial inference can be made on this point. But the question of ambition is worth considering in another light. Might it have been middle class political aspirations, perhaps first and foremost, that were limited? Recall again the example of the slightly earlier text, which promised no 'great Things' equivalent to those held up in the *Idea's* closing vision, as a reward for following its programme of study. Perhaps a certain diffidence in this regard, as much as a relative dearth of class resources, precluded support for the English School at any level beyond the one at which it actually existed in the early 1750s? But in any event, whether Franklin overestimated the ardency of Philadelphia's 'middling People' for offices of public trust, or not, it is clear that he over-estimated the openness of the late colonial power structure to an infusion from below. Room had been made in his exceptional case, but not until the Revolution did members of the middle class enter in significant numbers into the public life of the city and colony. Nowhere, in fact, is the gentlemen's continued control over the 'command posts' of local society more evident than in the dismal history of the English School itself. Of the twenty-four trustees appointed to make policy for the larger institution only Franklin and one other represented the middle class. Franklin, it is true, in recognition of the leading role he had taken in the enterprise from the start, had been elected president of the board, and from this position he was able within limits to look out for the interest of the English School and its constituency. But it was as he records it an uphill struggle against this overwhelming majority of 'Persons of Wealth and learning'.[102] Moreover, that majority voted him out of the presidency in 1756, thus overturning the major departure from custom that his election had represented, and at once clearing the way for upper class plans to expand the College and leaving the English School more than ever vulnerable to the indifference and even hostility of this constituency.[103]

It is interesting to speculate whether the *Idea* would have met a different fate had its publication coincided with the Revolution. For during that period of crisis a 'combination of artisans and lesser merchants' did, in a development not without its linguistic and communications aspects, come decisively to the fore in the military, political and civic leadership of the city.[104] And it happens that during the later years of the conflict and shortly thereafter new life was breathed into the English School, and steps were taken to incorporate certain features of the 1751 pamphlet into its curriculum.[105] However, this reversal, by no means complete in any case, proved only temporary. The dislocation of the war years ended, old patterns of class and power reasserted themselves to some extent, and once again the English School became poor relation to the larger, traditional institution. It was this situation that provoked the school's champion to his final, futile act of protest.[106]

By any measure, then, Franklin's was an *Idea* ahead of its time. Yet it was also an idea whose time would come. The terms of the text's rationale appear not to have been fully congruent with the realities of the historical situation in the Philadelphia, and the America, of 1751; but that does not mean they were wholly out of touch with those realities. Just as the programme of instruction set forth in the pamphlet seized upon certain definite potentials of the vernacular as a subject matter, so did the accompanying rationale reflect real tendencies or possibilities within that social historical situation. Their reality was attested to by Franklin's career (in which the deposition as the trustees' president constituted one of the only setbacks), and also by the developments of the Revolutionary period. And it would be confirmed by the history of a later period, in which not only would the basic rationale of the *Idea* be reasserted but the potentials of class, language and power intuited in that rationale come to fruition.

The NEA Rationale

This nineteenth-century rationale, a collectively articulated 'text' advocating newly sophisticated and coherent training in the vernacular language and literature, may be pieced together from the proceedings of the National Educational Association. It was this professional teachers' organization, founded shortly after mid-century, which sponsored the major committees on secondary instruction in the 1890s whose reports gave quasi-official definition to the subject of 'English' (and other modern components of the curriculum) at this level. Moreover, debate within the NEA throughout the latter part of the nineteenth century at once reflected and helped to propel the development of English study within the nation's new public high schools — the development eventually ratified by the Committee of Ten on Secondary School Studies and the Committee on College Entrance Requirements. Of course, NEA debate contributed to the shaping of the subject at other levels, as well, and in reconstructing a 'text' of vernacular advocacy the following discussion has drawn in several instances upon individual statements addressed to elementary (and in one case to higher) education, a procedure whose justification will subsequently become apparent.

Participants in the educational association's discourse on vernacular study frequently made a distinction between types of linguistic competence akin to the one articulated by Locke and theorized by Bernstein. 'Many people', observed one speaker, offering a virtual analysis of 'public language' or the 'restricted code', 'are satisfied with a surprisingly limited vocabulary'. Words like 'fixins' or 'doins', he contended, were being applied to a multitude of referents, reducing specificity and with it the 'power of perception and description'.[107] Another commentator, more pejorative in tone, decried the 'blundering crudities, the awkward infelicities, and the stammering poverty of speech of the masses of people'.[108] On the other hand of this distinction lay qualities since associated with formal/elaborated performance: 'accurate, copious, effective expression', in the words of the commentator just quoted; 'exactness or clearness of apprehension', readiness in generaliz[ing] from particulars and 'tracing order in the midst of variety', as yet another educator described the perceptual and conceptual dimensions of an enhanced verbal facility.[109] It is true that NEA speakers as a rule did not make Bernstein's, and for that matter Locke's, strong correlation of 'codes' with class. However, chance allusions are sometimes suggestive of the social locations presumed for the two types of usage. The reference above to the speech of the 'masses' provides one example. And another public school educator's quoting with approval Harvard President C.W. Eliot's dictum that an 'accurate and refined use' of language constitutes an essential end for the education of a 'lady or gentleman' suggests that the upper class — referred to, if at all in NEA proceedings, as the 'Brahmins' — may have supplied the model for this style of competence.[110]

Whatever vagueness may have existed as to class associations, how-ever, members of the organization were clear on the value of bringing pupils, who might otherwise spend their lives in 'vagueness and confusion' owing to untutored language habits,[111] into possession of a more disci-plined and flexible linguistic standard and the precision of consciousness presumably attainable through it. They were also emphatic about the value of the vernacular language and literature in serving this educational end. It may be true, one speaker conceded, that the study of Latin and Greek provided a certain command of language and the 'mental powers' comp-lementary to such command. But, he maintained, the curriculum at Eliot's Harvard and the great majority of American colleges and preparatory schools at this time notwithstanding, it was 'not the only or the best' means of doing so.[112] Another effectively completed his thought by declaring, in terms worthy of a Locke or a Franklin, 'The English Language is the great thing for us to teach, and we should make Latin and Greek tributary.'[113] In addition, the study of the vernacular in its printed forms received special emphasis in the NEA discourse.[114]

As to the extra-educational end of the linguistic mastery sought by these means, a good deal of consensus existed, as well. Actually, there appear to have been a number of such consensual aims. One of them was 'power'. This term echoes throughout the record of NEA promotion of English and appears, expressly connected with the higher competence argument, in certain of the individual presentations already quoted from. 'Expression — accurate, copious, effective expression', Henry E. Har-rington of the New Bedford, Massachusetts, High School assured his audience in 1875, 'is an incalculable power in the world'.[115] And in a statement that might be taken as an epitome of the 'NEA rationale', Cleveland superintendent of schools Andrew J. Rickoff specified this concept of 'power' somewhat, and also greatly expanded it. Having appropriated President Eliot's argument on behalf of superior linguistic capacity to the mission of public education, Rickoff went on to declare:

It is this that gives to men mastery over books, insight into the affairs of human life and directive power among men. If anywhere, in the world, this command over language is necessary, it is here in America where principles too subtle for expression in the language of the marketplace wield the power of kings.[116]

But if Rickoff's can be taken as *the* statement of this collectively articulated rationale, it (and other information presented thus far) leave important questions unanswered. To whom, that is, to what social constituency, was this vision of linguistic empowerment expected to appeal? Here, rather than in the matter of class affiliations of the two 'codes', is where the real vagueness of the NEA pronouncements lay. In public schools, yes, but where along the spectrum extending from the 'masses' to the 'Brahmins' were the pupils whose educational needs were being discussed by these various speakers to be found? Then, too, the 'incalculable power', the 'power of Kings'? Granted that Rickoff's 'directive power among men' begins to bring this beguiling concept down to earth, is there any way to translate it into concrete positions and functions in a socially constituted power structure that his and Harrington's and the other educator's pupils might hope to fill? Answers can be given to these questions only when more is known about the context in which this composite 'text' of vernacular advocacy took shape. What follows is a tentative foray, tentative because based on uncompleted research, into the realities of class, power and language behind the NEA rationale, and thereby into the social origins of 'English' in the late nineteenth century.

Context: 'New Middle Class', 'Bureaucratic Means', 'Critical Discourse'

One reason schoolmen in the nineteenth century so seldom made reference to the social background of their pupils is that they worked within the assumption that that background was broadly middle class. Public education in the United States represented a continuation of the English tradition, and retained a primary tie with the constituency that had developed historically with it. For the public high school, a direct institutional descendant of Franklin's English School, the relationship held with particular force. The very first of the new institutions, the Boston English High School, was established for the purpose of preparing youth for professions 'Mercantile or Mechanical'.[117] By way of further identification, David Labaree has recently reported that the 'proprietary (self-employed) middle class', clearly the direct social descendant of the artisan and lesser merchant community of colonial cities, furnished the 'founders, teachers, and students' of Philadelphia's Central High School, opened in 1838.[118] Work on the high schools from this perspective remains somewhat sketchy, but there is reason to accept Labaree's finding as generally valid,[119] and also to carry it forward in time to the period at issue here, for he contends that this same class and its educational interests remained 'organically bonded' to the public high school into the second half of the century. [120]

Over the latter part of the nineteenth century, though, a significant change overtook this constituency. Labaree describes it as a shift in occupational horizons, from business ownership to the professions. [121] Others have seen in this period a process of actual class formation, the emergence in Robert Wiebe's words of a 'new middle class'. The members of this predominantly urban group, drawn largely from the ranks of the existing (proprietary) middle class, responded to the unprecedented challenges of a rapidly evolving modern industrial order as so many opportunities: they flooded the traditional professions, elevated existing and new occupations to the level of professions, and entered prominently into the expanding corporate and service sectors of the economy. Withal they achieved a degree of cohesion — came to speak a 'common language', in Wiebe's words — to complement their new prosperity and visibility. [122] They also proved altogether more capable than their Philadelphia predecessors of, among other things, sustaining an educational innovation suited to their needs. In this case the innovation consisted, in part, of a greatly accelerated public high school movement and the alteration of the institution to serve the purposes of college preparation. Indeed, the new middle class has also been seen as the principal social force behind the creation of the modern American university in this same period. [123]

Further, this dynamic group showed itself either more ambitious for, or better able to seize, or both, positions of leadership, authority and influence in the society than the run of Franklin's 'middling People' had been. Of course, those positions were being redefined by the new configurations that society itself was assuming in the era of modern technology and capitalism. The new middle class responded to this opportunity by parlaying 'consciousness of [their] unique skills and functions' into the exercise of practical power. One avenue for this was the new professionalism. The group also virtually created the roles of 'expert' and 'administrator', and went far towards articulating what Wiebe, again, refers to as a 'bureaucratic vision' of the management of society. What is more, this grasp for the levers of power extended, in context of the progressive political movement, to offices *per se*. As it turns out, reformers imbued with the values of professionalism were not able to dislodge fully the hold of the upper classes, and at some levels that of new immigrant groups, over elective and appointive posts in government. Nevertheless, the effort left its mark, and attested to the nature of the aim: 'the heart of progressivism was the ambition of the new middle class to fulfill its destiny through bureaucratic means'. [124]

It may seem a far cry from the 'power of Kings' to 'bureaucratic means', but the second term did in this context roughly constitute the kernel of practical meaning in Rickoff's hyperbole. Professional, expert, administrative, this was the nature of the 'directive power among men' that he held out to the constituency of the public school as a reward of educational achievement. Indeed, he and his NEA colleagues exercised what leverage they did precisely by those means, and in a more general way may be taken as prototypical members of the new middle class, so that in urging this course upon their pupils they were doing, as Franklin had before them, not that much more than speaking for themselves.

Now of course having connected context with rationale to this extent, one piece of the picture remains missing, as has happened in similar junctures previously. Rickoff spoke of a 'command over *language*' as the immediate educational objective and the means to directive power. The NEA rationale was a rationale for the study of English. Thus further questions suggest themselves here. Did the new middle class make any special use of language, a 'more than ordinary' linguistic competence, in its thrust toward power? Might it have furnished the constituency, not only for the public high school movement of the late nineteenth century but also, and specifically, for the vernacular linguistic and literary subject coming into being within those institutions over this same time?

One further historical-sociological perspective allows for an affirmative answer to these questions. Sociologist Alvin Gouldner writes of the formation of a 'New Class' in the late nineteenth-century United States, a class which challenged for social power *and* which defined itself very largely through the cultivation of a 'distinctive language behavior', which he terms 'critical discourse'. The characteristics of this discourse, or 'culture' of discourse as it is more broadly referred to, Gouldner expressly relates to Bernstein's elaborated code. Moreover, he sees it as historically correlated to the decline of Latin and the rise of the vernacular, and also to the 'communications revolution in general and ... the development of printing technology in particular'. Finally, he locates the site for training in the discourse in the institution of public education, newly expanded in this period. In short, the various potentials going to make a certain use of language a key instrument for an up-and-coming class, and which were either not sufficiently developed in the middle of the eighteenth century or which Franklin's one-time peers could not recognize to seize upon, in approximation of his own success in this area, appears to have been realized in full by Gouldner's group. [125]

Yet before proclaiming a complete context found for the NEA rationale, and the discovery of an essential continuity extending from the 1751 *Idea* to the later period, it needs to be pointed out that Gouldner's New Class was and is composed of 'intellectuals', who presumably make special use of — and have a special dependence upon — their linguistic competence. A form of this same difficulty, it will be recalled, arose with Franklin (and Locke) as 'man of letters', and it may be answered in a similar manner in this case. For Gouldner obviously understands his intellectuals to constitute a large group — its members 'mass-produced' by public education — and it would not seem unreasonable to extend his analysis, perhaps modifying somewhat the emphasis he places on language *per se*, to the still larger collectivity that the term new middle class comprehends. Indeed it is not so hard to imagine something like 'critical discourse' as the 'common language' Wiebe identifies as a bond uniting the emerging population of professionals, experts and administrators. Finally, it is not hard to imagine that the educational basis for this specialized linguistic competence lay in the newly upgraded and transformed study of the vernacular put into place in the public schools, especially the public high schools, during this period; nor that this social group, flexing its growing economic and demographic muscle and exercising its already substantial professional authority (in the field of education, at the very least), provided the motive force for this curricular development, the emergence of 'English'.

Once again it needs to be said that I regard a definitive treatment of the social origins of modern English, even from a textual perspective, to be the task of future work rather than the accomplishment of the preceding few pages. What's more, at least some of the information in hand complicates the purpose for which this foray into the nineteenth century was in good part undertaken, i.e., to suggest the relevance of Franklin's intuitions to later developments.[126] Complications notwithstanding, though, the evidence for that relevance, the anticipatory reflection cast by the *Idea*, is impressive. The line of descent from the 'Merchants' and 'Handicraftsmen' who represented the intended constituency for the English School's programme of vernacular and other nonclassical study, to the new middle class consumers of high school English, appears clear enough. The linguistic mastery promised by Franklin to graduates of his programme is, when understood in the light of his own achievements in this respect and their context in the early stages of the 'communications revolution' made possible by print, essentially akin to the high-capacity 'discourse' which the later group would make a principal means to its 'Advancement'. That advancement, too, at least in so far as it involved accession to Mills' 'command posts of ... society', had been prefigured in the 'Public Offices of Trust' that had come to Franklin and which he in turn held out as attainable goals for the linguistically competent, well-educated middle class youth of his day. Finally, it might be added that the late nineteenth-century rationale was a little less self-centred, that is, centred on the ambitions, and to some extent the fears of its primary class constituency, than its eighteenth-century prototype had been. The subject of English came into being in a context of concern over the effects of foreign immigration, and with scarcely a thought to the linguistic educational needs of immigrant groups or the working class.[127]

True enough, in this last as in all other aspects the specifics of the situation had changed from Franklin's time to Rickoff's. Large-scale historical evolution, or revolution, had altered structures of class, social communication and power. This of course is what made for a different outcome than Franklin had been able to achieve in 1751. To him belongs the credit not for success but for intuiting the possibility of success, and the terms on which that success would come, for advanced vernacular subject matter. The *Idea of the English School* reflects deeply, if not in every way flatteringly, on the historical course of the social origins of English.

Conclusion

In place of a formal review of findings I would offer in closing only a brief further suggestion, based on the textual (and contextual) 'perspective' that has now been constructed. What stands out in this perspective is not only a particular social historical scenario for the emergence of English, but the constancy of the more generic — call them 'sociological' — parameters of this development. All of the texts of vernacular advocacy that have come under consideration here couched their arguments for the new subject matter at least implicitly in terms of class, language and power. While it probably deserved to be stated more often that it was that this was not the only form a rationale for advanced English study could and did take, its recurrent assertion over the two hundred year period of the subject's origination is instructive. Indeed, this persistence suggests the possibility — a possibility raised also, albeit from different perspectives, by other essays in this volume — that the same parameters may be equally relevant to the mature discipline we know as 'English' today. However, differently constituted the particulars of each and the relations among them may be from what they were in the eighteenth or for that matter the nineteenth century, and however mediated the entire situation may have become by the presence of a professional community of subject matter specialists pursuing to some extent its own interests and aspirations, the fundamental social realities of class, language and power will continue to play, as they have played, a determinative role in the history and politics of English.

Notes

1   ARCHER, M. (1979) *Social Origins of Educational Systems*, London, SAGE Publications, p. 1.
2   REID, W. (1985) 'Curricular Change and the Evolution of Educational Constituencies: The English Sixth Form in the Nineteenth Century', in Goodson (Ed.) *Social Histories of the Secondary Curriculum: Subjects for Study*, Lewes and Philadelphia, Falmer Press, pp. 293–5.
3   REID, W. and FILBY, J. (1982) *The Sixth: An Essay in Education and Democracy*, Lewes, Falmer Press, p. 38.
4   BURNS, G. (1980) 'Tradition and Revolution in the American Secondary Curriculum: The Cambridge High School Case', *Journal of Curriculum Studies*, 20,

2, pp. 99–118. GOODSON, I. (1981) 'Becoming an Academic Subject: patterns of explanation and evolution', *British Journal of Sociology of Education*, 2, 2, pp. 168–71. See also the discussion of the effective autonomy of the curriculum of Philadelphia's Central High School over most of the nineteenth century in LARABEE, D. (1988) *The Making of an American High School: The Credentials Market and the Central High School of Philadelphia, 1828–1939*, New Haven, Yale, pp. 3–4, 6, 34. I am indebted to a recent commentator on 'Tradition and Revolution' (whose name was omitted from the correspondence) for challenging my assumptions in the matter. But in the end I take my stand with Harvard's Charles W. ELIOT, who presided over major changes in his institution's course of study over the late nineteenth century, but nonetheless credited the public high schools with the leading, initiatory role in the development of the modern curriculum during this period. Eliot, C. (1899) 'Recent Changes in Secondary Education', in KRUG, E. (Ed.) (1961) *Charles W. Eliot and Popular Education*, New York, Teachers College, pp. 125, 129.

5   It needs also to be understood that while this emphasis should allow this essay to contribute something to the larger volume's theme of the 'politics' of English, what is at stake in the texts to be discussed is, once again, a *social* politics, involving not highly developed ideological claims but rather the more or less inarticulate efforts of a large class constituency to provide for its (linguistic) educational needs.

6   GOODSON, I. (1984) 'Subjects for Study: Towards a Social History of Curriculum', in GOODSON and BALL, S. (Eds) *Defining the Curriculum: Histories & Ethnographies*, Lewes, Falmer Press, p. 28. The distinction between historical analysis at the level of constituency development or 'class formation' and that dealing with larger-scale social changes is also discussed in REID (1985) *op cit.*, pp. 295, 307, and Hogan, D. (1982) 'Education and Class Formation: the peculiarities of the Americans', in Apple, M. (Ed.) *Cultural and Economic Production in Education: Essays on Class, Ideology and the State*, London, Routledge and Kegan Paul, pp. 35–6.

7   The discussion of class structure below in the text relies on the following principal sources: NASH, G. (1979) *The Urban Crucible: Social Change, Political Consciousness, and the Origins of the American Revolution*, Cambridge, MA, Harvard, pp. 14–21; DOERFLINGER, T. (1986) *A Vigorous Spirit of Enterprise: Merchants and Economic Development in Revolutionary Philadelphia*, Chapel Hill, University of North Carolina, pp. 15–60; BRIDENBAUGH, C. and J. (1942) *Rebels and Gentlemen: Philadelphia in the Age of Franklin*, Westport, Greenwood Press, pp. 3–19; RORABAUGH, W. (1986) *The Craft Apprentice: From Franklin to the Machine Age in America*, New York, Oxford, pp. 5–7; SMITH, B. (1981) 'The Material Lives of Laboring Philadelphians, 1750–1800', *William and Mary Quarterly*, 38, 2, pp. 163–202; LASLETT, P. (1965) *The World We Have Lost*, London, Methuen, pp. 26–49, 193; HILL, C. (1974) *Change and Continuity in Seventeenth-Century England*, London, Weidenfeld and Nicolson, pp. 208–14.

8   For a defence of this usage of the term see Hill, *op cit.*, p. 202, n. 63.

9   On Philadelphian artisans' general prosperity see Nash, *op cit.*, p. 121.

10   MILLS, C. (1956) *The Power Elite*, New York, Oxford, pp. 3–4.

11   DOMHOFF, G. (1970) *The Higher Circles: The Governing Class in America*, New York, Vintage, p. 107.

12   BRIDENBAUGH, *op cit.*, p. 13.

13 HANNA, W. (1964) *Benjamin Franklin and Pennsylvania Politics* (Stanford), p. 28.

14 HILL, *op cit.*, p. 214; RYERSON, R. (1978) *The Revolution is Now Begun: The Radical Committees of Philadelphia, 1765–1776*, Philadelphia, University of Pennsylvania, ch. 8. The term 'new men', used by contemporaries, is taken from Ryerson.

15 Quoted in ASHCRAFT, R. (1986) *Revolutionary Politics & Locke's Two Treatises of Government* Princeton, pp. 241, 250.

16 WATSON, F. (1909) *The Beginnings of the Teaching of Modern Subjects in England*, London, Pitman and Sons, pp. xxiv–xxxv; BURNS, G. (1984) 'From the "English School" Towards "English": Secondary Vernacular Study and the Origins of Modern American Education', Ph.D. diss., Yale University, pp. 288–332.

17 LOCKE, J. (1693) *Some Thoughts Concerning Education*, in AXTELL, J. (Ed.) *The Educational Writings of John Locke* (1968), Cambridge, Cambridge University Press, p. 325.

18 On the Renaissance/early modern educational revolution see STONE, L. (1964) 'The Educational Revolution in England, 1560–1640', *Past and Present*, 28, pp. 44–96; CHARLTON, K. (1965) *Education in Renaissance England*, London, Routledge and Kegan Paul, chs. 1–3; and CREMIN, L. (1970) *American Education: The Colonial Experience, 1603–1783*, New York, Harper and Row, pp. 170–3.

19 LOCKE, *op cit.*, pp. 277–8.

20 BERNSTEIN, B. (1971) 'A public language: some sociological implications of a linguistic form', in *Class, Codes, and Control*, London, Routledge and Kegan Paul, pp. 42–60. The public/formal language distinction is also explored in ATKINSON, P. (1985) *Language, Structure, and Reproduction: An Introduction to the Sociology of Basil Bernstein* (London, Methuen), 1985, pp. 39–43.

21 BERNSTEIN (1971) *op cit.*, pp. 42, 55. Here it should be noted that Bernstein has been charged with depicting public language/the restricted code as a type of 'linguistic deprivation'. These lists of characteristics would seem to give credence to the charge, but, in this same essay (p. 54) he does take pains to defend the energy and expressive richness of public language.

22 BERNSTEIN, B. (1982) 'Codes, modalities, and the process of cultural reproduction: a model', in APPLE, *op cit.*, p. 306; ATKINSON, *op cit.*, p. 53. Bernstein himself speaks of having moved away from 'linguistic indices' toward a general semantic and ideological orientation. Atkinson writes that Bernstein's argument is occupied not only with linguistics but with '*cultural* contrasts', although he goes on to caution that such a distinction goes against the '*structuralist*' grain of Bernstein's sociology.

23 LOCKE, *op cit.*, p. 280.

24 CRANSTON, M. (1957) *John Locke: A Biography*, New York, Macmillan, *passim*; JEFFREYS, M. (1967) *John Locke: Prophet of Common Sense*, London, Methuen, pp. 20, 30. The phrase 'assistant pen' ('in matters that nearly concerned the State and were fit to be made public') is Shaftesbury's grandson's, quoted in Cranston, p. 293.

25 Quoted in Cranston, *op cit.*, p. 244.

26 HEXTER, J. (1961) 'The Education of the Aristocracy in the Renaissance', in Hexter, *Reappraisals in History: New Views on History and Society in Early Modern Europe*, New York, Harper and Row, pp. 59–63; Charlton, *op cit.*, pp. 40, 76–85; MARROU, H. (1956) *A History of Education in Antiquity*, LAMB, G. (trans.) 3rd edn., London, Sheed and Ward, pp. 160–75, 273–84.

27 LOCKE, *op cit.*, pp. 280, 300.

28 *Ibid.*, p. 301.
29 Elements of this tradition, which had long shown favour to the native language, at least as a medium of instruction, are discussed in Charlton, *op cit.*, pp. 279–96; WATSON, F. (1909) *op cit.*, pp. xxiv–xxxv; PARKER, I. (1914) *Dissenting Academies in England*, Cambridge University Press, *passim*; HANS, N. (1951) *New Trends in Education in the XVIIIth Century*, London, Routledge and Kegan Paul, p. 64; and Burns *op cit.*, pp. 288–332.
30 *Ibid.*, p. 312.
31 CRANSTON, *op cit.*, pp. 3–10. On the upper class orientation of the *Thoughts* see also TARCOV, N. (1984) *Locke's Education for Liberty*, Chicago, University of Chicago, p. 3.
32 ASHCRAFT, *op cit.*, *passim*.
33 For example, the discussion of traditional upper class accomplishments is followed by the recommendation that a 'Manual Trade nay two or three' be taught. (Locke, *op cit.*, p. 314). It is apparent, however, that young gentlemen are doing the learning of these trades, which are to be practised as a means of genteel self-improvement.
34 LOCKE, *op cit.*, p. 268.
35 *Ibid.*
36 ANON. (1734–35) 'Some Thoughts on Education', in *American Weekly Mercury*, 31 December–7 January, 7 January–14 January. This and all subsequent references are to this unpaginated text.
37 The English tradition is discussed in BURNS (1988) *op cit.*, pp. 102–3, and at length in BURNS (1984) *op cit.*, pp. 243–87.
38 WATSON, *op cit.*, p. 263; COOTE, E. (1596) *The English School-Master*, London, Company of Stationers [1737], unpaginated preface.
39 CREMIN, *op cit.*, p. 395.
40 For an example of the claim see BRIDENBAUGH, C. (1955) *Cities in Revolt: Urban Life in America, 1743–1776*, New York, Knopf, p. 183. For the counterclaim BOTEIN, S. (1980) 'Printers and the American Revolution', in Bailyn, B. and Hench, J. (Eds) *The Press & the American Revolution*, Worcester, American Antiquarian Society, pp. 19–21.
41 NASH, *op cit.*, pp. 199–201.
42 CRANSTON, *op cit.*, pp. 386–7.
43 FRANKLIN, B. (1771) *The Autobiography*, LABAREE, L. (Ed.) (1964) New Haven, Yale, pp. 52–9.
44 FRANKLIN, B. (1722) 'Silence Dogood, No. 4', in Labaree, L. (Ed.) *The Papers of Benjamin Franklin* [1959] New Haven, vol. 1, pp. 15–16.
45 VAN DOREN, C. (1938) *Benjamin Franklin*, New York, Viking, 1938, p. 177; ROACH, H. (1961) 'Taxables in the City of Philadelphia, 1756', *Pennsylvania Magazine of History and Biography*, 22, 1, pp. 3–41.
46 FRANKLIN (1771) *op cit.*, pp. 196–7. On Franklin's later career see WRIGHT, E. (1986) *Franklin of Philadelphia*, Cambridge, MA, Harvard, pp. 111 ff.
47 VAN DOREN, *op cit.*, p. 260; HANNA, *op cit.*, pp. 28–30; CONNER, P. (1965) *Poor Richard's Politicks: Benjamin Franklin and His New American Order*, New York, Oxford, pp. 212–17.
48 FRANKLIN, B. (1747) *Plain Truth*, in *Papers*, vol. 3, pp. 199–200. On Franklin and the middle class and/or these organizations see OLTON, C. (1975) *Artisans for Independence: Philadelphia Mechanics and the American Revolution*, Syracuse, Syracuse

University, pp. 33–4; BRIDENBAUGH, C. (1955) *op. cit.*, pp. 283–91, 350; FAY, B. (1929) *Franklin, the Apostle of Modern Times*, Boston, Little, Brown, pp. vii, 119–21, 237.

49 FRANKLIN (1722) *op cit.*, pp. 15–16.
50 FRANKLIN (1771) *op cit.*, pp. 52–3, 62, 64, 72,
51 *Ibid.*, p. 60.
52 ONG, W. (1982) *Orality and Literacy: the Technologizing of the Word*, London, Methuen, pp. 162–3.
53 FRANKLIN (1722) *op cit.*, p. 16. Lewis Simpson has called my attention to the significance of this feature of the Dogood essay. For this and a generally stimulating treatment of Franklin *vis-à-vis* print culture, see Simpson, L. (1976) 'The Printer as Man of Letters: Franklin and the Symbolism of the Third Realm', in LEMAY, J. (Ed.) *The Oldest Revolutionary: Essays on Benjamin Franklin*, Philadelphia, University of Pennsylvania, pp. 3–20.
54 I have developed this point at greater length in BURNS (1987) 'Print Culture and Franklin's Conception of English Study', paper delivered at the Midwest History of Education Society annual meeting, 7 November 1987.
55 SIMPSON, *op cit.*, p. 8.
56 FRANKLIN (1771) *op cit.*, pp. 160, 173, 193, 200.
57 LARSON, D. (1986) 'Benevolent Persuasion: The Art of Benjamin Franklin's Philanthropic Papers', *Pennsylvania Magazine of History and Biography*, 110, p. 195.
58 FRANKLIN, (1771) *op cit.*, p. 200.
59 *Ibid.*, p. 124.
60 *Ibid.*; FRANKLIN, B. (1729) *The Nature and Necessity of a Paper Currency*, in *Papers*, vol. 1, pp. 139–57.
61 FRANKLIN (1771) *op cit.*, pp. 173–4; *Papers*, vol. 2, pp. 27–33, 37–65; vol. 4, pp. 130–3.
62 NASH, *op cit.*, pp. 210–12; STOUT, H. (1977) 'Religion, Communication, and the Ideological Origins of the American Revolution', *William and Mary Quarterly*, 34, 4, pp. 519–41.
63 Quoted in *Papers*, vol. 3, p. 186.
64 FRANKLIN (1771) *op cit.*, pp. 196–7; HANNA, *op cit.*, p. 49.
65 FRANKLIN (1771) *op cit.*, pp. 199–201.
66 *Ibid.*, pp. 192–6; CHEYNEY, E. (1940) *History of the University of Pennsylvania, 1740–1940*, Philadelphia, University of Pennsylvania, p. 29.
67 FRANKLIN (1771) *op cit.*, p. 197.
68 Quoted in SIMPSON, *op cit.*, p. 14.
69 FRANKLIN, B. (1789) 'Observations Relative to the Intentions of the Original Founders of the Academy in Philadelphia', in BIGELOW, J. (Ed.) [1881] *The Complete Works of Benjamin Franklin*, New York, Putnam's, vol. 10, p. 87.
70 FRANKLIN, B. (1749) *Proposals Relating to the Education of Youth in Pennsylvania*, in *Papers*, vol. 3, pp. 397–8.
71 *Ibid.*, pp. 405–9.
72 FRANKLIN, B. (1750) 'Paper on the Academy', in *Papers*, vol. 4, p. 36.
73 FRANKLIN (1749) *op cit.*, pp. 415–16.
74 *Ibid.*, p. 398.
75 FRANKLIN (1789) *op cit.*, p. 87; HANNA, *op cit.*, p. 49; HUTSON, *op cit.*, 306–7. This observation is also based on my general reading in Franklin sources. From this I have come to the conclusion that Franklin's portrayal, in the retrospective

'Observations', of his original educational initiative as a thoroughly populist venture is in significant respects a misleading one.

76 FRANKLIN (1789) *op cit.*, p. 87; *Constitution of the Academy of Philadelphia*, in *Papers*, vol. 3., pp. 424–5.

77 This reaction may be fact be inferred from FRANKLIN (1789), *op cit.*, p. 87.

78 Franklin to Samuel Johnson, 25 October 1750, in *Papers*, vol. 4, p. 72.

79 Johnson to Franklin, November 1750, *Papers*, vol. 4, p. 74.

80 FRANKLIN, B. (1751) *Idea of the English School*, in *Papers*, vol. 4, p. 105.

81 *Ibid.*, p. 108.

82 Franklin to Johnson, p. 72. In this place Franklin also seems to indicate that some upper class youth might elect to pursue their studies at the English School, although it is clear that this is not his principal expectation as to clientele.

83 Determination of parents' identity and income/occupational status is based on Minutes of the Board of Trustees of the College, Academy and Charitable School of Pennsylvania, 8 March 1757, vol. A1, pp. 80–2, and 'Book of Accounts', 1750/1-1757, MS 1558, Archives of the University of Pennsylvania; Roach, H. *op cit.*, p. 3–41.

84 FRANKLIN (1751) *op cit.*, pp. 101–7.

85 BURNS (1984) *op cit.*, pp. 384–417, and (1987) *op cit.*

86 FRANKLIN (1751) *op cit.*, p. 108.

87 ROSSITER, C. (1952) 'The Political Theory of Benjamin Franklin', *Pennsylvania Magazine of History and Biography*, 76, p. 269.

88 FRANKLIN (1751) *op cit.*, p. 108.

89 FRANKLIN (1789) *op cit.*, p. 114; Franklin quoted in 'Excerpts from the Papers of Dr. Benjamin Rush', *Pennsylvania Magazine of History and Biography*, 29, p. 27.

90 FRANKLIN (1751) *op cit.*, p. 108.

91 FRANKLIN (1750) *op cit.*, p. 36.

92 FRANKLIN, 'Observations Concerning the Increase of Mankind', in *Papers*, vol. 4, p. 234; WEAVER, G. (1957) 'Benjamin Franklin and the Pennsylvania Germans', *William and Mary Quarterly*, 14, pp. 539–41.

93 In addition, only one of the thirteen identifiable English School parents had a lower/working class background. See n. 89 above.

94 REID and FILBY, *op cit.*, p. 18.

95 The original treatment of this failure is Franklin's own (1789) 'Observations Relative to the Intentions of the Original Founders ...'. Secondary treatments include BRIDENBAUGH (1942) *op cit.*, ch. 2, and CREMIN, *op cit.*, pp. 402–4.

96 FRANKLIN (1789) *op cit.*, pp. 91–2. The account that follows is based on the sources listed in n. 95. On the methods of the English School's first master, David James Dove, see LYMAN, R. (1922) *English Grammar in American Schools Before 1850*, Chicago, University of Chicago Libraries, pp. 28, 52, and GRAYDON, A. (1811) *Memoirs of a Life, Chiefly Passed in Pennsylvania*, Harrisburg, Wyeth, pp. 14–16.

97 Minutes of the Board of Trustees, 8 March 1757, vol. A1, p. 192.

98 FRANKLIN (1789) *op cit.*, pp. 11–12; CHEYNEY, E. *op cit.*, pp. 154–5.

99 BRIDENBAUGH (1955) *op cit.*, pp. 283–4.

100 HALL, D. (1983) 'Introduction: The Uses of Literacy in New England, 1600–1850', in JOYCE, W. *et. al.* (Eds) *Printing and Society in Early America*, pp. 5–6; BROWN, R. (1983) 'Afterword: From Cohesion to Competition', in *ibid.*, pp. 300, 303.

101 OGILVIE (1964) *op cit.*, p. 57. Ogilvie points out among other things that no authoritative dictionary of English existed prior to 1755.

102 FRANKLIN (1789) *op cit.*, pp. 93–5.

103 On his deposition as president see Franklin to Ebenezer Kinnersley, 28 July 1759, in *Papers*, vol. 8, pp. 415–16, and KETCHAM, R. (1964) 'Benjamin Franklin and William Smith: New Light on an Old Philadelphia Quarrel', *Pennsylvania Magazine of History and Biography*, 88, pp. 145–54.

104 NASH (1979) *op cit.*, pp. 365–82; RYERSON, *op cit.*, chs. 7–8. The titles of Ryerson's chapters are suggestive: 'The "Wordy War" for Independence' and 'The Revolution of the Middle Classes'.

105 'Tuition, Money and Account Book of the University and "Schools", 21 Jun 1780-Aug 1782' and 'Laws relating to the Schools of the English School Arrangement' [1779-1789], MSS 1561 and 1127, Archives of the University of Pennsylvania.

106 NASH (1979) *op cit.*, p. 393; CHEYNEY, *op cit.*, pp. 147–54.

107 BLODGETT, J. (1870) 'Claims of English Grammar in Common Schools', in *Addresses and Journal of Proceedings of the National Educational Association of the United States* [volumes issued annually], pp. 164–5.

108 HARRINGTON, H. (1875) 'Language Teaching, Its Importance and Its Methods', in *ibid.*, p. 24.

109 STARK, A. (1877) 'The Place of English in the Higher Education', in *ibid.*, p. 24.

110 RICKOFF, A., (1879) 'Readjustment of Common School Studies Necessary', in *ibid.*, p. 47; MARBLE, A., 'Caste in Education', in *ibid.*, p. 25.

111 BLODGETT, *op cit.*, p. 165.

112 STARK, *op cit.*, pp. 24–5.

113 HOBBS, B. (1870) remark in discussion of Blodgett address, *op cit.*, p. 169.

114 HARRIS, W. (1870) 'The Theory of American Education', in *Proceedings of NEA*, pp. 188–9; MARBLE, *op cit.*, p. 26.

115 HARRINGTON, *op cit.*, p. 156.

116 RICKOFF, *op cit.*, p. 47.

117 Quoted in BROWN, E. (1903) *The Making of Our Middle Schools*, New York, Longmans, Green, pp. 299–300.

118 LABAREE, *op cit.*, pp. 2–3.

119 On constituency for the new public high schools see KATZ, M. (1968) *The Irony of Early School Reform*, Boston, Beacon, pp. 27–50. For a treatment which rebuts Katz but leaves open the possibility of a primary middle-class constituency, see VINOVSKIS, M. (1985) *The Origins of Public High Schools: A Reexamination of the Beverly High School Controversy*, Madison, University of Wisconsin, esp. pp. 69, 71, 114. See also COUNTS, G. (1922) *The Selective Character of American Secondary Education*, New York, Arno [1969], chs. 4–9, 15.

120 LABAREE, *op cit.*, p. 4.

121 *Ibid.*, p. 6.

122 WIEBE, R. (1967) *The Search for Order, 1877–1920*, New York, Hill and Wang, pp. 11–13, 128.

123 BLEDSTEIN, B. (1976) *The Culture of Professionalism: The Middle Class and the Development of Higher Education in America*, New York, Norton, *passim*. Bledstein's treatment of a (middle) class formation is cognate with Wiebe's in a number of respects. See especially pp. 36–9.

124 WIEBE, *op cit.*, ch. 7, p. 166.

125   GOULDNER, A. (1979) *The Future of Intellectuals and the Rise of the New Class*, New York, Seabury, pp. 1–8, 28–32.

126   Three differences between nineteenth-century developments and Franklin's 'intuitions' as revealed in the *Idea* may be briefly noted. (1) Later arguments for English placed much greater emphasis on the teaching of *literature* as opposed to language. (2) The presence of a body of professional educators, collectively articulating a rationale, and mediating the interests of the primary class constituency (to which they, of course, belonged) in more complex manner than a single spokesperson such as Franklin. (3) The upper class, through its agents in the pages of high-toned magazines, also advanced an argument on behalf of the subject, *for* the middle classes, but to an extra-educational end of 'culture' and tractability rather than 'power'. For an example of an argument of this type, sede [Anon.] (1878) 'Certain Dangerous Tendencies in American Life', *Atlantic Monthly*, 42, pp. 385–402.

127   WITT, P. (1968) 'The Beginnings of the Teaching of Vernacular Literature in the Secondary Schools of Massachusetts', Ph.D. diss., Harvard University School of Education, pp. 132, 138, 141–2. For a practical illustration of these exclusionary attitudes, with particular reference to the subject of English, see HULING, R. (1891) 'How English is Taught in One High School', in *Proceedings of NEA*, pp. 632–40.

Chapter 4

A Dividing Practice: 'Literature', English Teaching and Cultural Politics

Bill Green, School of Education, Murdoch University

To argue right from the outset for a view of English teaching as a form of cultural politics is, I suspect, to go very much against the grain. Not just against the grain of much current curriculum discussion regarding subject English but also against that of much current practice in English classrooms. It is as if the discourse of English teaching, on its various levels, refuses to contemplate the political, seeking instead to repress it, to expunge it actively from memory. And yet, refusing politics, it defines itself nonetheless *against* politics, in what amounts to a truly monstrous assertion of agency. Shakespeare's Ariel haunts the imagination of the profession as surely and emphatically now as it has ever done, and in attending to our dreams we need to bear in mind Freud's equally compelling fiction of the Unconscious. What, we may well ask, is the other side, the dark side, of our imaginings, our desires, our discourse?

In this paper, I propose a view of secondary English teaching as cultural politics.[1] I do so by focusing on the category 'literature' in the discourse of English teaching. By this I mean not only how literature has been talked about and conceived within the field but also, more radically, how English teaching as a specific social discourse has actively *constructed* literature, as both a cultural commodity and a practice with quite definite ideological and political effects. I want to situate this account within the context of what has been called the ideology-and-education debate.[2] I do so, however, by means of arguments and concepts drawn from the work of Michel Foucault. It is my contention that the category 'literature' has played a particular rôle in the practice of English teaching as cultural politics, such that it is important to recognize in English teaching a *contradictory politics*, with both progressive and reactionary moments and phases. The task as I see it is to reveal something of the *mythic* character of English teaching as it has hitherto sought to understand itself, so that we can seek to realize more of its genuinely utopian possibility.

A recent gathering of the international community of English teaching bore the title 'The Issues That Divide Us'. For me, this immediately evokes one of Foucault's most generative concepts: the notion of 'dividing practice'. He uses the concept in the context of his explorations of the problem of human subjectivity — the problem of the subject. How is it, he asks, that human beings are made, and make themselves, into 'subjects', particular forms of individuality socio-historically defined in accordance with certain operations of power? Foucault is especially fascinated by 'those processes of self-formation in which the person is active'.[3] For him what is striking in this intrication of subjectivity and power is its expression on the level of the ordinary, the 'natural' and the mundane:

> This form of power applies itself to immediate everyday life which categorizes the individual, marks him [*sic*] by his own individuality, attaches him to his own identity, imposes a law of truth on him which he must recognize and which others have to recognize in him. It is a form of power which makes individuals subjects.[4]

This is a particularly useful way of conceptualizing the practice of curriculum generally and specifically that of English teaching. The concept of 'individualizing power' is likely to be of particular value, for instance, in understanding the relationship between reading and self-production. Moreover, 'literature' itself may be productively regarded as a specific form of moral technology involving what has variously been described as the 'seminar of conscience'[5] and the '*techne* of self'.[6] Within the terms of this argument, then, literature is to be seen as directly linked, in accordance with a general socialization-effect, to the production of subjectivity.

It needs to be said that I am appropriating and modifying the concept of 'dividing practice' here. In this context, the expression refers to a combination of 'the three modes of objectification which transform human beings into subjects'[7] — that is, the establishment of a 'science', the organization of social division according to principles and procedures of exclusion, and the practices of self-formation. My view is that English teaching — particularly in its character as a school-based form of literary education, but not exclusively so — brings together these different kinds of 'subjectification'–'objectification' processes in a distinctive manner. What might be called 'the subject of English teaching' is very much a *hybrid* phenomenon, in various senses. It is interesting in this light to reflect on, firstly, what appears an endemic feature of English teaching right from the outset: its internal history of conflict and struggle,[8] and secondly, its role in the (re)production of larger, more systematic forms of social difference, discrimination and domination. Against this can be set its characteristic yearning for unity, harmony and consensus, as registered for instance in the aforementioned conference theme, clearly an ideological gesture *par excellence*.[9]

In what follows, I examine firstly the category 'literature' itself, proposing that it is inextricably bound up with the history and identity of subject English and the profession and practice of English teaching. I then consider, albeit briefly, instances of the division wrought by 'literature' within English teaching itself. Finally, I conclude with some observations concerning cultural politics and the possibility of developing a critical pedagogy in the context of English studies and English curriculum.

Literature and English Teaching

There can be little doubt that a close and even necessary relationship exists between literature and English teaching.[10] As Harold Rosen has noted: 'Whatever else is in doubt, no one has seriously questioned the claim that literature should be a central preoccupation of English teaching.'[11] While this is far from an uncontentious matter, despite Rosen's confidence, as a general observation it holds true. There are a number of ways in which this is so. If the focus is on English teachers, it quickly becomes clear that both their practices and their training revolves significantly around literature. There is now considerable research indicating that whatever else English teachers do, much of their time in classrooms is spent in teaching literature in one form or another.[12] Similarly, their constructs of what is involved in English teaching almost invariably centre on literature. Further, as Rosen has also noted, 'the formation of specialist English teachers has been overwhelmingly literary'.[13] In both their university education and their pre-service training, English teachers have been principally schooled in the practices and perspectives of literary study. Even those who have not gone through a specifically literary training ('non-specialists') find themselves in an expressly literary context and accordingly adapt, with varying degrees of success.

This orientation in English teaching is further evidenced on the level of research and policy, structured as it always is by particular governing paradigms. Notwithstanding the notorious disjunctions between classroom practice on the one hand and research and policy on the other, there has been a constant official emphasis on the importance of literature in English teaching (e.g. the Bullock Report). This has been variously conceived, but is markedly consistent all the same. In recent times what has been termed variously the 'Growth Model'[14] or 'English-as-Language'[15] paradigm has clearly dominated. This has involved a significant shift in perspective on literature and classroom literary study but, as I will argue later, it has meant neither abandoning the traditional category of 'literature' nor mounting a serious challenge to it. This means that *all* English teachers, whether specialists or not, have found themselves in a situation in which literature is significant and even critical to a proper sense of *professional* identity. At the same time, for many, it has also involved a considerable *personal* investment.

This is indicated, in a somewhat different context, in Noel King's observations on the history of English studies:

> ... one reason for paying attention to the Newbolt Report is to give a specific history to a set of teaching practices which otherwise might seem outside history, might seem always to have existed. And indeed if one accepts that any trajectory through secondary tertiary level English courses from the 1960s to the present is in large part a training in some combinations of Leavisism and new criticism ... then the Report would provide a surprising degree of autobiographical interest.[16]

Yet another perspective on the essential 'literariness' of English teaching focuses on the *institutional* nature of literature and education. Since this focus may be seen as contextualizing and organizing most if not all other considerations, it is this on which I will concentrate here. To refer to the 'institutional' nature of literature and education is to point to their function as specific sites for the regulation of the social production of meaning, including meaningful action. Social institutions are

> those enduring regulatory and organizing structures of any society, which constrain and control individuals and individuality ... the underlying principles and values according to which ... social practices are organized and coordinated.[17]

As such, institutions work to construct not only individuals and individuality but also forms or styles of individuality and hence the organization of individuals into *populations.*

Accordingly, both 'literature' and 'education' are to be recognized as social mechanisms for the mobilization, authorization and dissemination of certain specific discourses and, in varying ways, the refusal or the marginalization of others. Since discourses *produce* meanings, what is at issue here is precisely the question of *meaning* — or rather, the way in which discourse and power are intricated in the production of specific social meanings. What this involves is a recognition of both 'literature' and 'education' as arenas of ideological struggle, which must be understood explicitly as a struggle over meanings.[18] All this points to the need to perceive both 'literature' and 'education' as, right from the outset, problems of a political kind.

For our purposes here, it is necessary to subordinate literature to education, which is to see the former in the context of the latter.[19] From this perspective, education exists as an institutional practice responsible for the mobilization of the discourse (or rather the discursive ensemble) that is 'literature'. 'English teaching' refers simply to that pedagogy focused specifically around subject English, in the context of the secondary school. Of course, what is named here as 'subject English' is not at all self-evident and unproblematical, and part of the task of explicating the social practice of English teaching consists in engaging with the problem of 'English' as a school subject. Before that can be done, however, I need to examine something of what may be described as the social history of 'literature', both as a category and as a social practice.

On 'Literature'

Ian Reid has observed that the task of reconceptualizing literary education must begin with an *expansion* of the category 'literature'; moreover, 'the very idea of enlarging our concept of literature implies an anti-essentialist stance'.[20] For others arguing along similar lines, it is not simply a matter of making it 'a much more inclusive category' than hitherto it has been, but, more radically, a *refusal* of 'literature' as such.[21] At issue here is the manner in which history is realized as, or else actively transformed into, myth. Consequently, calling literature into question in this way is to *re*-call it to its history, and hence to initiate a project of demystification. This is obviously an important task, particularly in the current context of a widely-perceived general crisis in English studies and literature teaching.

Chris Baldick, among others, has pointed to the striking failure of criticism to consider its own history:

> Even leaving aside the very favourable conditions which it pro-
> vides for ideological assumptions of timelessness and naturalness,
> such a state of affairs is in itself an unhealthy one for literary
> studies, fostering within it a passive and indeed uncritical atti-
> tude.[22]

A very similar point, and clearly linked to this, may be made with regard to English teaching. To speak as Reid does of the need to take up 'an anti-essentialist stance' means among other things to foreground the historicity of categories such as 'literature' and 'the literary' and to perceive them not in terms of *intrinsic* qualities, defined as such from within, but rather, from without, as constructions in and by history. Literature must be seen as something *made*, in a number of senses, and not simply as something *given*. Part of what is involved in such a stance, as I see it, is recognizing the profound complicity of 'literature' and 'education', histor-ically and ideologically. This I suggest is the context in terms of which English teaching is best understood.

There are two ways in which this can be considered. One is to focus on language and what may be described as a project of national unity. The other focuses more closely on literature itself. In the first instance, we would need to consider the rise and development of compulsory mass schooling ('popular education') and its significance in the emergence and consolidation of the modern bourgeois state. This links up with a mounting crisis in the social, economic and ideological spheres, particularly focused in eighteenth-century Britain, and the move in response by dominant groups to secure a general hegemony. This was managed largely through the exercise of what Michel Foucault has called *disciplinary power* — that is, a power based upon the organization of individuality and the proliferation of technologies which were at once normative and normalizing.[23] Education became a particularly important site for such operations, on the one hand mediating between the family and the workplace and on the other providing an arena for the negotiation and structuring of identity in the movement between 'childhood' and 'adulthood'.

James Donald[24] has provided a most interesting account of the role and significance of language in these processes and strategies of cultural hegemony. His focus is 'the interplay between language and educational institutions in shaping both the state apparatus that emerged in England during the nineteenth century and also the forms of consciousness and subjectivity characteristic of that period'.[25] It is important to recognize, here, that these are not to be regarded simply as matters of historical interest but as bearing significantly on the configurations of the present. Language is neither merely a medium of communication nor a neutral agency in the social production of meaning; rather, it is an active force in the structuring of social life at the same time as it is itself shaped and determined by the play of social relations. As such it is 'both a site and a mechanism of cultural struggle'.[26] Donald goes on to point to the intrication of discourse and power in the intimate relationship between language and ideology:

> [L]anguage is politically important because of its ideological power — its meanings shape our perceptions and our experience of the world. Our consciousness is formed by the languages we encounter, when and where we encounter them, and our relationship to them. These relationships are possible because language actually constructs places for 'I', 'me' and 'you' within the symbolic world it signifies. We become social subjects as we enter culture. We enter culture by learning language.[27]

Of particular importance here is the notion of a close and necessary relation between language and subjectivity, and hence, by extension, thinking itself. From this perspective, language is to be seen as a critical site of surveillance and control precisely because it is linked so closely to thinking and the formation of subjectivities, and consequently is a crucial means to *social control*. This is what is at stake then in the on-going struggle over language.

Donald observes that this struggle was initially and most notably realized in and around the problem of *literacy*. For our purposes it suffices to note that this was in the first instance a matter relating specifically to *written* language. Schooling was intended to develop in the populace at large a specific competence with regard to written language. In practice, this meant differential access along primarily social class lines to reading and writing and so to knowledge, power and the means of 'cultural production'. With the emergence of a formal school curriculum organized in subject-specific terms, this meant that education was increasingly seen as synonymous with the development of what may be called 'cultural literacy'.[28] This needs to be seen, however, in terms of a political concern with the achievement of social order, a concern that was at least as important as the question of social welfare, if not more so.

What is of prime importance to recognize is the significant link between written language and social power (more particularly, those power-relations overdetermined by privilege). As various commentators have noted, the forging of a national language is an important strategy in the securing of a general cultural hegemony.[29] 'English' as the mother tongue ('standard English') signifies the outcome of this kind of struggle, although clearly it is one that is far from resolved, as is indicated in the constant surfacing of debates over 'correct' forms of usage. Here it must suffice merely to point to the close association between *national* language' and *'standard* language' and between these and *'written* language'. Controversies over usage and the like, and the 'literacy' debate generally, are, I suggest, best considered in this light.[30]

As might be expected, the question of 'literature' becomes important at this point. At the same time as and indeed deeply implicated in the cultural project of national unity organized in and through language, particular developments with regard to the category 'literature' are to be observed. Eagleton and others have asserted, rather provocatively, that 'Literature' as such does not exist. This should be seen specifically as a political intervention in the debate concerning 'English', one aim of which is to challenge what has been described previously as an *essentialism*. To question 'literature' in this fashion is to interrupt commonsense, based as it characteristically is on a *realist* epistemology. English teaching is certainly no exception to this. 'Literature' has been assumed all too readily in English teaching as essentially an unproblematical category, in an important sense integral to the *raison d'être* of the profession and discipline. What must be recognized, however, is that, from this perspective, 'literature' is a relatively recent invention, and one that must be seen emphatically as a paradigm instance of ideology at work. Raymond Williams has, for instance, suggested that literature is best understood as a concept.[31] This is to contrast it with that commonsense view which understands it as a particular body of (written) texts characterized necessarily and ontologically by qualities such as 'creativity', 'imagination', 'fictionality', 'originality' and 'artfulness' — that is to say, valued objects of a particular kind available for reading and appreciation, for the purposes of pleasure and edification that is at once both private and personal and public and institutional. Rather than a concrete particularity, the term 'literature' refers to an abstraction of a particular kind in that the processes of that abstraction, its *history*, have been either forgotten or else effectively refused. As Williams notes:

> In ordinary usage ['literature'] appears to be more than a specific description, and what is described is then, as a rule, so highly valued that there is a virtually immediate and unnoticed transfer of the specific values of particular works and kinds of work to what operates as a concept but is still firmly believed to be actual and practical.[32]

The point is, what are the implications and consequences of such a process? What, specifically, is at stake? Something of the character of English teaching as cultural politics begins to emerge very clearly in the light of such questions and such an argument. The first thing to recognize is that this was not a neutral or innocent occurrence; it didn't simply happen, in accordance with the laws of 'natural selection'. Rather, it was a specific response to changes in the social and political context. Faced with an ideological crisis, it became necessary to, as it were, 'invent' literature as part of a general hegemonic strategy.[33] This didn't happen all at once, of course, developing over a period of time, in direct relation to movements in other spheres, most notably that of education and compulsory mass schooling. Tony Davies has argued that, in the British context at least, literature played a 'decisive and determining role' in the shaping of a distinctive national consciousness that was the direct expression of dominant cultural interests. Moreover, it was intimately associated with the political mechanisms of schooling. Davies is quite explicit about this:

> ... following the semantic shift in the word itself, I want to argue that, faced with a crisis of ideological dominance and unable to resort either to the classics or to a science increasingly feared as the voice of a soulless materialism, education discovered and therefore created literature as the principal material and object of its institutions and practices.[34]

This is not to suggest that texts we would now identify as 'literary' in something like the restricted sense referred to here did not exist prior to this period. Obviously they did. But the particular *institutionalization* of the literary, a process that needs to be seen in relation to the formation of 'a disciplinary society',[35] emerged as a social force at this time and its effects are readily apparent across a range of surfaces. What is important to note, however, is that this process played a particular role in establishing and authorizing a distinctive national language, understood very precisely as the standard 'voice' and the voice of 'standards'. As Balibar asserts: 'the practice of a written language recognized and taught by the State cannot be dissociated from literary practice'.[36] This is because of the close association to be observed between the category 'literature' and *written* language. Part of the system of restrictions and exclusions associated with 'literature' has to do with the increasing significance of written language as a register of social division. The emergence of 'literature' is linked to a shift in emphasis and privilege from a predominantly oral, folk culture to one that was predominantly *literate* in the sense of being focused on and organized by the social relations of written language.[37] This was followed, as Williams notes, by a further process of restriction and selection, from a general association with all written or printed works to written works of a particular, valued kind.

At this point it is necessary to refer more specifically to English teaching. Its emergence as a distinctive practice in its own right needs to be seen in relation to, firstly, the production of what Davies calls 'literary ideology',[38] and secondly, the development and consolidation of compulsory mass schooling. Significantly, as it turns out, the two are intimately related. The specific emergence of subject English is linked to the movement towards specialization in the formal school curriculum, itself a matter of particular concern because it points to the organization and classification of knowledge in such a way as to make for the domestication of discourse and meaning. 'English' did not exist as a separate school subject prior to 1900;[39] since then, of course, it has very quickly established for itself a pre-eminent status, at the very heart of the curriculum at all levels of formal schooling. It is only relatively recently that this pre-eminence has been significantly challenged, and it is interesting to speculate as to why this has happened, given the argument presented here. With the development of a more fragmented and differentiated school curriculum, the particular functions of that ideological formation organized around the categories 'language', 'literacy' and 'literature' may well have been dispersed and effectively neutralized. Given the importance of this formation, however, to the cultural project of organizing subjectivities and social groups, a move towards the explicit deployment of formal curriculum space for these purposes was predictable. In this manner 'subject English' served in a very exact sense as a kind of *centring* mechanism, a principle of unity and unification.[40]

In this regard, an observation that Davies makes concerning the importance of literature (and hence, by extension, of English teaching) becomes more comprehensible and at least less contentious. Having noted the play of coercion and consent at work in the achievement, however tenuous, of linguistic and cultural hegemony, he goes on to imply a correlation between educational success and the distinctive kind of cultural politics that is in question here:

> For the rest of us, the successful ones who negotiate the transition from coercion to consent and learn to 'recognize' and internalize the natural superiority and universality of the dominant linguistic practice, literature plays a crucial role. It is crucial, evidently, for those who go on to study it, but no less so for those who proceed

to other subjects whose position in the curriculum is defined by the fact that *they are not literature*.[41]

It needs to be borne in mind that, up until quite recently, 'English' was the one compulsory subject in the school curriculum and indeed may well continue to be so in some contexts, either tacitly or explicitly. A less noticeable feature, but one which all the same has a compelling significance, is the manner in which competence in 'English' underpins schooling generally, right across the curriculum. This is not simply a technical competence with regard to reading and writing — or more broadly, *languaging* — but rather, what may be described as a specific *cultural* competence of the kind that Bourdieu associates with the notion of 'cultural capital'.[42] Given the genealogical and etymological linkages between 'literature' and 'literacy', and in turn their educational significance, the point that Davies is making becomes clearer. By extension, it involves an argument that English teaching must be seen right from the outset as a disciplinary mechanism, in Foucault's sense, a means for the production of a particular kind of 'cultured' subjectivity. Davies' account of what he calls 'literary ideology' is pertinent here. He points to the interpenetration and interdependence of the discourses of 'literature' and 'literary criticism', and argues that they must be seen as mutually constitutive and, in their relation, contextualized principally by the ideological operations of schooling. It is worth quoting him at some length:

> The relation between the two terms is mutually productive and reproductive: each depends upon the other, makes the other visible, as a necessary condition of its own existence and effect. Obviously, literary criticism — the name by which literary ideology most commonly goes — cannot exist without literature. But the reverse is equally true: *literature cannot exist without literary criticism*. I'm not speaking here only of the external conditions of their constitution within an ideological apparatus. Each is produced and reproduced *internally* within the other. And that reciprocal internalization, the constitutive condition of their existence and articulation one upon the other, is itself a determinate effect of their moral and educational function — specifically their function within the ideological institutions and practices ... of compulsory mass education.[43]

I propose, however, that the larger and more inclusive category here is 'literary education'. This enables a clearer and more adequate view of the relations between English teaching and literary ideology, and also of the complexities and specific character of that ideology at work. To speak exclusively of 'literary criticism' in this regard, as Davies does in effect, is to ignore the significant differences that exist between the tertiary and the secondary contexts and flatten out the complexity of the curriculum process, understood as an overdetermined ideological communication. In particular, it is to lose sight of the specificities of secondary schooling, especially with regard to English teaching. It also makes explicit the interface between 'criticism' and 'teaching' and consequently provides a richer perspective on the ideological practice of literary education, conceived specifically within the terms of the power–knowledge nexus. But my more immediate concern here is with the connections between literary ideology, so understood, and the notion of subjectivity.

In what was originally an address to the 1985 Annual Conference of the National Association for the Teaching of English, Terry Eagleton[44] issues a major challenge to mainstream English teaching as it currently conceives itself and as it has been traditionally constituted. The main thrust of his challenge consisted in questioning 'Literature', more specifically literature teaching, on moral and ideological grounds. In posing 'Literature' as a 'moral technology' which, together with other cultural mechanisms of a similar kind, works to instil certain forms of sensibility, discipline, behaviour and response in human beings (for, as he says, 'quite specific purposes of social control'), Eagleton sharply undercuts and so highlights some of the most fundamental premises of English teaching. He argues that the main effect of English teaching with regard to what, following Baldick, we can call its historical and social mission, has been the production of a particular kind of disinterested, intransitive *morality*:

> What Literature teaches is not so much this or that moral value — for after all, it's perfectly legitimate for one child to admire Piggy and another dislike him. It teaches us rather to be — let me rehearse some of the cherished terms — sensitive, imaginative, responsible, sympathetic, creative, perceptive, reflective. Notice the resounding intransivity of all of these familiar shibboleths. The task of the moral technology of Literature is to produce an historically peculiar form of human subject who is sensitive, receptive, imaginative and so on ... *about nothing in particular*.[45]

This he links to an ideology of abstract, formal *individualism* which, for him, must be seen within the context of the needs of capitalism. Despite what seems a congenital blindness it shares with Davies' account, as noted earlier, to the specificities of secondary schooling (to say nothing of primary schooling), there is much that is disturbing and unsettling in Eagleton's argument for those who are 'inside' English teaching, nothing perhaps more so than his apparent refusal, here at least,[46] of a utopian dimension to the whole enterprise. There would appear to be few 'spaces' in this line of argument and little room for manoeuvre in the service of a progressive politics, one in which English teaching has or could have an important role. All the same, such an argument cannot and should not be ignored, partly because it compels a radical reassessment of the practice of English teaching and of English teachers as ideological agents of a particular kind, constructed in certain ways, on the basis of certain kinds of training and experience. If English teaching is understood within the terms of literary ideology, and ideology in turn understood as 'a practice producing subjects',[47] then it is clear that the problem of subjectivity needs to be put more squarely on the agenda of English curriculum discussion. This would involve in particular a more critical, reflexive stance on the part of English teaching, not at all necessarily within the exclusive terms of Eagleton's particular brand of Marxism but, arguably, with reference also to something like Foucault's more positive and productive notions of power and subjectivity.[48] In this regard, we might fruitfully draw upon work such as that of Ian Hunter on the concept of 'literary discipline'[49] and seek to investigate the manner in which English teaching works in the service of a '*techne* of self', producing in students particular ways of being in the world and particular forms of conduct and character.

Inside English Teaching: Conflict and Consensus

The main thrust of my argument so far has been to propose the complicity of literature and English teaching as thoroughly intricated ideological practices, and hence as 'dividing practices' in Foucault's sense. This is perhaps clearer if we work with a notion of *literary practice* and point to the activities not just of writers and readers but also of publishers, editors and reviewers, as well as of teachers at every level, all of whom are actively engaged in the production and reproduction of 'literature' and literary ideology.[50] It is by no means simply English teaching, however, nor even the institution of education generally, that is 'culpable' in this regard. Rather, English teaching must be seen in the context of a systematic, although always contradictory, ensemble of practices working to achieve certain ideological effects. Further, it is not at all the case that this must *necessarily* be regarded in a negative, pejorative light.

But also clearly it is only partially useful to speak of English teaching — and also of literature, for that matter — as a single, homogeneous entity and an entirely unified practice. Competition and conflict within English teaching need to be recognized, as Stephen Ball[51] has argued, not just in terms of the historical development of subject English but also within individual English departments.[52] Certainly there is always contradiction and struggle within school systems as a whole, and there is also, notoriously, the matter of theory/practice relations to consider; in this regard, account must be made of the disjunction between the 'hegemony' that Growth Model theorizing has exercised on the level of policy, in Australia at least, and the experience of disarray, confusion and demoralization on the level of classrooms generally.[53] Even on the level of the individual teacher, there is likely to be conflict, in accordance with the principle of *multiple* and *contradictory* subjectivity. All of this points to the need to acknowledge and account for forms of struggle and division within English teaching. My concern here is specifically with those divisions and conflicts organized around the category 'literature'.

From this perspective, one of the most interesting features of post-Dartmouth developments in English teaching has been a recurring debate over the role and significance of literature. This has relatively recently been described in terms of 'the politics of discrimination',[54] a phrase which has striking resonance in the context of this present discussion. A somewhat earlier manifestation of this, and one which in varying forms still enjoys a currency, concerns criticisms of the Growth Model position which focus specifically on the status of literature in English curriculum theory and practice.[55] What characterizes these criticisms, particularly those of David Allen, Frank Whitehead and Fred Inglis,[56] is a sharp and concerted attack on what they see as the postulation of a *language*-centred view of subject English, at the expense of literature. More to the point, such critics see the Growth Model position (itself, of course, far from unified and homogeneous) as constituting an active refusal of literature as a significant category not only in English teaching but in human experience itself. Whitehead contends that 'in the real world of English teaching [James] Britton's influence has been disturbingly harmful'[57] and this is principally because it encourages a movement away from literature as 'at once the supreme source of enjoyment and the supreme creator of values'.[58] Similar sentiments are expressed by Inglis and Allen, in a manner and a language that is eloquent testimony to the investment and commitment that is characteristic of such arguments. For Inglis, there is a marked absence at the heart of Growth Model theorizing, a fatal debility, a *lifelessness*. In what I think can be taken as a general reference to literature, he has this to say: 'They [*sic*] fill one's mind to the brim. They alter the mind. They are profound and civilized in all their details. They become a part of one's life. But Britton cannot tell us what to do with such experiences.'[59] In a similar vein, having earlier noted that 'Britton's achievement has been great, but at very great cost',[60] Allen goes on to assert the following:

> [Literature — poetry, fiction and drama —] is central to English, for the reason that it is itself characteristic of the very life we seek to foster. It is the characteristic of literature (and of art in general) to distinguish the quick from the dead, it is endlessly curious, and vital: it seeks to know itself and what is not self; it is a created truth, but it exists only in that particular novel, that particular poem.[61]

The resonance in these statements in the light of the arguments being developed here should be readily apparent, and it is not my intention to elaborate on their implications here. What is important to understand is that the differences being signalled in these criticisms are clearly of an ideological nature, whatever else they may be. To grasp adequately what is involved in this debate requires that proper consideration is made of its literary-theoretical, political and pedagogical dimensions, as well as what can be described as its contextual and conjunctional features. More is at stake, however, than simply a debate within English teaching, conceived as a kind of 'in-house', internecine struggle. My contention is that it has a more general cultural significance, and represents a certain anxiety and instability in the larger ideological formation in which English teaching is implicated and in terms of which it is best understood. In order to provide some insight into what is involved here, I want to provide a brief account of what I see as the 'Growth Model' perspective on literature and literary education. [62]

One way of viewing the project of Growth Model theorizing overall is to recognize that in many ways it is defined by a general commitment to the notion of *agency*. This is to be understood expressly within the terms of an argument developed in certain contemporary forms of (neo-Marxist) social theory. [63] In this argument, 'agency' is seen in contrast to 'structure' as an organizing and explanatory principle. In essence, what may be called the discourse of agency valorizes human experience and action ('production'), while the discourse of structure puts its emphasis on the manner in which human beings are acted upon so as to ensure the maintenance and consolidation of the existing social order ('reproduction'); one is, so the argument runs, a 'humanist' or 'culturalist' position, the other is 'structuralist'. [64] In the case of Growth Model theorizing, perhaps the most striking expression of this commitment lies in its espousal of a particular notion of *authorship*. This is not to be seen naively as a kind of literary biographism, nor is it strictly speaking a matter of 'poetics' in the first instance; rather, it is to be seen in terms of a general emphasis on *writing*. Allen refers specifically to 'Britton's stress on literature as writing' [65] and clearly a similar claim might be made with reference to James Moffett, the other of the two chief architects of the 'Growth' paradigm. In itself such a view is, at best, limited and partial. However, it does indicate what I believe is an important and distinctive feature of the Growth Model position with regard to the question of literature: its commitment to the notion of *process*. [66] One manifestation of this concerns most directly matters of pedagogy and involves its emphasis on *learning*. My view is that Growth Model theorizing provides a basis for thinking constructively about literary education with specific regard to the socially-critical task of cultural production as it might be realized in and through pedagogy. Another clearly related manifestation of this process perspective, however, is to be located in its focus on *writing*.

Raymond Williams has noted that one consequence of that still dominant view of literature as at one and the same time both an objective entity (or body of entities) and, paradoxically, an 'immediate living experience', is what can be described as a reification of literary work. This involves among other things a refusal of the *compositional* dimension:

The very process that is specific, that of actual composition, has effectively disappeared or has been displaced to an interval and time-serving procedure in which writing of this kind is genuinely believed to be (however many questions are then begged) 'immediate living experience' itself. [67]

Clearly there are problems in this kind of formulation. [68] The relevant point here, however, concerns what I see as a convergence between this as an argument in literary and cultural scholarship and the Growth Model position generally. It is worth noting in this respect that Britton's personal project may be seen as emerging out of the *literacy* aspect of English curriculum, his first major publication being a book on grammar, and certainly a major thrust of his most influential work has concerned writing within the larger context of literacy and learning. This emphasis on writing *need* not in any way mean either a refusal or even a slighting of literature, as some have suggested. Indeed, Britton has commented rather bemusedly, in response to such criticisms, that his own inclinations have always been towards a strong commitment to literature in education (and also in 'life'). [69] Similarly, Nancy Martin has noted that

> in the pedagogical writing about English teaching since Dartmouth, a myth has grown up that the 'growth model' of English takes no account of literature ... that part [of the Darmouth programme] which articulates the notion of a universe of discourse in which one of the uses of language — and a highly significant one — is literature has not been assimilated, it has, in fact, been quite overlooked, so that many people think it isn't there. [70]

Two points can be made here, very briefly. Firstly, one should not overlook the likelihood that it has been, in part, a *strategic* decision by the mainstream in Growth Model theorizing to focus on 'writing' rather than 'literature'. Interestingly, one commentator notes this as a possibility only to downplay and finally dismiss its possible significance: 'the full contribution of literature, received achievement, was not as fully endorsed, its use not so fully encouraged. Was it assumed that literature was sufficiently entrenched to look after itself?' [71] Secondly, such an argument as Allen presents here is structured by what is in effect an illicit and unnecessary polarization (*literature: literacy*); it rests upon a fundamental misunderstanding of the interrelation and interpenetration of 'literature' and 'literacy', both conceptually and institutionally, in the formulation of subject English. [72] It seems to me that a (constructive) recuperation of the Growth Model's project in this regard would be to see it as effectively, if often tacitly, refusing this kind of polarization. This is not to deny the contradictory nature of its enterprise nor is it to exaggerate its self-understandings in this matter. But it is to suggest that the situation is far more complex than either the criticisms allow or curriculum discussion so far has been able to recognize.

Perhaps the most important point to consider here concerns what appears a decisive foregrounding of the notion of (cultural) production. This is what is at issue in Williams' explorations of 'literature' as a concept; and similarly the notion of *authorship* in Growth Model thinking involves, as I see it, a radical commitment to the idea of cultural production and to the problems and possibilities of its pedagogical realization. James Moffett's[73] deliberate use of the term 'authoring' is significant here in its binding together of the *authentic* practice of writing ('composing'), agency and authority. It is not only writing (as 'composition') that is in question however, but also reading, conceived specifically as *production*. This includes the development of a view of reading as writing — or rather, of a pedagogy which seeks to realize readings in and through the practice of writing.[74] The more general political implications of such developments are clear. What is not as clear is the very emphatic challenge that they present, in my view, to the category of literature as it has been traditionally conceived. The semantic shift is important: from 'product' to 'process'; from 'literature' to 'reading' and 'writing' ('reading-writing'). This then is part of the radical implication of the Growth Model project for literary studies and literary education: it represents an attempted 'recovery' of the productivity of literary practice, specifically in the context of curriculum.

This is not to suggest, however, that this project is free of problems of its own; quite the contrary. I have suggested elsewhere that, for all its important and undeniable advances, it remains intensely problematical not only in the neo-Arnoldian echoes of its rather ambiguous attitude towards 'art', but also in its commitment to a largely uncritical, *essentialist* 'response' paradigm.[75] 'Literature' as such is still largely taken-for-granted, serving as a pre-existent category with a 'natural' and enduring referent, authorized and underwritten by the Real. This commitment on the level of a governing 'poetics' is in turn realized on the level of classroom practice in, among other things, a significant ambivalence with regard to pedagogic authority and the category of 'experience'. Part of the problem here is what may well be a necessary *non*-correspondence among the structural elements of 'poetics', 'politics' and 'pedagogy' making up any given project of literary education. In this regard, I would suggest that the specific contribution of the Growth Model project is to be observed in the realm of pedagogy, although clearly it cannot be seen exclusively in these terms. Indeed, in the larger perspective, its advances in one sphere are to be explicitly related to, and contrasted with, its problems and dilemmas in other spheres. My point is that this is to be seen as an indication of its *contradictory* nature, as a site of significant ideological tension.

What must be recognized, then, is that while there is conflict on one level between parties and positions represented in this discussion, on another, more abstract level they share both an allegiance and a general consensus and speak from a common ideological position. This is not to gloss over their differences, which are real and significant enough; rather, it is to locate their respective discourses in certain quite specific conditions of possibility which by and large they share. Each works upon the basis of a deep-seated investment in a particular kind of what has been described here as *literary ideology*, which contextualizes them and structures both their understandings and their action.[76] Both, in differing ways, are to be understood in the final analysis in relation to the operations and effects of a certain '*techne* of self', that is, a general moral technology. In this regard, Hunter's observation of what he calls 'the unstable transition from the regulation of norms to the regulation of images',[77] in terms of which moral regulation is achieved 'by allowing images to be adjusted in relation to "experience" rather than via the imposition of norms',[78] has in my view a striking pertinence to recent developments in English curriculum, as has King's historical account of '"English" as a field of infinite and intimate self-correction'.[79] There are clearly significant continuities, as well as disjunctions and real developments, to be observed in the movement from Newbolt to Bullock, and also beyond.

All the same, I would argue that Britton and his associates, and others within the Growth Model or English-as-Language paradigm, do offer an important reworking of the ideological formation that is in question here, a *re*-articulation that certainly merits serious attention. Their challenge to 'Literature', although limited in the final analysis, nonetheless is progressive, as is their focus on writing. Clearly then, the debate within the culture of English teaching between those associated broadly with 'language' and those who identify with 'literature' very much involves a struggle over meaning and hence is a striking instance in itself of cultural politics.

Against the Grain — or, How Practical is the Political?

A further instance of 'division' within English teaching, relevant specifically to this present discussion, involves taking into consideration its implications for classroom practice. The danger exists, once again, that there is a sharp disjunction, a chasm, between what is being proposed on the level of theory and what happens, and what is possible, on the level of classrooms — in practice.[80] Just as importantly, there is obviously a need to consider not only where interventions might most productively be made but also where energy and attention need to be directed. Given the persistence in classrooms of the more 'traditional' paradigms (despite the dominance of what Ball[81] calls the 'socio-linguistic paradigm' on the level of policy), it is of particular urgency to consider right from the outset the practical feasibility of a critical pedagogy, one which is realized actively as practical theory and links up coherently with a reconceptualized view of English teaching and literary education within the framework of what has been described as the socially-critical curriculum.[82] It may be that there are significant structural and institutional factors on the level of teachers' work[83] and the lived experience of classrooms that work specifically *against* the radical proposals concerning literature and discourse which are in question here. The point to consider then would be: How is it that the discourse of English teaching, however reconceptualized, is necessarily subsumed within the larger, more inclusive discourse of curriculum so as to further the general ideological project of schooling? Put simply, we need to consider what is *possible* in the present circumstances, as well as what is desirable.

To begin with, it needs to be asked, very directly, *How practical is the political?* This is a question which needs to be taken very seriously indeed. It touches specifically on the conditions of ordinary classroom life and on teachers' *experience*. As many classroom teachers can readily testify, it is often hard enough getting students to *read* literature at all, let alone contemplate its 'deconstruction'. And when they do read, often the teaching task is seen then as getting them to read 'properly', which is construed in most instances both as *re*-reading and as close attention to 'the words on the page'. It seems that teaching literature *can* become a more or less technical matter of developing 'text-attack' skills in a manner analogous to much earlier literacy teaching with its emphasis on 'word-attack' skills, with often similar results and effects. That it *doesn't*, in many classrooms at least, is ample and eloquent testimony to the mindful efforts of English teachers actively engaged, whether they know it or not, in the critical-ideological work of meaning-production.

But such efforts, significant as they are, can be circumscribed or else rendered more or less 'impotent' on other levels if that is all that is going on, and if English teaching remains locked into what can be described as a structure-agency dualism. Positioned in this way, there may well be, in real terms, little room for manoeuvre and perhaps at best merely local and regional 'spaces' and 'escapes'.[84] A pessimistic scenario, granted; but only if — and this is my point — English teaching remains locked into a logic and a theoretical perspective which, *despite itself*, actively sets limits on what is possible. This is not to underestimate the difficulties, which obviously are considerable. But it is to claim that a socially critical stance, informed by the arguments presented in this paper, is more than merely a pipe-dream.

With regard to classroom practice, the critique offered here of the category 'literature' involves not only *reading* against the grain but also *teaching* against the grain.[85] There is an important sense in which taking a critical stance such as is implied and advocated here means acting, as it were, 'unnaturally'; it means making trouble for oneself and for others.[86] In the usual view of things, 'critical' reading and teaching is contrasted with 'natural' reading and teaching, so that the former is seen as adjunctive at best and at worst antithetical to the 'natural' stance. But this of course is to ignore the fact that the so-called 'natural' mode — naked, unadorned reading and teaching — is, except in certain privileged circumstances, a difficult and fraught business. If it were a straightforward matter of simply doing what comes naturally, then our teaching of literature and of reading would be by and large a smooth and untrammelled affair. But it is not like that, and literature teaching in the context of English curriculum is arguably in a state of crisis, one which is likely only to deepen. Part of the problem is certainly the 'system' and the very recalcitrance of the world teachers find themselves in, in the ideological climate of the late 1980s. But part is located in English teaching itself and in the discourse that structures its practice, and hence produces us as 'subjects', teachers and students alike. As Garth Boomer[87] asserts in another context: 'Teachers teach most profoundly what they are at the core.'

Consequently we might well ask, *How political is the practical?* What is it in English teachers' current practice and their current understandings (their 'constructs') that contributes to the glossing of social divisiveness as 'second nature'? How do we, in moving with the flow of things in the course of managing the complexity of life in classrooms, become, as it were, accomplices in our own and others' oppression? More specifically, how is the divisiveness at the very heart of the concept 'literature' actively (re)produced in our everyday practice?

Three points I want to make here, and that must suffice for the moment; clearly it is a matter of urgency which must be addressed, however, as soon and as actively as possible, *despite* its complexity and its difficulty. The first concerns an argument developed by Valerie Walkerdine[88] in the specific context of mathematics learning and nursery children, involving what I would describe as a discourse-theoretical perspective on curriculum. This argument has some interesting implications for literature teaching. Given that literary curriculum typically involves a specific set of social relations and social practices predicated on certain ideological assumptions, and *not* on natural laws and axioms, it follows that immersion in other forms of discourse is possible. The first step consists in recognizing and accepting that reading practices are always both *learned* and *socio-historically determined*. There is never, at any level of schooling, a first-order, 'natural' reading practice which then becomes the basis for higher-order and possibly more 'critical' forms of reading. For instance, 'practical criticism', as it is called, is far from the mere formalization of a technique for close reading, understood as a disciplined attention to text. It is, rather, a highly elaborate mechanism for producing certain kinds of reading effects, including a distinctive form of reader-positioning, and hence a quite specific reader-subject.[89] There are, of course, analogous practices in early literacy curriculum.

My second point leads directly on from this and involves an assertion that the realm of 'the practical' must be understood as coinciding, at every point, with the realm of 'the ideological'. Practical dilemmas in, for instance, the teaching of aesthetic reading, in Louise Rosenblatt's sense,[90] always have an ideological dimension. Similarly, ideological dilemmas always involve practical decisions and problems. For instance, Ian Reid's proposals for re-thinking literary curriculum in accordance with the principles of *integration* and *interaction*[91] clearly represent a significant challenge to much English teaching as it is currently practised, presenting considerable practical difficulties for English teachers in the ordinary classroom situation. To a very real extent it requires that English teaching, specifically with regard to literary education, proceed very much *against the grain.* How this is to be reconciled with the institutional nature of compulsory mass schooling, particularly as that is realized on the level of teachers' *experience,* is, to say the least, unclear. What is clear is that a start must be made somewhere, however 'imperfect' and 'impure' it might be; there is no use in sitting back and waiting for the Millennium, or even a change in government. A critical pedagogy begins in the classroom, preferably in a situation where collaboration and collective action are actively encouraged, not only among students but among teachers as well. Although the task is far from simple, qualitatively different social relations and social practices must be encouraged and even, if necessary, institutionalized. In this regard, progressive forms of English teaching might well work towards a properly critical theorization of the notion of *classroom regime,*[92] and seek to incorporate it in a practical-theory of English curriculum.

Thirdly, the pedagogic difficulties associated with recent appraisals of the category 'literature' should not be underestimated. This is what tends to happen, I believe, when the debate works on the assumption that classrooms are merely the site of application of theory. What needs to be grasped, however, is that there are important institutional and material conditions for current-traditional practices in English teaching. The ideological practices of 'commentary', 'authorship' and 'disciplinary enquiry' (i.e. *proper* enquiry), which Foucault[93] draws attention to as principles of constraint and control with regard to discourse and meaning, enable English teaching to perform its historical-cultural task as 'an apparatus of moral training "linked to" a highly specific governmental technology and rationality'.[94] The classroom has its own specificity, its own regional autonomy; it is also, and has been so historically, *functional* in the larger project of social discipline.

Literary-educational critiques of the concept of 'authorship', for instance, informed by poststructuralist scholarship, which fail to theorize the problem of the classroom or else tend to see it merely in terms of application, miss the point.[95] Linked as it is to a particular notion of textuality, the concept among other things enables teachers to manage the complexity of classrooms and also, by extension, 'master' the (subversive) flow of textuality conceived as 'free-play'.[96] This has wider social implications and a manifestly political import. It means recognizing, specifically in English teaching, text-based pedagogy as a social management strategy. Calls for the profession to move away from current-traditional principles of pedagogic authority can only generate conflict and cause division, if they are cast *simply* in 'the language of critique' and not also in 'the language of possibility'.[97] The point is, the category 'literature' has served quite specific purposes in the social practice of English teaching, and these need to be investigated and accounted for if there is to be any real advance in furthering the cause of critical-democratic schooling. This is not something to be achieved merely by exhorting teachers to 'lift their game'.

To conclude this section: my point is that the category 'literature' is clearly divisive in its effects, on a number of levels. In this case, the conflict is between those who work with a critical notion of the literary and perceive 'literature' as itself a *problem* and those for whom literature is more a *resource* to be worked with and from, towards a more or less critical engagement with 'experience'. It is not, however, simply the case that the difficulty lies less in literature itself than in how it is conceived in the context of curriculum. In the latter view, the problem is largely one of 'bad teaching'. I have endeavoured to argue that the distinction in itself is, strictly speaking, untenable. Given then that English teaching is constituted in a particular relationship to literary ideology as presented in this discussion, there is little wonder that recent challenges to and reformulations of the ideological formation that is in question here are perceived as, in a very exact sense, *scandalous*. No wonder also that the profession generally is so 'divided' in this regard.

Conclusion

Following Gramsci, it is useful to speak of *contradiction* in the constitution of subjectivity and hence in the realms of consciousness and identity. English teaching is, as I have argued, intimately involved in the production of dispositions, attitudes, sensibility and perception, as well as quite specific capacities. In the seminar of conscience, the student reads (and hence writes) him or herself, a process which is at first mediated by the moral-therapeutic presence of the teacher, a model figure as well as a Model Reader, to appropriate Eco's[98] phrase, but increasingly it is taken over by the student and accepted as a sign of active autonomy. In this way, the student is constructed as a certain kind of (authorized) individuality: a 'subject'.

But clearly this is to overstate the case, and in doing so, to fall victim to the rigid and doctrinaire logic of the reproduction thesis. More specifically, it denies human activity, creativity, resistance and production. Human beings are not only structured and positioned by the discourses that traverse them; they also, using the resources available to them in and through those discourses, assert their presence and announce themselves, their *agency*. The process of 'subjectification', in the various senses of that word, is never preordained and must in every instance be fought out and struggled over. The task is one of moving *within* structures, *against* structures, in what Connell[99] describes as 'invention within limits', in the course of which the possibility may present itself of moving *beyond* these present limits.

It is in this sense that English teaching is to be regarded as an instance of cultural politics, with a dynamic interplay of progressive and reactionary elements. The ideological work that is conducted in and through the discourse of English teaching is never monolithic or homogeneous; rather, it is contradictory and shifting, although always overdetermined by the organizing logic of the dominant cultural bloc. If it *is* the case that one can speak of the constitution of subjectivity in and through English teaching, in the micro-processes of the classroom as well as on other levels of activity, including textbook publishing, research and policy, then it is important to recognize this as complex, contested and contradictory. It is a process which is in every sense on-going, as an event in time which at once changes and endures, in a constant dialectic of sameness and difference. In this respect, it is absolutely imperative not to lose sight of the fact that Foucault's notion of 'dividing practice' is not to be seen in automatically pejorative terms; rather, it has a positive and productive dimension, actively producing new forms of subjectivity and hence new knowledges and new forms of human possibility. In the case of English teaching, what is required is, firstly, a recognition of its character as ideology, and secondly, a concerted attempt, at every level, to seize upon its progressive and utopian elements and organize them into a coherent counter-hegemonic discourse.

Literature, therefore, is not simply a resource for curriculum but, in an important sense, an instance of curriculum in itself. Hence, what is done in the classroom, in working with literature, is crucially important; teachers may either help secure the intermeshing of the discourses of literature and curriculum in such a way as to amplify the effects of the ideological communication of schooling, or they may work actively against the grain so as to allow for the expression of critical and emancipatory meanings. In this sense, (English) classroom practice is emphatically a site of cultural politics, and the interface between literary education and English teaching is an exemplary instance of ideological struggle. As such, it warrants further critical-sociological investigation.

Notes

An earlier version of this paper was presented at the Fourth International Conference on the Teaching of English, Carleton University, Ottawa, Canada, 11–16 May 1986.

1 I am using the phrase 'cultural politics' here to refer to the process of ideological struggle generally, understood however quite specifically in terms of textual practice. For a succinct account, see BATSLEER, J. *et al.* (1985) *Rewriting English*, London, Methuen.

2 GREEN, B. (1986) 'Reading Reproduction Theory: On the Ideology-and-Education debate', *Discourse: Australian Journal of Educational Studies,*. Vol. 6, No. 2, April, pp. 1–31.

3 RABINOW, P. (1984) 'Introduction', in RABINOW, P. (Ed.), *The Foucault Reader*, New York, Pantheon Books, p. 11.

4 FOUCAULT, M. (1982) 'The Subject and Power', in DREYFUS, H.L. and RABINOW, P. (Eds), *Michel Foucault: Beyond Structuralism and Hermeneutics*, Brighton, Harvester Press, p. 212.

5 HUNTER, I. (1984a) 'Literary Discipline', *Southern Review*, Vol. 17, No. 2, July, pp. 129–34.

6 KING, N. (1987) '"The Teacher Must Exist Before the Pupil': The Newbolt Report on the Teaching of English in England, 1921', *Literature and History*, Vol. 13, No. 1, pp. 14–37.

7 FOUCAULT, *op. cit.*, p. 208.

8 BALL, S. (1985) 'English for the English since 1906', in GOODSON, I. (Ed.), *Social Histories of the Secondary Curriculum: Subjects for Study*, Lewes, Falmer Press, pp. 53–88.

9 Cf. Dixon (1967/75): 'The premature sense of failure in a divisive school can only prepare pupils for a divided society.' Against this is posed 'the unstreamed or unsorted school' and the principle of 'heterogeneity', itself 'an issue that has divided [English] teachers in the past' — something presumably transcended in the post-Dartmouth era; in DIXON, J. (1967/75) *Growth Through English*, 3rd Edn, Oxford, Oxford University Press, p. 102.

10 GREEN, B. (1988) 'Literature as Curriculum Frame: A Critical Perspective', in HART, K. (Ed.) *Shifting Frames: English/Literature/Writing*, Typereader Publications No. 2, Victoria (Aust.), Centre for Studies in Literary Education, Deakin University, pp. 46–71.

11 ROSEN, H. (1981) *Neither Bleak House nor Liberty Hall: English in the Curriculum*, London, Institute of Education, London University, p. 4.

12 BARNES, DOUGLAS and BARNES, DOROTHY, (1984) *Versions of English*, London, Heinemann Educational Books (with Stephen Clarke).

13 ROSEN, *op. cit.*, p. 5.

14 DIXON, *op. cit.*

15 BALL, S. (1987) 'Relations, Structures and Conditions in Curriculum Change: A Political History of English Teaching 1970–1985', in GOODSON, I. (Ed.), *International Perspectives in Curriculum History*, London, Croom Helm, pp. 17–45.

16 KING, *op. cit.*, p. 23.

17 O'SULLIVAN, T. *et. al.* (1983) *Key Concepts in Communication*, London, Methuen, p. 116.

18 FROW, J. (1985) 'Discourse and Power', *Economy and Society*, Vol. 14, No. 2, pp. 193–214.

19 A similar move, for different reasons, is made in: HUNTER, I. (1987) 'Culture, Education and English: Building "the Principal Scene of the Real Life of Children"', *Economy and Society*, Vol. 16, No. 4, pp. 568–88.

20   REID, I. (1984) *The Making of Literature*, Adelaide, Australian Association for the Teaching of English, p. 6.

21   EAGLETON, T. (1983) *Literary Theory: An Introduction*, London, Blackwell; BENNETT, T. (1985) 'Really Useless "Knowledge": A Political Critique of Aesthetics', *Thesis Eleven*, No. 12, pp. 28–52.

22   BALDICK, C. (1983) *The Social Mission of English Criticism 1848–1932*, Oxford, Clarendon Press, p. 3.

23   See also: SMART, B. (1983) *Foucault, Marxism and Critique*, London, Routledge and Kegan Paul.

24   DONALD, J. (1982) 'Language, Literacy and Schooling', *Unit 29: The State and Popular Culture (1)*, Open University Press, pp. 42–74; DONALD, J. (1983), 'How Illiteracy Become a Problem (And Literacy Stopped being One)', *Boston University Journal of Education*, Vol. 165, No. 1, pp. 12–34.

25   DONALD (1982), *ibid.*, p. 43.

26   *Ibid.*, p. 47.

27   *Ibid.*, p. 46.

28   A difficult and problematical concept which is currently being deployed with particular enthusiasm, and which can be linked up in interesting ways, I believe, with notions of educational crisis and 'conservative restoration'. See: HIRSCH, E.D. (1987) *Cultural Literacy: What Every American Needs to Know*, Boston, Houghton Mifflin; also: SHOR, I. (1985) *Culture Wars: School and Society in the Conservation Restoration 1969–1984*, Boston, Routledge and Kegan Paul.

29   BISSERET, N. (1979) *Education, Class Language and Ideology*, London, Routledge and Kegan Paul.

30   DONALD (1983), *op. cit.*

31   WILLIAMS, R. (1977) *Marxism and Literature*, Oxford, Oxford University Press, p. 45.

32   *Ibid.*, p. 45.

33   DAVIES, T. (1981) 'Education, Ideology and Literature' in BENNETT, T. *et. al.*, (Eds.) *Culture, Ideology and Social Process*, London, Open University Press, pp. 251–60.

34   *Ibid.*, p. 253.

35   FOUCAULT, M. (1977) *Discipline and Punish*, Harmondsworth, Penguin Books; SMART (1983) *op. cit.*

36   BALIBAR, R. (1983) 'National Language, Education, Literature', in BARKER, F. *et. al.*, *The Politics of Theory*, Colchester, University of Essex, pp. 134–47.

37   GROSSMAN, L. (1974) 'Literary Education and Democracy', in MACKSEY, R. (Ed.), *Velocities of Change*, Baltimore, The Johns Hopkins University Press, pp. 3–31.

38   DAVIES (1981) *op. cit.*, p. 257.

39   BALL (1983), *op. cit.*

40   BATSLEER *et. al.*, (1985), *op. cit.*

41   DAVIES (1981), *op. cit.*, p. 258.

42   BOURDIEU, P. and PASSERON, J.C. (1977) *Reproduction in Education, Society and Culture*, London, Sage.

43   DAVIES (1981), *op. cit.*, p. 257.

44   EAGLETON, T. (1985/6) 'The Subject of Literature', *Cultural Critique*, Vol. 2, pp. 95–104.

45   *Ibid.*

46 He has referred elsewhere to the *utopian* dimensions of literary practice, but has certainly not sought to elaborate on this side of his argument to any great extent: EAGLETON, T. (1981) 'The End of Criticism', *Southern Review*, Vol. 14, No. 2, pp. 99–106.

47 MOUFFE, C. (1979) 'Hegemony and Ideology in Gramsci', in MOUFFE, C. (Ed.), *Gramsci and Marxist Theory*, London, Routledge and Kegan Paul, p. 187.

48 FOUCAULT (1977) *op. cit.*; FOUCAULT, M. (1980) *Power/Knowledge: Selected Interviews and Other Writings 1972–1977* (edited by Colin Gordon), Sussex, The Harvester Press. See also: DONALD, J. (1985), 'Beacons of the Future: Schooling, Subjection and Subjectification', in BEECHEY, V. and DONALD, J. (Eds.), *Subjectivity and Social Relations*, Milton Keynes, Open University Press, pp. 214–49.

49 HUNTER (1984a) *op. cit.*

50 See REID, I. (1984), *op. cit.*

51 BALL (1985), *op. cit.*

52 BALL, S. and LACEY, C. (1980) 'Subject Disciplines as The Opportunity for Group Action: A Measured Critique of Subject Sub-Cultures', in WOODS, P. (Ed.), *Teacher Strategies*, London, Croom Helm, pp. 149–77.

53 PIPER, K. (1983) *Curriculum Style and English Language*, Victoria, ACER, Hawthorn.

54 BEYNON, J. *et al.* (1983) 'The Politics of Discrimination: Media Studies in English Teaching, *English in Education*, Vol. 17, No. 3, Autumn, pp. 3–14.

55 BALL (1987), *op. cit.*

56 ALLEN, D. (1980) *English Teaching Since 1965: How Much Growth?* London, Heinemann Educational Books; WHITEHEAD, F. (1976) 'Stunting the Growth', *The Use of English*, Vol. 27, pp. 11–17; WHITEHEAD, F. (1978) 'What's the Use, Indeed?', *The Use of English*, Vol. 28, pp. 15–22; INGLIS, F. (1975) *Ideology and the Imagination*, Cambridge, Cambridge University Press.

57 WHITEHEAD (1978), *Ibid.*, p. 15.

58 *Ibid.*, p. 22.

59 Cited in ALLEN (1980), *op. cit.*, p. 67.

60 ALLEN (1980), *Ibid.*, p. 67.

61 *Ibid.*, p. 111.

62 DIXON (1967/75), *op. cit.*

63 GREEN, B. (1986), *op. cit.*

64 GIROUX, H. (1983) *Theory and Resistance in Education: A Pedagogy for the Opposition*, Massachusetts, Bergin and Garvey.

65 ALLEN (1980), *op. cit.*, p. 38.

66 See WILLIAMS, R. (n.d.) *Writing in Society*, London, Verso Editions.

67 WILLIAMS (1977), *op. cit.*, p. 67.

68 One of which is certainly the fact that Williams' project is itself to be seen within the framework of culturalist Marxism, as is exemplified here in what might be described as his 'productivist' stance.

69 BRITTON, J. (1982) *Prospect and Retrospect: Selected Essays of James Britton* (edited by Gordon Pradl), Montclair, N.J., Boynton/Cook, p. 211.

70 MARTIN, N. (1983) *Mostly About Writing*, Montclair, N.J., Boynton/Cook, p. 43.

71 ALLEN (1980), *op. cit.*, p. 64.

72 GREEN (1988), *op. cit.*

73 MOFFETT, J. (1981) *Coming On Center: English Education in Evolution*, Montclair, N.J., Boynton/Cook.

74 CORCORAN, B. and EVANS, E. (Eds) (1987) *Readers, Texts, Teachers*, Montclair, N.J., Boynton/Cook; ADAMS, P. (1983) 'Responding to Literature: What Kinds of Writing?' in BROWN, L. *et al.*, *A Single Impulse: Developing Responses to Literature*, Education Department of South Australia, pp. 35–67.

75 GREEN, B. (1984) 'Yes, but ... "A Single Impulse"' (review-article), *English In Australia*, No. 68, June, pp. 60–6.

76 I have developed this argument in greater detail elsewhere; see Green, (1988), *op. cit.*

77 HUNTER, I. (1984b) 'Laughter and Warmth: Sex Education in Victorian Secondary Schools', in BOTSMAN, P. and HARLEY, R. (Eds), *Sex, Politics and Representation*, Local Consumption, Series 5 (Sydney), p. 72.

78 *Ibid.*, p. 73.

79 KING (1987), *op. cit.*

80 BALL (1987), *op. cit.*

81 BALL (1985), *op. cit.*

82 KEMMIS, S., COLE, P. and SUGGETT, D. (1983) *Orientations to Curriculum and Transition: Towards the Socially-Critical School*, Victoria (Aust.), Victorian Institute of Secondary Education.

83 CONNELL, B. (1985) *Teachers' Work*, Sydney, George Allen and Unwin.

84 See, for instance: MEDWAY, P. (1980) *Finding A Language*, Surrey, Chameleon Books.

85 BOOMER, G. (1988) 'Teaching Against the Grain', in GREEN, B. (Ed.), *Metaphors and Meanings: Essays on English Teaching by Garth Boomer*, Adelaide, Australian Association for the Teaching of English.

86 LEMKE, J.L. (1984) 'Making Trouble', in LEMKE, J.L. *Semiotics and Education*, Toronto Semiotics Circle, University of Toronto.

87 BOOMER, G. (1988) 'Struggling in English', in Green (Ed.), *op. cit.*

88 WALKERDINE, V. (1982) 'From Context to Text: A Psychosemiotic Approach to Abstract Thought', in BEVERIDGE, M. (Ed.), *Children Thinking Through Language*, London, Edward Arnold, pp. 129–55.

89 BOWEN, J. (1987) 'Practical Criticism, Critical Practice: I.A. Richards and the Discipline of "English"', *Literature and History*, Vol. 13, No. 1, pp. 77–94.

90 ROSENBLATT, L. (1982) 'The Literary Transaction: Evocation and Response', *Theory Into Practice*, Vol. 21, No. 4, Autumn, pp. 268–77.

91 REID (1984), *op. cit.*, p. 9.

92 I use this phrase in a sense drawn from Foucault (1980), *op. cit.* and BOOMER, G. (1983) *Towards a Science of English Teaching*, paper delivered at the National Conference of the Canadian Council for the Teaching of English, Montreal, May.

93 FOUCAULT, M. (1981) 'The Order of Discourse', in YOUNG, R. (Ed.), *Untying the Text: A Post-Structuralist Reader*, London, Routledge and Kegan Paul, pp. 48–78.

94 HUNTER, I. (1987), *op. cit.*

95 For example: REID (1984), *op. cit.*; GILBERT, P. (1988), 'Authorship and Creativity in the Classroom: Re-reading the Traditional Frames', in HART, K. (Ed.), *Shifting Frames: English/Literature/Writing*, Victoria (Aust.), Typereader Publications No. 2, Centre for Studies in Literary Education, Deakin University, pp. 24–39. Not that either of these figures is unaware of problems and difficulties in this regard; indeed, Reid's book, albeit brief, is something of a manual for progressive literature teaching.

96 CROWLEY, S. (1986) 'writing and Writing', in ATKINS, G.D. and JOHNSON, M.L. (Eds), *Writing and Reading Differently: Deconstruction and the Teaching of Composition and Literature*, Lawrence, Kansas, University Press of Kansas, pp. 93–100.

97 GIROUX (1983) *op. cit.*

98 ECO, U. (1979) *The Role of the Reader: Explorations in the Semiotics of Texts*, Bloomington, Indiana University Press.

99 CONNELL, B. (1983) *Which Way Is Up? Essays on Class, Sex and Culture*, Sydney, George Allen and Unwin.

Chapter 5

The Ideology and Politics of English Grammar: An 1894 Newfoundland Example

Laurence Walker, University of Lethbridge

Abstract

An English grammar examination conducted in Newfoundland in 1894 is used as a focal point for an interpretation of grammar teaching as an expression of curriculum ideologies and group interests. By the end of the nineteenth century a complex and abstract body of propositions about the structure of language had been elevated to the status of worthwhile and necessary knowledge for teaching and evaluation, placing experience of formal grammar above other kinds of experience with the mother tongue in the curriculum of English studies. The sources of this elevation in curriculum-relevant ideologies of learning and language, and in class interests, are presented. Their influence on the pedagogical discourse of English studies since the mid-nineteenth century is illustrated from the Newfoundland record, with wider reference to the Canadian context which the British colony joined constitutionally in 1949. The exercise suggests that the proclamation of grammar's role as a basic in the curriculum serves, innocently or wilfully, purposes other than the effective use of the mother tongue.

Introduction

Time moves and the angle of incidence of the light shifts; the audience perceives a different kind of truth.[1]

Grammar is not a difficult study. However, we must keep our wits about us.[2]

On Monday 25 June 1894 at 2.30 in the afternoon in the Colony of Newfoundland candidates for the Junior Grade[3] examination in English

Grammar, who were required to be at least 12 years of age, turned over their papers and began to answer the following questions:

1 Define: Adjective, Gender, Imperative Mood, Syntax.
3 Parse every word in the following sentence: 'To do this properly requires time.'
4 How are the Past Tense and the Past Participles formed in (a) Strong Verbs, (b) Weak Verbs? Give the Past Tense and Past Participle of : find, catch, rub, drive, sing, think, bless, hang, mean.
5 Analyse:
(a) Here shall be done a deed of dreadful note.
(b) I told you all that an hour ago.
6 Correct the following sentences, giving your reasons: -
(a) Either he or I are at fault.
(b) Let you and I take a walk.
(c) It is not me who say so.[4]

When that ordeal had ended at 4.30 p.m., candidates had a fifteen-minute break before returning to the examination room to write a composition. Candidates had to choose one of four topics, the narrative choice being 'William of Orange's second (successful) attempt to land in England', with an eight-point outline provided to guide the candidates in organizing their essay.[5]

1894 was the first year of operation for the Colony's new Council of Higher Education, set up by the government to prescribe syllabuses and textbooks and to organize examinations for Newfoundland secondary schools in an attempt to bring some uniformity to the curriculum offered by diverse denominational schools by 'focus [ing] the learning and culture' of different schools (Andrews, 1985a, p. 21) and providing standards to guide teachers, students and the public. The Council had been the brainchild of Brother Slattery, a teacher with the Irish Christian Brothers, a religious order which operated schools in the colony (Burke, 1975). He had won the $100 prize offered by the Colonial Government for the best essay addressing the problems of education in Newfoundland, and the government enacted legislation to implement his proposals. The Council contracted with the Joint Examining Board of Cambridge and London Universities for the setting and marking of the examinations. This contract was later switched to the College of Preceptors, an affiliate of London University. This British connection, perhaps, accounts for a 1912 composition topic: 'O! to be in England, Now that April's there.'[6]

The 1894 Grammar paper was similar to those set for that general age level in any of the provinces or territories of Canada at the end of the nineteenth century. With a British examining board setting the questions, it is hardly surprising that the grammatical knowledge demanded by the Newfoundland examination was also of the same kind taught and examined in British schools at that time (Shayer, 1971, pp. 19–24). In terms of

Laurence Walker

English studies, knowledge of the formal grammar of the language was assumed to be an important part of the answer to the curriculum question of what knowledge is of most worth. The worth of grammar in the eyes of the Newfoundland Council of Higher Education was shown by the number of marks allocated to its study in the syllabus it drew up for the junior grade studies. English Grammar was grouped with spelling and composition. Out of a total of 700 marks for this paper, 150 were for grammatical definitions, classifications and accidence (inflections), 100 were for elementary syntax, 100 for easy parsing, and 50 were for analysis of easy sentences, leaving only 300 marks for spelling and composition. Interestingly, English literature was grouped with geography and was worth 300 marks.[7] Clearly English had not yet emerged as a well defined school subject, and grammar was the predominant component of the loose aggregation of topics related to English studies.

As a commonplace of the time, in the sense of an assumption that was taken for granted in the world view of educators and the educated, the ability to define grammatical terms, to parse words, and to analyse sentences, all based in a complex body of propositional information about language forms and structure, was secure in the discourse of education in the late nineteenth century. Four main sources for this security can be identified: grammar's particular contribution to a curriculum based in a mental discipline theory of learning; its role as a guardian of linguistic propriety within a fundamentalist conception of language; its status as a prerequisite for language use within a theory-into-practice epistemology of language learning; and, in a political sense, its compatibility with certain explicit and implicit group interests.

Grammar's Role in a Mental Discipline Theory of Learning

Although the year 1894 saw the publication in the United States of the report of the Committee of Ten which defined English as a school subject rather than as a collection of separate subjects, and which emphasized the development of reasoning as the prime focus of the curriculum, mental discipline was the dominant theory of learning that controlled what was taught in schools in the 1890s. Faculty psychology saw the human mind as consisting of a hierarchy of several faculties such as memory, reason, will, imagination and conscience. A mentally fit person was one in whom all the faculties were well developed. Consequently a good education was achieved through the selection of those subjects which were well suited to the strengthening of particular faculties. Grammar, sometimes called 'the logic of the common schools',[8] was particularly well suited, as a complex but systematic and coherent classification of knowledge about language, to the exercise of the memory and the reason. Lennie's Grammar, for example, a widely used textbook in the Canadian provinces and territories

164

into the 1880s, and referred to in the Newfoundland record (Burke, 1975), reflected a mental discipline approach. It divided grammar into the four traditional classifications of Orthography, Etymology, Syntax and Prosody, from which proliferated a steep hierarchy of sub-categories of parts of speech, inflections, rules and structural elements, all to be memorized. For example, after defining the preposition, Lennie listed, in alphabetical order, 62 prepositions 'to be got accurately by heart' (1869, p. 50). That at least one teacher made sure his pupils did 'get' them accurately is attested by Agnes Dean Cameron's 1902 recollection of her schooling in Victoria thirty years earlier:

> Lennie's Grammar was a more indirect good as old Mr. Scottinger expounded it. His method was very simple. We learned the book of holus-bolus from preface to postscript, rules, examples, fine print, footnotes, with a large contempt for the claims of any one part to paramount importance. The reasoning was very plain: grammar is the science which teaches us to read, write, and speak the English language correctly. If we learned all the grammar there was, could we miss it? Hold up any of the boys and girls of that school at midnight on a lonely highway with, 'Name the prepositions!', and out of the darkness will come 'About, above, according to, around, at, athwart, before, behind, below, beyond, by, concerning, down, during, except, excepting, for, from, in, into, instead of, etc.' ... Ask him for the example of the pluperfect tense, and you will learn that 'All the judges had taken their place before Sir Roger came.' (Cameron, 1902, p. 137)

Memorization was likely endemic in the teaching and learning of grammar in Newfoundland in 1894. The Examiners' Report on the Junior Grade grammar examination for that year included the comment that although the average of marks had been fairly high, the favourable impression produced had to be modified by 'the consideration that a considerable proportion of the marks was gained by mere memory work; the questions which involved thought were not, on the whole, so well done'.[9]

However, already in the 1890s faculty psychology and mental discipline were under attack as James, and later Thorndike, reported negative results in their experimental studies of the transfer effects of learning (Kleibard, 1986, p. 106). The Social Efficiency movement was proposing a radically different basis for the curriculum. Scientific analysis of society's needs and of the individual's abilities replaced the notion of general mental faculties with lists of precise and functional objectives. Knowledge was now to be judged on the basis of its direct relevance and utility. The rationale for grammar teaching had to be changed from a humanist belief in its general disciplinary value to claims for its explanatory power in helping students discriminate and justify approved language forms. Several changes in school grammar sprang from this shift, and these changes are reflected in the Newfoundland record. First of all English studies began to show a closer relationship between grammar and composition, the latter being the 'proper edifice and crown, of which Grammar, Spelling and Word Building are but the base and scaffolding'.[10] This epistemology had been reflected in advice to teachers from the examiners in 1915 'that the grammar be regarded as a practical help in the expression of human thoughts and ideas, not as a set of rules for solving a more or less arbitrary puzzle'.[11] This functional perspective was also represented in the recommendation on the English curriculum for grades 1 through 8 brought forward in 1934 by the Commission of Enquiry into the Curriculum. 'Only the minimum essentials of formal grammar should be taught', it said, 'and these for practical utility and not as a formal exercise' (in Andrews, 1985a, p. 171). The second change was a reduction in the sheer amount of grammar to be learned as only those terms and rules that illuminated errors revealed in pupils' usage or by surveys of general usage could be justified on functional grounds. By 1916 the English grammar examinations in Newfoundland at the Primary (grade 6) and Preliminary (grades 7 and 8) Levels were beginning to have fewer questions of a purely formal nature, and items were appearing requiring the manipulation of language according to grammatical instructions, for example, turning statements using given words as particular parts of speech. However, in spite of the growth of a more functional approach to curriculum, rituals from the older formal study of grammar survived in the form of parsing questions which lasted until the early 1930s and in the form of clause analysis questions which endured until 1970, although the test material for clausal analysis changed from complex and sometimes lofty prose or poetry selections to easier single sentences. For example, the examiners reported that the passage they had chosen for analysis for the grade 9 examination in 1934 was easy. Perhaps they meant easy to analyse because it is not easy to understand. The passage was:

> When I came to my castle, I fled into it like one pursued; whether I went over by the ladder or went in at the hole which I called a door, I cannot remember; for never frightened have fled to cover with more terror of mind than I to this retreat.[12]

In contrast, the equivalent question in 1936 required candidates to 'pick out each of the subordinate clauses and show how each clause is related to some word in some other clause' from a short selection of poetry, considered by the examiners to be difficult:

> 'Tis a common proof
> That lowliness is young Ambition's ladder
> Whereto the climber upwards turns his face;
> But when he once attains the utmost round,

He then unto the ladder turns his back,
Looks into the clouds, scorning the base degrees
By which he did ascend.[13]

Four years later clausal analysis was a much simpler task, even for grade 11 students (the grade 9 external examination had been abolished in 1937). On the grade 11 English Language paper, candidates were required to give a general analysis of only a single sentence: 'One day I met a strange-looking man who asked whether I could tell him about an old house where he had lived when he was a boy.'[14]

In documenting changes in the prevailing ideology of curriculum insofar as these changes affected grammar teaching, it is necessary to distinguish between changes in the official discourse — syllabuses, official policy statements, and examination reports — and changes in actual classroom teaching. As Patterson (1986) cautioned, the influence of Progressive Education in Canada in the 1930s and 40s was more apparent in the thinking of department of education officials than in the practice of classroom teachers.

For example, complaints about memorization remained a constant theme in the reports on the Newfoundland English Language examinations for many years after 1894, showing that the legacy of faculty psychology and mental discipline survived in classroom practice in spite of its official demise. In 1901 the examiner complained that in the Primary Level grammar paper there had been 'meaningless reproduction of what had evidently been committed to memory without being understood'.[15] In 1915 the report on the Primary Level English grammar paper noted that in the answers 'terms were used and matter given which could hardly have been understood at this (Grade 6) stage'.[16] Sixteen years later the grade 7 and 8 examiner noted that 'Hundreds gave a good definition of gerund and then proceeded to name all the six words in the passage, with -ing ending, as gerunds.'[17] In 1934 a comment showed that memorization also played a part in composition at the grade 9 level: 'In a few cases essays were written that had been learnt by heart', the subject being 'A Winter Landscape'.[18] The examiner also noted, rather triumphantly, that 'a group of very pretentious essays on 'A Shipwreck', all with the same wording, were discounted accordingly'.[19]

Of course, it was not just a matter of residual survival of older ideologies that preserved memorization as a learning method. Poorly trained teachers, lack of proper facilities, and overcrowded one-room schools, characteristic of schooling in Newfoundland and Canada in the early part of the twentieth century, made reform difficult to implement. Moreover, the very examination system that was designed to raise and maintain educational standards served to coerce teachers and students into a programme of instruction that emphasized preparation for examinations rather than learning. This was an especially severe inhibiting factor in

Newfoundland education. This was made apparent in 1933 in a report by a British school inspector who had been commissioned to advise on education in the Colony. The Council of Higher Education's examination system had been in operation for forty years, and the number of levels of external examinations had been increased from the original two to as many as seven covering grades 6 to 12. In 1932 the setting and marking of examinations had been moved from Britain to the Common Examining Board of the Maritime Provinces and Newfoundland (Andews, 1985a, p. 142). In his report, Inspector Richardson spoke of the 'profound influence' of the examination system. 'Every child', he said, 'is regarded at any rate through the greater part of his school life as a potential examination candidate', and is put through 'the same machine irrespective of his individual qualities and capacities', the curriculum machine being 'predominantly of a formal and artificial nature'. He noted also that public opinion tends to judge schools and teachers by examination results (in Andrews, 1985a, p. 164). Since it was the practice in Newfoundland to publish the results of these public examinations in the newspapers, candidates being listed in order of marks obtained, there was a particular piognancy to Richardson's final comment.

Richardson noted a special inappropriateness about the examination-driven curriculum in Newfoundland. Whereas in Britain the examination syllabuses were used in secondary schools, which only 10 per cent of children over 11 years of age attended — presumably the most able selection — in the Colony the formal, abstract programme was used for all older children attending school (Andrews, 1985a, p. 166). There is some retroactive explanation in this comparison for the examiners' rather tautological comment on the Primary Level grammar examination in 1900 'The paper set appears to have been beyond the capabilities of the candidates. This is to be regretted because otherwise they would undoubtedly have acquitted themselves better than they have done.'[20]

A Fundamentalist Ideology of Language

There is an interesting parallel between the predominant nineteenth-century conception of language and a twentieth-century religious ideology that clarifies the power of the prevailing ideology of language in the final decade of the last century. A fundamentalist stance on religion asserts that truth, or reality, lies outside or beyond human experience, as some other-worldly, unwavering, absolute set of laws and precepts. These are abiding, unchanging, and dependable for all time. They are available to people in certain written works in which God's will is revealed through words that were divinely inspired. Fundamentalist Christians, for example, believe in the 'inerrancy' of Scripture, especially in the verbal form of the King James version. Being 'God-breathed', it has the 'quality of being free from error in all its statements and affirmations' (Falwell, 1981, p. 8). Preaching, in this fundamentalist tradition, is more a matter of reiteration than of asking after the meanings on which belief is based (Barr, 1966, p. 203).

A relevant characteristic of Christian fundamentalism, as noted by Barr (1966), is that it is in radical opposition to the general culture (p. 203). The target that fundamentalists denounce is that pervasive ideology referred to as 'secular humanism' which elevates transient human values over abiding spiritual ones, and which locates goodness and creativity in the person rather than in some external, divine source (Ramm, 1974, p. 235). As Brubacher (1986) wrote: 'whereas formerly humans were seen in relation to the world that defined them, now the world is seen in relation to humans, deriving its meaning from them' (p. 293). The opposition between these two cosmologies is reflected in the twentieth-century curriculum debate on whether language learning in school is a matter of mastering an external body of authoritative knowledge or whether it is the nurture of an internal developmental process grounded in the individual learner's experience. A fundamentalist position on language — sometimes referred to as the classical view (Lloyd-Jones, 1972) — such as prevailed as the major assumption of school instruction in English in the late 1800s would say that there exists outside human beings a body of rules and definitions that are stable and fixed. These definitions and rules establish the true forms of language (Standard English, for example). They define the language world that individuals seek to enter, and they can be enshrined in authoritative textbooks. Fries (1927) pointed out the parallel between religious and linguistic authority in his discussion of the character of school grammar texts:

> Although the present-day popular views of grammar do not, in medieval fashion, find 'divine inspiration in the eight parts of speech' and veiled references to the Trinity in the 'three persons of verbal conjugation', yet they do look upon the rules of the common school grammars as the infallible measure of correct language, and the one defence against the forces of corruption that continually beset it. (p. 221).

The moral certainty that linguistic fundamentalism gave to the traditional teaching of grammar is hard to recapitulate from a modern perspective, influenced by more pluralistic, 'secular humanist' theories, which assert the central role of the individual in the reconstruction of language out of personal experience in the making of meaning, and which accept the authentic variability of language forms in the service of variable functions, relationships and communities. In the 1890s, linguistic propriety was a singular doctrine, and, in accordance with the wider academic curriculum of the time, it was external to the individual child. Grammar was a body of knowledge that had to be mastered as a prerequisite to proper speaking and writing upon which, together with polite manners and an approved religion, depended full participation in respectable society.

Propriety in speech and writing has been a Canadian preoccupation for a long time, and Fries's (1927) reference to grammar instruction as a defence against the forces of linguistic corruption would have been approved by many generations of Canadians. From the beginnings of public schooling in the Maritime Provinces, for example, school officials frequently complained about the poor quality of spoken language used by both teachers and pupils. In 1845 the Prince Edward Island School Visitors (inspectors) criticized teachers who habitually spoke poor English themselves and who allowed their pupils to display 'indistinctness of articulation and vulgar and provincial dialects'.[21] This concern that teachers be better models of correct English usage was reflected in the 1851 by-laws of the Durham, Nova Scotia, Teachers' Association. After the statement that the object of the Association was to hear papers presented by members, another by-law maintained that it was the duty of members to criticize 'in a constructive spirit' any errors of pronunciation and grammar that they noted in the presentations. Fines were specified for members who were derelict in their duty.[22]

A firm belief in an absolute and singular external standard of language was demonstrated by the Reverend C. Geike's 1857 address to the Canadian Institute on the subject of the deterioration of Canadian English. His main argument was that neologisms were rampant in English as it was spoken and written in North America and that these represented unnecessary deviations from the standard established by British usage. For example, he noted that in England, 'beef is hung, gates are hung, and curtains are hung, but felons are hanged; in Canada, felons, beef, gates and curtains, are all treated in the same way'.[23] The term 'Canadian English', Geike complained, is 'expressive of a corrupt dialect growing up amongst our population, and gradually finding access to our periodical literature, until it threatens to produce a language as unlike our noble mother tongue as the negro patua [sic], or the Chinese pidgeon English'.[24] He suggested that common school teachers should correct children under their care, 'whenever they utter slang or corrupt English, not only in the school, but in the playground, and on the streets'.[25]

The clergyman's words must have gone unheeded by the general course of usage development in Canada. Writing at about the time of the First World War, in the preface to a book of language drills, Ryerson Press Editor, Lorne Pierce, launched a vehement attack on the general standard of spoken language in North America: 'The standard of everyday speech in Canada and the United States surely must be the worst in the civilized world. The unmusical huffle, the slurred, strident, ill-bred cackle of most people is hard to bear, but the accompanying vulgarisms make conversation a travesty upon culture.'[26] As late as 1940, a Canadian provincial curriculum guide was referring to children's 'vicious language habits' as justification for teaching proper language forms.[27]

If the teaching of formal grammar was assumed to be a necessary part of the defence of the mother tongue against the corrosions of the colonial vernaculars in Canada, in Newfoundland it was a vital instrument in an urgent task. The Colony's isolation from the mainstream of spoken and literary English (Story, 1957), and the individual isolation of its coastal fishing communities, had produced a pattern of spoken English that, in spite of local geographical variations, constituted an identifiable Newfoundland dialect. Patterson (1896) noted the survival of older forms of English that dated from the original settlements. He wrote '... the rude speech of the unlettered fishermen was really part of the language of Shakespeare, Milton, and Chaucer' (p. 67). However, the prestige of the sources of the dialect has not, at least until recently, done much to offset the sense in Newfoundlanders that their language was inferior to that of other English speakers. Perhaps this feeling of linguistic inferiority was part of the general lack of confidence in native ability that the Superintendent of Church of England Schools referred to in his 1893 comments about the new Council of Higher Education. 'I am hopeful', the Rev. Canon William Pilot wrote, 'that this new endeavour will lead to a greater and more rapid growth of knowledge, and help create a wider sympathy for native talent, and lessen that tendency to its depreciation that is so essentially colonial' (in Andrews, 1985a, p. 21).

It is unlikely that linguistic self-confidence among Newfoundland pupils was enhanced by the authoritarian teaching of the formal system and rules of Standard English as though it were a second language with little in common with local usage. From time to time the external examiners reported recurring provincialisms in the Newfoundland papers as mistakes, apparently unwilling to accord the dialect any status as a systematic variety of English. In 1913, for example, in the report on the Preliminary composition paper, they noted that 'it was a common provincialism to speak of "securing" fish with salt where the English word is to "cure". "Trouting", though easily understood, is not usually found in an English dictionary.'[28] Frequently noted was what the examiners called a lack of agreement between subject and verb, 'a marked tendency to use the third person singular regardless of the number and person of the subject'.[29] This comment reveals the failure of the Mainland examiners to realize that what they called a 'lack of agreement' was simply a different rule of agreement in the Newfoundland dialect. In that dialect speech the 's' inflection is added to each present tense form regardless of person or number, to produce, for example, 'I eats, you eats, he eats, we eats', etc. Dialect variation in the use of past tense and participial forms caused irritation on the parts of examiners too. In 1950, for example, the examiners noted that on the grade 11 English Language paper 'the most glaring grammatical errors consisted of using past tenses for past participles and vice versa'.[30]

The low status accorded to dialect by Newfoundland curriculum developers was revealed in the 1940 *Handbook to the Course of Study: English*.[31] Under 'Idiom', which was defined as 'the right way of phrasing things as generally agreed upon by English speaking people', the Handbook noted that: 'Wait while (for till) he comes — We stopped off at Halifax — Mother lives inside Long Pond — are respectively good Yorkshire, good American and good Newfoundland, but all bad English.'[32]

There is a sense of the bludgeoning effect of grammar teaching within the hegemony of Standard English over local patterns of speech in an unwitting comment by the 1939 grade 11 examiner for English Language. After complaining about the poor stylistic quality of the essays, he wrote: 'the conversations of the average student are not without wit, and certainly do have a freshness of viewpoint. Why must the pupil lose these when he takes up his pen? After all, essays are but written chats between author and reader.'[33] The same failure, from a fundamentalist position on language, to understand the nature of dialect is shown in the 'Catch-22' admonition to pupils that appeared year after year on the English Language paper that in using dialogue in the narrative option for the composition they should use speech that was 'natural, but not incorrect or ungrammatical'.

There is no doubt that instruction in grammar was seen as part of the campaign to rid written work at least of the vestiges of dialect and impose the singular authority of Standard English. In 1954 the grade 9 examiner allowed himself an indignant outburst about what he saw as the effects of a decline in grammar teaching in Newfoundland schools. This indignation was perhaps encouraged by an official repudiation in Canada of progressive education principles after the end of the Second World War as part of a conservative reaction culminating in the 1953 publication of Hilda Neatby's vigorous attack on progressive education, *So Little for the Mind*. The examiner quoted from an editorial in Newfoundland's major newspaper, the *St. John's Evening Telegram*, in which the editorial writer had alleged that the teaching of grammar had been cut back to the mere identification of the parts of speech. The editorial went on:

> This is a crime. An atrocity. Language is one of the greatest achievements of mankind. The English language is one of the greatest and noblest of the languages of either past or present. To deny children an opportunity for scientific insight into its structure is to deny them a fundamental part of our heritage.[34]

To this claim of cultural deprivation, the examiner then added his conviction that 'since so much depends on knowing the fundamentals of English grammar, teachers should give it more attention. In ordinary conversation or in the written composition, correct English can only be used if the user has a thorough knowledge of the rules of grammar.'[35]

A marked contrast with this authoritarian fundamentalism in language teaching is provided by a brief outbreak of linguistic romanticism in a 1971 examination paper. By this time Newfoundland had been a Canadian province for twenty-two years, examination patterns had undergone several changes, and papers were now set and marked in Newfoundland itself. Optional question 4 on the grade 11 General English Language paper was as follows:

> Presented below is a somewhat difficult situation and four alternative ways of handling it. Try to decide why each alternative might have been chosen. Then describe the reason for each choice.
>
> A man asks you and two friends to volunteer for a church project. One friend replies, 'I don't got not time for that stuff.' The second says, 'I don't got no time either.' Then the man asks you. Why might you reply in each of the following ways? (That is for each choice, give in a couple of sentences what your reasoning might be.)
>
> (a) I don't got no time either.
> (b) I'm sorry but I don't have the time.
> (c) Sorry, but I ain't got the time.
> (d) I would most assuredly like to assist your worthy cause but other commitments prevent my affiliation at this time. [36]

This question seems to have been more creative than successful. The Readers' Report noted that only a small number of students had attempted the question. It had been well handled except that some candidates had been confused about what was really expected and attempted to correct the sentences in terms of good or bad English. [37] Even the Chief Reader was moved to comment that this question had detracted from the otherwise high quality of the examination as 'most students who answered the question had not the slightest notion of what was wanted as an answer'. [38] Although in subsequent years the English Language papers continued a focus on usage rather than formal grammar, setters avoided creative questions such as number 4.

In spite of its psychometric shortcomings, question 4 is interesting because it was obviously based in a very different ideology of language from that which gave rise to traditional grammar questions involving parsing and analysis and to usage questions requiring correction of grammatical errors. The issue that the question asked candidates to address is the relationship between language and its context and the way language adapts itself to situation, topic, social relationships and function, producing not the notion of linguistic correctness in the fundamenalist sense but the sociolinguistic principle of appropriateness of language form in particular social contexts. Replacing the single, all-purpose norm is the notion of levels of usage, or registers of language. It seems to be assumed that worthwhile knowledge about language is no longer limited to formal categories and rules but has been extended to include conventions of social use that affect language as a flexible communication system. It is interesting to note from the Readers' comments that some candidates had tried to interpret the question in terms of the older, normative ideology. External examinations do not easily breach ideological boundaries.

Epistemology of Language Learning

The 1894 grammar paper in Newfoundland rested on two assumptions about language learning: the first that language use depended upon prior mastery of information about language, or a theory-into-practice epistemology; and the second that the most useful information (or the only information) to be mastered was a body of propositional knowledge about language forms. From a modern, more pluralistic perspective, it is hard to appreciate the weight of these two commonplaces on the late nineteenth-century curriculum. Twentieth-century philosophy has separated propositional and procedural knowledge (Ryle, 1949; Scheffler, 1965). Twentieth-century research, it is widely accepted, has shown that the teaching of propositions about language does not transfer to the procedural use of language (Braddock *et al.*, 1963; Elley *et al.*, 1976); and twentieth-century experiential theories of language learning have been proclaimed and successfully implemented on at least a minor scale. In addition, the modern educational consciousness is aware that theory and practice have made available to curriculum planners alternative kinds of information about language: information about the relationships between words and their meanings — semantics, incorporated into, for example, the Province of Alberta's junior high school English language arts curriculum in 1954;[39] information about language as a communication system, affecting programmes in the late 1970s; information about the psychological processes of language development — psycholinguistics, influential in language research and programmes in the 1960s and 70s; and information about the social uses of language — sociolinguistics, salient in contemporary thinking about language and language teaching.

Although the propositional curriculum for English studies was in the ascendancy in classrooms in the 1890s, the educational discourse of the time was not unanimous in support of the theory-into-practice epistemology of language learning. In fact opposition to it in a general philosophical sense had a long history. Groome (1980), in a discussion of religious education, identified two broad epistemological positions that have confronted each other throughout the history of Western education. One is the experiential position on knowledge and learning which asserts that knowledge exists in the act of knowing, in the experiencing and the doing; the other is the objective view of knowledge that sees it as a commodity or as information that exists outside the knower as theory and that permits and leads to practice. The first, according to Groome (1980), can be traced from the Old Testament view of knowing God through living a good life in obedience to his word. Commenius, Locke, Rousseau, Pestalozzi, Froebel, Herbart and Dewey were heirs to that experiential philosophy. The second comes from the Greeks with their emphasis on contemplative knowing, passed on through Aquinas, Luther and Descartes.

With specific regard to English studies, since the 1870s and the formation of the Froebel Society in Britain, there had been a growing interest in the application of experiential curriculum ideas to language teaching in British schools (Mathieson, 1975, p. 57). Recommendations that composition could start with children's own lives and experiences rather than with grammar exercises, and that interest and creativity were more important than mental exercise were even finding their way into official British Department of Education documents by the 1890s Mathieson, 1975, p. 58). The same ideas had been applied in the United States by innovative teachers such as Colonel Francis Parker of Massachusetts in the 1870s, including, for example, the replacement of formal grammar exercises by natural language activities such as letter writing (Kleibard, 1986, p. 42).

There was evidence that these child-centred ideas had penetrated some of the provincial educational establishments in Canada by the 1890s. In Nova Scotia, for example, the 1888 report of the Supervisor of Schools in Halifax recommended that formal grammar instruction be delayed until grade 8 and that language growth before that level should be fostered by a curriculum that emphasized 'conversations in which the pupils take part, descriptions by them in their own words of what they observe, and frequent written abstracts of their lessons in History and the Science of Common Things' (in Wood, 1979–80, p. 18). However, these ideas appear to have had little impact on the classroom experience of young Nova Scotians. Wood (1979–80) cited poorly trained teachers, conservatism in the general population on matters of schooling, and conflict between child-centred and utilitarian branches of the educational reform movement in the province as reasons for the robust survival of the traditional theory-into-practice English language arts curriculum until at least the programme revisions of 1932 (p. 21).

In Newfoundland evidence of any shift away from the traditional theory-into-practice curriculum to an experiential epistemology is hard to find in the first half of the twentieth century. The system of external examinations, that 'monster which made curriculum development at levels under its influence virtually impossible' (Andrews, 1985b, p. 334), helped to preserve the teaching of English as information because it was so much easier to examine mastery of information than to test development of procedural language abilities. When, by the 1970s, English examinations were attempting to measure students' use of language as readers and writers, there was much controversy about the extent to which such examinations could be based on precise curriculum objectives and about the difficulties students experienced as they tried to review the year's work in preparation for the tests.[40]

Educational reform which influenced the curriculum of all Canadian provinces in the 1930s under the loose umbrella term, 'progressive education', introduced, to some extent, the language of the experiential English curriculum into Newfoundland. A strong statement, for example, appeared in the 1940 *Handbook to the Course of Study: English*. 'Language is a medium for the expression of one's self. English curricula, therefore, must provide much flexibility based upon the individual pupil's environment, experiences, vocational and avocational interests.'[41] However, that ringing assertion was offset by the lengthy section on grammar teaching in the grades 7 and 8 section. In spite of exhortations to teach the functions rather than the forms of grammatical units, and recommendations to follow a scientific, inductive sequence, the content to be taught remained bulky, traditional and examinable. In addition there was in the document a great preoccupation at each grade level with the importance of removing error from pupils' speech and writing. It seems as though, as in the case of other Canadian jurisdictions at the time (Patterson, 1986), the Newfoundland Department of Education, in its embrace of progressive ideas, flinched from a genuine endorsement of experience as a valid basis for language learning.

English Grammar and Curriculum Politics

From a complacement point of view, the school curriculum comprises that knowledge and those skills that are of the most worth in terms of the goals of education and in terms of the developmental nature of children. The assumed authoritative status of the wider pool of knowledge from which curriculum content can be drawn reflects its derivation and verification by standard procedures within the scholarly and applied disciplines. Other than in its selection and in its methods of presentation, the intrinsic validity of knowledge, in this naive view, is not open to question. However, the Cartesian duality of mind and world, separating the knowing subject from the object of knowing and thereby permitting notions of the objectivity of knowledge, is now widely challenged, even as applied to the natural sciences (Geertz, 1964, pp. 39–40; Gutting, 1980, p. 1). An alternative epistemology, following Wittgenstein, Heidegger and Dewey (Rorty, 1979), proposes a reality and knowledge of it that are culturally formed and pluralistic. A compelling version of this argument is that realities are constituted through our symbolic representations, principally language (Williams, 1979; Frow, 1986), and that these 'cultural worlds' reflect tensions and struggles among different groups and interests in society. As

Kress and Hodge (1979) wrote, 'in its use by a speaker language ... is a version of the world, offered to, imposed on, exacted by someone else' (p. 9). This epistemology gives issues of the school curriculum a new dimension. The question of what knowledge is of most worth becomes mixed up with the question of whose knowledge is of most worth, and the curriculum, no longer a neutral selection from objective knowledge, becomes an issue of cultural politics. In Apple's (1979) words, 'The knowledge that gets into schools ... is a form of cultural capital that ... often reflects the perspectives of powerful segments of our social collectivity' (p. 8). This amounts to the claim that the school curriculum is ideological in that what is taught is influenced by particular dominant worldviews that represent and support, innocently or wilfully, certain relationships of power in society.

To the extent that this view of the general curriculum has validity, it may provide a helpful explanation of the pre-eminence of grammar in the late nineteenth-century teaching of English studies. Morgan (1987), denying that English as a school subject is either simply a 'set of neutral processes, techniques, or skills' or a '"power of articulateness" acquired through a critical exposure to the ... masterpieces of English literature' (p. 1), maintained that the 'culture of English teaching ... has always been the site for the promotion of some experiences over others, some kinds of identity over others ...' (p. 6). Standard English, or so-called propriety in speech and writing, which grammar teaching was assumed to develop, could be considered as a kind of 'experience' or 'identity' in Morgan's terms, which schools sought to legitimate at the expense of other more local, more colloquial, more vernacular forms of language experiences and identities.

The curriculum assessed by the 1894 grammar examination in Newfoundland might then be considered as support for some interests in Newfoundland society. However, before looking at the issue in terms of Newfoundland society, it must be remembered that the island colony was by no means an educational island. Thinly populated, poor in resources, and consisting of small, isolated communities strung along an immense coastline, Newfoundland's educational ideas and systems were largely imported until at least the middle of the twentieth century. The denominational school systems were created by churchmen from England and Ireland, and it was to England that the Council on Higher Education looked for the setting and marking of its examinations until the 1930s, when those tasks were organized from Nova Scotia. Nova Scotia also provided the model for Newfoundland's major curriculum revision in 1934. Consequently any political factors operating in Newfoundland's English studies curriculum were not home-grown.

Several covert political factors buttressed the explicit rationale for the importation of formal grammar teaching, for its pre-eminence in the loose aggregation of studies that constituted English as a set of school subjects at the end of the nineteenth century, and for the form that its teaching took. One such factor was the attempt to make the study of the mother tongue a respectable academic subject in its own right (Shayer, 1971; Ball, 1985) by basing its content and pedagogy on the more prestigious model of Latin. The tough questions on arcane terms to be defined and English words to be parsed using ill-fitting, Latin-based categories owed something to the struggle to establish English as a reputable part of the school curriculum in competition with the established classical tradition.

The slow growth of English towards unified curriculum status is shown in the titles of the subjects and examinations papers that made up mother-tongue study in Newfoundland after 1894. In the 1890s the different components of mother tongue study had not coalesced into a unified school subject. The term 'English' as a noun did not appear in the syllabuses of that period. 'English' always appeared as an adjective labelling separate papers in English Grammar, English Composition, and English Literature, the latter, as noted earlier, being grouped with Geography. By 1915 the syllabuses were using English as a generic noun, acknowledging the relationship among its different components. By the 1930s English had two sub-categories, Language and Literature. It wasn't until the 1970s that English as a singular subject appeared in the syllabus. Again this status issue was more related to the emergence of an 'English' lobby in British education (Ball, 1985) than to any pressure from within Newfoundland's own teaching profession.

Grammar's second hidden agenda was its contribution to the achievement of that nineteenth-century ambition, respectability. To be considered respectable a person had to follow an approved religion, demonstrate refined manners and taste, and speak and write proper English (Prentice, 1977, p. 68). Any deviation in one of these could undermine a person's status and cause suspicions of more general disrepute associated with the lower orders and their tendency towards illiterate speech, rough manners and criminal dispositions. Thus the elevated language of the nineteenth-century standard was associated with high personal status and, through its civilizing influence, with social stability and the safety of property and the state. The ruling classes, therefore, had a stake in Standard English and in grammar teaching as a way to promote it, just as lower class people did in their aspirations for their children's advancement. Standard speech and successful learning of grammar were, therefore, widely regarded as prerequisites of social advancement.

A third force supporting Grammar as a clearly bounded school subject is revealed by Bernstein's theoretical explorations of the structural relationships among family, school and work (Bernstein, 1973; Atkinson, 1985). Two concepts are significant: classification and framing. Classification refers generally to cultural and symbolic boundaries and may be applied to family types, relationships and roles; to the workplace where job classifications and specializations can be marked; or to the school with its role boundaries and its classification of pupils according to age, gender and ability. Curriculum boundaries divide proper and everyday knowledge, and they define the domains of school subjects as well as the categories of their internal taxonomies of knowledge and skills. Boundaries may be strong or weak. Framing refers to the degree of autonomy permitted in the intersection among participants; for example, the extent to which teachers and pupils are free to decide the content, sequencing and pace of lessons. Strong framing reduces the options. The classification and framing character of a curriculum have message value as a code. A curriculum which has strong classification and framing qualities is called a 'collection' code; a curriculum with weak classification and framing is called an 'integrated' code. These curriculum codes may be continuous or discontinuous with the primary socialization code of the pupil's family and with the code of the workplace or of the institution of higher education to which the pupil aspires. Discontinuity will produce conflict either between school and home or between school and other institutions.

Clearly the traditional, academic curriculum revealed by the 1890s Newfoundland syllabuses, including the strictly bounded and framed aggregation of English subjects, represented a collection code. As such it represented a continuity with the codes of both family and work. On the one hand, families within the predominantly coastal fishing economy were classified on religious and occupational grounds, and roles within families were clearly specified by age and gender. On the other hand, work, for those who would succeed in school — success being unambiguously marked by survival in the examination system — and move out of the primary occupations of the fishery, would also be strongly classified on the industrial model or bounded by the clear middle class status of non-labouring work. In other words, the collection curriculum was well suited to the late nineteenth-century social structure of the Colony, even though, of course, its ideology was wholly imported. At the end of the nineteenth century the colonial government's attempts to diversify the economy by promoting industrial development (Alexander, 1980) was creating a demand for an industrial workforce. The collection curriculum would also have been continuous with the ideology of the Newfoundland middle class which controlled the schools. Bernstein (1973) characterized the ideology, or code, that underlies the socialization patterns of what he called the 'old middle class', oriented to reproduction of the material economic order of society, as one of strong classification and framing to produce specific, unambiguous role identities and relatively inflexible role performances (p. 122). He made the strong claim that 'visible pedagogy' associated with the collection curriculum, had its source in this middle class socialization pattern (p. 122). While the pedagogical roots of grammar as a school subject may be more diverse, its character, as revealed by the Newfoundland examinations, was a perfect fit with Bernstein's concept of the collection curriculum. It had an explicit hierarchical and sequenced content with absolutely clear taxonomic boundaries; it was unequivocal in its prescriptive pronouncements on the boundaries between proper and improper forms of language, and, above all, its preoccupation with language as propositional information allowed for explicit and unambiguous criteria for evaluation. You could memorize the definitions or you couldn't; you could parse the words or you couldn't; you could separate the subordinate clauses from the principal clauses or you couldn't. The evidence was in the examination result published in the newspaper. In other words, the formation and survival of grammar teaching in spite of opposition in the official and explicit discourse of English studies may have been aided and abetted by its compatibility with and support for patterns of relationships and roles in the larger society. Arguments for alternative English studies curriculum, in this view, were faced with a powerful, though largely unseen, adversary.

Conclusion

This historical excursion into the discourse of grammar teaching in the colony and then province of Newfoundland has suggested that what qualifies as approved knowledge in the English studies curriculum is not simply a product of dispassionate, rational inquiry and debate. Logical arguments against the worth of propositional knowledge about language, such as those advanced by the confident official consensus against grammar teaching that prevails in Canadian language arts education today[42] have to contend with the commonplaces and assumptions of ideological commitments to authoritarian, fundamentalist views of language, and to a theory-into-practice conception of language learning and with the implicit influence of political interests. While some of these assumptions may survive only as relics or perhaps penances of extinct paradigms, others are very much alive in both professional and lay convictions that strongly affect practice in the English language arts classroom. There is perhaps some useful clarification in that recognition for the ongoing debate about the efficacy of grammar teaching. Moreover, it is perhaps salutary to acknowledge that just as grammar teaching in 1894 was supported by a complex and covert apparatus of ideological and political commitments, the apparent consensus in 1987 against grammar teaching is also embedded in ideologies and group interests. While some might find that claim unnecessarily provocative (ideologies being what they are), others might find that the interrogation of personal assumptions induces a humility about conviction that could contribute to what Nunberg (1983) called for as 'a return to civil discussion of the problems of grammar and their social importance' (p. 45).

Notes

This chapter is based on a study funded by the Social Sciences and Humanities Research Council of Canada.

1 CONLOGUE, R. 'Hamlet: a man for all seasons'. *Globe and Mail Newspaper*, 22 March 1986. The quotation, attributed to Ralph Berry, was part of the argument that interpretations of the play have changed through the history of its stage presentations.

2 LANG, S.E. (1909) *An Introductory English Grammar*, Toronto, Copp Clark.

3 In 1894 there were two levels of external examinations in the colony, junior for those pupils who had reached their twelfth birthday and senior for those aged at least 16. By the early 1920s the number of levels had increased to seven: Senior Associate (grade 12), Junior Associate (grade 11), Second Year Intermediate (grade 10), First Year Intermediate (grade 9), Second Year Preliminary (grade 8), First Year Preliminary (grade 7), and Primary (grade 6). Thereafter the number of levels began to decrease.

4 Calendar of the Council of Higher Education, Newfoundland, St. John's 1894, p. 107.

5 *Ibid.*

6 Report and Syllabus for 1912 of the Council of Higher Education, Newfoundland, St. John's, 1912, p. 99.

7 Calendar of the Council of Higher Education, Newfoundland, St. John's, 1894, pp. 12–13.

8 Twenty-Third Annual Report of the Public Schools of the Province of British Columbia 1893–94, Victoria, B.C., 1894, p. 183.

9 Calendar of the Council of Higher Education, Newfoundland, St. John's, 1894, p. 96.

10 Report of the Examinations for 1917 of the Council of Higher Education, Newfoundland, St. John's, 1917, p. 4.

11 Report of the Public Schools Under the Church of England Boards for the Year Ended June 30, 1915, St. John's, 1916, p. vii.

12 Report of the Examinations Conducted by the Council of Higher Education, Newfoundland, St. John's, 1934, p. 52.

13 Report of the Examinations Conducted by the Council of Higher Education, Newfoundland, St. John's, 1936, p. 27.

14 Report of the Examinations Conducted by the Council of Higher Education, Newfoundland, St. John's, 1940, p. 51.

15 Calendar of the Council of Higher Education, Newfoundland, St. John's, 1901, p. 60.

16 Report of the Examinations for 1915 of the Council of Higher Education, Newfoundland, St. John's, 1915, p. 9.

17 Report of the Examinations Conducted by the Council of Higher Education, Newfoundland, St. John's, 1931, p. 21.

18 Report of the Examinations Conducted by the Council of Higher Education, Newfoundland, St. John's, 1934, p. 21.

19 *Ibid.*

20 Calendar of the Council of Higher Education, Newfoundland, St. John's, 1900, p. 58.

21 Journal of the Legislative Council of Prince Edward Island, Charlottetown, 1845, p. 13.
22 Report on the Schools of Nova Scotia for the Year 1851 by the Superintendent of Education, Halifax, 1852, p. 63.
23. GEIKE, Rev. A.C. (1857) 'Canadian English', *Journal of Education for Lower Canada*, 1, January, pp. 128–31.
24 *Ibid.*
25 *Ibid.*
26 ARCHIBALD, R.M. dewolfe (1921) *The King's English Drill*, Toronto, Ryerson, p. 3.
27 British Columbia Department of Education, *Programme of Studies for the Elementary School*, Victoria, 1940, p. 81.
28 Report of the Examinations for 1913 of the Council of Higher Education, Newfoundland, St. John's, 1913, p. 14.
29 Report of the Examinations Conducted by the Council of Higher Education, Newfoundland, St. John's, 1948, p. 25.
30 Public Examinations Conducted by the Department of Education, Newfoundland, St John's, 1950, p. 20.
31 Newfoundland Department of Education, *Handbook to the Course of Study: English*, St. John's, 1940.
32 *Ibid.*, p. 145.
33 Report of the Examinations Conducted by the Council of Higher Education, Newfoundland, St. John's, 1939, p. 11.
34 Public Examinations Conducted by the Department of Education, Newfoundland, St. John's, 1954, p. 15.
35 *Ibid.*
36 Public Examinations Conducted by the Department of Education, Newfoundland, St. John's, 1971, p. 9.
37 *Ibid.*, p. 14.
38 *Ibid.*, p. 13.
39 In 1954 the Alberta Department of Education prescribed a new series of textbooks for junior high school English. *Words and Ideas, 1–3*, by H.S. Baker and C. Campbell, included a strong emphasis on semantics.
40 Public Examinations Conducted by the Department of Education, Newfoundland, St. John's, 1975, p. 42.
41 Newfoundland Department of Education, *Handbook to the Course of Study: English*, St. John's, 1940, p. 128.
42 For example, the Canadian Council of Teachers of English passed a motion at its May 1987 annual meeting urging that the teaching of grammar be replaced by activities 'known to foster literacy'.

References

ALEXANDER, D. (1980) 'Newfoundland's traditional economy and development to 1934', in Hiller, J. and Neary, P. (Eds) *Newfoundland in the Nineteenth and Twentieth Centuries: Essays in Interpretation*, Toronto, University of Toronto Press, pp. 17–39.
ANDREWS, R.L. (1985a) *Integration and Other Developments in Newfoundland Education 1915–1949*, St. John's, Harry Cuff Publications.

ANDREWS, R.L. (1985b) *Post-Confederation Developments in Newfoundland Education 1949–1975*, St. John's, Harry Cuff Publications.

APPLE, M. (1979) *Ideology and Curriculum*, London, Routledge and Kegan Paul.

ATKINSON, P. (1985) *Language, Structure and Reproduction: an Introduction to the Sociology of Basil Bernstein*, London, Methuen.

BALL, S. (1985) 'English for the English since 1906', in Goodson, I (Ed.) *Social Histories of the Secondary Curriculum: Subjects for Study*, London and Philadelphia, Falmer Press, pp. 53–88.

BARR, J. (1966) *Old and New in Interpretation: a Study of the Two Testaments*, London, SCM Press.

BERNSTEIN, B. (1973) *Class, Codes and Control (Volume 3)*, London, Routledge and Kegan Paul.

BRADDOCK, R., LLOYD – JONES, R. and SCHOER, L. (1963) *Research in Written Composition*, Champaign, Illinois, National Council of Teachers of English.

BRUBACHER, J. (1986) 'Secular humanism and higher education', *The Educational Forum*, 50, 3, pp. 291–3.

BURKE, L. (1975) 'Some Irish contributors and contributions to Newfoundland education in the last century', M.Litt, Thesis, University of Dublin.

CAMERON, A.D. (1902) 'The old Broughton Street School', *Educational Journal of Western Canada*, 4, 5, pp. 136–7.

ELLEY, W.B., BARHAM, I.H., LAMB, H. and WYLLIE, M. (1976) 'The role of grammar in a secondary school English curriculum', *Research in the Teaching of English*, 10, 1, pp. 5–21.

FALWELL, J. (1981) *The Fundamentalist Phenomenon*, New York, Doubleday.

FRIES, C.C. (1927) 'The Rules of Common School Grammars', *Proceedings of the Modern Languages Association*, 42, pp. 221–37.

FROW, J. (1986) *Marxism and Literary History*, Cambridge, Mass., Harvard University Press.

GEERTZ, C. (1964) 'Ideology as a cultural system', in Apter, D.E. (Ed.) *Ideology and Discontent*, New York, pp. 47–76.

GROOME, T. (1980) *Christian Religious Education: Sharing our Story and Vision*, San Francisco, Harper and Row.

GUTTING, G. (1980) (Ed.) *Paradigms and Revolutions: Appraisals and Applications of Thomas Kuhn's Philosophy of Science*, Notre Dame, Ind., Notre Dame University Press.

KLEIBARD, H. (1986) *The Struggle for the American Curriculum, 1893–1958*, Boston and London, Routledge and Kegan Paul.

KRESS, G. and HODGE, R. (1979) *Language as Ideology*, London, Routledge and Kegan Paul.

LLOYD-JONES, R. (1972) 'Romantic revels — I am not you', *College Composition and Communication*, 23, 3, pp. 251–7.

LENNIE, W. (1869) *The Principles of English Grammar*, Toronto, Adam Miller.

MATHIESON, M. (1975) *The Preachers of Culture: a Study of English and its Teachers*, London, George Allen and Unwin.

MORGAN, B. (1987) 'The Englishness of English teaching', paper presented at the annual conference of the Canadian Society for the Study of Education, Hamilton, Ontario.

NEATBY, H. (1953) *So Little for the Mind*, Toronto, Clarke, Irwin.

NUNBERG, G. (1983) 'The decline of grammar', *Atlantic Monthly*, December, pp. 31–46.

PATTERSON, G. (1896) 'Notes on the Dialect of the People of Newfoundland', *Nova Scotia Institute of Science: Proceedings and Transactions*, 9, pp. 44–78.

PATTERSON, R.S. (1986) 'The implementation of progressive education in Canada, 1930–45', in Kach, N., Maxurek, K., Patterson, R.S. and DeFaveri, I. (Eds) *Essays on Canadian Education*, Calgary Detselig Enterprises, pp. 79–96.

PRENTICE, A. (1977) *The School Promoters: Education and Social Class in Mid-Nineteenth Century Upper Canada*, Toronto, McClelland and Stewart.

RAMM, B. (1974) *A Handbook of Contemporary Theology*, Grand Rapids, Michigan, Eerdmans.

RORTY, R. (1979) *Philosophy and the Mirror of Nature*, Princeton, Princeton University Press.

RYLE, G. (1949) *The Concept of Mind*, New York, Barnes and Nobel.

SCHEFFLER, I. (1965) *Conditions of Knowledge: an Introduction to Epistemology and Education*, Chicago, Scott Foresman.

SHAYER, D. (1972) *The Teaching of English in Schools 1900–1970*, London, Routledge and Kegan Paul.

STORY, G.M. (1957) 'Newfoundland English usage', *Encyclopedia Canadiana*, Vol. 7, Toronot, Grolier of Canada, pp. 321–2.

WILLIAMS, R. (1979) *Politics and Letters: Interviews with the New Left Review*, London, Verso.

WOOD, A. (1979–1980) 'Turn the schoolroom into a workshop: Nova Scotia's New Education initiatives in the language arts, 1888–1910', *Nova Scotia Journal of Education*, 6, 4, pp. 17–22.

Chapter 6

Foreign Language Teaching as an Instrument of Policy in the Cultural and Societal Orientation of a Nation: The Case of English Teaching in Norway

Björg Brandtzaeg Gundem, Institute for Educational Research
University of Oslo

Abstract

The article discusses the development of English teaching and its relation-ship to German teaching in Norwegian elementary and secondary schools from the last century up to the present time. Initially it is argued that the modern language teaching of a nation is linked to its societal, political and cultural orientation, and to its historical development in relation to other nations. The case of modern language teaching in Norway is outlined in this perspective. It is also stressed that the democratization of Norwegian society, with an accompanying emphasis on equality and practical knowl-edge in education, was a decisive factor in the removal of the classical languages from the curriculum at the end of the last century, and that the democratization of the Norwegian school system of the 1960s and 1970s focusing on equal opportunities and equity made possible the present situation in which no other language but English is compulsory in elementary and secondary schooling.

General Discussion

Historical studies of different nations' foreign language teaching pro-grammes may reveal that the teaching of foreign languages is both an inherent part of and a means of promoting a particular cultural and societal orientation. The expressions 'part of' and 'means of' indicate a complex relationship encompassing intentional as well as causal forces as central influences.

These influences affect the ways in which a country relates to particular other nations in cultural matters like literature, art, music and languages, and higher education, as well as in economics and in social and political life. Thus factors like trade, shipping, craft and tourism, in the context of the present-day internationalization of business and trade, have regularly been cited as arguments for programmes in modern language teaching.

Along with these factors social and political ideals have also played a part. The democratization of Norwegian society and the emphasis on equality have without doubt led to a turning away from nations cultivating elitism; countries practising political parliamentarianism have accordingly seemed more attractive than those associated with empire building or Nazism.

The way a nation orients itself in matters of cultural and social life in relation to other nations will certainly be influenced by the history of its relations with those nations. Trade blockades, war and military occupation, for example, leave behind traces that may cause a foreign nation's language to fall out of favour despite the high value which may still be placed on its cultural tradition. Moreover, the way a nation directs itself in matters like culture and social conditions will influence not only which modern languages are chosen, which schools they are taught in and to which pupils, but also the aims and objectives, the content, teaching methods and teaching aids specified by teaching guides and prescribed curricula.

In modern language teaching there may exist a discrepancy of interest between cultural concerns on the one hand and political and economic concerns on the other. The material needs and interests of a modern society may indicate that it is first and foremost practical language skills that are required, stressing the instrumental and not the intrinsic value of the language involved. Communicative skill in, for example, English is in demand without the necessity for an understanding of British institutions and literature. Even where a cultural affinity exists, the pressing situation of modern society requires an emphasis on functional aspects.

Generally speaking the practical aspect of modern language competence has been predominant in our part of the world from the 1950s till the 1970s. Modern language subjects have become instruments to achieve a useful and flexible general education in compliance with the needs of the individual and the demands of modern society. Consequently the traditional content of modern language subjects, such as literary texts and the history and civilization of the country, as well as meaning conveyed through the specific nature of the language involved, has been minimized, neglected or, at best, trivialized.

Historical Perspective

The connection between the development of culture and society on the one hand and the development of language teaching in schools on the other is in Norway probably best illustrated by the rather abrupt and rapid change from classical to modern language teaching at the end of the last century.

The Education Ordinance of 1809 made room for the teaching of the mother tongue and also introduced modern languages as oral subjects in the 'learned school', a secondary school for boys of the upper classes built on a classical curriculum. Modern language teaching failed completely, however, because of the lack of qualified teachers and the looseness of the regulation: 'English' should be taught 'when and where it is possible'. In spite of a rather broad curriculum it was the humanistic emphasis on English civilization and culture and not the practical emphasis on functional communication that dominated.

Thus very little happened until the Education Act of 1869, as a result of which the situation in the secondary schools changed drastically. The fight against classical education and the domination of the schools by the 'dead' languages was fierce. There was enormous strength in this political and cultural revolt built on a national and democratic foundation. Science and modern language teaching were finding their natural places within secondary education. What emerged was a working compromise between 'classicism' and 'realism', in which the teaching of English enjoyed a status subordinate to the teaching of German.

The Education Act of 1896 made things clearer. An account from 1927 explains what happened:

> On 18 June 1896 a decisive battle was fought in the Odelsting (the larger division of the Norwegian Parliament) between the 'Latin school' and 'the non-Latin school'. ... By a majority of 46 against 39 Latin and Greek were abolished as teaching subjects in the secondary schools. The fact that the Lagting (the smaller division of the Norwegian Parliament) on 10 July according to the proposal of the Minister for Church and Education passed an annotation to paragraph 10 smuggling Latin back into some schools through the back door, meant in this connection very little. The interesting fact is that on 18 June 1896 the teaching of classical languages in the higher schools was buried by the Odelsting. ... A national public movement helped by practical life, science and modern linguistics had brought this battle to its happy ending. A growing number of Norwegians had come to look upon the classical languages in secondary schooling as the main hindrance to the development of this school in a national and practical direction. [1]

In the new school system that emerged after the 1896 Education Act, German kept its strong position as the first modern language. It is, however, remarkable that all options for *examen artium*, the final examination necessary for university admittance, included German, English and French as compulsory subjects. The break-through of modern languages in the higher secondary schools was a fact. And it was the emphasis on practical knowledge and a broad liberal education linked to parliamentarism and to a democratic society built on a national foundation that made this break with classical education and the classical languages possible.

Turning to compulsory primary education, to the *folkeskole*, a common school for ages 7–14, we find a similar situation. The demand for foreign language teaching was intensified for reasons to do with craft, trade and shipping. The Education Act of 1889 had ordained foreign language teaching as an optional subject, mainly because teaching programmes of English already existed in elementary schooling, especially on the south coast where trade with England was flourishing. Since the Education Act of 1889 did not say which foreign language was to be taught in the common school, local school boards were free to choose English or German.

So we may say that at the beginning of the twentieth century we have a situation in Norwegian schools where modern language teaching had not only found its place, but even dominated the curriculum. And it was only a beginning. In 1964 a professor of education characterized the curriculum of the Norwegian upper secondary school (the *gymnasium*) as essentially a specialized course in modern language teaching.[2]

Today the situation is different. Articles in professional periodicals reveal frustration with the 'state of the art'.[3] There is especially great concern about the quality and future of second and third foreign language teaching in Norwegian schools.

In the following section the development of foreign language teaching in Norway in the twentieth century, focusing on the relationship between English and German, will be outlined. An attempt will be made to explain the historical development as well as the present situation of English and German as school subjects in Norwegian schools. An objective will be to show how political and social circumstances influence foreign language teaching in a context wider than the mere pedagogical one. It will be argued that this context continues the tradition characterized by the break away from the classical education and classical languages. But now it is the hegemony of two modern languages that is at stake.

The Years Towards the 1930s

Summary

The most important reform in the upper secondary school resulting from the 1896 Education Act was that English became a main subject on the arts side — in the way that Latin was once a central humanistic subject — through its focus on British literature and history. A well known educationalist expressed the humanistic case in this way:

> The fact that the study of texts makes pupils really acquire valuable knowledge, by forcing them, as it were, to penetrate lines of thought with complete comprehension, has made English into a subject that under favourable conditions will do much for the spiritual growth of the pupils. Here it does not suffice to learn by heart. The thought must be acquired and rightly understood ... Language is becoming a servant of the thought.[4]

German, however, had also gained more influence. Before this time German had been a subject taught mainly in the lower grades of the secondary school. Now it became compulsory for *examen artium* regardless of options.

This was a period of reorganization and reform with several school commissions working. Around 1927 a new school structure emerged. All secondary schooling was from now on based on a completed seven-year compulsory elementary education or common school (*folkeskolen*: ages 7–14). The lower secondary school (*realskolen*: ages 14–17) got its own final examination. The *gymnasium* (ages 14–19) leading to *examen artium* became a five year school, divided in the last three years into three 'sides', science, Latin and English, with English, French and German as compulsory subjects in all three.

Even if German had the stronger position (except on the 'English side'), this was the heyday of English teaching in the Norwegian upper secondary school. The Norwegian pupil with English as a main subject had an amazingly thorough and wide knowledge of British history, literature and civilization as well as orthography and grammar. Oral proficiency was, however, wanting.

English or German in the Folkeskole *or Common School?*

The question, 'English or German in the common school?' was a constant dilemma which was continuously debated right from the introduction of a foreign language subject as an option in 1889. Until the end of the 1920s, the problem was solved by letting the local school boards decide. But it was a highly unsatisfactory situation. The different school commissions at work during this period were eager for more stable arrangements, out of consideration for the secondary schools and the common school itself, because of the confusion and loss of time and money created by the present situation.

Studies revealed great discrepancy between the preference expressed by the secondary schools and the elementary or common schools about which language to teach. The first considered German most suitable to their type of school. The latter preferred English because it was of more practical use and pedagogically more easily acquired. Other studies indicated that in towns such as Kristiania (now Oslo), where the pupils could choose between English and German, the greater part of the pupils opted for English. The conclusion was clear:

> There is no doubt that the greater part of our population in the towns and in the rural districts have a greater demand for learning English than German. This is a direct consequence of the geographical position of our country, our foreign connections and our trade. It suffices to mention our shipping and our relationship to America. On the other hand one has to admit that certain parts of our country, where the greater part of our industry is located, will be in favour of German; the same applies to craft. But numbers in the latter areas cannot be compared with those preferring English.[5]

The Education Acts of 1936 introduced English as a part of the ordinary curriculum of the common school. Although it was still an optional subject, being required for entrance to secondary schooling it acquired a special status very unlike the other subjects in the common school.

A factor of great importance in this connection was that a specific education for the training of teachers of English for the common school was established from 1938. Even if the curriculum was academically orientated and not unlike a university course, it contributed not only to a thorough training of teachers of English, but also to the consolidation of the position of English as a subject in the common school.

During the German occupation in the Second World War, English in the common school was in many towns replaced by German. This change did not work out well, mainly because of the unwillingness of teachers to undertake the teaching and because, naturally enough, few teachers in the common school had any formal qualifications for teaching the German language.

Some Main Features of the Period After 1945

English Becomes Compulsory in Elementary Education

Turning to the period immediately after 1945 one of the most important events which consolidated English teaching in the common school was that the Education Act of 1959 ensured that if local communities introduced English as a subject (as nearly all did) then it was compulsory for *all* pupils to take it.

Curriculum Revision as a Consequence of War and Occupation

In the secondary school, the most important event was the curriculum revision that was a direct consequence of war and occupation.

Immediately after the liberation, on 8 September 1945, the Council for Instruction (*undervisningsrådet*) sent a circular to all schools asking for opinions on the present curriculum and proposals for reform. Many proposals were sent in. In foreign language teaching there was a general agreement that German had to concede teaching hours especially to English and, particularly, that students taking science for their final examination, *examen artium*, ought to have their German teaching reduced in favour of English.

Naturally enough there was much discussion. Some people wanted to abolish all German teaching in Norwegian schools once and for all. There would be no need for the German language either in oral communication or in more technological and educational contexts. Others warned against decisions based on emotional reactions due to war and occupation and stressed the cultural heritage the German language represented. Even the problem of teachers of German becoming superfluous entered the debate. A committee working on the revision of examinations proposed that there should be no written examinations in German.

In the end German kept its status as a compulsory second foreign language in the secondary school for all pupils, though substantial reduction in teaching hours gave the subject little chance of thriving.

Developments Towards the 1980s

The Introduction of the nine-year Basic School and Consequences for the English/German Relationship

With the Education Act of 1959 and the 'Experimental Syllabus' (*Laereplan for forsök med 9-årig skole*) which followed shortly afterwards, the structure of the new basic school emerged. The lower secondary school (*realskolen*) disappeared. Consequently the entrance qualifications for the *gymnasium* (higher secondary schooling) changed drastically, as did those for the teaching of foreign languages. How did this affect the relationship between English and German teaching?

It is not difficult to demonstrate that the teaching of English in the new basic school was enormously strengthened. Compulsory English for everybody from the fourth to the ninth year of school was justified in terms of the needs of the individual and the demands of modern society as well as the equality principle. English for everybody became a means towards the democratization of the Norwegian society.

The key to an understanding of this lies in the structure of the 'unbroken' and unstreamed Norwegian compulsory seven-year — now nine-year — common school, a unique phenomenon in Europe from the 1920s to the 1960s. In this undifferentiated elementary school system English was the only subject having an elitist taint and a selective function, being optional, but necessary as an entrance ticket to secondary schooling.[6]

It was consequently very clearly stated in the School Long Term Programme from 1952 of the Norwegian Labour Party, *Arbeiderpartiet*, that a first step to further the democratization of the Norwegian basic compulsory school, as a means towards the democratization of Norwegian society in a social democratic direction, was to make English a compulsory subject for all pupils in that school.

The official legitimation was, however, first and foremost the demand for practical language skills in English:

> The technical expansion that has taken place during the post-war period has made it necessary to make new demands on the teaching of foreign languages. Technical innovations within the area of communication and consequent closer contact with the rest of the world have created a growing demand for practical language skills that can be applied — especially in English.[7]

This quotation from the preliminary draft for the curriculum guidelines of the new basic school is followed by the description of a series of situations that will demand a working knowledge of English by the ordinary Norwegian man and woman. There is a reference also to the recommendations of the Council of Europe for modern language teaching advocating practical language skills.

The effect on the status of German teaching was drastic. It lost its status as a compulsory subject, and French was introduced as an option on equal terms.

The Situation in the Secondary School (the Gymnasium)

In the upper secondary school, on the other hand, it looked for a time as if German would consolidate its status as a compulsory language. The number of teaching hours devoted to it increased, and the 1962 report of the Secondary School Commission strongly advocated a strengthening of all foreign language teaching, including German.

The most decisive event, however, was the appearance of the report from the Commission preparing a new structure for secondary schooling for all youth in the age group 16–19. The role of foreign language teaching was discussed in the first report of 1967.[8]

The structure of the present situation can now be discerned. The key issue was: what kind of foreign language competence should be the target as part of both liberal education and vocational training, and as a basis for further and higher education? The influence of Swedish studies of the demands placed on secondary schooling by industry, the civil service and higher education was explicitly acknowledged. As a consequence English was given first priority in vocational training. English was likewise valued as indispensible for higher education, although German was also part of the picture. It was, however, stated that the distance between French and German was diminishing, and that French might prove to become as important for Norwegians as German had once been.

The Situation Today

German has lost its status as a compulsory subject both in the basic and in the secondary schools. A decisive change took place when it was decided that only English was required as the entrance requirement for secondary schooling and that only one language, English, should be a compulsory language for *examen artium*, the final examination in upper secondary education.

Discussion

Summing Up

The turning point for the status of English and German as school subjects in Norwegian schools came after the Second World War. The reduction of teaching hours and curriculum devoted to German in the higher secondary school indicated particularly clearly that the Norwegian people and the Norwegian education system preferred to look westward and wanted foreign language teaching to contribute to this.

Close contact with Britain and the United States during the war, military alliances like NATO, international organizations like the Council of Europe and the United Nations further strengthened Anglo-Saxon ties.

At the same time the English language emerged, to a degree nobody would have dreamt of, as a world language and as a working international communication tool. Located as it is in a corner of the world, the Norwegian nation depends on English for trade and shipping, industry and travel. These factors make English the obvious choice and reinforce the pragmatic argument when the choice has to be justified politically and educationally.

Other factors that can contribute to explaining this development are bound up with the specific nature of the languages involved, the kind of educational structure being aimed at, and the target pupils.

Foreign Language Teaching as a Means to a Practical Liberal Education

What kind of formation and education does a nation want and for whom? The development of foreign language teaching and especially the English/German relationship in Norwegian education ought to be viewed from this perspective as well.

At the end of the last century when the question of English or German for the common school was raised, English was preferred in the interests of the common school, while German was felt best to serve pupils' continuing education in the secondary school. During the 1930s English won the battle for hegemony in the common elementary school. When German gradually lost its dominance in the secondary school, this was partly due to the democratization of secondary schooling, and indirectly a consequence of the type of formation and education that was sought through the acquisition of foreign language skills. It may be that German as a school subject was too difficult a language for an undifferentiated and unstreamed nine-year basic school, and for a secondary school catering for the greater part of the population of pupils. We do not have to peruse the educational periodicals for long in order to find articles from the 1960s and 1970s indicating the problem: 'Is German so difficult?' and 'German: The Problem Subject' are typical headings.

In Oslo at the beginning of the 1970s the bad results and the lack of knowledge of the pupils taking their final examination from the lower secondary school in German, created considerable disturbance in the upper secondary schools (the *gymnasium*). Indeed, it became a source of political unrest that the subject produced a large quantity of 'school failures'. Representatives from the German Teachers' Association demanded other types of examination and drastic changes to improve teaching and standards.

German, it appears, suffered the same fate as did the classical languages by the end of last century. It was not in accordance with the spirit of the time. As a compulsory subject for lower secondary school entrance it became an obstacle to the creation of a democratic basic school and of a secondary school catering for all pupils.

It may be fair to ask what kind of foreign language teaching did suit the 'spirit of the time'? What kind of modern language teaching is suited to a technological, specialized and democratized society? The language must not be too difficult but must be accessible to all. The teaching must have practical aim and be suitable for all pupils and to all types of schooling. It should give practical skills and not formal knowledge.

The school subject English was flexible where German was not, a criterion which counted particularly in the nine-year basic school. In the higher secondary school it met at first with problems, since it no longer derived status from a content of British literature and civilization, history and institutions. Shakespeare and Trevellyan are still for the few. 'Received pronunciation' is competing with American, and even Australian English may be accepted, and other variants besides, such as 'English for Special Purposes'.

The high point in the emphasis on instrumental aims in modern language teaching may now have been passed. The aims of English teaching specified in the 1987 Curriculum Guidelines for the basic nine-year school may suggest so. There it is stated that in the basic school English is meant to be a 'subject for communication, skills, experience and involvement, and knowledge'.[9] The fact that all these are regarded as important aims and objectives for the teaching of English may indicate that a change has occurred, away from the very narrow and practically orientated aims dominating the 1960s and 1970s teaching of English in Norwegian schools, towards a more comprehensive view of the role of modern language teaching in the life of the individual and of the nation.

Another point is also to be noted. Comparing the present situation of modern language teaching in Norwegian schools to the recommendations from different commissions and resolutions passed at conferences during the last two decades, a marked discrepancy emerges. The common factor of all recommendations has been an explicit statement of the need for more time and resources spent on foreign language teaching, and a necessity for mastery of and competence in several modern languages, especially English and French. It thus seems reasonable to assume that considerations very different from these prevailed when the initiatives leading to the present situation were staked out.

Notes

1 BJÖRGE, J. (1927) 'Fra debatten om latinskolen' ('From the debate about the Latin school'), in BOYESEN, E. and WILDHAGEN, F. Chr. (Eds) *Tidskifte*, Oslo, Aschehoug, p. 24 (my translation).

2 DAHL, H. (1964) 'Språkopplaeringens plass i skolen sett fra historisk synsvinkel' (Language teaching in education from a historical perspective'), in *Språkforskning og språkopplaering*, Oslo, Studentersamfundets Fri Undervisning, pp. 35–44.

3 I am especially referring to *Språk og språkundervising* ('Language and Language Teaching'), the periodical of the Association of Modern Language Teachers, and *Skoleforum*, the periodical of the Secondary School Teachers' Association.

4 HÖST, S. (1927) 'Engelsk i det sproglig-historiske gymnasium' ('English at the arts side of the upper secondary school'), in *Tidskifte*, Oslo, Aschehoug, pp. 137–41. (my translation).

5 DEN PARLAMENTARISKE SKOLEKOMMISJON III. 'Utkast til lov om folkeskolen i byene' (The parliamentary school commission III. 'Proposition for education act for the town schools'), p. 55 (my translation).

6 DET NORSKE ARBEIDERPARTI (1952) 'Langtidsprogram for skolen' ('The School Long Term Programme',) (my translation).

7   *Forarbeid til Normalplan for grunnskolen* (1970) ('Preliminary draft of the set curriculum for the basic school'), Oslo, Aschehoug, p. 125 (my translation).

8   KIRKE OG UNDERVISNINGSDEPARTEMENTET (1967) *Innstilling 1 om det videregående skoleverket fra Skolekomiteen av 1967* (Report no. 1 regarding secondary schooling from the 1965 School Commission), Oslo, pp. 38–50.

9   *Mönsterplan for grunnskolen, M 87* (1987) Aschehoug, Oslo ('Curriculum Guide for the Basic School'), (my translation).

Chapter 7

The 'Englishness' of English Teaching

Robert Morgan

Introduction

English as a school subject in Ontario is 'back in the hot seat again', to quote a headline from one of the province's leading newspapers.[1] Recently the Ontario government reaffirmed the centrality of this curricular area for state education by requiring a minimum of five compulsory 'English credits' for secondary school graduation, while simultaneously permitting students to take as many as three English credits during their final year. This boom in English studies has come with a significant rider however. In February of 1987 mandatory examinations in English were announced for all students at an advanced academic level, and a separate *Handbook* was issued to insure the uniform implementation of this examination across the province during the 1987-88 school year.[2] English studies is likely to become the wedge used to reintroduce standardized examinations into provincial schools after a twenty year hiatus.

The new *English Curriculum Guideline* (1987), a directive on *Ontario Academic Courses*, and an accompanying *Handbook* on examinations intervene in the current liberal moment by retraining English teachers in a very particular discourse, one concretized as ways of properly formulating questions, designing tests, and schemas for their evaluation. Methodologies exemplified by examinations are expected in turn to infiltrate the daily routines of English classrooms,[3] teachers being advised that mastering the official discourse will better 'adapt their current practices' to ministry standards. This process is not to be left to chance, however, with the ministry instituting an 'Examination Review' of sample 'Language and Literature' papers from 'every secondary school in Ontario' during 1988.[4] The proposed review instrument rates student papers on twenty-two separate criteria, and the examined exams will be returned 'with comments to the individual schools via the director of education or the principal ...'[5] Teachers are not blind to the fact that not only students are being evaluated by the proposed examinations.

In spite of ministry claims that a new and 'really quite radical approach'[6] is set in motion by these directives, what is striking about such documents is their attempt to reinstate a very traditional version of discursive inquiry, one reaching back to the early 1870s within Ontario schooling. In fact, apart from the massive impact of psycholinguistics and an increasing emphasis upon individual and group work, contemporary 'English studies' at the secondary level has remained largely impervious to recent theoretical writing on language and literature,[7] insulated from discussions about the cultural politics of its chosen forms, and resistant to the insights of historical sociology. Brian Doyle, for example, has remarked that unlike many other areas where 'the question of the significance of a discipline's own past for a reflexive understanding of its present operations has to some extent been posed,'[8] practitioners of English have been slow to examine their own history, remaining content for the most part with the image reflected in ministry documents of English as *the* central subject of the secondary school curriculum.

Yet, as Raymond Williams has remarked, sometimes 'the most basic concepts ... from which we begin, are seen to be not concepts but problems, not analytic problems either, but historical movements that are still unresolved ...'[9] If we are to understand those problematic categories which inform our practice, Williams recommends archaeology: that is, we must turn to history, attempting 'to recover the substance from which their forms were cast'.[10] Subjected to this kind of historical scrutiny, 'English studies' stands revealed as just such a questionable category, invented as an institutional division of knowledge a little over a century ago. It has become visible as a historically deposited artifact, a composite and often contradictory 'jumble of discourses'[11] spoken by state institutions. There is an accumulating body of evidence, for instance, that the term 'Literature' and its affiliated categories, 'literary criticism', 'literary periods', 'literary history', are inherently ideological designations,[12] not so much trans-historical essences as particular, historically instituted relationships to discourse.[13] Perhaps the most powerful of these reifications is the attempt to establish at the centre of State schooling a set of indisputably 'acknowledged classics' as legitimate specimens of a 'National Literature'. Such texts become the required readings of the classroom, a pedagogic literary canon embodying that imaginary community, 'the nation'.[14] Historically examined all of these terms can be recovered as forms of practice, social constructions fought for and later refunctioned in specific ways.[15]

What is truly 'radical' (in the sense of 'rooted') about the Ontario Ministry documents, then, is their effort to turn back the clock and rehabilitate many of the nineteenth-century concepts listed above. For instance, in spite of the espoused 'multiculturalism' of recent Ontario government pronouncements on the teaching of English, the stress continues to fall upon a monochromatic and stable nationalism. The expressions 'acknowledged classics' and 'national literature' are taken directly from recent ministry documents.[16] What I explore in greater detail below is how the early discipline of English studies utilized such concepts, building an 'imaginary unity of the social formation as the 'nation'',[17] and beyond it a belief in an organic Anglo-Saxon empire, in a way that has left its traces within the subject up to the present time. Contemporary directives continue to champion the 'centrality of Literature' with its 'special place as [the] foundation of Canadian culture'.[18] Though differences between 'races' and ethnicities are now licensed as 'opportunities to observe and appreciate the cultural mosaic', they are still ultimately recuperated upon the field of an unproblematic 'national identity and unity', itself embodied educationally in a literary canon.[19] Such claims are quite remarkable given that Canada is a country where the Constitutional ink has scarcely dried,[20] and which has been continually wracked throughout its history by regional, religious and linguistic differences. It is with scepticism, therefore, that we read a section entitled 'The Central Focus of English' in the most recent *Guideline* (1987), which endorses a homogeneous 'English-speaking society' with an imaginary 'Ontario dialect' at its centre. Although this final construct is offered as a simple linguistic fact, it is in reality a State attempt to demarcate a particular political boundary via language. English studies in a Canadian context, then, continues to be a key site of citizenship training, or in the words of the current ministry guidelines, 'a subtle and powerful force in building the character of a nation and its people'.[21]

Simultaneously, yet in contrast with its nation-building properties, very deeply rooted ways of conceiving of the subject as the privileged pedagogic locus for the student's moral introspection are envisioned by ministry directives. From the moment of its inception the territory which English studies progressively came to work turned away from the repressive regime of the grammarian, and promoted instead certain pleasures and capacities in the student now seen as a unique 'individual'.[22] Michel Foucault has called this process 'subjectification': that is, the 'way a human being turns him or herself into a subject' by means of the discourses and practical routines made available within a discipline and in which students take an 'active' part.[23] Significantly the birth of English studies coincided with the rise of an industrial bourgeoisie and the need felt by ruling class groups for new ways of forming 'free', moral, and affective subjectivity in the drastically altered social and economic circumstances of the late nineteenth century. Current attention in pedagogical discourse to the analysis of 'literary characters', the 'development of personal taste', 'unique personal responses', and individual 'discrimination',[24] is consistent with this projection of English as a secularized 'seminar of conscience'.[25] The most frequently used word in contemporary documents on the teaching of English is 'personal'. According to the 1979 Ontario *Guideline*, for example, English studies is chiefly in the business of 'personal growth', developing 'personal values', and helping students articulate their 'personal aims and goals'.[26] This ideology is explicitly endorsed by a boxed and highlighted quotation on p. 20: 'English is above all a personal discipline, concerned with personal behaviour and personal choices and tastes. The receptive language skills, listening, and reading are aspects of personal behaviour ...'[27] This document provides an excellent example of the way in which a very public realm — the language and literature of State-sponsored texts — is converted into a purely private and 'personal' matter.

Barbara H. Smith has observed that 'questions of literary value and evaluation' are regularly begged by contemporary pedagogical discussions, which are confined instead to debates about 'the *proper methods and objectives of the academic study of literature*'.[28] While we are swept along by this methodology madness, committed to an excess of practice, urgent questions about the categories and conditions of intelligibility, the actual communities and material situations we practise in are ignored. Part of this learned stupidity is the suppression of the sociality of discursive forms and their historically varied functions, thus ratifying by default the established forms of discursive authority embodied in arbitrary genre divisions, or dogmatic distinctions between poetry and prose. When the social and historical relations of power within which these distinctions take on a social life remain implicit, hidden, for example, behind terms like 'Literature' or 'the classics', then, as Smith notes, 'assumptions about the desired and expected functions of the texts so classified and about the interests of their appropriate audiences ... [are] less likely to be questioned or challenged, or even noticed. Thus the privileging power of evaluative authority may be very great, even when it is manifested inarticulately.'[29]

One of the symptoms that there are indeed competing social functions for English studies is the convenient slippage within official discourse between an undifferentiated and polar set of terms: 'public' and 'private', a seamless 'society' on the one hand and the sovereign, decontextualized 'individual' on the other.[30] Though English studies is clearly an ethics of language orchestrated by the State, ministry documents appear untroubled by the contradictory claims they advance, fostering a conception of English as at once a political and a non-political practice. The most severely individualizing approaches sit side by side with assertions about its nation-building properties. At their most expansive such claims extend as far as the belief that 'English language and literature', properly taught and appreciated, reflects the immutable truths of the human condition. While acting as a theory of social value at a number of levels, a liberal humanist English studies has shunned theory itself as too abstract, relying instead on authoritarian conceptions of 'intuition', 'insight', and spontaneous 'feeling'.

Reinforcing the poverty of historical imagination at the heart of English studies have been the lazy common-sense catch-all 'human nature', and precritical conceptions of 'experience'. The 1987 *Guideline*, for instance, celebrates the unmediated 'vicarious experiences emanating from literature'.[31] In this regard Catherine Belsey contends that English teaching has always been scandalized by any proposed relationship between what it sees as 'the transcendent (Literature), the contingent (history), and the merely strategic (politics)'.[32] She makes clear, however, that severing such connections, while simultaneously foregrounding the decontextualized 'experiences' which Literature is felt to access unproblematically for pupils, results not only in political amnesia, but in an aloof quietism:

> The function ... of conventional [English practice] is to reinstate the continuity of felt life ... No history: no politics. Because if there has never been change at a fundamental level, there is no rational grounds for commitment to change. No politics — or rather no overt politics, since there is, of course, no political neutrality in the assertion of an unchanging essential human nature.[33]

The failure to go behind favoured terms, then, has meant evading a careful working through of the specific historical connections between nation and signification, the textual and the sexual, culture and class — relationships which the pedagogic practice of English is nonetheless always active in constructing.[34]

The bridge between the political and the personal is built of course by a pedagogy informed by curricular directives and provincial examinations. Both institute, in Foucault's terms, forms of 'hierarchical surveillance, continuous registration, perpetual assessment and classification',[35] but which are encountered, 'humanized', on the ground as the pleasurable routines of the English classroom, pedagogic techniques for writing and reading, 'for setting up and developing relationships with the self, for self-reflection, self-knowledge, self-examination, for the decipherment of the self by oneself ...'[36] These 'panoptic'[37] and 'pastoral' forms of power enact a 'government by individualization'[38] to the extent that individuals come to adopt unconsciously the institutional norms embedded in the habitual daily performances of 'English', or more precisely and radically, around which a literate subjectivity — the very notion of individuality itself — is formed within State schooling. In this sense English studies continues to fulfil a set of functions which determined its birth: the formation of both public 'citizen' and private 'subjectivity'. Yet, characteristically represented as either a disinterested 'aesthetic' or a positivist 'linguistic' knowledge, English studies has remained miraculously uncontaminated by the grime of 'isms', continuing to function as one of the modern State's more effective forms of cultural politics.

This suppleness of English studies, its manner of circulating social values and pursuing cultural objectives in very experiential, individualized and indirect forms, was a discovery made by the founders of English pedagogy. Adam Smith, 'the first professor of English',[39] for example, feared the corrosive effects his *laissez-faire* economic formulations would have on any sense of community. He therefore turned to education and his own tentative experiments with the teaching of literary selections in the vernacular as a possible antidote to his economic theory. Smith believed that Literature, properly taught, would develop in his students 'the spectator within us'. This could best be achieved by exciting the 'moral sentiments' in a process whereby the student-disciple 'enters by sympathy into the sentiments of the master [writers]' or 'what is really good company'.[40] Smith's pioneering linkage of social psychology, *belles lettres* and the organic State was operationalized for his students as the writing of 'character sketches', evaluations of valorized authors and their literary characters. Such studies would encourage pupils to reflect upon their own personalities.

The architect of English studies in Ontario, George Paxton Young, had a similar agenda to Smith's. Young wrote a series of influential reports for the Department of Education between 1864 and 1868 which proposed a morally refining 'aesthetic' education accomplished through vernacular texts taught in 'a different sort of school', new 'English High Schools'.[41] His inspiration for these reforms came from reading a new generation of English liberal intellectuals such as Matthew Arnold and John Seeley. In particular, he relied upon the latter's essay, 'English in Schools',[42] for many of his suggestions, especially Seeley's notion that pupils do not understand the English language properly 'owing to the fact that they had never been taught English'.[43] This is not an absurd claim if we understand it to mean the production of a particular mode of reading and its consequent meanings: the pedagogical use of English language and literature for the 'civilizing of a nation'.[44] Seeley was especially concerned about that 'new ... but rude class' which possesses none of the 'politeness' or 'perfection in our aristocracy',

> none of these domestic traditions, no inherited refinement, no common stock of literature forming an intellectual atmosphere around every child. If we teach this class what we have hitherto taught the other [i.e. the ruling] class, the result will not be the same. For them the schoolmaster must do more because the parents and the home have done much less. To them he must become a kind of priest or missionary of culture.[45]

Yet Seeley's interests extended far beyond England. Selections from his most influential work, the imperialist blueprint *The Expansion of England* (1883),[46] were recommended reading for teachers and students,[47] and the 'Seeley Society' for the promotion of Empire was championed by the editor of the *Canadian Educational Monthly*.[48] Like Seeley, Young was also concerned about that 'small number of cultivated men [who] will always live in the midst of a vast half-barbarous population' and the need systematically to 'enlarge' the latter group's views, especially during those adolescent 'years in which the missionaries of civility and cultivation can [still] reach [them]'.[49] For the emerging middle and working classes, Young saw that the classical languages were as relevant 'as Chinese'.[50] In order best to achieve 'the formation of moral character', therefore, he counselled teachers to 'rely more ... on the English than on the Classical [languages]', utilizing only those literary works which 'contain a considerable number of interesting selections, exhibiting human character in all its phases, recording in particular those actions of great and good men ...'[51] Such texts 'exhibit[ed] virtue in living concrete embodiment' in contrast to the arid sermonizing of the previous era.[52] In this way moral training would be 'given most *naturally*, — most impressive, and with the greatest likelihood of abiding effect,— in connection with the study, by the pupils, of the words of good English Authors'.[53] Illustrating his intentions by citing a lesson he himself had given to a class of adolescent girls on Shakespeare's *Merchant of Venice*, he concluded: 'Here was a lesson in practical Christian Ethics, given incidentally, in no dry dogmatic fashion, but in connection with words of such singular sweetness that they can scarcely be read intelligently without entering into the soul and becoming part of its convictions for ever. Why should not such lessons be a regular feature of the classes of English literature in our Schools?'[54] Franklin Court has observed that Adam Smith's preoccupations have remained essentially our own, 'inform[ing] the fundamental design of the teaching of English literature up to the present'.[55] This comment applies with equal force to Paxton Young's discovery that English studies had the capacity to win hearts and minds precisely because of its 'indirection'.[56]

The story of modern English studies, then, is a tracing of the gradual empowerment and refining of such techniques, especially the pedagogic manipulation of the 'powers of writing' to rewrite the student's subjectivity. In a sense, to narrate the history of the teaching of English we require another type of history of the 'subject' altogether than the traditional ones: that is, a history of the forms of human subjectivity projected by English studies as a site where particular discourses and practical routines are enacted, others silenced, still other capacities and connections never envisioned or fostered at all. From this perspective, English is a training in how to say 'I', and the establishment of the social horizons within which this utterance takes place. In arguing for the basic 'homogeneity of the English-speaking races' in 1877, Elihu Burritt remarked that '"We" is the grandest word a human tongue can utter, when the heart expresses by its interest in the populations of a continent, its fellow-feeling with the commonwealths of an Empire. ... Each has learned to say "We" first and "I" afterwards, and their "We" means and embraces the whole nation and its interests.'[57] Ideologically unsaturated even at the level of its smallest pronouns, language plays a constitutive role in informing subjectivity within education, and therefore in facilitating either the reproduction, contestation, or the transformation of the forms of social life we encounter. The pedagogic space within which students read and write is always located within the wider agendas of a whole culture, particularly as these are defined by the State. Mikail Bahktin remarks that 'people do not [so much] "accept" their native language, it is in their native language that they first reach awareness'.[58] School literacy constitutes a second, State-sponsored linguistic birth, an attempt to make 'second nature' particular orientations to society and self through the agency of a schooled language. It is relevant to the subsequent development of English studies in Ontario that its earliest advocates shared a very particular 'image repertoire',[59] one which promoted the expansion of a global English Empire.

Identity and Otherness in English Studies

Any reckoning of the historical role of the institution of English studies, humanist mythologies about its timeless and universal human values notwithstanding, must take account of the subject's historical role as a 'literary department of state' from the beginning.[60] Archaeologists of English quickly discover its role in state formation, as well as the reciprocal side of this process, the fact that 'state bodies' and 'other forces invented English ... as a discourse, a subject, an ideology'.[61] It has always been 'worldly' in the way Edward Said claims literary texts are: 'always enmeshed in circumstance, time, place and society — in short, ... in the world, and hence worldly'.[62] Though it characteristically appeared in forms which were pleasurable, indirect and understated, English studies was one of the more positive shapes State power assumed. Acting as a field of 'governance' in Foucault's terms,[63] it consisted of an ensemble of procedures for working with language and literary texts to develop 'a whole complex of "savoir"', that is, a commissioning of ways of knowing and equally of being ignorant.[64] In an important sense, then, the State made and continuously remakes this discourse on language as a determination of which contexts and capacities prevail in the organization of social life in general. English pedagogy is always the site for the production of some experiences over others, some ways of speaking/writing, and consequently some kinds of identity in preference to others. Semiotic practices generally are central to the social formation in this way, operating to constitute and to regulate, to give voice to or to render silent particular interests, to bring into communication and alignment various groups or else to split them apart.[65] What has been consistently suppressed for English studies is the built-in nature of this dividing operation, the manner in which an initial partitioning and 'instituting'[66] moment established the very structure and possibility of 'English' knowledge *per se*: the production of legitimate Identity against alien Otherness, a placing along with a corresponding displacing.

It is only recently that an understanding of school English as a 'political act' of this kind,[67] an operation of power, and not in some add-on or optional feature kind of way, but as an intrinsic and indispensible element of the discursive practices of the classroom, has become the focus of scholarly interest. I have suggested two possible reasons for this omission until now. First, there has been a historical blindness to the social and institutional conditions which gave rise to English studies as a mode of cultural understanding in the first place, one distinct from other forms of pedagogy. As Gayatri Spivak remarks, the necessity and 'means of production of explanations is, of course, a very important part of the ideology of cultural explanations that cannot be distinguished, in fact, from the explanations themselves'.[68] Secondly, the ongoing institutional and theoretical commitments embedded within English studies have remained buried in part because of a pervasive vitalism which favoured 'literary experiences' over 'literary theory'. In the rest of this chapter, I want to focus on how these two suppressions reinforced each other during the first half of English's curricular history within Ontario, in effect drawing an invisible boundary around our thinking which could be called the 'Englishness' of English teaching. By this last phrase I intend to highlight the conditions of privilege which established a particular set of texts and the methods of their circulation at the centre of schooling.

It is important to recall in this connection that while a humanitarian English studies advertised itself as a generous, all-encompassing, liberalizing culture of the feelings, it was just as frequently the exact opposite, an ideologically loaded and exclusionary set of practices. Relevant for a more self-conscious English studies, therefore, is Edward Said's redefinition of the term 'culture' as a dynamic relationship, an ongoing dividing operation between centre and margin, enlightened inside and barbarian outside:

> ... culture must be seen as much for what it is not and for what it triumphs over when it is consecrated by the State as for what it positively is. This means that culture is a system of discriminations and evaluations ... for a particular class in the State able to identify with it; and it also means that culture is a system of exclusions legislated from above but enacted throughout its polity, by which such things as anarchy, disorder, irrationality, inferiority, bad taste, and immorality are identified, then deposited outside the culture and kept there by the power of the State and its institutions.[69]

It is impossible from this perspective to divorce the rise of an aesthetically and racially organized English studies from the zenith of British imperialism, whose school editions of 'Standard Authors' served as its literary armature. Thus at one level the expansiveness of the claim that English literature embodied the essential truths of 'the human condition' is no more than the cultural counterpart to the military domination of a global empire, part of a 'trajectory of "Westering"'.[70] Significantly, English as a school subject began in the colonies, in Africa, India, Scotland and Ontario long before it was initiated within secondary schooling at 'home'.[71] Though demands for a secondary English studies were not lacking at the centre, these outposts of Empire functioned as the laboratories in which it took its initial shape.[72] It was here, in the words of Benjamin Disraeli quoted in the 1870 *Journal of Education* (Ontario), that

English literature demonstrated its 'exuberant reproductiveness':

> There is a vigour and a versatility in our literature and in its power
> of expression which has sustained the commanding influence of the
> English language. ... but I think it can be accounted for. I attribute
> it in a great degree to the wide circle to which the English writer
> appeals. ... he can effect the feelings and influence the conduct of
> every transatlantic city. His productions soothe the labour and
> solace the life of the workers of the antipodes.[73]

Yet this dissemination was hardly spontaneous, nor reassuring. What
England did was to systematize and popularize language and literature as
forms of ruling, sending its philologists, teachers, literary anthologies,
grammar texts, newspapers and publications around the world with the
intention of reforming or 'Anglifying' (to use a term supplied by an early
English governor of Upper Canada) diverse populations.[74] Between 1815
and the end of the First World War European powers generally, and the
English empire most of all, increased their domination from 35 to 85 per
cent of the world's land mass.[75] We can no longer dissociate the birth of
English studies from this long compact with cultural imperialism. 'English
culture', English language, English Literature were as essential to the
consolidation of English 'power and progress' as English armies had been
in implanting them.[76]

Understanding English studies within this kind of power-knowledge
framework is therefore long over-due. One possible entry for such an
approach is suggested by Said's writing on 'Orientalism'.[77] For Said,
Orientalism is 'the discursive imposition of a political doctrine over the
Orient ... the appropriation, transformation and, in short, the occupation of
a weaker culture by a stronger'.[78] Throughout his work Said deploys the
insight of poststructuralism that language is always caught in the creation
of difference, but he historicizes and concretizes this awareness by detailing
those institutional forms and practices by which racial, ethnic, class and
gender markings are not only at work within language and the literary, but
take on a flesh and blood existence within the social order. The value of his
method for a rethinking of English studies should be apparent since as an
enterprise it is the other half of the dialectical relationship Said sketches. If
Orientalism is a 'corporate institution for dealing with the Orient —
dealing with it by making statements about it, authorizing views of it,
describing it, by teaching it, ... ruling over it',[79] then English studies is a
corporate institution for imaging many of these very same social relations
and affiliations, though now seen from the opposite side of the mirror, the
specular centre. Particularly in the colonies the pedagogy of English
provides us with an opportunity to observe the representation of cultural
relations at their point of intersection between dominant and subordinated
cultures when plotted along racial-linguistic lines. As Philip Dodd points
out, we must not see 'Englishness' as a settled or unitary notion, rather it

signified the unstable relationship of a dominant cosmopolitan centre to the periphery, of us Anglo-Saxons against them, 'natives', 'foreigners', 'aliens'.[80] In short, school texts always exist in relation to social text, and school English with Englishness.

Corroborating Said's call for attention to the exclusions enacted within English studies, Homi Bhabha has remarked that 'the field of the "true" emerges as a visible effect of knowledge/power only after the regulatory and displacing division of the true and the false. ... Such a bringing to light is never [just] a *prevision*; it is always a question of the *provision* of visibility as a capacity, a strategy, an agency but also ... an *elision* of sight ...'[81] Our encouragement of student readers to look through transparent texts in an effort to find significant meanings and vital experiences beyond them is better understood therefore as the production of particular reality-effects made possible by the discourse circulated within English classrooms, one ultimately dependent upon an 'authority to differentiate' located within the State.

> Transparency is the action of the distribution and arrangement of differential spaces, positions, knowledges in relation to each other, relative to a differential, not inherent, sense of order. This effects a regulation of spaces and places that is authoritatively assigned; it puts the addressee into the proper frame or condition for some action or result. Such a mode of governance addresses itself to a form of conduct that is achieved through a reality effect that equivocates between the sense of *disposal*, as the bestowal of a frame of reference, and *disposition*, as mental inclination, a frame of mind.[82]

As we shall see, this blurring of the line between English and 'Englishness', discourse and disposition, a language and a mentality, was a persistent feature of the writing on vernacular pedagogy by Ontario educators.

For Said the practical routines and common-sense approaches of the English classroom could just as equally be described, therefore, as 'impractical' and 'habitual strategies' which 'split literature and criticism off from wider social practices', effectively blocking our awareness of the way English is always 'intercalated in a wider field of power and action ...'[83] By extrapolating from Said's method of analysing 'Orientalism', we can posit three overlapping levels which apply to 'English' as a language, a literature, and a school subject. First, and typically, we can see it as an institutional division of knowledge which evolved in the late nineteenth century, the school 'discipline' we're all familiar with. But, secondly, and prior to this, we need to become aware of a long history of cultural politics which inscribed intra- and trans-cultural relations within a language, a set of enacted 'discriminations and evaluations' which the later action of institutionalizing the same literary text over a wide area helped to circulate, thus promoting notions of a particular cultural space and those who lived within it, as well as those without.[84] In relation to this second horizon, the discipline of English studies is a kind of organized corporate embodiment with its own productivity and mediations. Finally, arising from the first two levels, we can think of English as 'Englishness', i.e. a set of 'ideological suppositions, images, and fantasies' fostered by language, theories of language, and the literary — what Said refers to as the 'imaginative geography' a discourse stages.

The very designation 'English' discloses this dynamic. It is easy to forget that behind the gallery of individual authors and texts what English studies transmitted most of all was the notion of race. It was in fact intended to embody this conception from its founding moment. Henry Gates has argued that this conjunction of race and literature was not accidental but historically given: 'The growth of canonical national literatures was coterminous with the shared assumption among intellectuals that race was a 'thing', an ineffaceable quantity, which irresistibly determined the shape and contour of thought and feeling as surely as it did the shape and contour of human anatomy.'[85] The illusion of 'race' functioned 'as a metonym for muddled thinking about the relation of genetics, intention, meaning, and culture',[86] and assisted in the construction of Otherness within Western representations. The pedagogy of English language and literature in Ontario as elsewhere was complicit with this 'racy'[87] discourse, helping to 'will a sense of natural difference into our formulations' of cultural life,[88] endowing the emergent 'Canadian nation' and the Empire it was part of with the inevitability of biology refracted through language.

Though George Paxton Young's descendants have largely acquiesced in a view of English studies as a holistic, liberal, individualized, and affective form of educational literacy which transcends time and place, it was and is a highly specific and evaluative set of moral-political practices. Championed as that form which linguistic competence takes at an advanced level, secondary school English later became central to debates about one's intelligence or educability — orientations with which current ministry intentions to use it in a gatekeeping capacity are consistent. It was equally, however, a form of cultural imperialism. It is necessary, then, to restore the pedagogy of English to its role as an ethical praxis within a historical field, making it visible once again as 'an integral and not merely an accessory part of the social processes of differentiation, exclusion, incorporation, and rule'.[89]

The Englishness of English Teaching in Ontario

Two other factors which made for a racially organized English studies by the late nineteenth century need to be mentioned. The first is the important role played by what Linda Dowling has called 'romantic philology' which conceptualized language as *Volksstimme*, the unified and unifying expression of a homogeneous cultural group.[90] The intellectual roots of this orientation can be traced to the philological problematic initiated by German writers like Johann Herder, Friedrich Schlegel,[91] Friedrich Schiller,[92] and Johann David Michaelis. The latter, for example, exalted the vernacular as a historical record, a living archive of 'the race', making etymological study equivalent to attending closely to 'the voice of the people'.[93] For Herder, whose *Treatise Upon The Origin of Language* was published in England in 1827, a language revealed the 'genius of a people', and the harmony between State and individual citizen was mirrored in 'folk' stories or 'specimens' of their poetry.[94] Subsequent to such developments, conceptions of authorship and anthology were able to function in such a way that they appeared to incorporate and embody the life of an organic group, 'a people', 'the nation', and did not just represent the words of an isolated writer or random collection of writers.[95] Preoccupations with English literature as the index of a timeless 'English character', or a concern with literary works as embodiments of an essential 'English mind' were also within this problematic. It is at this same juncture that we can locate the editions of 'Standard English Writers' which circled the globe. By the mid–nineteenth century such texts were felt to represent more than the privileged voices of admired writers, but rather disclosed the essence of a race, distilled its national historical culture and imperial destiny. One of the topics for composition at University College in Toronto in 1861, for example, was 'The connection between literary excellence and natural greatness, as exhibited in English history'.[96]

Secondly, and allied with this development, was a linguistic Darwinism by the end of the century.[97] Statements by Ontario educators and others during this period indicate a widespread ambition for a 'world English'.[98] Darwinist theories of language held that some forms of speech were more 'fitted' and capacious than others, evolving or degenerating in accordance with the vigour of a race. Overlaying this position was an older religious belief that language reflected the providential destinies of 'chosen' or unchosen peoples. By the end of the century such theories reinforced each other in assigning to English language and literature a special racial mission.

In a remarkable 1867 tract, *The Mission of Great Britain to the World, Or some of the Lessons which she is now Teaching*, a number of these linguistic assumptions merge. Its author, James George, an Ontario minister, professed that the very first of 'the lessons God has commissioned [England] to teach' the planet was 'a noble language, embodying the richest scientific and literary treasures' found anywhere.[99] For George, each language accorded with the mentality of a 'people'.

> Hence a highly civilized race, will ever have, a highly accomplished language. The English language strikingly illustrates this. It is very generally held, that a certain mixture of blood, drawn from the

noblest branches of the human family, produces the finest race of men. ... The English tongue, is in all senses a very noble one. ... But now, mark it — Great Britain is on a grand scale, engaged in teaching this noble tongue to the world.[100]

The long-term benefits of this teaching would be the gradual homogenization of human speech and the great purity, moral order, truth and comparative peace' which accompanied it. George is chillingly prophetic in asserting that while English will not 'wholly eclipse the minor dynasties of tongues', it will effectively marginalize them: 'The probability is that many of these will continue still to exist, but occupy a very minor and subordinate place', surviving 'only as the obscure Patois of the world, while English will become the grand medium ...'[101] At the end of his introductory remarks George discloses the pedagogical metaphor underlying his approach: a vision of England as school-'Mistress', 'commissioned to teach a universal language to the world'. While he is aware of the arrogance of this position, he feels it is justified by the actual progress of the English language's 'imperial reign' around the world. He explicitly locates his vision within the realpolitic of imperial expansion in a way that other writers tend to elide.

I hope it is not spoken ignorantly, nor in a tone of arrogant patriotism, when I say that the English language is eminently fitted for this purpose, and that things for a generation past seem to point to its final accomplishment. ... There is no need for aping a prophetic strain in this matter. I ask you simply to look at present appearances, and say, if these do not sufficiently foretell the future. Is not the teacher fairly seated for the high task. Are not the forms all placed, are not the classes — the nations — all assembling [within, in an earlier phrase, the 'English School']? Do you not see that I am indulging in no groundless, or vain prediction; but that it rests on the strongest probability — that our English speech shall become the universal speech of all men.[102]

The advantage of starting with George's text is that it presents clearly an image lurking behind many later educational tracts — that of the Empire as a giant classroom for the teaching of English.

Homogenization was also the theme of the official historiographer of the Education Department, John George Hodgins. A prolific author and editor in his own right, Hodgins believed that literary texts, properly taught, would transform the alien races entering Ontario during the last half of the nineteenth century. In an article entitled 'Canadian National Homogeneity', he complains of the rapid 'relays of these nationalities [who] come to us from Europe faster, and in greater numbers, than we can absorb and Canadianize them'.[103] His recommendations on how to best assimilate this population gave priority to the German method of employing a set of national 'classics' within state schooling: '... gradually and surely to absorb these diverse elements, so as to Canadianize the whole. Without question the school is the place in which the work must be done, and there it can be done most securely and pleasantly.'[104] As early as 1857 Hodgins had made an effort to supply this need by publishing an anthology, *Selections for Public Recitations in Schools*.[105] This text had the Department of Education's blessing,[106] Hodgins stating that its purpose was 'to meet a want much felt in many of our schools' not merely to cultivate 'a taste for correct speaking and recitation', but more importantly to assist teachers in inculcating the political sentiments which 'should be imbibed by Young Canadians who ... should be taught to love and venerate that great fatherland, whose annals are so rich in heroic incident and noble achievement'.[107] The selections attempted to imprint upon students an England that was the spiritual centre of the universe. In his subsequent *School Speaker and Reciter* (1868), Hodgins continued this ritualization of patriotic Englishness.[108] Like many later school anthologies, this text attempts to form the subjectivities of students around an England so haunting it becomes more real than their actual experience of colonial life.

The chief superintendent of the province, Egerton Ryerson, also desired 'to familiarize our youth with the varied and rarest productions of British authors' for political purposes.[109] Strongly opposed to the flood of cheap American books crossing the Canadian border, Ryerson alternately believed they either exerted a 'silent and imperceptible ... influence against the established Government of the Country'[110] or were openly of 'the most inflammatory anti-British' character.[111] He privately confided that such texts had helped to foster the 1837 'Rebellion' in Upper Canada.[112] Similarly, the English publisher, John Murray, whose inexpensive 'Colonial Library' editions circled the globe, remarked to Sir Francis Bond Head, governor of Upper Canada at the time of the 1837 uprising, that his colonial volumes had originally been marketed as a 'substitute to the Canadas and other Colonies for the Yankee publications hitherto poured into them and which besides damaging the copyrights of British Authors by the piracy of their Works, are sapping the principles and loyalty of the Subjects of the Queen by the democratic tendency of the native American publications'.[113] Quintessential English literary treasures then were not just for sale at 'home', but assisted in politically immunizing colonial populations 'abroad' who might otherwise have been seduced by democratic ideals.

What fuelled this approach among an Ontario Anglo-Saxon elite was a growing paranoia they might lose their supremacy in the face of increasing numbers of immigrants, at first from Ireland, and later from eastern Europe. Foremost amongst the charges levelled at such groups was that of cultural 'degeneracy', with linguistic inferiority its prime instance.[114] At the 1870 Ontario Teachers' Convention both of the invited speakers expressed their xenophobia in unambiguous terms. Doctor Nelles of Victoria College stressed the urgent need for the state to fashion a 'common enlightenment' or 'culture of the conscience on a large scale' in view of the 'vermin' he found about him: 'this foreign element ... [is] the chief danger to our schools' and must be countered by the raising of a 'rational generation capable of outnumbering them and controlling them'. Part of this required that 'boys and girls hear only correct and elegant speech'.[115] The second speaker, poet and anthologist Edward Hartley Dewart, referred to this same problem as that of 'power towards the mass of the people ... [that is] the most ignorant and vicious classes ... holding the balance of power in this country'. Like Matthew Arnold, Dewart saw in poetry a form of concrete morality which 'proclaims the same truth [as religion], that mind is greater than matter'.[116]

Shakespeare as Proto-imperalist

Shakespeare played a central role in this homogenizing process for Upper Canadian educators, coming to represent the ultimate sign of English literary-cultural authority, the best distillation of Englishness, and thus all that was sacred to colonial elites. This concern eventually established his plays in Ontario as a way of indexing upper school grades, each grade taking as its focus a different play for study during the year — a situation that has not substantially changed since its inception in 1871.[117] By 1865 Reverend Hamilton's *Classic Reader*, a text Hodgins had recommended as companion to his own *School Speaker and Reciter*, contained no less than seventeen selections by Shakespeare, far in excess of previous school editions, while the authorized *Fifth Reader* of 1868 included seven items from this source, more than any other writer.

Henry Scadding, the founder of the Toronto Atheneum and a teacher at the prestigious Upper Canada College, is symptomatic of this colonial Bardolatry and the extent to which it could go.[118] For Scadding, Shakespeare played an indispensible role in reproducing an 'imperial' or 'home' culture, since more than other writers he exemplified 'the soundness and richness of the great bulk of our Literature, and of ... its place and possible use in the education of the English-speaking races'.[119] Like George, Scadding starts from the premise that 'the English-speaking tribes of the globe seem destined more or less to assimilate' the races they come in contact with.[120] English literature was pre-eminently suited to this quiet assimilation since it matched a quality in the 'national' or 'English character':

> the undemonstrativeness of the English character ... The English race proper, when transplanted from their native homes, do not see any especial need for asserting their nationality. It has not been

their habit to do so ... They indeed are aware of their prominence in the world — that they are as a city on the hill cannot be hid — but this conspicuousness they know that neither they nor their fore-fathers have ever sought. It has been brought about for them wondrously in the providential government of God, without having been aimed at. [121]

While the settlement of Upper Canada had been 'to a remarkable extent homogeneous' until now, Scadding is concerned about the 'races [which] will supply the staple population on the western slopes of our northern Andes', but concludes that 'from whatever quarter the bone and muscle necessary for subduing the soil may come, we may be sure that the great North-American mixed people already in possession will furnish the intellect, and finally the religion and civilization for all'. [122] Shakespeare's works are ideally suited for this 'civilizing' operation since they are exemplary of the 'clear masculine, right-judging intellects' of Englishmen, and can therefore serve 'as the standard classics of the English language. How thoroughly characteristic of England, of the free intellect of England are the Productions of the great Poet ... We can scarcely imagine any other European society producing the infinitely varied Shakespeare ...' [123] In another pamphlet entitled 'Shakespeare The Seer — The Interpreter', he outlined the educational benefits of 'our national poet', the way Shakespeare supplies a vital 'nutriment [of] the Imagination in the modern civilized man ... a power ... in the elevating and refining of men', [124] by providing 'idealities', 'beautiful visions and intuitions' which allow us to see into the 'essences .. of things'. [125] This not only makes his work prophetic, but also eminently useful in training those 'less-gifted but sympathetic minds' in a society, in 'giv[ing] understanding to the simple'. [126] Thus for Scadding, Shakespear is

> Virtually a Type of Colonist ... appreciated among the junior members of the family of nations, — among the human down-rootings from the great mother-tree of England. He will be recognized amongst them as exhibiting and embodying in his history ... the BEAVER-INSTINCT — the instinct which ... perpetuates, as it originated, the great colonizing movements of the present day. [127]

Finally, in a remarkable series of expanding statements at the end of this document, Scadding characterizes Shakespeare as the 'autochthon-poet', 'the Genius of a Race', 'of the whole English-Speaking World, to whom 'altars' should be set up around the world. [128] He is 'the best Exponent of British Character', and 'English Literature' the best 'Bond of Union Among the English-Speaking Peoples', because it is 'a seed grain in various parts of the earth ... In the course of centuries, how will the great globe be girt with nations of our blood and speech! How full of interest is the reflection, that, everywhere, wherever our race penetrates and plants itself, there it takes with it and deposits, as the seed of further mental products, the fundamental works of such a literature.'[129] The extravagance of these claims would be absurd were it not for the centrality of Shakespeare within educational practice, and the reinforcement of Scadding's sentiments in articles like 'Our English Shakespeare',[130] the prefaces to school texts,[131] or the statements of Canadian politicians. In 1936, for example, a prime minister of Canada, Arthur Meighen, invested Shakespeare with these same racial burdens in his remarks before the Canadian Club entitled 'The Greatest Englishman of History'.[132] Meighen states that as the recipient of 'the richest strains of English blood', Shakespeare expresses 'the genius of his race ... [and is] a champion of the Reign of Law'.[133] This identification of Shakespeare with the power of the state and established authority has a long reach, confirming the observation that within education the mask of Shakespeare 'has been made to speak mainly for the [political] right ...'[134]

When in 1873 Taine's influential *History of English Literature* was published in English, it confirmed an already established 'English mind/race' approach, positing race as one of 'three primordial forces' which constitute literature (along with 'epoch' and 'surroundings'). Race here signified a psychological-literary, 'inner', and 'moral' disposition, and not only a physiological typification. England is chosen to exemplify this analysis, says Taine, because English literature shows 'the recondite mechanism whereby the Saxon barbarian has been transformed into the Englishman of to-day'. Thus an ancient tribe of Saxons are confirmed as 'the primary springs', 'the source' materials from which an alchemical recovery of Englishness could be accomplished within a literary-evolutionary model.[135] The overall effect of romantic philology, Taine's work, the remarks of figures like George and Scadding, and the educational policies implemented by Ryerson and Hodgins, was to authorize what can only be described as a vigorous 'Saxonism' within late nineteenth-century Ontario: that is, a belief that English language and literature were the legacies of a legendary Saxon race.

By 1889 James McBrien, school inspector for Ontario County, demanded increased curricular attention for English by asking, 'What is English literature but the embodiment of English soul or character, and that of her noblest sons with all their God inspired thoughts, principles, and purposes?'[136] Similarly, a column in the *Canada Educational Monthly* of 1894 by Samuel Thurber defined English literature in the following terms:

> We must not consider our literature merely as the work of isolated men expressing private thoughts and feelings. Only those utterances which the race adopts are literature. When the race adopts a writer, it does this because it finds in him an adequate representative and exponent of itself. Literature therefore is the voice of the

> nation asserting its ideals, confessing its fears. ... There is no
> influence discoverable in the school curriculum so directly and
> exactly fitted to uplift young souls as contact with old literature. [137]

Speaking as chief textbook editor of the Department of Education, D.J.
Goggin defined a literary textbook as a suitable collection of 'the great
classics of the race'. [138] Literary Readers were particularly important to
Goggin since 'for thousands' they are 'their first introduction to our British
classics ...' [139] While for early Ontario educators the promotion of a Saxon
literary heritage seemed crucial, the later trajectory of this early version of
Englishness saw its gradual displacement by notions of the 'Queen's
English', [140] 'Pure English', [141] and finally just plain 'English'. However,
many of the same racial dynamics were still intact, though less visible, in
these later incarnations, informing English studies up to the present.

An articulate summary of the Darwinian approach and its implications
for language pedagogy within an English colony is provided by John
Reade's 'Language and Conquest — A Retrospect and a Forecast', a speech
given before the Royal Society of Canada in 1882.

> Real, permanent conquest is something more than that of mere
> physical force; and, though it may be initiated by the rough
> methods of war, is confirmed and perpetuated by moral agencies. It
> is a conquest of mind by mind, a conquest in which the victor is a
> teacher and the vanquished a learner. It is, in fact, a conquest of
> civilization. Among the evidences of this kind of conquest by
> which a people's ideas of politics, of ethics and of religion are
> gradually but surely changed, that of language holds a prominent
> place. [142]

We must remember that the counterpart of nineteenth-century philology was ethnology, their mutal focus the mapping of social identities. [143]
A literary/linguistic Saxonism emerged from just this discursive grid,
reaffirmed it, and was not merely the literary celebration of individual
poetic voices in isolation. If Macaulay could dismiss all of Oriental
literature with the remark that it was not worth a single shelf of English
classics, it was because of this discourse. [144] Reade's categories demonstrate
the close ties between ethnography, racism, and language study when he
elaborates upon the way in which 'grades of language ... separate one race
of men from another'. [145] According to his classification system 'The Aryan
family is very definitely marked off from that of the Semites, while the
differentiation is still more decided between either of these and the great
hordes of tongues outside their common language.' [146] The very 'value of
philology' for him rests upon the fact that it is 'an infallible criterion' for
'distinguish[ing] some of the Semitic peoples from the mass of the
dark-white nations ... where from mere physique we would hesitate in
pronouncing a decision'. [147] Later Reade published a series of articles on

'Nation-Building' in a prominent Ontario periodical, *The Week*, in which he locates Canada as part of that 'western movement of the Aryans, bearing in skilful hands and active brains the seeds of the world's greatest civilisation'.[148] Some of his poems later appeared in school anthologies in support of these themes.[149]

A chosen race discursive formation can also be detected in the discourse of prominent Ontario educators. William Houston, the librarian at the Ontario legislature and a frequent speaker at teachers' conventions, located English within the 'great Teutonic family' which, in turn, was nested within the 'Aryan'.[150] The same distinction, Aryan/Semitic, was crucial to the director of teaching training schools in Ontario, S.A. Morgan.[151] By the late 1890s Matthew Arnold's metaphoric-racial cultural co-ordinates ('Hebraism and Hellenism', 'Barbarians, Philistines') had become accepted currency of pedagogical literary discussions.[152] In a talk before teachers on 'Our Debt as Teachers to Matthew Arnold', for example, David R. Keys who 'was the English department'[153] at the University of Toronto in the 1880s, quoted with approval Arnold's remark 'Look on America; it is the same race; whether we are first or they, Anglo-Saxonism triumphs.'[154] Similarly, the first professor of English literature at this same university and later its president, Daniel Wilson, defined the purpose of English studies as the demonstration of 'how indissolubly the history of the [English] language is identified in all ways with that of the English race ...'[155] It entailed learning 'reverence' for English literary productions, and 'to sympathize in the feeling with which in a great crisis in England's history, her poet Wordsworth ... exclaimed:

We must be free or die, who speak the tongue
That Shakespeare spake; the faith and morals hold
That Milton held.[156]

His counterpart at Queen's University at Kingston, George Grant, put the matter still more bluntly in 1897: 'We have a mission on earth as truly as ancient Israel had. ... Our mission was to make this world the home of freedom, of justice, and of peace, and to secure these ends the British Empire was the highest secular instrument the world has ever known.'[157] An arm of this imperialism, English studies increasingly took on the terms of the evangelical discourses it had supplanted.

Later approaches stressing 'aesthetic appreciation' only refined the ideological configuration we are examining, leaving unaltered its fundamental outline. A.S. Morrison, for instance, a prolific contributor to educational periodicals, argued that poetry should become an 'intuitive culture' to pupils.[158] Yet in his *The Art Gallery of the English Language* (1886) the English poetry used for this purpose was to be chosen from a portrait gallery of national-historical glories 'guarded by succeeding generations, the offspring of the Viking'.[159] Teachers, the 'high priest[s]' of this culture, were to officiate 'at many an altar to many a neophyte, whose plastic mind and nascent tastes have not only to be regulated, but verily formed at the promoting of the minister'.[160] In a subtler way W.J. Alexander, the first occupant of the Chair of English at the University of Toronto (1889 to 1926), endorsed the essential civilizing values and cosmopolitan spirit of English, or 'Literature as instrument of culture'. This instrument was especially needed in those 'small, secluded, and backward communit[ies] ...' such as are found 'in new countries like our own' where 'the variety and range of interest ... is small'. For Alexander, in other words, it is the English ideal of 'gentility', and the 'man of culture' that literature promotes.[161] Beyond his conception of English studies as 'truly liberal culture' also lurked an organicist conception of the state. The society which 'higher literature brings us into contact with' is 'the truest aristocracy of the human race in their happiest mood. ... It is in no figurative sense, but in sober truth, that I call this "society". ... like all good society, [it is] difficult of access.'[162] While students are to begin with individual authors, their ultimate and 'final task as students of English literature ... [is] the task of tracing out and imaging the development of national thought ...'[163] As the editor of numerous secondary school anthologies, Alexander was able to concretize this approach for teachers.

Another editor of school texts, O.J. Stevenson, was in an even better position to train a cadre of teachers in their effective use as 'Lecturer in Methods in English and Chief Instructor in English' at the Faculty of Education, University of Toronto.[164] He too demonstrated this complicity between English pedagogy and English power. In his 1904 doctoral thesis he outlined the 'law of literary production', that is, literature as a record of the irresistible march of human 'progress', and its implications for teachers. Here he informs us that literature transfigures its material, overlooking for example 'the disagreeable elements ... the toil, weariness, the poverty and ignorance of the peasant' in the interests of an 'idealised' and 'universal' portrait, or 'the truth purged of irrelevant details'.[165] Like his colleagues, his discursive politics alternates between communing with 'the author's spirit' and 'poetry as formative of character'.[166] But there is no ambiguity for him regarding the ultimate purpose of the literature class.

> Its purpose is, and must continue to be, distinctly ethical. It is by the study of literature more than any other means that the child must learn to estimate the relative importance of the facts of human life, to interpret the conduct in the world about him, and to shape his own life in conformity with social laws ... As a result of an intelligent study of good literature, the individual should ... become a more efficient member of a society ... [and] the child is enabled to appreciate the value of those facts of the history of his own community, nation, or race, the knowledge of which he must possess in order to discharge the duties of citizenship intelligently. ... The student who wishes to estimate the importance of the

institutions among which he lives, may learn the facts concerning their rise and development from the pages of history, but it is in literature proper that he must seek for the reflection of their value in contributing to human progress. [167]

Since literary texts embodied both 'the progress of the individual and of the race', [168] Stevenson asks, 'should the presentation of material follow the order of development of the race?' [169] While he refers this question for 'final settlement to the psychologist', it is clear from his other comments that the answer is 'yes'. Poetry will provide the emotional charge, for instance, to the dry 'facts concerning the expansion of English trade, and the extension of English Empire ...' [170] It is to Tennyson's imperialist hymn 'Boadicea' that we must turn if we want to feel destiny stir in our veins. [171]

These interconnections between empire and English studies enjoyed their ultimate flowering in a series of jingoistic texts produced for schools between 1893 and 1919. A 1901 school Reader published simultaneously in Toronto and London (England), for example, surveyed the Imperial idea in its various literary-historical manifestations. Entitled *Britain Over the Sea*, its premise was that since 'poets, dramatists, novelists, [and] essayists' are the 'unconscious historians of a nation's life and progress', a full comprehension of the British Empire entailed a 'right understanding and appreciation' of literary works. [172] Thus Marvell, Milton, Burke, Wordsworth, Carlyle and Tennyson are excerpted to the extent that their works register the 'expansion' of England around the globe. The author explicitly acknowledges the inspiration of 'Sir John Seeley' for this project, relinquishing none of his jingoism.

> It has been said that cultivated minds have a natural wish to spread the special type of civilization which they enjoy, and it is this larger and more thoughtful view of the growth of Greater Britain that the example of England should impress upon her neighbours. She should teach them to recognize an all-impelling power for good that drives the common aspiration of the Anglo-Saxon race to found and support a great Empire beyond the seas, so that the world might come to see in the British Empire the demonstration of a great scientific truth, in the survival of the race whose natural aptitude best fits it to carry on and maintain the best form of human government. [173]

Another anthologist who traced the interconnections between language and empire was the premier and former minister of education of the province, George Ross. [174] Once again, nation and empire, race and language are inextricably linked for Ross. For example, a proper 'Canadian sentiment' is founded upon 'the energy which has characterized the Saxon race ... the Saxon does not rest merely on the advancement of the civilization of any country he possesses, but he immediately begins to transform it so that it possesses in its outward appearance, as well as in the spirit of its institutions, some characteristics of the Anglo-Saxon mind.[175] In a speech before the Ontario Teachers' Association in 1884, Ross cites with approval Professor Eliot of John Hopkins Univesity regarding the centrality of English language and literature:

> It cannot be doubted that English literature is beyond all comparison the amplest, most various, and most splendid literature which the world has ever seen ... It may further be said of the English language that it is the native tongue of nations which are pre-eminent by force of character, enterprise and wealth, and whose political and social institutions have a higher moral interest and greater promise that any which mankind has hitherto invented.[176]

By 1905 Ross could remark that 'Imperialism' was a relatively new word in people's vocabularies a few years ago, though it 'is not a new word now...'[177] In this speech he therefore sets out to answer the question, 'How did we come to think Imperially?'[178] In fact it was Ross himself who was not only instrumental in establishing the credibility of imperialism within educational circles, but its promotion around the world.[179] He succinctly identifies the relation which held for most Ontario educators between a patriotic Canadian nationalism and imperialism.

> There is no antagonism in my opinion between Canadianism and Imperialism. The one is but the expansion of the other. To be a true Canadian, under existing conditions, is to place yourself in harmony with the spirit of the empire ... with its interest in all that refines and ennobles the human race ... That is imperialism as I understand it. That is Canadianism as I would want it to be ...[180]

In 1893 Ross issued his *Patriotic Recitations and Arbor Day Exercises*.[181] In its preface he encouraged teachers to regard the volume as a resource manual in 'Civics', a way of 'preparing [their] pupils for properly appreciating the purposes of a national holiday and other important events in the history of the country'.[182] On its dedication page it bore a quotation from Bismark: 'We owe to our schools the thankful task of strengthening the feeling that we are all Germans.' Teachers were instructed to use the text to explain to the student the dominant political order, from 'the school section in which he [*sic*] lives to the Government of the Empire in which he belongs'.[183] Many of its Canadian selections were by imperialists such as W.W. Campbell, Agnes Machar, George Grant and Ross himself. Significantly the final third of the anthology was devoted to English authors. The volume, then, was a means of concretizing Ross's proposition that impirialism and Canadian nationalism were fully compatible. It was also a 'break text' in the sense that it made explicit an imperialism latent in many previous school anthologies, recasting their selections in this light. Finally, it set the tone for a later generation of school texts which adopted the same perspective in more subtle, poetic forms, such as the 1909 *Fourth Book*, and J.E. Wetherill's two supplemental Readers, *Poems of the Love of Country* (1912), and *The Great War in Verse and Prose* (1919).[184] The *Fourth Book* contained the most blatant and propagandistic gems, such as Frederick Scott's 'A Hymn of Empire' and W.E. Henley's 'England, My England'. Henley's poem, for instance, celebrated an England 'whose mailed hand keeps the keys/ Of ... teeming destinies',[185] a position that made him the darling of the British Israel movement which held that Anglo-Saxons were the lost tribe of Israel, God's chosen people.[186] Like other poems in these volumes, Henley's verses epitomize the long historical interweaving of language, race and empire.

Another anthology which explicitly addressed these relationships was Gage's *Literary Selections for Advanced Classes in Public and High Schools* (1901).[187] Opposite the title page it featured King Edward VII's photograph in full military regalia. Containing excerpts from Joseph Addison, Richard Trench and Max Muller, the predominate purpose of much of this texts was to illustrate 'the genius and natural temper of the English'.[188] Among its selections was J.G. Lyons' pungent Saxonist hymn, 'Triumphs of the English Language', an item which had appeared in officially endorsed school Readers as early as 1868.[189] Here Lyons' poem was less obtrusively retitled 'The English Language'.[190] It explicitly thematizes the role of literature within a dynamic imperialism, recruiting Shakespeare and Milton to the project of disseminating English throughout the world. Other exemplary figures are also enlisted: Robinson Crusoe, Isaac Newton, King Alfred — all exemplify the imperial mission and become auspicious colonizers. Even more revealing is William Story's 'English Speech', which suggests that the English language is itself an imperial apparatus — extracting what it needs from the language of other countries ('Not from one metal alone the perfectest mirror is shapen') and historical epochs, purifying the residue, turning it into 'imported wealth'.[191] The resultant language is mainly a weapon, a 'good stout English', 'mine and my ancestors' tongue', which the poem's metaphors superimpose on other imperialist competencies: geographic conquest, naval power, equestrian mastery, even providing a veiled reference to the plundering of foreign artifacts for English museums. The overall effect of the poem is to integrate the English language with other modalities of belligerent rule. Not unexpectedly the poem ends by denigrating 'feeble Italian', and 'French with its nasal lisp'.

Another function of such anthologies in a colonial setting was to mediate between a variety of social voices, embodying the 'nation' by holding in relation Irish, English, French and Native peoples through the selected themes, images and, more invisibly, the inclusions and exclusions enacted. Anthologies and literary curricula generally in this sense are powers of representation,[192] a mapping of social identities along racial, ethnic, gender and class lines. There are important links here between the concept of 'representation' as employed within literature or language theory, and the political 'representativeness' of the state: in each a claim is made to provide for others a service of reconciliation, a simple reflection of realities which they only record. Yet such texts not only described, they proscribed social life, including as excluded the differences they constructed and contained.[193] At the level of the literary anthology, for instance, poetic animations of the Native as noble savage,[194] of the Irish as sentimental or comic,[195] of the English as sober and rational, were staged upon an aesthetic field where racial essences met and were recuperated in a particular way, a paper landscape for the production of 'complementary' but hierarchized identities reworked into an organic whole within the covers of a single book.

Williams Spanos has referred to this operation of the anthology as a 're-collective' one: not a simple 'recollection' of 'our heritage', but rather 'a history of subtle coercions', assimilating cultural and historical differences in the interests of a 'Proper' image of 'Man'.[196] While at first glance, school anthologies appeared to be omniscient samplers of various cultural voices and historical periods, and thus a type of social memory students were held accountable for ('memory work'), they were equally a form of State cannibalism justifying and embodying the 'nation' by offering students a metaphorical and departicularized genealogy.[197] By systematically manipulating cultural identities, diagramming them in relation to a dominant and invisible axis, they amounted to a form of textual imperialism.[198] The panoptic school Reader can therefore be regarded as a theatrical space — that of the State — and not merely a window on 'Man and His World',[199] as the title of an officially approved and widely used Ontario English textbook of the 1970s prompted us to believe. It is interesting that while English teachers carefully attend to the rhetoric of specific poems or narratives, the profession as a whole has almost completely ignored the totalizing rhetorical techniques of anthology and curriculum.

The predominance of 'English' authors in school literary anthologies and the referential universe they instantiated (English scenery, landmarks, heroes) was a clear message to the diverse peoples who settled here during the period I examine, an assimilationist's signal that the terms 'Motherland' or 'home' really designated but one legitimate set of memories and identities. There is at work here a series of relays of the kind Roland Barthes describes in 'Myth Today'[200] whereby a race (English), a language (English), a landscape (England), and a literature (English) form a semiological chain in which each signifier preys upon the meanings of the previous term, the end result being a set of school texts which embody quintessential 'Englishness'. In the discourse of Scadding, Ryerson, Ross and other early Ontario educators, concepts such as 'literature', 'nation' and 'empire' could all be coordinated with one another because race was the explanatory category beneath all of them. The point to stress is that while the term 'race' was supposedly an objective category which literature simply reflected, it was, in Henry Gates's apt phrase, 'a dangerous trope' accomplished as much by school Readers as by other social practices.[201]

Moreover, although the 'racial' exclusion described above was enacted at the formation of English disciplinarity, it continued to haunt the literary-pedagogical from the 'inside' after this founding moment, persisting as the distorted images of other social groups found in school anthologies. French Canadians, for instance, were represented in Wetherell's *Poems of the Love of Country* by the 'habitant verse of W.H. Drummond, a form of speech akin to 'talking nigger' for blacks. The following sample gives the flavour here:

> Dat's about de way we're leeving', dat's a few t'ing we're seein'
> W'en de nice warm summer sun is shinin' down on Canadaw,
> An' no matter w'at I'm hearin, still I never feel lak bein'
> No oder stranger feller, me, but only habitant.[202]

The pressure of what was ruled 'outside' was continual once the original lines were drawn. It is important, therefore, not to see boundary setting as simply an innocent enabling device, a kind of institutional blindness which provides us with offsetting insights at a reasonable cost. Rather, the disciplinary boundaries of English were always 'ambivalent demarcations' in Samuel Weber's terms,[203] forms of active denial and suppression with real social costs, dispossessions of other classes and women. Additionally, a 'racy' language and literature functioned to restrict and delimit immigrant groups seen as 'strange' or 'alien'. In their vigorous endorsement of Saxonism, Ontario Readers therefore played an important part in legitimizing those social forces beyond the school which attempted to assimilate 'the foreigner' to a self-evidently progressive and inevitable Englishness.[204] In this sense imperialism was just as much a set of literary-pedagogical practices as it was an international economic or military order.

Empire Day as Literary Display

One of the pedagogical forms which developed by the end of the century for cultivating patriotic and imperial subjectivities was a ceremony called 'Empire Day'. Robert Stamp has traced the process whereby Clementina Fessenden's concern for racially inspired patriotic ritual combined with George Ross's zealous imperialism to produce an annual school ceremony across the province by 1899.[205] Their mutal brainchild proved so effective that Ross sold the idea not only to his fellow provincial premiers, but to influential imperialists in England who in turn promulgated it around the globe.[206] Fessenden could accurately observe in 1914 that 'the Empire story' was annually retold to more than twenty million children in imperial territories, thus becoming 'a valuable imperial asset' in its own right, 'to be counted on as needs be'.[207] The racial charge of this ceremony is conveyed by Governor-General Earl Grey's remark to the assembled school children of Toronto in 1909 that the day was a means of pledging 'to be true to the traditions and to the mission of your race'.[208]

What I want to stress about this ritual is its literariness. It was not only a cultural form created by two people who had already demonstrated their literary-national concern, nor did it just consist of flag-waving drills, though these were its standard feature.[209] Rather it was preeminently a form of literary embodiment. In nurturing pupils throughout the year on the patriotic discourse supplied by school Readers, teachers were also asked to keep Empire Day in one corner of their curricular vision, assisting pupils in preparing recitations and readings some of which invariably came from the texts we have examined. The preface of the 1926 'teacher's manual' for school Readers advised, 'Special lessons may be chosen for special occasions such as Christmas and Empire Day ...'[210]

Empire Day can be partially understood as the ritualization of the literary genre Ross had taught the province to read. Its first celebration in May of 1899 came six years after the publication of his own *Patriotic Recitations*, and produced the same values in more theatrical and public ways. In his initial instructions to teachers on the conduct of the Day there is even a veiled reference to this text. In the morning teachers were to utilize

> readings by Canadian and British authors ... [and] interesting historical incidents in connections with our own country. The aim of the teacher in all his references to Canada and the Empire should be, to make Canadian patriotism intelligent, comprehensive and strong.
>
> The afternoon, commencing at 2:30 might be occupied with patriotic recitations, songs, and readings by the pupils and speeches by trustees, clergymen and such other persons as may be available. The trustees and public generally should be invited to be present at these exercises.[211]

Similar circulars were issued annually, invariably referring to the utility of English 'literature', 'its distinguished authors', and advising 'patriotic recitations, songs, readings' as the principal means of fostering nationalism-cum-imperialism.[212] In reality celebrating empire meant celebrating Englishmen as heroic figures most frequently drawn from royal, military or literary hagiologies. The preferred saints in the latter case were Shakespeare, Burke, Goldsmith, Tennyson and Dickens.[213] The official programme for schools in 1914 incorporated many of the poems in the anthologies referred to above, including F.G. Scott's 'The Hymn of Empire'.[214] In 1906 Ross's successor as minister of education, Robert Pyne, fine tuned patriotic observances still further by officially endorsing for school use the 'patriotic programmes' provided by the 'Imperial Order of the Daughters of the Empire'.[215] These were to be implemented 'on the Fridays of each month'. A typical programme involved a motto (usually a few lines from Tennyson),[216] a couple of readings, a recitation and a song.[217] Perhaps the most spectacular embodiment of the literary occurred in 1899 when the girls of the Toronto Normal School paraded in white dresses and performed a tableau illustrating the poems of Rudyard Kipling which ended with 'graceful evolutions' to the strains of 'The British Grenadiers'.[218] Similarly, school texts like Agnes Machar's *Stories of the British Empire* (1914) provided short heroic narratives 'for young and busy folks' in order that they might better appreciate the 'great privilege ... great responsibility' of belonging to an Empire.[219] Behind such stories Machar insisted was that single 'wonderful Story of our British Empire ... [and] a sense of its Divine purpose, its final mission to humanity, as the end for which the shoot of Saxon freedom, planted in British soil, has grown into the greatest Empire this world has ever seen'.[220] Other imperial organizations sprang up during this period and fostered the literary-imperial. The League of Empire, for instance, held an annual competition for 'the Lord Meath Empire Day Challenge Cup' and 'League of Empire Prizes' for the best essay 'written in Schools on May 24th (Empire Day), or some day adjacent ...'[221] The set topics in 1921 were, 'For what great ideals does the British Empire stand?', 'Show how the overseas Empire grew', or 'What constitutes "Patriotism"?' I recall similar competitions sponsored by the Imperial Order of the Daughters of the Empire when I was in public school.

Wider Still and Wider[222]

There is a revealing and symptomatic slippage in the discourse of early twentieth-century advocates of English studies. Their claims for the civilizing properties of English as the sweetest of all the humanities still disclose the marks of its racial and imperial birth. In a study on 'The Bearing of English Upon the National Life', for instance, produced for the English Association (of England) in 1910, C.H. Herford argued that English studies was 'exceptionally fruitful' as an 'educational instrument' for adapting individual 'conduct' to national life.[223] It accomplished this because it 'mould[ed] ... what may roughly be called the mind of England'.[224] And since this 'tribal or national mind' was characterized by 'matter-of-fact practicality, mechanical ingenuity, masterful self-assertion, political sagacity, and shrewd common sense', a heritage of 'spiritual wealth' in brief, it could be asserted 'without any blustering patriotism ... [as] of great and enduring significance', not only within England for the English 'at home', but for the rest of us as well — in Herford's words an essential facet of 'the history of civilization and of mankind ... an indispensible part of what [is] called in education the Humanities ...'[225]

A belief in the superiority of the Anglo-Saxon 'race', then, and its duty to civilize the 'subject' or 'backward races' of the earth ('the white man's burden' according to Rudyard Kipling), endowed a humanist English studies with a similar mission. Appearing on the same panel ('Imperial Co-operation in Education') as S.A. Morgan at the 1921 Leaue of Empire conference in Toronto, J.H. Fowler of Bristol recommended 'English Literature as a Bond of Empire'.[226] He urged the assembled imperialists in Convocation Hall to grasp 'the importance of the study of English language and literature as an essential part of school training on the grounds of practical utility, an enlightened patriotism, and the humane ideal in education'.[227] In words recalling the rhetoric of Henry Scadding sixty years earlier, Fowler claimed literature facilitated not only a 'bond of sentiment', but a 'bond of race', making available

> 'the common heritage', 'the sacred fire from the hearth of the mother city' which British colonists carry all over the world, which is the British point of view, the British way of looking at life. It is traditional and instinctive, and it expresses itself in deeds — the deeds of statesmen, soldiers, farmers, mechanics, traders; but it finds expression in thought and words as well, and its finest expression in thought and words is that English literature which is the common dower of the race, and should be the greatest bond between them. Do we make the most of this priceless possession? It is not a foolish boast but the statement of an unchallenged fact, to say that in English literature we have one of the ... greatest literatures of the world — a crowning achievement of the spirit of man — the best that has been thought in the world upon all the themes that vitally touch humanity expressed in the best way... That literature was not produced for specialists: it has a message for all — for settlers in the wilds... as truly as for students and their professors ... It is something better even than a bond of Empire. It is — if it be really impressed upon the feeling of the race — an assurance that the race shall give to humanity the best and highest of which it is capable.[228]

At the end of the period I survey stands the Newbolt Report, *The Teaching of English in England*, published in 1921. It too celebrated English as 'Englishness', a way of forming 'good citizens' and serving the nation by providing a 'common culture', while simultaneously seeing it as the vehicle of a 'new humanism'.[229] In 1923 Newbolt attended the 'National Council of Education' at the University of Toronto on 'Education and Citizenship' where, along with Baden-Powell, he was awarded an honorary degree. He gave two lectures at this conference, both of which drew upon his earlier Report and advocated the power of an English studies as a form of 'humanism' to consolidate the nation.

> We claim further that an English humanism, including the study of
> literature, of history, and of language as an instrument of thought
> and expression, if made actual by being brought closely into touch
> with the main preoccupations of the students, might go far not
> only to enable the education of the industrial worker, but also to
> bridge the gulf between industry and culture.[230]

In his second talk Newbolt reinforced the linkages between 'our language,
our literature, our national life', claiming that 'a liberal education' was
a 'gift proposed by the State in undertaking the elementary training of
its citizens'.[231] Others at the conference like E. Crummy of Winnipeg
and B.R. Barnett of Toronto framed their own remarks in Newbolt's
discourse.[232]

But what is rarely commented upon is Newbolt's desire to export this
Englishness to the colonies. In the preface to his 1922 anthology, *A Book of
Verse Chosen for Students at Home and Abroad*, a text published continuously
over this decade, he illustrates the culmination of the linguistic and literary
strategies I've been tracing.

> The anthology now offered was first designed as a book to be used
> by students in India or the Dominions, where a knowledge of
> English literature is, in a sense, almost more necessary than it has
> hitherto been considered in our own country. This is natural
> enough, for English — the language of the Empire — is an old and
> rich language, whose every word is laden with associations; ... To a
> home-born Englishman they come in some degree by use, by
> tradition, and by easy education: but by one another continent or
> another race they must be carefully acquired, and this can only be
> done by familarity with the writings where they are exemplified.
> Even more than this is involved: it is of importance for every
> citizen of the Empire to understand the working of the historic
> English mind, and the English mind cannot be studied with any
> depth or certainty unless in the field of English Literature, and
> especially of English Poetry. It was desired, then, to furnish an
> introduction to English thought and language ... [for those] who
> meet in it the ideas and associations of a culture from which their
> own has diverged or which their race has not yet accepted.[233]

Newbolt's linkage of race and language was only the refinement by
1922 of very deeply rooted orientations to English studies, ones which
now wore the mantle of Empire at the moment of its decline. This union of
power and literary discourse occurred because educators understood that
the English Empire was more than just the red patches on the school globe.
It was also, in the words of Edward Hartley Dewart, a 'collective moral
and intellectual activity', a 'princely literature' which fashioned 'hearts'.[234]
Essayist Stephen Leacock also valued education because it was a form of

cultural politics. In an address entitled 'Empire and Education' in 1907, he revised conventional wisdom to read 'The hand that rules the blackboard rocks the world'.[235] 'Historic English mind' embodied in the English language or the canonic texts of its Literature and posed against 'other' languages or literatures was an enduring theme of educators in Ontario and elsewhere. Even the alternatives on offer in Newbolt's final line — deviation or assimilation — still linger.

One of the legacies of this linkage was that humanist versions of English have had racial features systematically built into them which were taken for granted until fairly recently. Professors of English at the University of Toronto like H.V. Routh, for instance, felt a literary 'neo-humanism' provided 'insight' into an essential 'human nature' everywhere and timelessly the same.[236] However, in his *The Diffusion of English Culture* (1941) Routh provided a primer for English teachers as 'British emissaries' who disseminated 'British culture' in colonial settings around the globe, cautioning them about the dangers of being 'un-English'.[237] Likewise in *English Character and the English Literary Tradition* (1952), Malcolm Wallace, principal and professor emeritus of English at University College (Toronto), and member of the Society for Pure English, maintained that an unbroken and 'living continuing tradition' of English letters was the best photograph of 'English character'. He even revived Kipling's notorious phrase, 'the white man's burden', remarking that it was 'ceasing to be a phrase for cynicism'.[238]

Recent objections to the representation of Jews in *Merchant of Venice* or blacks in *Huckleberry Finn*, texts often used within Ontario schools, can only be met therefore with indignant surprise if we ignore the way literary works were initially formed and later refunctioned within schooling as part of specific relations of power and domination. Generally the so-called 'Third World' has been misrepresented or exoticized in school literature (i.e. when it is visible at all), as in that standard of secondary curricula, Joseph Conrad's *Heart of Darkness*.[239] School anthologies have never been immune from the discrimination and prejudices of the society they inhabit. Imperial relations inscribed the poetries and fictions studied in school partly because ethnocentricity works 'at the limits of logocentricity, the unknown territory mapped neatly on to the familiar' polarities set up within any discourse.[240] English studies has been in this respect a form of 'dream-work' serving to justify western superiority and domination.[241]

Moreover, as Gates has remarked, the formalist preoccupation of the twentieth century with linguistic or literary technique has only 'bracketed or suspended' such questions: 'there was no need to speak of matters of race, since the race of the authors was 'the same'.'[242] The authorized text I used as a high school student illustrates this claim. Its preface states that the selections included are

necessarily almost entirely English. Yet this is not a serious disadvantage, for English literature is representative of western-European culture in general. All culture is to some extent racial, for the thought-experience of a people is conditioned by its own national heritage. But there is sufficient contact with other races and other cultures to provide a refreshing stimulus to literature without displacing its essential qualities.[243]

Direct evidence of 'sufficient contact' amounted to selections from Edward Fitzgerald's exoticizing 'The Rubaiyat of Omar Khayyam' and James Flecker's aestheticized 'Golden Journey to Samarkand'[244] — i.e. an imposed version of the 'Orient as stereotype and phantasm' in Malek Alloula's apt phrase.[245] Published six years after Wallace's focus on essential Englishness, this text reveals racialism alive and well within contemporary English studies. It is time to utilize texts in which other cultures represent themselves, thereby exposing the contradictory claims of a liberal English studies to be both universal and national.

Finally, the thematic of the 'inside/outside' extends beyond the English classroom affecting forms of perception in the wider community into which school English is inserted, and helps to make sense of the continuing colonial mentality found in statements like the following:

> Somehow the idea was planted in me that the English landscape had a spiritual legitimacy that our Canadian landscape did not, because it was always the English landscape we read about ... England was where stories were set, where people had adventures; England became the land of story books for me. English woods, English meadows, lanes and villages stirred feelings that ours did not, as did the words for features of the English landscape not encountered in Canada ... England became more real than our own world, because of the books we lived in from childhood.[246]

> We children of post-war Canada were reared on English writers. Our first literary excursions were with Peter Rabbit, Christopher Robin and Enid Blyton. At summer camp we were steeped in the lore of Robin Hood in our own smiling Glens. In high school we were comparing and contrasting the landscape of Hardy, Austen and D. H. Lawrence.
> Indeed the mists of dale and health belong to our childhood as much as to the people who are born and bred among them. Little wonder we are so strongly drawn to visit England again and again. ... Perhaps the best [area visited] was Clovelly. No writers have come from or written about Clovelly. Yet here, on the north coast of Devon — King Arthur's Coastline — everything came together from the images of literature.[247]

This is overstated of course. The influence of American media was just as formative during the lifetime of these two writers. But its truth lies in the fact that, regardless of a pervasive American influence in the wider culture, the occasional Canadian studies course, or the rhetoric of 'language processes' within education, most secondary English courses still foster 'Englishness', that is, a racially constituted sameness and otherness which appears natural by operating within the language of the classroom.

Conclusion

Recently and radically a number of questions have been posed for a more self-conscious English studies: the legacy of a historical or 'instituting' moment and the nature of the 'disciplinary' boundaries it established, the subsequent institutionality of a practice, and the social interests it has served as a form of cultural production. In spite of its renewal in Ontario, as elsewhere, English has become an increasingly problematic category to spend one's working life within even at its most photogenic moments; at its worst it is little more than an archaic 'disciplinary ghetto'[248], a sadly inadequate way to understand the operation of social-linguistic products in an 'age of mechanical reproduction'. The frequent suggestion that English should be superseded by other forms of curricular organization, such as that designated by the term 'cultural studies', is only outrageous to guild interests while it is widely discussed elsewhere.[249] Beyond the minor revisions of methodology in professional journal or Ministry directives, therefore, there are pressing questions for the current practice of English studies, ones which can no longer be avoided even by those unwilling to peer over departmental hedgerows or beyond the professional circle.

I have argued throughout that the teaching of English in Ontario schools was from its inception in 1871 a set of practices which enacted cultural politics at the level of theories of language and of the literary. This was hardly a situation unique to Ontario, however, since the founding of English studies generally can be located within the expansion of a global English empire. More specifically, in a colonial situation it arose out of the perceived needs of an English elite attempting to secure their cultural hegemony by extending and revitalizing a normalizing language curriculum in the unstable circumstances of late nineteenth-century immigration, growing nationalism, and the shifting class relations of early industrializ-ation. An ironic offshot of this formative period has been a claim of ideological innocence, the belief that somehow English studies transcends politics, a myth which has plagued English pedagogy to the present day. This fiction is harder to maintain given the historical facts of English's constitutive relation to state and empire formation, as well as the explicit statements of founding figures that the study of 'higher' English was 'Englishness', a racial and imperial positioning, not merely advanced language training. This is not to say, however, that the ideology sold was the ideology bought by the pupils it was intended for. There is a need, for example, for accounts of what it was like to experience such texts and teaching from the perspective of students, and thus to see what registered and what was refused, as well as how it affected their writing and reading beyond the schoolroom.

Part of a more self-conscious recovery of English studies, therefore, would mean recognizing the importance of curricular history. In an important sense 'subjects are their histories',[250] and what we think 'English' really is as a discipline, turns out in fact to be a residue of its historical appearances, a condensation of various discourses only partially grasped when their historicity, their conditions of actualization are removed. In this light we need to understand present English pedagogy as littered/layered with the contradictory discursive forms of the past. The power embedded in linguistic practices does not disclose itself easily to a historical archaeology; it is necessary to account for the multiple refunctioning of forms in a variety of situations. Moreover, literary and linguistic pedagogy has always been a triangulation between several factors: curriculum guidelines and requirements, what seems to work with a particular generation of students, the theoretical and practical knowledge available to teachers, etc. But to put it this way is to point to the State, to historical communities/generations, and discursive forms which, when unpacked, are always social relations — in Foucault's terms, 'relations of power'.[251]

Related to a calculation of English practice and confirmed by the documents surveyed, there is a need to see, in Gayatri Spivak's trenchant phrase, 'the productive undecidability of the borderlines of politics, art, law and philosophy as they sustain and are sustained by the identity of a composite entity such as the state ...'[252] If there is to be a more progressive teaching of language and literacy, then borders will have to be crossed between 'fields of study' usually kept apart, into a fuller awareness of history and politics. The early history of English studies suggests that such separations are artificial at any rate, since English routinely internalized and depended upon a 'range of naturalized and idealized concepts available in [the wider] culture'.[253] This should lead us in turn to see in our present as well that 'literary idealization is necessarily in dialogue with, and embedded in all other idealizations by which our culture sustains and justifies itself ...'[254]

What a historical approach to the teaching of English has to offer the present is that present returned to it as a pedagogical moment socially organized, regulated and historically defined by means of a number of ongoing political struggles. Perhaps the greatest disadvantage of presenting a seamless and ahistorical 'English' has been the effacement of the racial and imperial dynamics implicit in the term 'English' itself. In a colonial and multicultural society it was just as often as a weapon against others (French, first peoples, recent immigrants) as it was a celebration of universal humanity. Though French-Canadians, for instance, were represented in school anthologies, it was through the demeaning voice of William Henry

Drummond's 'Habitant'. These conflicts are more easily suppressed if we think of 'language' as simply a medium with technical specificities, and literary forms as merely matters of genre, tone and taste, rather than what they really are — forms of social life. To foreground historical conflict, therefore, means reformulating an awareness of 'English' as neither unitary nor neutral knowledge, but the political construction of a plurality of discourses operating behind the labels 'language', 'literacy', and the 'literary'. It also entails that such discourses are continually in flux, and that by seeing English studies as a construction it becomes an arrangement constantly rearranged, and thus alterable in our present.

In turn what is lost to a profession ignorant of its own history is the weave of ideology in the discourse of English studies from its inception. Margaret Mathieson notes that our formidable historical ignorance contributes to the 'martyr's preparation' we provide novice English teachers.[255] As 'cultural missionaries' they are largely ignorant of the historical commitments of their practice, of the formidable political presence of the forms of language pedagogy they inherit. In contrast, by restoring the political historicity of English teaching, we make it possible to grasp the institutional conditions of a practice, its historical shifts, internal contradictions, relationships with other adjacent or antagonistic discourses, and the normalizations implicit in its operation. Potentially this means that teachers might relocate themselves among the actual communities and historical situations they find themselves in. At any rate, it is no longer sufficient to accept 'English' on its own traditional and self-serving terms, a rhetoric which has been 'pugnaciously antihistorical'[256] and politically neutralizing. What Henry Giroux has termed the 'liberatory memory'[257] of history, and the provision of a historical vocabulary, is beginning to inform current debates on English studies.

Notes

1 'Education: Back in the hot seat again', *Toronto Star*, Saturday 24 January 1987, pp. B1, B8.

2 Cf. 'Ontario sets a standard for English exams' [headline], *Toronto Star*, 28 February 1987, pp. A1, A12.

3 Ontario Ministry of Education, *Handbok for Designing and Marking*, March 1986, p. 22.

4 Ontario Ministry of Education, 'Memorandum to Directors of Education, Principals of Secondary Schools, Principals of Inspected Private Schools', 2 December 1987, p. 3.

5 *Ibid.*, pp. 3–5.

6 *Toronto Star*, 28 February 1987, p. A1.

7 Terence Hawkes's editorial introduction to Methuen's *New Accents* series provides the relevant manifesto. HAWKES, T. in Salmusinszky, I. (1987), *Criticism in Society*, New York, Methuen, p. ix.

8   DOYLE, B. (1982) 'The hidden history of English studies' in WIDDOWSON, P. (Ed.), *Re-reading English*, London, Methuen, pp. 17–31, p. 17.

9   WILLIAMS, R. quoted in GREEN, M. (1982) 'The Centre for Contemporary Cultural Studies', in WIDDOWSON, P. (Ed.) *Re-reading English*, London, Methuen, pp. 77–90.

10 *Ibid.*, p. 78.

11 HUNTER, I. (1984) 'Literary Discipline', *Southern Review*, Vol. 17, No. 2, July, pp. 129–34, p. 131.

12 EAGLETON, T. (1984) 'The Rise of English Studies', *Southern Review*, No. 17, March, pp. 18–32, p. 18.

13 Cf. WILLIAMS, R. (1961) *The Long Revolution*, London, Chatto and Windus; FROW, J. (1986), *Marxism and Literary History*, Cambridge, Harvard UP; GODZICH, W. and SPADACCINI, N. (Eds) (1986) *Literature Among Discourses*, Minneapolis, University of Minnesota Press; and EAGLETON, T. (1984) *The Function of Criticism*, London, Verso.

14 Cf. ANDERSON, B. (1983) *Imagined Communities, Reflections on the Origin and Spread of Nationalism*, London, Verso. For a recent use of literature to distill an essential England, see BAKER, K. (1988) *The Faber Book of English History in Verse*, London, Faber.

15 Cf. COOK-GUMPERZ, J. (Ed.) (1986) *The Social Construction of Literacy*, Cambridge, University of Cambridge Press.

16 Ontario Ministry of Education, *Ontario Academic Courses*, Senior Division, 1984, pp. 5–6; English *Curriculum Guideline*, 1987, pp. 2, 7.

17 DAVIES, T. (1978) 'Education, Ideology and Literature', *Red Letters*, No. 7, pp. 4–13, p. 13.

18 English *Guideline*, 1987, p. 7.

19 *Ibid.*, p. 7. For a discussion of the problems with a 'multicultural' perspective, see YOUNG, J. (1987), *Breaking the Mosaic: Ethnic Identities in Canadian Schooling*, Toronto, Garamond Press.

20 The Canadian constitution was 'repatriated' on 17 April 1982.

21 English *Curriculum Guideline*, 1987, p. 2.

22 Cf. FOUCAULT, M. (1979) *Discipline and Punish*, trans. Alan Sheridan, New York, Vintage Books, p. 194: 'We must cease once and for all to describe the effects of power in negative terms: it "excludes", it "represses", it "censors", it "abstracts", it "masks", it "conceals". In fact, power produces; it produces reality; it produces domains of objects and rituals of truth. The individual and the knowledge that may be gained of him belong to this production.'

23 FOUCAULT, M., quoted in RABINOW, P. (Ed.) (1984), *The Foucault Reader*, New York, Pantheon Books, p. 11.

24 Ontario Ministry of Education, *Curriculum Guideline*, 1987, pp. 2, 4, 17.

25 Cf. HUNTER, I. (1984), 'Literary Discipline, *Southern Review*, Vol. 17, No. 2, July, pp. 129–34.

26 The Ontario Ministry of Education, *English*, Intermediate Division Curriculum Guideline, 1977, p. 3.

27 *Ibid.*, p. 20.

28 SMITH, B.H. (1983), 'Contingencies of Value', *Critical Inquiry*, Vol. 10, No. 1, September, pp. 1–35, pp. 1, 2.

29 *Ibid.*, p. 26.

30 Cf. Toronto Board of Education, *Values Teaching and the Language Arts/English*

Program, May, 1987. While acknowledging a shift away from earlier assumptions regarding a set of 'common values' which English curricula would inculcate, and towards a contemporary concern for the needs of the 'individual' pupil, this document goes on to argue English studies should be 'concerned with producing citizens', p. 10.

31 English *Guideline*, 1987, p. 6. Contrast with this Foucault's understanding of 'experience' as itself 'the correlation between fields of knowledge, types of normativity, and [the] forms of subjectivity' promoted by a discursive regime. FOUCAULT, M. (1986) *The Uses of Pleasure*, New York, Vintage Books, p. 4.

32 BELSEY, C. (1983), 'Literature, History, Politics', *Literature and History*, Vol. 9, No. 1, Spring, pp. 17–27, p. 17.

33 *Ibid.*, p. 18.

34 Cf. DOYLE, B. (1986) 'The Invention of English', in COLLS, R. and DODD, P. *Englishness: Politics and Culture, 1880–1920*, London, Croom Helm, pp. 89–115, p. 111.

35 FOUCAULT, M. (1979) p. 220.

36 FOUCAULT, M. (1986) p. 29.

37 FOUCAULT, M. (1979) p. 221–8.

38 FOUCAULT, M. (1982) 'The Subject and Power', *Critical Inquiry*, No. 8, Summer, pp. 777–95, p. 781.

39 COURT, F.E. (1985) 'Adam Smith and the Teaching of English Literature', *History of Education Quarterly*, Vol. 25, No. 3, Fall, pp. 325–40, p. 326.

40 *Ibid.*, pp. 329, 332.

41 YOUNG, G.P. in HODGINS, J.G. *Documenting History of Education*, [DHE hereafter], Vol. 20, 1868, p. 116.

42 SEELEY, J. (1870) 'English in Schools', in *Lectures and Essays*, London, Macmillan and Co., pp. 217–44. This was originally given as a speech in 1867.

43 Seeley as quoted in George Paxton Young's report for the 1868, DHE, Vol. 20, Chapter XIII, p. 115.

44 SEELEY, J. (1870) p. 219.

45 *Ibid.*, pp. 218–19.

46 SEELEY, J. (1883) *The Expansion of England*, London, Macmillan and Co.

47 Cf. 'Patriotic Programmes for October, November, December, January, February 1906–1907', *Annual Report*, pp. 133–5.

48 Editorial 'The Empire', *Canadian Educational Monthly*, Vol. 17, 1895, p. 352.

49 SEELEY, J. (1870) pp. 240, 238.

50 Cf. *Annual Report* (1864–1868).

51 *Annual Report* (1865) Appendix B, p. 78.

52 *Ibid.*, p. 78.

53 YOUNG, G.P., *Annual Report*, (1867–1868) pp. 119–20.

54 *Ibid.*, p. 119.

55 *Ibid.*, p. 337.

56 The current name of the official journal of the Ontario Council of Teachers of English is in fact *Indirections*.

57 BURRITT, E. (1877) 'The integration of the British Empire', in *Canadian Monthly and National Review*, Vol. 12, pp. 124–33.

58 BAHKTIN, M. quoted in EMERSON, C. (1983) 'The Outer Word and Inner Speech', *Critical Inquiry*, Vol. 10, December, p. 245–64.

59 Cf. BARTHES, R. (1973)*Mythologies*, trans. Lavers, A. London, Paladin.

60 The expression is Matthew Arnold's in his report on the French School system. It is contained in RYERSON, E. (1868) *A Special Report on the Systems and State of Popular Education on the Continent of Europe, in the British Isles, and the United States of America*, Toronto, Printed at the Leader Steam Press.

61 GOULDEN, H. and HARTLEY, J. (1982) 'Nor should such Topics as Homosexuality, Masturbation, Frigidity, Premature Ejaculation or the Menopause be Regarded as Unmentionable', in *Literature, Teaching, Politics*, No. 1, pp. 4–20, p. 14.

62 SAID, E. (1983) *The World, the Text and the Critic*, Cambridge, Harvard UP, p. 35.

63 For Foucault's notion of forms of knowledge as 'governance', see his 'Governmentality', *Ideology and Consciousness*, No. 6, Autumn 1979, pp. 5–21.

64 Cf. SAID, E. (1974) 'An Ethics of Language', *Diacritics*, Vol. 4, pp. 28–37, p. 35.

65 Cf. GUATTARI, F. (1984) 'Capitalist Systems, Structures and Processes' in *Molecular Revolution*, Harmondsworth, Penguin, pp. 273–87.

66 Cf. WEBER, S. (1987) *Institution and Interpretation*, Minneapolis, University of Minnesota Press.

67 Cf. FORGACS, D. and NOWELL-SMITH, G. (Eds) (1985) *Antonio Gramsci: Selections from Cultural Writings*, Cambridge, Harvard UP, p. 184.

68 SPIVAK, G. (1987) *In Other Worlds: Essays in Cultural Politics*, New York, Methuen, p. 105.

69 SAID, E. (1983) p. 11.

70 SAID, E. (1985) 'Orientalism Reconsidered', *Cultural Critique*, No. 1, Fall, pp. 89–107, p. 94.

71 For the reasons for this long delay in vernacular secondary education in Britain, see HOLLINGSWORTH, B. (1974) 'The Mother Tongue and the Public Schools in the 1860's', *British Journal of Educational Studies*, Vol. 22, pp. 312–23.

72 Cf. BATSLEER, J., DAVIES, T., O'ROURKE, R. and WEEDON, C. (1985) *Rewriting English*, London, Methuen.

73 *Journal of Education*, Editorial, 'Mr. Disraeli on English Literature', Vol. 23, 1870, pp. 52–3.

74 Cf. COHN, B.S. (1985) 'The Command of Language and The Language of Command', unpublished paper, Department of Anthropology, University of Chicago, June 1985; and SAID, E. (1979) *Orientalism*, New York, Vintage Books.

75 Cf. KIERNAN, V. (1969) *The Lords of Humankind: European Attitudes Towards the Outside World in the Imperial Age*, London, Weidenfeld and Nicholson, pp. 3–28.

76 Cf. MORRIS, J. (1982) *The Spectacle of Empire*, 'Style, Effect, and the Pax Britannica', London, Faber and Faber.

77 In additon to the works cited so far, see SAID, E. (1979) *Orientalism*, New York, Vintage Books.

78 SALUSINSZKY, I. (1987) 'Edward Said', Chapter Six of his *Criticism in Society*, New York, Methuen, pp. 123–48, p. 125.

79 SAID, E. (1978) p. 3.

80 DODD, P. (1986) 'Englishness and The National Culture', in *Englishness: Politics and Culture 1880–1920*, London, Croom Helm, pp. 1–28.

81 BHAHBA, H.K. (1985) 'Signs Taken for Wonders: Questions of Ambivalence and Authority under a Tree Outside Delhi, May 1817', *Critical Inquiry*, Vol. 12, Autumn, pp. 144–65, p. 152. My emphasis.

82 *Ibid.*, p. 151. My emphasis.

83 Said in SALUSINSZKY, I. (1987), p. 123.

84 SAID, E. (1985) pp. 90–1; SAID, E. (1983) p. 11.

85 GATES, H. (1985) 'Writing "Race" and the Difference it Makes', Editor's Introduction, *Critical Inquiry*, Vol. 12, No. 1, Autumn, pp. 1–20, p. 3.

86 *Ibid.*, p.15.

87 Cf. FESSENDEN, C. (1899) 'The Development of a National Literature', *Journal and Transactions of the Wentworth Historical Society*, Vol. 2, pp. 74–5.

88 GATES, H. (1985), p. 5.

89 SAID, E. (1978) 'The Problem of Textuality: Two Exemplary Positions', *Critical Inquiry*, No. 4, Summer, pp. 673–714, p. 704.

90 Cf. DOWLING, L. (1986) *Language and Decadence in the Victorian Fin de Siècle*, Princeton, Princeton UP.

91 For a description of Schlegel's racist philology, see SAID, E. (1979) pp. 98–9.

92 Cf. LLOYD, D. (1985–1986) 'Arnold, Ferguson, Schiller: Aesthetic Culture and the Politics of Aesthetics', in *Cultural Critique*, Vol. 2, Winter pp. 137–68.

93 Cf. AARSLEFF, H. (1983[1967]) *The Study of Language in England, 1780–1860*, Minneapolis, University of Minnesota Press, pp. 143–7.

94 *Ibid.*, pp. 147–53.

95 Cf. FROW, J. (1986) p. 180.

96 Quoted in JOHNSON, N. (1986) 'An Historical Perspective on the Role of Composition Instruction in English Education in Canada', paper given at the Ottawa International Conference on the Teaching of English, Carleton University, Ottawa, 11–16 May, p. 14.

97 Cf. DOWLING, L. (1986) p. 79. Dowling refers us to the editor of the influential manifesto of 1868, *Essays On A Liberal Education*, Frederic W. Farrar. His 'Philology and Darwinism' two years later argued that regarding 'the preservation of the best and strongest form in the struggle for life, Mr. Darwin's hypothesis may be confirmed and verified by the entirely independent researchers of the comparative philologist.'

98 For an early version of linguistic manifest destiny, see TAYLOR, B. (1874) 'The Spread of the English Language', *Journal of Education* (Ontario), Vol. 27, p. 90. See also WEST, M. (1934) 'English as a World Language', *American Speech*, Vol. 9, No. 3, October, pp. 163–74. West's project was to simplify everyday speech in order to come up with a version of English that would travel the world, so that it could be 'something that every foreigner can put into his head' (p. 174). West was a faculty member at the Ontario College of Education. See also BAILEY, R.W. and GORLACH, M. (1982) *English as a World Language*, Ann Arbor, University of Michigan Press.

99 GEORGE, [Rev.] J. (1867) *The Mission of Great Britain to the World, Or some of the Lessons which she is now Teaching*, A lecture delivered at Stratford, Toronto, Dudley and Burns, p. 4.

100 *Ibid.*, p. 4.

101 *Ibid.*, p. 6.

102 *Ibid.*, pp. 5, 6–7.

103 HODGINS, J.G. (1886) 'Candian National Homogeneity', *The Educational Weekly*, No. 64, March, p. 181.

104 *Ibid.*, p. 181.

105 Originally a major section of his *The School House*, Toronto: Printed for the Department of Public Instruction for Upper Canada by Lovell and Gibson, 1857, pp. 165–210, it was made available in pamphlet form for schools.

106 The title page states, 'Edited by Authority of the Chief Superintendent of Education for Upper Canada'.

107 *Ibid.*, p. iv.

108 HODGINS, J.G. (1868) *The School Speaker and Reciter*, Montreal, John Lovell.

109 RYERSON, E. (1842) 'Inaugural Address on the Nature and Advantages of an English and Liberal Education', delivered at the opening of Victoria College, 21 June 1842, pamphlet, Victoria College Archives, University of Toronto, printed at the Guardian Office, p. 12.

110 Egerton Ryerson cited in HODGINS, J.G., *DHE*, Vol. 7, p. 111.

111 'The National Readers in Our Schools', Editorial, *Journal of Education*, Vol. 19, 1866, pp. 37–9, p. 38.

112 Cited in HODGINS, J.G., *DHE*, Vol. 19, Chapter XII, pp. 68–9.

113 John Murray quoted in PARKER, G. (1985) *The Beginnings of The Book Trade in Canada*, Toronto, University of Toronto Press, p. 109.

114 Cf. GEIKE, [Rev.] A.C. (1857) 'Canadian English', *The Canadian Journal*, Transactions of the Canadian Institute, Vol. 2, pp. 344–55; and CHAMBERS, J.K. (1986) 'Lawless and Vulgar Innovations': Victorian Views of Canadian English', Department of Linguistics, University of Toronto.

115 NELLES, [Rev. Dr.] S. (1870) 'President's Address', *Annual Report and Proceedings of the Ontario Educational Association*, pp. 13–26.

116 DEWART, E.H. (1870) 'Characteristics and Tendencies of the Times', *Annual Report and Proceedings of the Ontario Educational Association*, pp. 26–38.

117 Appropriately Shakespeare was the first author whose work appeared in the curriculum independent of anthology or historical survey, and under the banner of the 'actual text of an author's work'.

118 Cf. HODGINS, T. (Ed.) (1857) *The Educational Directory and Calendar for 1857–58*, Toronto, Maclear and Co., p. 54.

119 SCADDING, H. (1897) 'Shakespeare The Seer — The Interpreter', 'Address delivered before the St. George Society of Toronto, in the Cathedral of St. James, April 23, 1864', Toronto, The Copp, Clark Co., p. 4.

120 SCADDING, H. (1860) 'English Civilization Undemonstrative', 'Address to the St. George Society in the Cathedral of St. James', Toronto, Rowsell and Hutchinson.

121 *Ibid.*, p. 5.

122 *Ibid.*, p. 13.

123 *Ibid.*, p. 9.

124 SCADDING, H. (1864) pp. 10, 13.

125 *Ibid.*, p. 14.

126 *Ibid.*, p. 13, 5.

127 *Ibid.*, p. 22.

128 *Ibid.*, p. 24.

129 *Ibid.*, p. 22.

130 KING, J. (1876) 'Our English Shakespeare', *Canadian Monthly and National Review*, Vol. 10, pp. 501–14; 'O.S.' (1880) 'What's Shakespeare?', *Rose Belford's Canadian Monthly and National Review*, Vol. 4, pp. 408–21. 'O.S.' quotes Emerson's statement that Shakespeare is 'the man who carries the Saxon race with him'.

131 Cf. HUDSON [Rev.] H. (1885) *Shakespeare's Merchant of Venice*, 'With introduction, and notes explanatory and critical ... for use in schools and classes', Boston, Ginn, Heath and Co.

132 MEIGHEN, A. (1936) *The Greatest Englishmen of History*, Ottawa, Buntin Reid.

133   *Ibid.*, pp. 33, 35.
134   SINFIELD, A. (1985) 'Give an account of Shakespeare and Education, showing why you think they are effective and what you have appreciated about them. Support your comments with precise references', in Dollimore, J. and Sinfield, A. (Eds) *Political Shakespeare*, Manchester, Manchester UP, pp. 134–57, p. 136.
135   TAINE, H.A. (1873) *History of English Literature*, trans. H. Van Laun, New York, John W. Lovell Co., pp. 30–3.
136   DEPARTMENT OF EDUCATION (Ontario) (1889) *Annual Report*, 134–5, p. 135.
137   THURBER, S. (1894) 'English in Secondary Schools: Some Considerations as to its Aims and its Needs', *Canadian Educational Monthly*, pp. 369–73, pp. 369–70.
138   GOGGIN, D.J. (1908) 'What Constitutes a Good Text-Book', *Annual Reports and Proceedings of the OEA*, pp. 248–56, p. 255.
139   *Ibid.*, p. 249.
140   This term, if not popular by 1864, became so due to the publication of a book with this title by Henry Alford, Dean of Canterbury: *The Queen's English*, London, George Bell, and Sons, 1897.
141   Cf. 'Pure English' (editorial), *Educational Weekly* (Ontario), No. 68, 22 April 1886, p. 251. In 1913 the 'Society for Pure English' (SPE) was founded in England by Robert Bridges and Walter Raleigh. Supported by eminent literary figures like Walter De La Mare, Thomas Hardy, A.C. Bradley, and Henry Newbolt, it counted among its Candian subscribers two members of the University of Toronto, G.M. Wong and M.W. Wallace. Its mandate was to establish a kind of Literary Academy made up of 'men of letters, and the better class of journalists' who could 'guide' the language during the rapid expansion of English around the world. Anything 'alien', 'un-English', or out of 'touch with the national means of expression', and thus tending 'towards degeneration', would be expunged. The terms of Romantic philology were adopted, language legislators approving of words 'made of English material, which are easily understood and naturally spoken by English-speaking people'. *SPE Tract*, No. XL, pp. 646–53; and *SPE Tract*, No. I, pp. 5–11.
142   READE, J. (1882–1883) 'Language and Conquest — A Retrospect and a Forecast', *Proceedings and Transactions of Royal Society of Canada*, Vol. 1, pp. 17–33, p. 17.
143   LLOYD, D. (1985–1986) pp. 148–9.
144   Macaulay cited in AARSLEFF, H. (1983) p. 139.
145   READE, J. (1882) p. 17.
146   *Ibid.*, p. 17.
147   *Ibid.*, p. 17.
148   READE, J. (1887–1888) 'Nation-Building', *The Week*, 1887, Part I, pp. 479–80; Part II, pp. 591–2; Part III, pp. 624–5; Part IV, pp. 688–9; 1888, Part V, pp. 36–7, p. 480. In part three he assessed the 'meagre' role played by the 'aborigines in building up our Canadian nationality ...', pp. 624–5.
149   Cf. Reade in WETHERILL, J.E. (1912) *Poems for the Love of Country*, Toronto, Macmillan Co., pp. 75–6.
150   HOUSTON, W. (1884) 'The Study and Teaching of English', *Annual Reports and Proceedings of the OEA*, pp. 54–70, pp. 69–70.
151   MORGAN, S.A. (1892) 'Metaphysical Theories on the Origin and Development of Language', An Address before the Hamilton Association, 1892, *Journal and Proceedings of the Hamilton Association*, No. 7, 1891–2 [Printed at the Hamilton Spectator Printing Co., 1892], pp. 174–85.

152 Cf. PARKENHAM, W. and MARSHALL, J. (1895) *Literature 1896, Selections*, Toronto, Copp, Clark Co.

153 HARRIS, R. (1987) 'English Studies at Toronto', a study of the University of Toronto's role in developing English as an academic discipline, forthcoming, p. 23.

154 KEYS, D.R. (1896) 'Our Debt as Teachers to Matthew Arnold', *Annual Report and Proceedings of the Ontario Educational Association*, pp. 126–36, p. 131.

155 WILSON, D., speaking at convocation in June 1888; quoted in Harris, R. (1987), p. 23.

156 The lines are from Wordsworth's poem, 'It is not to be thought of', which appeared in Wetherell (1912).

157 George Grant quoted in BERGER, C. (1970) *The Sense of Power, Studies in Canadian Imperialism 1867–1914*, Toronto, University of Toronto Press.

158 MORRISON, A.M. (1890) 'The Moral and the Poetic Instinct in Man', part five of a series, *Canada Educational Monthly*, pp. 205–10.

159 MORRISON, A.H. (1886) *The Art Gallery of the English Language*, Toronto, Williamson and Co., p. 282.

160 *Ibid.*, p. iii.

161 ALEXANDER, W.J. (Ed.) (1900) *Tennyson: Selected Poems*, 'Containing the Literature prescribed for the Junior Matriculation and Junior Leaving Examinations', Toronto: Copp, Clark Co., pp. xx–xxi.

162 *Ibid.*, pp. 12–13.

163 ALEXANDER, W.J. (1889) 'The Study of Literature', Inaugural Lecture delivered in Convocation Hall, 12 October, 1889, Toronto, Rowsell and Hutchinson, pp. 30–2.

164 Cf. 'Calendar' Faculty of Education, 1909–1910, p. 23.

165 STEVENSON, O.J. (1904) *The Study of Literature*, Toronto, Morang and Co., p. 6.

166 STEVENSON, O.J. and MARSHALL, J. (1899) *Select Poems*, Toronto, Copp, Clark Co., pp. xviii–xix.

167 STEVENSON, O.J. (1904) pp. 7–8.

168 *Ibid.*, p. 10.

169 STEVENSON, O.J. (1904) p. 23.

170 *Ibid.*, p. 22.

171 *Ibid.*, p. 22.

172 LEE, E. (1901) *Britain over the Sea*, A Reader For Schools, Toronto, George N. Morang and Co., pp. xi–xii.

173 *Ibid.*, pp. xliv–xlv.

174 Ross became Minister of Education in 1883, and Premier in the fall of 1899. He left office in 1905.

175 ROSS, G. (1904–1905) 'The Evolution of Canadian Sentiment', *Empire Club of Canada Speeches*, pp. 252–67, p. 257.

176 ROSS, G. (1884) 'President's Address', *Annual Reports and Proceedings of the OEA*, pp. 29–35, pp. 30–1.

177 ROSS, G. (1904–1905) p. 252.

178 *Ibid.*, p. 259.

179 Cf. BERGER, C. (1970).

180 ROSS, G. in *The London Advertiser*, 28 September 1900, as quoted in PAGE, R.J.D. (Ed.) (1972) *Imperialism and Canada, 1895–1903*, Toronto, Holt, Reinhart and Winston, pp. 37–8.

181 ROSS, G. (1893) *Patriotic Recitations and Arbor Day Exercises*, Toronto, Warwick Bros. and Rutter.

182 ROSS, G. (1893) p. v.

183 ROSS, G. (1893) p. v.

184 WETHERELL, J.E. (1912) *Poems for the Love of Country*, Toronto, Macmillan Co;
WETHERELL, J.E. (1919) *The Great War in Verse and Prose*, 'Printed by Order of the
Legislative Assembly of Ontario', Toronto, A.T. Wilgress.

185 *Fourth Book* (1909), p. 364.

186 Cf. BIRCH, T.A. (1956) *The English Mind as Reflected in Literature*, Montreal; Renouf
Publishing Co., pp. 270–1. A professor of English Literature at the University of
Montreal, Birch's book itself is testimony to the contemporary reach of a racially
organizsed English.

187 *Literary Selections for Advanced Classes in Public and High Schools*, Toronto, W.J. Gage
and Co., 1901 [No author given].

188 *Ibid.*, p. 142.

189 Lyons' poem first appeared in the *Advanced Reader* authorized for secondary
schools in Nova Scotia, and was subsequently reprinted in the Ontario *Fifth
Reader* of 1868. Nova Scotia Council of Public Instruction (1865) *The Advanced
Reader*, No. 7 of the Nova Scotia School Series, Halifax, A. and W. Mackinlay, pp.
109–10; Ontario *Fifth Reader* (1868) pp. 424–5.

190 *Ibid.*, pp. 153–5.

191 *Ibid.*, pp. 149–53.

192 Cf. COLLS, R. and DODD, P. (1986) *Englishness: Politics and Culture, 1880–1920*,
London, Croom Helm, pp. 1–61.

193 Cf. WHITE, A. (1983) 'The Dismal Sacred Word', in *Literature/Teaching/Politics*,
No. 2, pp. 4–15, p. 13.

194 Cf. WESTON, P.J. (1984) 'The Noble Savage as Bourgeois Subject', *Literature and
History*, Vol. 10, No. 1, Spring, pp. 59–71; CARR, H. (1986) 'The Myth of
Hiawatha', *Literature and History*, Vol. 12, No. 1, Spring, pp. 58–78.

195 Cf. 'The Celtic Race' (1851) a selection reprinted from Knox's *Races of Man* in the
Journal of Education for 1851. Here the Celts are seen as 'warm-hearted, full of
deep sympathies, dreamers ... warlike', etc., p. 167.

196 SPANOS, W.V. (1985) 'The Apollonian Investment of Modern Humanist Education: The Examples of Matthew Arnold, Irving Babbitt, and I.A. Richards',
Cultural Critique, Vol. 1, Fall, pp. 8–72, p. 9.

197 Cf. ALONSO, A.M. (1988) 'The Effects of Truth: Re-Presentations of the Past and
the Imagining of Community', *Journal of Historical Sociology*, Vol. 1, No. 1.

198 Cf. Edward Said's conception of a 'textual attitude' in *Orientalism* (1979) New
York, Vintage Books, p. 92.

199 ROSS, M. and STEVENS, J. (1961) *Man and His World*, Toronto, J.M. Dent and Sons

200 BARTHES, R. (1973) 'Myth Today' in *Mythologies*, trans. A. Lavers, London,
Paladin, pp. 109–59.

201 GATES, H. (1985) p. 5.

202 From 'The Habitant's Summer' in Wetherell, J.E. (1912) pp. 94–5.

203 Cf. WEBER, S. (1987), p. 148.

204 Cf. JAENEN, C.J. (1972) 'The Public School: Agency of Integration and Assimilation', a paper presented at the Eighth Annual Conference of the Canadian
Association of American Studies, University of Toronto, 27 October.

205 STAMP, R. (1973) 'Empire Day in the Schools of Ontario: the training of young
imperialists', *Journal of Canadian Studies*, Vol. 8, No. 3, pp. 32–42.

206 Cf. MCDONALD, N. (1980) 'Forming the National Character, 1867–1914',

Ph.D. Thesis, Ontario Institute for Studies in Education, University of Toronto, pp. 403–4.

207   *Ibid.*, p. 405.
208   Earl Grey in 1909, quoted in STAMP, R. (1973), p. 38.
209   Cf. *British Empire Drill* 'For 12 or 16 Boys', Toronto, Educational Publishing Co., 191- [no author given].
210   Ontario Government (1926) *Notes on the Ontario Readers*, 'Ontario Teachers' Manuals, Authorized', Toronto, Ryerson Press, p. vi.
211   Department of Education (Ontario) (1899) *Annual Report*, pp. 17–18.
212   For example, see the Department of Education (Ontario) (1905) 'Regulations and Circulars, Empire Day', *Annual Report*, Appendix F, p. 87.
213   Cf. Department of Education (Ontario) (1912) *Empire Day in Ontario*, Toronto, L.K. Cameron, p. 10.
214   Department of Education (Ontario) (1914) *Empire Day in Ontario*, Toronto, L.K. Cameron, p. 5.
215   Department of Education (Ontario) (1906) 'Patriotic Programmes for October, November, December, January, February, 1906–1907', *Annual Report*, p. 133–5.
216   For example, Tennyson's 'To England under Indian skies,/To those dark millions of her realm!/ To Canada whom we love and prize,/ What ever Statesman hold the helm' Quoted in the 1906 'Programme', p. 134.
217   The readings for November, 1906, are from J. Seeley's *Expansion of Empire*, Charles Dickens's *Christmas Carol*, Goldman's *The Empire and the Century*, and a final song, 'True Born Englishman'.
218   STAMP, R. (1973) p. 36.
219   MACHAR, A.M. (1914) *Stories of the British Empire*, Toronto, William Briggs, p. x.
220   *Ibid.*, p. x.
221   'Essay Competitions', *The School*, Vol. 9, No. 7, 1921, p. 507.
222   This phrase comes from the coronation ode, 'Land of Hope and Glory' by A.C. Benson. Put to the tune of Edward Elgar's 'Pomp and Circumstance', Benson's poem is still celebrated, most notably by England's Conservative party.
223   HERFORD, C.H. (1910) 'The Bearing of English Studies Upon the National Life', The English Association, Leaflet No. 15, p. 1. See also an earlier tract on this subject, WYLD, H.C. (1906) *The Place of the Mother-Tongue in National Education*, London, John Murray.
224   *Ibid.*, p. 1.
225   *Ibid.*, pp. 1, 14.
226   'League of Empire Programme', Second Meeting of the Imperial Conference of Teachers' Associations, Toronto, 10–12 August 1921.
227   *Ibid.*, p. 50.
228   *Ibid.*, pp. 50–1.
229   Cf. KING, N. (1987) 'The Teacher Must Exist Before the Pupil': The Newbolt Report on the Teaching of English in England, 1921', *Literature and History*, Vol. 13, No. 1, Spring, pp. 14–37. Also MATHIESON, M. (1975) *The Preachers of Culture: A Study of English and Its Teachers*, London, George Allen and Unwin, pp. 69–88.
230   'National Council of Education Conference on Education and Citizenship' [pamphlet], Toronto, Ontario, 4–8 April, 1923. Held 'in co-operation with the Ontario Educational Association', pp. 24, 20–1.
231   *Ibid.*, p. 21.

232 *Ibid.*, pp. 20–1. Crummy, for instance, states that 'literature is replete and resplendent with biographies' which provide 'glowing examples' of moral life.

233 NEWBOLT, H. (1922) *A Book of Verse Chosen for Students at Home and Abroad*, London, G. Bell and Sons.

234 DEWART, [Rev.] E.H. (1885) 'Self Education: The Cultivation of the mind and of the Body', Toronto *Globe*, 11 March 1885.

235 LEACOCK, S. (1906–1907) 'Empire and Education', *Empire Club Speeches*, pp. 280–99, p. 291.

236 ROUTH, H.V. (1943) 'Humanism: Past, Present and Future', in *Essays by Divers Hands*, Oxford, Oxford UP, pp. 1–15.

237 ROUTH, H.V. (1941) *The Diffusion of English Culture Outside England*, Cambridge, Cambridge UP, pp. 43–55. Routh's chapter titles give the flavour: 'Diplomatic Relations and the Influence of Culture'; 'The English Teacher's Opportunity Abroad ...'; 'The Language of Humanism and the Future'; 'The English Teacher's Opportunity Abroad [*sic*] ...'

238 WALLACE, M.W. (1952) *English Character and the English Literary Tradition*, Toronto, University of Toronto Press, p. 76.

239 Cf. ACHEBE, C. (1975) 'An Image of Africa', *Scrutiny*, 18 February, pp. 31–43; JANMOHAMED, A.R. (1985) 'The Economy of Manichean Allegory: The Function of Racial Difference in Colonialist Literature', *Critical Inquiry*, Vol. 12, No. 1, pp. 59–87.

240 BHABHA, H.K. (1983) 'Difference, Discrimination and the Discourse of Colonialism', in BARKER, F. *et. al.* (Eds) (1983) *The Politics of Theory*, Colchester, University of Essex, pp. 194–211, p. 196.

241 Cf. BHABHA, H. (1985) pp. 147, 164.

242 GATES, H. (1985) p. 4.

243 KINGSTON, E.F. (Ed.) (1959) *Poems to Remember*, Toronto, J.M. Dent and Sons, p. v–vi.

244 *Ibid.*, pp. 54–5, 362–3, 431.

245 ALLOULA, M. (1986) *The Colonial Harem*, trans. Myrna and Wlad Godzich, Minneapolis, University of Minnesota Press, pp. 3–5.

246 MACNEIL, R. (1989) *Wordstruck*, New York, Viking.

247 ENRIGHT, J. (1987) 'Literary Pilgrimage', *Toronto Star*, 1 August, p. G1.

248 SAID, E. (1983), p. 25.

249 Cf. EAGLETON, T. (1983) *Literary Theory*, Oxford, Basil Blackwell; EAGLETON, T. (1984) 'The Rise of English Studies', *Southern Review*, No. 17, March, pp. 18–32; EAGLETON, T. (1987) 'The End of English', *Textual Practice*, Vol. 1, No. 1, Spring, pp. 1–9; and WIDDOWSON, P. (1982).

250 INGLIS, F. (1985) *The Management of Ignorance: A Political Theory of the Curriculum*, Oxford, Basil Blackwell, p. 39.

251 FOUCAULT, M. (1980) *Power/Knowledge*, Brighton, Harvester, p. 114.

252 SPIVAK, G. (1982) 'The Politics of Interpretations', *Critical Inquiry*, Vol. 9, No. 1, pp. 259–78, p. 262.

253 NELSON, C. (1986) 'Against English: Theory and the Limits of the Discipline', *ADE Bulletin*, No. 85, Winter, pp. 1–6, p. 4.

254 *Ibid.*, p. 4.

255 MATHIESON, M. (1975) p. 210.

256 AARSLEFF, H. (1983) p. xv.

257 GIROUX, H. (1987) 'Literacy, Voice, and the Pedagogy of Political Empowerment', unpublished paper, University of Miami, Ohio, p. 17.

Chapter 8

Contested Terrain: English Education in South Africa 1948–1987

Hilary Janks, University of The Witwatersrand

This story of English education in South Africa begins with a description of state control of education. Language policy and the teaching of literature are examined in relation to the racial segregation of education, the state's policy of Christian National Education, the unequal distribution of educational resources, and the function of education in providing the labour needs of capital.

Resistance to state control is introduced at this stage but is not fully described until after a discussion of two state syllabuses. The comparison of English syllabuses for black and white students is included to illustrate current thinking about English education in the state system. Most significant here is the mismatch between such thinking and actual practice. The material conditions in which teachers and students in South Africa work constrain praxis. An understanding of state syllabuses is also important for an understanding of the draft proposals for People's English.

People's English concludes this story. People's Education for People's Power, of which People's English is a part, grows out of a continuing struggle to resist Apartheid education. The history of resistance to education and the state's repression of this resistance predates 1948 and is unlikely to end in 1987. The historical account offered is highly selective.

State Control of Education

State control in South Africa affects fundamental aspects of human life. Where you live, which hospital you go to, what work you do, what you are allowed to say, what you are allowed to see and read are all controlled by a formidable array of legislation. Apartheid capitalism determines people's lives and it is reinforced and maintained by the school system.

There are seventeen departments of education in South Africa. Black education outside the bantustans (the so-called independent states) is under the control of the Department of Education and Training (DET). There are separate departments for 'coloureds' (people of mixed race) and 'Indians' (people of Asian origin). White education is controlled by four separate departments, one for each of the four provinces in South Africa (Cape, Natal, Transvaal and the Orange Free State). In addition to these seven departments of education, there is a department for each of the bantustans: KaNgwane, Gazankulu, Lebowa, KwaNdebele, KwaZulu, QwaQwa, Ciskei, Transkei, Bophuthatswana and Venda. This fragmentation reveals the rigid racial segregation in education which is a non-negotiable feature of Apartheid. The duplication which results is costly and divisive and educational provision is unequal, preparing pupils ultimately for different forms of labour. A clear example of this is that education is compulsory to the age of 16 for 'coloureds' and whites and to the age of 15 for 'Indians' but is not compulsory at any age for African blacks. Despite the proliferation of departments, education policy is governed by acts of parliament and there is *de facto* centralized state control. The Department of Education and Training is, in addition, controlled largely by whites.

Language Policy

Any attempt to describe English teaching and learning in South Africa has to confront the divisions legislated into the school system. Mother-tongue speakers of English are schooled separately from speakers of other languages. In white education, English and Afrikaans-speaking children attend separate schools but are required to study the other official language for all twelve years of their schooling. English and Afrikaans have been the two official languages of South Africa since 1926, despite the fact that neither of these languages is the mother-tongue of the majority of the population. For black children who speak one or more of the vernacular African languages, English is a second or often a third or a fourth language. To speak of it as a second language, however, is to misrepresent the situation: many of these children never come into contact with mother-tongue speakers of English until they leave school and seek employment. While this is usually the case in rural schools, it is equally true in the urban ghettos. For many of these children, learning English is more like learning a foreign language despite the fact that from Standard 3[1] the fifth year of primary education, English is also the medium-of-instruction in schools. Why English is the medium-of-instruction will become clear later. It is important to note that, as medium, English is not simply a subject within the curriculum but is the means of access to education *per se*.

The whole concept of English as a *second* language is being contested. Subtle undertones of 'second-language, second-class' exist in the society. The belief that English is owned by mother-tongue speakers who are the guardians of its 'correctness' is being resisted by many non-mother-tongue speakers of English. This resistance takes two forms. The one is a Gramscian striving for excellence[2] and a rejection of 'non-standard' English for blacks. The other, recognizing that 'standard' English is the minority dialect of the dominant classes, values the tendency of language to indigenization (the development of new forms specific to local groups of speakers) and maintains that it is possible for colonized people to appropriate English for their own ends.

> We appropriated these colonial languages, domesticated them in order to express an African sensibility, traditional, modern, rural or urban, political or religious: the ultimate phase of emancipation.[3]

The tendency to indigenization includes both 'non-standard' grammatical forms such as the widespread use of the present continuous tense for stative verbs as well as the evolution of new meanings for 'standard' English words. 'Brother' for example is not restricted to notions of blood brother in a nuclear family. It could refer to a 'cousin' in an extended family in cultures where kinship ties are different from western culture or it could mean 'comrade', brother in the struggle against oppression. Furthermore appropriation requires at times a deliberate rejection of western encodings. In communities where children are frequently born out of wedlock, the notion of 'illegitimate children' needs to be seen as a western concept, thus validating and empowering different cultural practices.

Without this appropriation, English remains functional, a means of economic access. In a capitalist society functional English 'can further reinforce the instrumentalization of people as units of labour'.[4]

Preparing black people for the working class has been a feature of Bantu education since its inception in 1953. In a speech delivered to the Senate, 7 June 1954, Dr Verwoerd, then Minister of Native Affairs said,

> There is no place for [the Bantu] in the European community above the level of certain forms of labour. Within his own community, however, all doors are open. For that reason it is of no avail for him to receive a training which has as its aim absorption in the European[5] community, where he cannot be absorbed. Until now, he has been subjected to a school system which drew him away from his own community and misled him by showing him the green pastures of European society in which he was not allowed to graze.[6]

Bantu education was also predicated on a specific language policy.

> We believe that the teaching and education of the native must be grounded in the life and world view of the whites, most especially those of the Boer[7] nation as the senior white trustee of the native, and that the native must be led to a *mutatis mutandis* yet independent acceptance of the Christian and National principles in our teaching.

We believe that the mother-tongue must be the basis of native education and teaching but that the two official languages must be taught as subjects because they are the official languages, and to the native, the keys to the cultural loans that are necessary to his own cultural progress. On the grounds of the cultural infancy of the native, we believe that it is the right and task of the state, in collaboration with the Christian Protestant Churches, to give and control native Education.[8]

The Bantu Education Act (1953) legislated that mother-tongue medium-of-instruction be extended one year at a time in black primary education. This policy was always rejected by the black population and was seen as a form of oppression. Their views were disregarded. Mother-tongue medium-of-instruction had significant negative consequences.

1   Primary schools could be ethnically divided as different ethnic groups spoke different vernacular African languages. This supported the state view of the black majority as a number of ethnic minorities.
2   The switch to English and Afrikaans as medium-of-instruction in secondary school proved extremely difficult for many students. Difficulty with language is a contributory factor to the high failure rate in black education.
3   Students who did not go on to secondary education left school with little knowledge of English.
4   The knowledge of English in the community, gradually built up by English medium-of-instruction in the English mission schools prior to Bantu education, was eroded.

The 1953 Act also introduced the 50/50 rule. This meant that in secondary school half the subjects in the curriculum were studied through the medium of English and the other half through the medium of Afrikaans.

The compulsory use by African pupils of both Afrikaans and English as medium cannot be justified on Educational grounds ... Should a decision be taken to select a foreign language as medium such a decision is a grave matter ... Once such a language has been selected, it is completely unnecessary ... to compel the use of yet another language as medium and in this way to double the burden of mastery.[9]

When in 1975 a decision was taken to push back the 50/50 rule into the final, Standard 5 year of primary school,[10] Afrikaans as medium-of-instruction was strongly resisted. This provided the flash-point for the 1976 Soweto uprising.

The 1976 uprisings led to a change of policy. The present situation is that mother-tongue is the medium for the first four years of primary education after which parents may choose the medium-of-instruction. English as medium-of-instruction is the almost universal choice of the black community. There are many reasons for this. As an international language, English provides access to the rest of the world in general and to the rest of Africa in particular; it is seen to provide greater access to employment and to tertiary education; Afrikaans has been more readily seen as the language of the oppressor despite the colonial guilt of English. Given the many different African languages spoken by the black community, there is a clear need for a lingua franca and English functions as a linking language.

Ten years after 1976, cautionary voices can be heard. Bearing western values and cultural assumptions, English can become a dangerous form of entrapment.[11] Work by the National Language Project in the Western Cape aims to develop English as a linking language while at the same time recognizing the importance of strengthening the African language of the region. It is important, however, to remember that at the time, in 1976, the ousting of Afrikaans, and the right to choose English was a political victory paid for in blood. Hector Pieterson, the first person killed in the 1976 uprisings, was a primary school child. Before examining the resistance to state education in any detail, it is necessary to develop further the picture of existing structures.

Christian National Education

Calls by black students for equal educational opportunity within a unitary system of education have, when taken up by the broad democratic movement, resulted in a critical look at white education, the most privileged sector of education in South Africa. Predicated on the Afrikaner[12] ideology of Christian National Education (CNE) and fostering racism as well as sexism and elitism, white education (both English and Afrikaans) maintains and reproduces Apartheid capitalism. The rejection of Bantu education has not therefore taken the form of a call for white education for all, but has rather been extended to an all-encompassing rejection of Apartheid education. The process of formulating alternatives has begun, and a grassroots movement, known as People's Education for People's Power, which will be discussed later, is growing.

The policy of Christian National Education is based on the puritanical Calvinist creeds of the three Dutch Reformed Churches and on fervent Afrikaner nationalism which aims to preserve and strengthen everything Afrikaners value: *their* country, *their* language, *their* history and *their* culture. The Broederbond (translated: the brotherhood), the secret Afrikaner society committed to total Afrikaner control of the country, ensured that key posts in the country were and are filled by Broeders.

No sector was — and is — more completely dominated by the Bond than education ... An analysis of the Bond's 1977 membership lists (obtained by Serfontein by clandestine means) reveals that educationalists comprised the single largest group (20.36%). These included not only people involved in Afrikaans [educational] institutions, but also those of other [racial] groups. [13]

Christian National Education, serving the interests of the ruling minority in South Africa, is the official policy of education in South Africa. The effects of this policy penetrate all aspects of school life. Religious assemblies, Republic Day celebrations, school cadets (military-style marching and rifle practice), youth preparedness (a course in patriotism and moral preparation), strict discipline and respect for authority are rigid features of white education. In the Transvaal Education Department sex, politics and religion may not be debated or explored in the classroom. If this were adhered to rigidly it would render the teaching of literature impossible. Manifestations of the tight narrowness of Christian National Education are apparent in two disturbing instances of education department control: the Cape Education Department ordered the burning of all prescribed school copies of *Boesman and Lena* by Athol Fuguard in 1985 and in the late 1970s the Transvaal Education Department instructed teachers to cover copies of *The Great Gatsby* in brown paper, because the line-drawing on the Penguin edition was considered too suggestive for 16-year-old students.

The Teaching of Literature

Official statements about education maintain that education is ideologically neutral. This is clearly not the case. As far as English teaching is concerned this is best illustrated by an examination of the literature texts which have been prescribed for public examinations. In white education, selections tend to be made from the Leavisite tradition of high culture with British high culture predominating. Meaning is seen to be inherent in the text and it can be extracted by practical criticism. In recent years some South African literature has been prescribed. The works chosen are exclusively by white writers and most of them offer very little challenge to the status quo. *Cry the Beloved Country* (Paton, 1948), despite its conservatism, was not set in the Transvaal until 1985 (nearly forty years after the novel was written) and then only because *Down Second Avenue* (Mphahlele, 1959) was withdrawn as too subversive, and a replacement had to be found hurriedly.

In black education the only discernible policy is that the literature prescribed should in no way relate to the political and social interests or aspirations of the students. There appears to be no coherent literary or educational philosophy. This is best illustrated by an example from Reid (1982). [14] She draws attention to the apparently random prescriptions for

1979. In 1979 *Leon Solves the Mystery* by Topsy Smith was prescribed. This trite book, set in an English-type public school, is as little known in South Africa as in the rest of the world. In 1980 the same students were expected to study Hardy's *Mayor of Casterbridge*, followed in 1981 by Gallico's *Scruffy* as their matriculation [15] setwork. In black education, South African literature is rarely set.

> Young black people see models for their way of living and judging not in their own country but in a far off country unknown to them and inaccessible to them. This can lead to lack of interest in, and more seriously, the undervaluing of their own civilization and environment. Daffodils and red roses are what the poets write about so why bother to look at the cosmos. [16]

It is not difficult to understand why the education departments have rarely set the literature of their own country, written in English. Much of this literature deals explicitly with the brutality of repression and the torment of life under Apartheid capitalism. But it speaks also of black consciousness, of courage and of the indomitable strength of communities. South African literature speaks with the 'voices of the land' [17] which cannot be silenced but may not be prescribed. Counter-hegemonic literature is rigorously excluded by all the state departments of education.

Control is further extended to literature which may be purchased for school libraries and English stock rooms. In white education only books listed in the official Book Guide may be acquired by schools. This is a subtle and effective form of censorship. Given that a vast range of material deemed politically subversive, blasphemous or pornographic is already banned for sale or possession in South Africa by statutory censorship committees, it is significant that additional forms of censorship are deemed necessary to 'protect' the youth. The following list of some authors excluded by the Book Guide has been included to give a sense of the narrow-mindedness which determines acceptability: R. Cormier, S.E. Hinton, S. Townsend, P. Zindel, J. Blume.

The Unequal Distribution of Resources

The unequal distribution of educational resources ensures that school libraries and English stock rooms barely exist in black education. Until 1985 black students were expected to buy all their own text books and stationery. Since 1985 some schools have been provided with stationery and text books and all schools have been supplied with class readers. Black students are still expected to buy their own books, prescribed for public examinations. In white education text books, class readers, prescribed books and stationery have always been provided free of charge. [18]

An understanding of the unequal distribution of resources is a starting

Table 8.1   Unequal distribution of resources

(a) *Per capita expenditure by the state during 1984|5*
on pupils of the different racial groups

African blacks	R 293.86
Coloured	708.32
Indian	1,182.00
White	1,926.00

(b) *Pupil|teacher ratios 1984*
(excluding the 'independent homelands')

African blacks	41.2 to 1
Coloured	25.4 to 1
Indian	22.5 to 1
White	18.7 to 1

(c) *Unqualified teachers 1984*
(These percentages are calculated on a minimum qualification for a teacher
of a post-matriculation teacher's certificate or diploma)

African blacks	70.2% are unqualified
Coloured	41.9% are unqualified
Indian	11.2% are unqualified

point for an understanding of Apartheid education. The statistics in Table 8.1 have been taken from the most recent Institute of Race Relations Survey (1985).

The numbers of unqualified teachers in white schools were not available, but the proportions in 1983 in Natal and Cape Schools were 8.1 per cent and 2.3 per cent respectively. These percentages are calculated on a minimum qualification. White education has a far higher percentage of degreed teachers than any other sector.[19]

Some material details may reveal more vividly than the statistics the contrast between white privilege and the neglect afforded to the majority of the population. Many white schools have libraries, now fashionably elevated to 'media centres', with computers and wide-ranging audio-visual equipment. They have school halls, playing fields, swimming pools and gymnasia. Many black schools in contrast lack electricity, duplicating facilities, and books. In some schools the toilets often do not function and there is rarely enough ground for more than one ungrassed football field. Lacking a new coat of paint with little money for ongoing building maintenance, the classrooms are often bleak and depressing. It is hardly surprising that black students who perceive their education as 'gutter education' resort to boycotting schools and to seeking alternatives.

A Class Analysis of Bantu Education

It is not enough to explain 'gutter education' as a form of racial oppression. It is an effective means of providing an ongoing source of cheap labour. Black education has played a significant role in the reproduction of labour suited to the needs of a capitalist economy since the 1930s, even before the Nationalist Party came to power. The reproduction of labour involves the reproduction of appropriate skills as well as the reproduction of attitudes and values appropriate to the social relations of production. The Eiselen Commission, charged with designing Bantu education, maintained that pupils should 'possess such qualities as punctuality, initiative, self-confidence, sense of duty, persistence, sociability, mannerliness, neatness, reliability, power to concentrate, etc'.[20] in order to be useful members of society.

Speeches in the early 1950s by prominent Nationalist politicians make explicit the function of Bantu Education: 'I am in thorough agreement with the view that we should so conduct our schools that the native who attends those schools will know that to a great extent he must be the labourer in the country.'[21] These views date back to the inception of Bantu education.

The 1980s have seen a restructuring of education. The state's reform strategy was launched partly to meet the employment needs of capital while at the same time ensuring that the dominant classes maintain power and control. Industry's need for black people to fill semi-skilled, skilled, clerical and managerial positions led to a massive increase in state spending on black education. Black student enrolment rose dramatically necessitating an expansion of school building programmes. 'The political aim was to fragment black opposition through stratification .... to intensify class differentials while reducing racial ones.'[22]

Reformist strategy is changing the way in which the labour force is being reproduced. It is bolstering the development of a more easily co-optable black middle class by giving more emphasis to class division and less to race. Despite a substantial increase of expenditure on education, student resistance to state education has, as we shall see, continued to deny legitimacy to DET education.

Ideological conflict, the unequal distribution of resources, the reproduction of labour and the language difficulties faced by school pupils learning through a foreign medium provide greater insight into education in South Africa than the comparison of English syllabuses which follows.

Comparison of a DET and a TED English Syllabus

In 1986 the Transvaal Education Department (white) and the Department of Education and Training (black) published their new English syllabuses. These syllabuses will be analysed to establish the current views of English education in the state controlled system. This will also provide a background for understanding the draft proposals for English teaching published by the People's English Commission in November, 1986.

To cut through the complexity created by a multitude of syllabuses only the Standard 8[23] syllabuses of these two education departments will be compared.

1   Both syllabuses are skills-based and contain different sections for the four skills listening, speaking, reading and writing.

2   Both syllabuses stress that these skills should not be taught in isolation, but that skills teaching should be integrated. The Transvaal Education Department (TED) further stipulates that language activities must also integrate with 'the multiple experiences of pupils as individuals and as members of communities in an historical context'.[24]

3   Both syllabuses recognize that South Africa is a multi-lingual society. The Department of Education and Training (DET) syllabus sees English as a means of assisting pupils 'to meet the challenge of living in a multi-lingual environment'.[25] The TED syllabus states that 'pupils should come to realize that languages have social, political, national and international implications'.[26] The DET syllabus therefore offers English as a means of access to communication, the TED syllabus pleads for the acknowledgment of and respect for the different languages in South Africa.

4   Both syllabuses aim to develop communicative competence in the pupils and stress the importance of interactive, communicative methods.

5   The DET syllabus stresses functional competence across the four skills for 'social, educational and occupational purposes'.[27] This emphasis is also evident in the TED syllabus but it is underpinned by numerous references to individual development and personal growth. Aiming to foster self-confidence, originality, creativity, self-understanding, etc., the TED syllabus tends to a liberal-humanist position. This represents fairly 'enlightened' thinking within the overall framework of the Transvaal Education Department but remains a far cry from the demands for empowerment of People's Education.

6   Both syllabuses stress the importance of language across the curriculum but neither syllabus has the power to establish language policies within schools or to influence other subjects within the curriculum. It is significant that in 1986 both syllabuses call for language across the curriculum policies, indicating clearly that such policies do not as yet exist. This is particularly critical in black education where English, the medium-of-instruction, is not mother-tongue.

7   Both syllabuses emphasize language in relation to function, audience and context and stress the importance of appropriateness. Neither syllabus recognizes that appropriateness is normative. Norms that count in a society are socially constructed. Neither

syllabus recommends that the language norms within the society be questioned or challenged. Neither syllabus offers any challenge to the status quo.

8   The TED syllabus states that 'language is best explored and experienced in an atmosphere of free and open enquiry'.[28] How this is to be achieved where discussion of sex, politics and religion are excluded from the classroom and under repressive States of Emergency where a range of statements is legally defined as subversive and where banned persons may not be quoted, remains an unresolved contradiction.

9   Both syllabuses advocate a language-in-use approach as the skills orientation would suggest. 'There is little place for the old-fashioned formal grammar lesson; language must be studied as it is actually used in speech and writing. Pupils should be taught English, not about English.'[29] This statement effectively captures the attitude to language in the TED syllabus as well. Here study of language is confined to providing pupils with 'a metalanguage that will enable them to talk about their increasingly complex work'.[30]

  Despite the overall language-in-use approach there is a strong emphasis on language structures in the DET syllabus. A detailed list of structures that have to be covered is provided. Although this is consistent with the needs of students whose mother-tongue is not English, it creates a conflicting pull within this syllabus. For teachers, untrained in communicative methodology, the temptation to focus on the different structures in isolation is hard to resist.

10 The DET prescribes three books for school study in the Standard 8 year: 'one prose work (a novel or a collection of short stories or extracts), a selection of poems and a play (or collection of plays)'. The TED prescribes 600 lines of poetry and six works which must include 'at least one play, at least one novel, at least one antholoIgy of short stories'. Some of the poetry should be South African as well as at least one of the six works. The inclusion of some South African material at all levels of the secondary school was first introduced in the 1986 TED syllabus and should be considered as a major break-through. The number of prescribed texts was doubled in an attempt to encourage more extensive reading and to discourage the 'set-book syndrome'. Past practice in schools had pupils studying one set-work per term in great detail. At Standard 8 level, TED teachers select the works for their particular classes; in the DET the actual texts are prescribed each year for all Standard 8 pupils nationally by a syllabus committee.

  Given the different composition of the TED and DET syllabus committees, given the differences between learning English as mother-tongue and as second or third language, and given the vastly different classroom practice in the TED and the DET, the similarities between these two syllabuses are far more striking than their differences. The explanation for this is that both syllabuses have been influenced by international trends in the teaching of English as mother-tongue and as second language. Both syllabuses reflect the growing understanding of the relationship between language and learning and the current influence of communicative approaches.

Differences in Examinations and Classroom Practice

The differences lie in classroom practice and in the kinds of questions set in the public examinations. The backwash effect of these examinations controls classroom practice more effectively than any syllabus. At the same time slow changes in classroom practice affect what can be asked in examinations. If teachers are unable to understand or teach the new syllabuses, then their students will be poorly prepared to write examinations based on them. Existing examinations are probably a fairer reflection than the new syllabuses of what students and teachers are doing in practice.

TED literature questions ask for an analysis of character or theme. The emphasis is on practical criticism. The DET literature questions focus on content, who said what to whom in what context. The TED language papers require an understanding of how the language is working in different selected passages. The papers written by DET candidates require students, for example, to rewrite sentences in the passive voice or reported speech and to explain the meaning of idioms. All the examination papers show little understanding of literary theory or modern linguistics. The TED papers require some analysis, the DET papers rely fairly heavily on recall of information.

The differences in classroom practice relate to the material circumstances which prevent teachers from transforming these syllabuses into meaningful classroom activity. Teaching in black schools, for example, has traditionally been based on a transmission model where pupils are passive recipients of information provided by the teacher. Language has been taught using chorus drills, rote repetition and gap-filling exercises. Literature is seen as content. Culturally, teachers are seen as authorities who possess knowledge which they impart to learners. The switch to an interactive, communicative methodology is difficult under any circumstances. Where the teachers are poorly qualified and insecure in relation to their subject matter, allowing pupils to ask questions and make their own meanings can be very threatening. In overcrowded classrooms group-work is difficult and it is difficult to mark and monitor pupils' production when every class you teach has up to fifty pupils in it. (Pupil-teacher ratios do not reflect the fact that English classes are always larger because it is a compulsory component of the curriculum). Moreover, pupils schooled in passivity often do not adapt to participatory, communicative learning with any more ease than their teachers.

Very little in-service training is provided for teachers in South Africa and what there is, is tightly controlled by the state education departments. The new syllabuses, top-down interventions, dictate new approaches to teachers who are expected to implement them with little guidance or support. No national non-racial professional association of English teachers exists as yet. Teachers' associations are as ideologically and racially divided as the rest of the country. The few non-racial democratic teachers' organizations that do exist have as yet no unified national structure, although there are moves to establish one, and they are too small for the luxury of further sub-division into subject-specific organizations. Teachers belonging to progressive[31] teachers' organizations face dismissal from their teaching posts, unexplained transfers, police harassment, raids and detention without trial. This is equally true for the many courageous teachers who bring progressive thinking into their classrooms. Tolerance of opposing views is not something for which Afrikaner nationalism is well known. Constant repression plays havoc with organizational structures.

Resistance to State Education

Given the effectiveness of state repression, the persistence of conflict is a testimony to the strength and determination of people to resist domination. In South Africa, education is one of the major sites of struggle. The synopsis which follows is a brief and simplistic summary of Hyslop's (1987) complex analysis of school student movements and state education policy.[32]

A number of factors coalesced in the mid 1970s to produce student rebellion. These include the partial restructuring of Bantu education to meet the needs of industrial capital, a dramatic increase in the number of secondary school students, high unemployment of secondary school drop-outs and the growth of the Black Consciousness movement in the late 60s. On 16 June 1976, police shot some demonstrating Soweto students. This led to widespread student uprisings affecting 160 communities. Protests and school boycotts continued sporadically until late 1977. Student struggles (1980–81) were marked by school boycotts and high levels of student politicization, particularly in the Western Cape. In early 1984 a renewed series of boycotts began in Attridgeville near Pretoria and in Cradock in the Eastern Cape. These were sparked by grievances that were specifically educational.

With a massive police and army presence in the townships, school boycotts inevitably resulted in large-scale police–student confrontations.

Police used armoured vehicles, tear-gas, *sjamboks*[33] and bullets. Students set up street barricades and armed themselves with stones and petrol bombs. These running battles in the streets left many students injured and dead and led to the arrest and detention of many more.

In August 1984 the state held elections for the 'coloured' and 'Indian' houses of the new tricameral parliament. Rejecting these as co-optive and incorporating institutions, students organized school boycotts as part of a general call for a boycott of these elections. In September 1984 police killings and rent riots in the Vaal Triangle led to large-scale, national school strikes. By 1985 student demands were no longer only educational. They included broad political demands such as the release of detainees and the removal of troops from the townships. 'Educational grievances became simply one aspect of their experience of overall oppression.'[34] By the end of 1985 students were calling for 1986 to be the year of no schooling and the rallying cry was 'Liberation first now, education later'. In late 1985 the Soweto Parents Crisis Committee was formed as parents were concerned about the dangers inherent in an indefinite school boycott.

Establishment of the National Education Crisis Committee

The Soweto Parents Crisis Committee convened a National Education Consultative Conference on the Crisis in Education at the end of 1985. The notion of People's Education for People's Power grew out of this conference. People's Education for People's Power maintained that students should struggle for the attainment of their educational priorities rather than withdraw from the education system. A national body was set up, the National Education Crisis Committee (NECC) and it was agreed that a grassroots network of Parent-Teacher-Student Associations (PTSAs) would be organized across the country. Mass meetings following the National Conference supported the NECC proposal that students end the boycott and return to school late, after the return date set by the DET, conditional on the state's meeting NECC demands by the end of March 1986.

A subsequent conference was held in March 1986 to discuss the state's inadequate response to the December demands. At that conference a People's Education Secretariat was established and it was agreed that priority would be given to reconsidering the History and English syllabuses. As a result it was agreed to continue with the return to school.

People's Education for People's Power

By October 1986 People's Education History and English Commissions had been established by the NECC. The commissions consisted of academics, teachers and students. In practice the initial work was often undertaken by academics. This work then formed the basis for consultation with the teachers and students. Membership of the commissions is not public knowledge in order to protect individuals from state harassment. In November 1986 the English Commission released its draft proposals for People's English to the press. By December all but one of the NECC office-bearers were in detention and discussions relating to People's Education syllabuses in schools were declared prohibited under the State of Emergency and subject to vast punitive action by the state.[35] Published prior to the new regulations, the draft proposals for People's English constitute the last public document available for discussion.

People's Education for People's Power is intended to apply to *all* South Africans and is tied to the United Democratic Front, the broad, non-racial, democratic movement[36] which aims to establish a government based on one-person, one-vote in a unitary state.

Fundamental to the evolution of People's Education for People's Power is the process of consultation. Parent-Teacher-Student associations, street, block and area committees, trade unions and student organizations are closely involved with the conceptualization and implementation of People's Education for People's Power. It is part of a long-term, 'mass-based undertaking by a whole society to transform itself'.[37]

This transformative function underlies the aims put forward in the draft proposals for People's English.

People's English

People's English aims to assist all learners:

> to understand the evils of apartheid and to think and speak in non-racist, non-sexist and non-elitist ways;
> to determine their own destinies and free themselves from oppression;
> to play a creative role in the achievement of a non-racial democratic South Africa;
> to use English effectively for their own purposes;
> to express and consider the issues and questions of their time;
> to transform themselves into full and active members of their society;
> to proceed with their studies.[38]

The specific proposals relating to method, language competence and content are predicated on an understanding of education as process. Process in the broad sense includes the establishment of community-based structures, the evolution of appropriate forms of consultation and the development of support systems for teachers which aim to empower them to work comfortably with innovative approaches to teaching and learning. In a narrower sense

> Process ... means exploration through language. It involves discussion and revision, and an understanding of how parts relate to the whole. Process values the contributions of all the learners and makes every member of the group responsible for the learning experience. The teacher's role is to make this possible. [39]

This notion of process is diametrically opposed to the transmission model of education and to the rote memorization of facts, endemic in all state education. It underlies the interactive methods proposed by the English commission: discussion, debate, argument, speeches; group and pair work; sharing and pooling of ideas; collecting and recording community-based experiences; the telling and retelling of stories; community participation; research; dramatization; performance and song; co-operation not competition; collective development not and individualistic selfishness; thinking not memorizing. Learners should also gain experience of the processes of production. They should design and produce newsletters, pamphlets, notices and posters. People's English believes alternative methods to be as important as, if not more important than, alternative content.

People's English should enable learners to develop confidence in their ability to form opinions and to draw conclusions. 'What the group or class discovers and reveals is the truth for those people at that time, capable of revision or reconsideration at a later stage, but not to be verified or corrected by outside received opinion.[40] The study of texts should be based on a range of approaches giving rise to multiple readings. Such study should not be confined to the single dominant method of practical criticism currently entrenched in schools. Notions about the kinds of texts that can legitimately be explored need to be expanded to include:

> popular culture; biographies and life histories; oral literature including song; talks by people of the community; written literature from the whole world (including translations but particularly from our place and time); newsletters, pamphlets, newspapers, advertisements, magazines, public documents and statements by politicians; essays, speeches, sermons and orations; cartoons; material from radio, television and film; texts from other subjects in the curriculum.[41]

People's English should enable learners to read texts and to resist them where necessary. The ideological functioning of all language must be explored and the plurality of meaning must be teased out so that learners are capable of formulating critical responses to texts. Meaning is not fixed but dialogic.[42] Learners need to understand the relationship between language and power and work currently being done by critical linguists[43] is being used by the English Commission in designing materials that will help teachers and students to deconstruct the language of hegemonic discourse.

If English is ultimately to empower students and serve as a vehicle for liberation, language competence must include the ability:

> to say and write what one means
> to hear what is said and what is hidden
> to defend one's point of view, to argue, to persuade
> to negotiate
> to create, to reflect, to invent
> to explore relationships, personal, structural, political
> to speak, read and write with confidence
> to make one's voice heard.[44]

Such competence should fulfil the aim of enabling learners to use English effectively for their *own* purposes.

In its attempt to re-examine the English syllabus, the English Commission is engaged in reconstructing the boundaries of this traditional school subject. Meetings between the People's Education History and English Commissions, for example, have recognized areas of common concern, and collaboration on a joint History-English workbook has been suggested. By rejecting the traditional notion of texts suitable for study in English, it becomes possible to examine the language of newspapers, political pamphlets, documents, letters, literature, eyewitness accounts, etc. Much of this discourse is the source material of the historian. In a combined History-English workbook students could be encouraged to use the methods of historians, discourse analysts and critical linguists to arrive at multiple readings of texts. Still in its infancy, the work of the People's English Commission is likely to produce a very different idea of what English is from the one presently entrenched in the system.

State propaganda maintains that all this is dangerous, a threat to the security of the state, radical and communistic, 'an exercise in ideological indoctrination that embodies the antithesis of the educational ideal'.[45] Yet People's English for People's Power is not unrelated to what is currently being advocated for English classrooms in societies freer than our own

> The teaching of English is powerful stuff ... It's hardly surprising that teachers of English are an irritant to the government ... We are clearly not in the business of teaching our pupils to be obedient workers, docile citizens and eager consumers. Instead we are primarily concerned with putting our pupils in charge of their own lives. Learning to be sensitive to the ways others use language, which means in part to recognise manipulation, deception and coercion, protects our pupils from exploitation.[46]

In South Africa such thinking is outlawed. Part of a broad attempt to reconsider People's Education for People's Power, People's English *is* subversive for the very reason that it aims to empower all students and, in particular, those who have been systematically and ruthlessly denied access to political and economic power by three centuries of white rule. The struggle over English is part of a much broader struggle for the emancipation of an oppressed majority and the liberation of an entire nation. English education is contested terrain and rightly so.

Author's Note: March 1988

In December 1987 the last remaining member of the NECC executive was detained indefinitely. On 24 February 1988 the state effectively banned seventeen organizations by placing extremely severe restrictions on their activities. Included in these organizations were the United Democratic Front, the NECC, NEUSA (a progressive teachers' organization), and most of the black student organizations.

Notes

1   Primary education in South Africa takes seven years: Sub A, Sub B (also known as Grade 1 and Grade 2) followed by Standards 1–5. The fifth year of schooling is Standard 3. The final year of primary school is Standard 5. Secondary education takes five years: Standards 6–10. The final year of secondary school is also known as matriculation, the year in which students write public school-leaving or university-entrance-certificate examinations. Movement up through the system is theoretically based on students' attaining a satisfactory standard of achievement thereby earning promotion to the next standard. In practice promotion is often related to age, material necessity or political demands. In times of extended school boycotts, for example, whole standards have been promoted to make room for new students entering the system from below or in response to student demands captured by the slogan 'Pass one, pass all'.

2   GRAMSCI, A. *Notebooks* in HOARE, Q. and SMITH, G.N. (1971) (Eds) *Selections from the Prison Notebooks of Antonio Gramsci*, London, Lawrence and Wishart, p. 325. 'It is true that every language contains the elements of a conception of the world and of a culture, it could also be true that from anyone's language one can assess the greater or lesser complexity of his conception of the world. Someone who only speaks dialect, or understands the standard language incompletely, necessarily has an intuition of the world which is more or less limited and provincial, which is fossilised and anachronistic in relation to the major currents of thought which dominate world history. His interests will be limited, more or less corporate or economistic, not universal ... It is at the least necessary to learn the national language properly. A great culture can be translated into the language of another

Hilary Janks

great culture, that is to say a great national language with historic richness and complexity, and it can translate any other great culture and can be a world-wide means of expression. But a dialect cannot do this.'

3 MPHAHLELE, E. (1983–1984) 'Prometheus in chains: the fate of English in South Africa', *English Academy Review*, Vol. 2, p. 90.

4 NDEBELE, N.S. (1986) 'The English Language and Social Change', keynote paper delivered at the Jubilee Conference of the English Academy of South Africa, Johannesburg, September 1986, p. 18.

5 *European*: a euphemistic expression referring to white South Africans.

6 ROSE, B. and TUNMER, R. (1975) *Documents in South African Education*, Johannesburg, A.D. Donker, p. 266.

7 *Boer*: the Afrikaans word for 'farmer' used to refer to Afrikaners in general. Afrikaners are the descendants of the original Dutch colonizers. Afrikaans is the language they speak.

8 Article 15, Christian National Education Pamphlet, in Rose, B. and Tunmer, R., *op. cit.*, pp. 127–8.

9 Memorandum by The African Teachers Association of South Africa, quoted in DE LANGE, J.P. (1981) *Investigation into Education. Report of the Work Committee: Languages and Language Instruction*, Pretoria, Human Sciences Research Council, pp. 48–9.

10 See note 1 above.

11 NDEBELE, N.S. *op. cit.*

12 See note 7 above.

13 RANDALL, P. (1982) *Little England on the Veld*, Johannesburg, Ravan, p. 187.

14 REID, J. (1982) *English Literature in South African Senior Schools: A Critique of Set-Books*, Centre for African Studies, University of Cape Town, Communications No. 7.

15 See note 1 above.

16 *Ibid. Cosmos*: a well known South African wild flower not originally indigenous.

17 CRONIN, J. (1983) *Inside*, Johannesburg, Ravan, p. 58.

18 *Race Relations Survey* (1985) 50th ed., Johannesburg, Institute of South African Race Relations.

19 *Ibid.*

20 Eiselen Report quoted in Christie, P. and Collins, C. (1984) 'Bantu Education: Apartheid ideology and labour reproduction', in Kallaway, P. (Ed.), *Apartheid and Education*, Johannesburg, Ravan.

21 *Ibid.*, p. 176.

22 HYSLOP, J. (1987) 'School Student Movements and State Education Policy: 1972–1987', paper presented at the 1987 Conference of the Association of Sociologists of South Africa, pp. 8–9.

23 See note 1 above.

24 Transvaal Education Department (1986) *Syllabus for English First Language Higher Grade, Standards 8–10*, p. 1.

25 Department of Education and Training (1986) *Syllabus for English Standard 8*, p. 1.

26 Transvaal Education Department (1986), *op. cit.*, p. 1.

27 Department of Education and Training (1986), *op. cit.*, p. 1.

28 Transvaal Education Department (1986), *op. cit.*, p. 2.

29 Department of Education and Training (1986), *op. cit.*, p. 7.

30 Transvaal Education Department (1986), *op. cit.*, p. 41.

31 *Progressive*: Currently used to describe people on the left from a range of different

260

extra-parliamentary positions, united in their opposition to Apartheid and the Nationalist Government and in their support for the broad non-racial democratic movement known as the United Democratic Front.

32 HYSLOP, J. (1987), *op. cit.*

33 *Sjambok*: a whip used by the South African police.

34 HYSLOP, J. (1987), *op. cit.*

35 Government Gazette, 9 January 1987.

36 See note 31 above.

37 GARDINER, M. (1987) 'Liberating Language People's English for the Future', *Lengwitch*, Vol. 4, No. 1, March, 1987, p. 36–40.

38 National Education Crisis Committee (1986) 'People's English for People's Power: draft proposals', Press Release, 27 November, p. 1.

39 *Ibid.*, p. 1.

40 GARDINER, M. (1987), *op. cit.*, p. 8.

41 National Education Crisis Committee, *op. cit.*, pp. 2–3.

42 VOLOSINOV, V.N. (1973) *Marxism and the Philosophy of Language*, tr. by Matejka, L. and Titunik, I.R., Cambridge, Massachusetts, Harvard University Press.

43 JANKS, H. (1986) 'Critical linguistics and the teaching of language', paper delivered at the Kenton-on Jukskei Conference, Johannesburg, October 1986; MCKENZIE, M. (1986) 'Critical linguistics and practical stylistics: teaching the People's English instead of the Queen's English', paper delivered at the Kenton-on Jukskei Conference, Johannesburg, October 1986; MCKENZIE, M. (1987) 'Free indirect speech in a fettered insecure society', *Language and Communication*, Vol. 7, No. 2, pp. 153–9.

44 National Education Crisis Committee, *op. cit.*, p. 2.

45 News Comment, 15 July 1987, South African Broadcasting Corporation.

46 DOMBEY, H. (1987) 'What's the use of English? Powerful stuff', *The Times Educational Supplement*, 1 May, p. 6.

Notes on Contributors

Stephen Ball

Stephen Ball is Professor of Sociology of Education in the Centre for Educational Studies at King's College, London. His research has been concerned with the policy and practice of comprehensive education. See *Beachside Comprehensive* (Cambridge University Press, 1981) and *The Micropolitics of the School* (Methuen, 1987). He is co-editor of *The Struggle for Democratic Education: Equality and Participation in Sweden* with Staffan Larsson (Falmer Press, 1989).

Björg Brandtzaeg Gundem

Björg Brandtzaeg Gundem graduated in education at Oslo University, where she also received her doctoral degree. She is presently Associate Professor in Education at the Institute for Educational Research, Oslo University, where she teaches and gives advice to graduate students in the fields of educatonal foundations, curriculum theory and curriculum history. Her research interests are higher education, 'didactics', curriculum history and curriculum theory. She is currently starting up a research project on the history and current practices of curriculum administration in Norway. Recent publications are *Skolens oppgave og innhold* (The Aims and Content of Schooling) (1987), 2nd ed. (Universitetsforlaget) and *Engelskfaget i folke-skolen: Pavirkning og gjennomslag 1870–1970* (The School Subject English in the Common School: Influences and Impact 1870–1970), (in press), (Universitetsforlaget). She has published a range of articles in Scandinavian and international publications like the conference papers of the International Standing Conference for the History of Education, ISCHE.

Gerald Burns

Gerald Burns holds a Ph.D. in American Studies from Yale University and is currently Assistant Professor of English and American Studies at

Wesleyan University (in Middleton, Connecticut, USA). In addition to research on English he has published on the history of the secondary curriculum, most recently 'Tradition and Revolution in the American Secondary Curriculum: The Cambridge High School Case', in *Journal of Curriculum Studies* 20 (March–April 1988). He also writes on American literature and culture.

David Gardiner

David Gardiner teaches English at Langley Park Boys School in Bromley, London. When studying as an undergraduate in Cambridge he was taught by F. R. Leavis.

Ivor Goodson

Ivor Goodson is Professor of Education in the Faculty of Education at the University of Western Ontario. Following doctoral studies at the London School of Economics, he trained as a teacher at the Institute of Education in London. He taught in two innovative comprehensive schools in England before moving to the University of Sussex. He took up his present position in 1986. More recently he has held a number of visiting professorships: at the University of Uppsala and King's College, London. He is the author of *School Subjects and Curriculum Change* and *The Making of Curriculum: Collected Essays*; co-author of *European Dimensions and Secondary School Curriculum*; editor of *Social Histories of the Secondary Curriculum* and *International Perspectives in Curriculum Histories*; and co-editor (with Stephen Ball) of *Defining the Curriculum* and *Teachers Lives and Careers*. He is the founding editor of the *Journal of Education Policy* and a national editor of *Qualitative Studies in Education*.

Bill Green

Bill Green is currently a Lecturer in English Curriculum Studies in the School of Education, Murdoch University, Western Australia. He was previously an English teacher in Western Australian secondary schools. He was educated at the University of Western Australia and Murdoch University. Past publications include an edited volume *Metaphors and Meanings: Essays on English Teaching* by Garth Boomer (A.A.T.E., Adelaide, 1988) and articles on literacy, ideology and English teaching. Current research interests include curriculum theorizing, cultural studies , the politics of school literacy, English teaching and literary education, and the relationship between technology and textual practice.

263

Hilary Janks

Hilary Janks is a graduate of the University of the Witwatersrand, Johannesburg, South Africa. She has higher degrees in both English Literature and Applied Linguistics. Her research area is the relationship between language and ideology and the implications of this relationship for classroom practices. She has worked as a lecturer in English education at the University of the Witwatersrand since 1977. She is jointly responsible for training high school English teachers who intend teaching English either as mother-tongue or as a second language. She serves on the advisory committees of a number of alternative education projects. She has published three papers on language and power: *Reaching for the cosmos, Critical linguistics and the teaching of language* and *Language, myth and disempowerment.* Since 1984 she has annually edited a collection of classroom materials on the relationship between language and society entitled *A Book About Language.*

Alex Kenny

Alex Kenny studied English at The Polytechnic of North London, where he was student of Malcolm Evans. Whilst there he studied Critical Theory and submitted a paper on Media Studies. He is currently working at Stepney Green School in East London, where he teaches English and Media Studies. His research interests are in Language and Learning, the social construction of culture, and Media Studies. He is an active member of the NUT and the Socialist Teachers' Alliance.

Peter Medway

Peter Medway has been a Senior Research Fellow at the University of Leeds since 1985. He has taught in schools in various parts of England and has lectured widely on English and Language Learning in Britain, North America and Australia. His Ph. D. thesis was a study of teachers' implicit definitions of English. He is author of *Finding a Language.*

Robert Morgan

Robert Morgan obtained his B.A. from the University of Western Ontario, his M.Ed. from the Ontario Institute for Studies in Education and his Ph.D. from the University of Toronto. He is Assistant Professor of Cultural Studies and Graduate Methodologies Program at Trent University, Peterborough, Ontario. Apart from teaching English and media studies for many years, his other research interests are critical theory as it relates to education, English studies, language and society.

Laurence Walker

Laurence Walker is an Associate Professor of Education at the University of Lethbridge. His university education was obtained at Durham, Nottingham and at the University of Alberta where he completed graduate work in reading education. He has taught in schools in England, Alberta, and Newfoundland, and at Memorial University of Newfoundland and Mount St Vincent University in Nova Scotia. An interest in the relationships between oral and written language has led to research on the influence of dialect on reading and writing, and on the teaching of grammer from a historical point of view. He has published in *Curriculum Inquiry, Visible Languge, Reading Research Quarterly, Canadian Journal of Education,* and *English Quarterly*.

Index